Linguistics and aphasia

LANGUAGE IN SOCIAL LIFE SERIES

Series Editor: Professor Christopher N. Candlin

Language and power
Norman Fairclough

Discourse and the translator
Basil Hatim and Ian Mason

Planning language, planning inequality
James W. Tollefson

Language and ideology in children's fiction
John Stephens

Linguistics and aphasia
Ruth Lesser and Lesley Milroy

Linguistics and aphasia:

psycholinguistic and pragmatic aspects of intervention

Ruth Lesser
Lesley Milroy

Longman
London and New York

Longman Group UK Limited
Longman House, Burnt Mill,
Harlow, Essex CM20 2JE, England
and Associated Companies throughout the world.

*Published in the United States of America
by Longman Publishing, New York*

© Longman Group UK Limited 1993

First published 1993
ISBN 0–582–02221–5

British Library Cataloguing-in-Publication Data
A catalogue record for this book is available from the British
Library

Library of Congress Cataloging-in-Publication Data
Lesser, Ruth.
    Linguistics and aphasia: psycholinguistics and pragmatic
    aspects of intervention/Ruth Lesser and Lesley Milroy.
        p.   cm. — (Language in social life series)
    Includes bibliographical references and index.
ISBM 0–582–02221–5
1. Aphasia. 2. Psycholinguistics. I. Milroy, Lesley.
II. Title. III. Series.
    [DNLM: 1. Aphasia. 2. Psycholinguistics.   WL 340.5 L638La]
RC425.L57 1993
616.85′52—dc20
DNLM/DLC
for Library of Congress   91–11601
                                                                 CIP

Set by 8V in 10/12 pt Palatino

Produced by Longman Singapore Publishers (Pte) Ltd.
Printed in Singapore

Dedication

To the students of the Department of Speech, University of Newcastle upon Tyne, and to the dedicated therapists who are their clinical supervisors.

Contents

General Editor's Preface

In their authorial Introduction to this most recent contribution to the *Language in Social Life Series*, Ruth Lesser and Lesley Milroy emphasise the interdisciplinary nature of their subject matter, aphasia, and show in helpful and practical detail throughout the book how the diversity of aphasias and their effects on communication requires a diversity of approaches both for research and intervention. In particular, they focus on the contributions to its study and practice from psycholinguistics and pragmatics, the former emphasising more the source of disturbance in the relationships between linguistic structure and language processing, the latter more the effects of aphasia in terms of impairments to communicative interaction. This associa-tion of 'source' and 'effect' is of course not unidirectional and in stressing the mutuality of the psycholinguistic and the pragmatic the authors add powerful weight from their perspective of disorder to the need expressed by researchers into 'ordered' language for greater interaction between the social and the cognitive. Not that the call for such interdependence is new, it is after all inherent in the work of Vygotsky and indeed in many writers in the field of educational linguistics and psychology who have found it unhelpful to separate context and use from content and form. It is, however, recent in aphasiology and has yet to be incorporated fully both in research paradigms and in clinical practice. Hence one of the values of this book.

In highlighting this mutuality, however, one must be careful not to diminish the very real distinctions that apply to both traditions and which, certainly in the older, more established and it has to be said, at this time more coherent, psycholinguistic approach, has built up an impressive body of experimental research and intervention practices, the character of which is amply illustrated here. Nor should one rush into attempting to construe one tradition in terms of the principles and practices of the other. This is especially important in the still volatile area of pragmatics where early work in the context of aphasia naturally sought to see pragmatic disorder as parallel, but at a 'higher' linguistic level, to the better charted disorders of phonology, lexis and grammar. The identification of units of pragmatic disorder in terms of the inappropriate performance of isolatable speech acts realised in particular utterances is a case in point. The focus at that time and in large measure still now, was on the performance of the aphasic patient, detached for analysis and treatment, as it were, from particular communicative contexts and without a discoursal perspective. Not that research into the pragmatics of aphasia in its beginnings twenty or more years ago was any different to other parallel applications of pragmatics at that time to other fields of applied linguistic endeavour, second language acquisition studies being a clear case in point. Indeed the parallels are striking in terms of research agendas, though less so in terms of applications. However, as the characterisation of pragmatics has moved from its linguistic-philosophical beginnings in speech act theory, through the work of Grice, to an accommodation with relevant work in the analysis of discourse and conversation, so there has been a recognition that we need to research the interactions of aphasic patients with their partners and their interlocutors in natural settings, and to see successful and unsuccessful communication as a joint responsibility, affected by particular social conditions. One particular area of considerable interest is thus in the nature of repair, both self-repair by patients and other-repair by partners, and in the management of deixis.

It is important also to realise that these distinct contributing disciplines have their own research methodologies, their own definitions of what constitutes permissible data and in particular their own methods of reporting their findings. In stressing their interdependence, then, one should not seek to force a marriage on the paradigms too hard. As in other areas of applied linguistic research, and I return to that of second language acquisition, the experimental and the ethnographic orientation each has its adherents, its particular practices and its related but distinctive objectives. The striking quality of this book is that it presents both positions, both orientations, and, significantly, shows how they can not only be usefully combined in aphasia management but also, more controversially perhaps, how both paradigms need to accommodate the other in research. I suspect that it will be at this researcher and theoretician level that this accommodation will prove hardest to achieve. Strong disciplinary allegiances make interdisciplinary work, especially in the contentious field of language, difficult to realise and difficult to fund. Nonetheless, the evidence and the practices charted here suggest the importance of this accommodation, for both theoretical and practical reasons.

We are thus at an exciting moment in aphasia research and in the practical management of aphasia, one where we can attempt at least to bring under one roof the contributing disciplines of psychology, philosopy, sociology and anthropology, together with relevant models of linguistics, as they impinge on and offer candidate explanations for language disorders and suggest appropriate modes of treatment and intervention. More than that, however, we can look at aphasia research and management as a paradigm case in applied linguistics; one which not only displays the interdependence of research and practice in the study of language, the brain and social context, but one which as a social and personal *problem*, provides a challenge and a means for bringing together relevant disciplinary research. It is evident from the chapters of this book that Ruth Lesser and Lesley Milroy have been able to identify the considerable benefits such collaboration can bring in terms of new research questions and new patterns of treatment. What they do not say, of course, is how this mutuality and this collaboration can be best achieved amongst researchers and between them and practitioners. That is the question that this book raises for the training institutions and their professional and academic structures, in terms of linking research and practice, constructing appropriate interdisciplinary curricula and in facilitating the establishment of mixed research teams. The two authors of this book, from somewhat different disciplinary perspectives but with a mutuality of interest and engagement, indicate how this collaboration can be most productively achieved.

Christopher N Candlin
General Editor

Acknowledgements

This book was written very much in response to our perceptions as teachers of speech-language therapy students, both of their needs and of the needs of their patients. We are therefore indebted to students in the Department of Speech at the University of Newcastle upon Tyne during the 1980s who acted as helpful, enthusiastic and responsive guinea pigs in enabling many of the ideas developed in this book to be tested. Sometimes, however, their involvement was closer than this. We are particularly indebted to Lisa Perkins, who, both as an undergraduate and a postgraduate researcher, has worked closely with us. Her work is acknowledged as we discuss it at various points in the text. Thanks are also due to Catriona Fleming, Naomi Conway and Gail Barnsley who, in the course of writing their undergraduate dissertations, helped us to develop our approach. We gratefully acknowledge the help of the following, in providing us with transcriptions of both normal and aphasic conversation: Catherine Booth, Mandy Chadwick, Moira Conlon, Catherine Crockford, Pat Fenwick, Karen Finnie, Suzanne Platt, Jennifer Smith, Jo Vanderlinden, Helen Watson, Anne Whitworth. Our thanks also go to the many aphasic patients who have allowed themselves to be subjects of psycholinguistic investigations by ourselves and our students; our respect and admiration for these patients and their families continues to increase over the years.

We are grateful to our series editor, Chris Candlin, for the careful and conscientious way in which he dealt with our manuscript and for his many helpful suggestions at all stages of composition.

Transcription conventions

Excerpts of data cited from other works are reproduced with minimal modification to the original transcription conventions. The conventions used for transcribing our own material, adapted from those of Levinson (1983: 370), are as follows:

Italic	Simultaneous speech
(0.0)	Pauses or gaps in tenths of seconds
(.)	Micropause
(2 syll)	Uncertain passage of transcription, with number of syllables indicated where possible. Round brackets are also used to enclose inferred glosses on indistinct utterances
.hhh	Audible in-breath
= =	Latched utterances with no gap
CAPS	Relatively loud speech
:	Lengthened syllable
?	Not a punctuation mark, but marks a rising intonation contour
/	Marks a tone group boundary in longer utterances

Phonetic symbols used are those of the International Phonetics Association.

PART I:
THE BACKGROUND

ONE

Introduction

Aphasia, the language impairment in adults which can follow various kinds of brain injuries such as strokes, is a topic which has been explored by researchers from the different perspectives of medical, cognitive and linguistic sciences. Much of this work is of interest both to the speech-language therapists whose task it is to treat aphasic patients and to relatives and friends who wish to understand more about the impairment and learn to cope with its consequences on their lives. Aphasia is also an intrinsically interesting topic, holding a fascination for many people from the wide range of theoretical and applied disciplines concerned with language and communication. We are aware of this widespread interest on the part of both specialists and non-specialists, and have therefore written this book with a rather heterogeneous range of readers in mind.

Our focus is, however, rather narrower than these opening comments imply. Much recent research in aphasiology, in relation both to the management of the aphasic patient and to the modelling and explanation of patterns of language deficit, has followed advances in two rather divergent sub-disciplines of linguistics – psycholinguistics and pragmatics. Both of these sub-disciplines are also *interdisciplinary*, being centrally connected to linguistics but facing away from it in quite different directions. Psycholinguistics interfaces with various branches of psychology and the neurological and cognitive sciences, pragmatics chiefly with philosophy, anthropology and sociology and to a lesser extent psychology. The main purpose of this book is to examine the impact of recent developments in psycholinguistics and pragmatics on aphasia research and on the practical management of aphasia.

Although this book is intended to be accessible to non-specialists, we have particularly tried to write it in a way which is helpful and informative to aphasia therapists. However, we have also kept in mind cognate professionals such as educationists, psychologists and those from a range of medical (including psychiatric) specialisms who want to understand more about the character of acquired language disorders and of disordered discourse. For this reason, the second introductory chapter of this book provides a brief survey of some clinical aspects of aphasia for non-specialists. In the main part of the book, we have tried to provide an informative evaluation and synthesis of some recent developments which have influenced aphasia studies. A more important goal perhaps is the provision of a basis for evaluating current research and for planning research projects, both major and minor. Most important of all, we hope to offer here an illuminating perspective on the routine management of aphasia.

The level of knowledge which can be assumed by the authors of an interdisciplinary book with an interdisciplinary readership is rather problematic, and we shall try to outline our policy here. Our decision to 'anchor' the work by directing it primarily towards aphasia therapists, rather than, for example linguists, means that for the main part of the book we assume not only a certain level, but a certain kind of knowledge. For example, both education in speech-language pathology-therapy and the general aphasiological literature often make quite detailed reference to certain *syntactic* theories and syntactic descriptive techniques. On the other hand, *pragmatic* theory and techniques for describing conversation are much less well integrated into either educational syllabuses or the research literature. We therefore deal relatively rapidly with quite difficult syntactic material, limiting our comments to points of contact with psycholinguistic theory. Basic references are provided to fill gaps for interested readers, while Crystal (1991) offers an up-to-date glossary of linguistic terminology. However, we treat even those pragmatic concepts which linguists might find relatively straightforward in some detail. This is because the application of pragmatic concepts in aphasia is particularly difficult and contentious. This problem is not unique to aphasia studies, but pertains generally to attempts to apply pragmatic concepts, and is particularly apparent in other clinical linguistic areas such as the study of schizophrenia and dementia. Similarly, the application of psycholinguistic theory to aphasia is only just becoming an essential component of education in speech-language pathology-therapy, though it has perhaps advanced more rapidly in Britain than in many other English-speaking countries, since the new discipline of cognitive neuropsychology which incorporates this application was initiated there. In psycholinguistics, too, we have been selective, and described only those developments which seem to us to have direct applications in the analysis of aphasia and in planning remediation.

Although this strategy of selectivity may entail the provision of too much information for some readers and too little for others at various points in the book, we have attempted to compensate for unevenness of coverage by supplying a summary of key topics at the end of each chapter, in order to allow readers to omit that chapter if they wish. In short, we have tried to judge the amount, type and level of information necessary for current purposes, as defined by the goals set out in this introduction.

CHAPTER SUMMARIES

After this introductory Part I, the book is divided into two further parts. Part II deals with the models and methods which are used in the two sub-disciplines of linguistics we have selected. Part III discusses the implications of the issues raised for planning intervention in aphasia, and discusses some ways in which these have actually been applied.

Chapter 3, the first in Part II, provides a context by outlining the different kinds of contribution to aphasiological study offered by linguistics. In doing so, it provides an anchor for later chapters by locating, in particular, the field of pragmatics in relation to the discipline of linguistics as a whole. A somewhat more selective review is offered of a number of issues in linguistic theory of psycholinguistic relevance which are taken up later in Chapters 4 and 5. The question of how far linguistic theories can be viewed as 'psychologically real' is discussed, as this is particularly pertinent to the design and interpretation of psycholinguistic investigations which make extensive reference to 'mentalist' theories of the type pioneered by Chomsky (1965).

Chapters 4 and 5 describe some of the psycholinguistic models which have been applied in the interpretation of the disorders of aphasic individuals. These have been most fully developed (although still underspecified) in respect of the mental processing of single lexical items, and this forms the theme of Chapter 4. Less well elaborated and experimentally tested through aphasia is the model of sentence processing which is described in Chapter 5. Nevertheless discussion of these models is necessary as they have already begun to be directly applied in aphasia therapy.

Chapters 6 to 9 deal particularly with pragmatics in relation to aphasia therapy. It is important to remember that pragmatics, like psycholinguistics, is a very active research area, but is plagued with contentious issues, ill-defined concepts and partly developed methods. The purpose of these chapters is to select, describe and evaluate topics and approaches which seem to be particularly pertinent to the management of aphasia, rather than to duplicate existing texts. Chapters 6 and 7 on the one hand and 8 and 9 on the other are organized as complementary. Chapters 6 and 7 concentrate initially on the principles underlying discourse and conversational structure, rather than presenting a template for analysing bodies of data. Chapters 8 and 9 present an account of the mechanisms of negotiating a conversation and suggest procedures for approaching real and consequently intractable data. This division corresponds roughly to two major approaches to conversation, the linguistic/philosophy-of-language approach and the ethnomethodology/conversational analysis approach, respectively referred to by Owen (1989) as 'top-down' and 'bottom-up' modes of analysis.

While Chapters 8 and 9 offer a relatively straightforward exposition of a conversation analysis approach to both normal and aphasic conversation, we need to comment briefly on the content and organization of Chapters 6 and 7. As with the chapters on psycholinguistics, the principle underlying the selection of topics for detailed discussion is their particular relevance to aphasia. For example it has often been reported that aphasic people have difficulties with articles, pronouns and verb tenses, although discussion of these difficulties is less often placed within a coherent conceptual framework. All three categories can illuminatingly be considered under the overlapping headings of *deixis* and *definiteness*, and we have discussed such central topics as straightforwardly as possible in relation to aphasia, referring frequently to examples.

We have also considered critically, with attention to potential applications, the underlying assumptions of the theories of Searle and Grice which have wide currency in the applied literature but have been subject to some criticism within pragmatics. The overall goal of these chapters is to examine the various strands of the complex of models and approaches which comprise a sociolinguistically orientated pragmatics. We shall argue that this orientation is potentially best able to provide a more principled basis for therapeutic intervention and for evaluation of existing assessment instruments. These are discussed in Chapter 11.

Part III of the book deals with the implications for therapy of the observations made in Part II. We have not attempted a synthesis of the psycholinguistic and pragmatic approaches, but have devoted separate chapters to each (Chapters 10 and 11 respectively). This is because at present the underlying philosophies of each are quite different. The psycholinguistic orientation to aphasia therapy is essentially that of experimental psychology, and is based on the testing of model-motivated hypotheses. The intervention which derives from this is often direct didactic work on language (although it may also incorporate the teaching of substitutory language strategies – as discussed in Chapter 8). In contrast, the pragmatic approach is observational and eclectic, without exclusive commitment to a particular theory or model. The intervention which derives from the pragmatic approach is generally concerned with the development of compensatory strategies to achieve functional communication, and with management of the patient's communicatory environment. It is primarily facilitative rather than didactic – though again there are exceptions, as is shown in Chapter 11. Therefore, rather than attempting to construct a combined psycholinguistic/pragmatic model, we look in the concluding chapter at the areas in which these two approaches overlap, both from a theoretical and a clinical perspective.

TWO

Aphasia: the clinical background

This chapter gives a brief account of the nature and aetiologies of
aphasia, and its prognosis for recovery, as a preliminary to the
later chapters in this book which concern intervention aimed at
promoting or accelerating that recovery. The chapter is intended
to be primarily of interest to non-specialists in aphasia, and
readers who are aphasia therapists may wish to move straight to
Chapter 3.

THE CAUSES AND NATURE OF APHASIA

Aphasia can take many forms. Indeed some would argue that
there are as many forms of aphasia as there are individuals who
suffer from it. But patterns emerge which show commonalities in
sub-components of the disorder, even though each individual's
combinations of particular dysfunctioning sub-components may
differ, as well as response and adjustment to the condition. All
aphasic people have in common (by definition) that they have
suffered some form of brain damage (from stroke, head-injury,
tumour, metabolic disorder, toxicity or other aetiology), which
has destroyed neuronal cells in parts of the brain on which
language seems to be critically dependent. In most individuals
this will be in a central zone of the left cerebral hemisphere, and
will involve destruction of parts of the cerebral cortex and
connecting fibres, although sub-cortical damage can also interfere
with language. Typically the damage which causes aphasia is
unilateral; it affects only, or predominantly, one of the cerebral
hemispheres, in contrast to other neurological conditions which
lead to articulatory or intellectual disorders in which the damage
more typically affects both sides of the brain.

Right cerebral damage can also have consequences for language, even in people whose left hemispheres are dominant for language, but the changes which occur after unilateral right hemisphere damage are generally more subtle (affecting prosody, semantic discrimination and affective uses of language, for example) and are not usually given the label of aphasic.

We give below some samples of aphasic speech from patients who have suffered left cerebral damage. The first is a conversation between two elderly members of a Speech after Stroke Club, discussing their school days. Both have a longstanding aphasia.

(1) (Fleming, 1989)

1. M (2) erm (.) d you (1.0) d you er what school wan you?
2.   (points to B)
3. B (1.0) buts
4. M (1.0) buts?
5. B yes
6. M (1.0) buts
7. B yes
8. M yes
9. B er (.) d you oh dear (2) erm (4) erm (2) sums // sums
10. M oh yes yes
11. M er er maths?
12. B (1.0) yeh er mmhm (1) erm er
13. M maths
14. M (1.0) erm (2) are er er good maths?
15. B yes yes mmhm
16. M yes

It is clear that verbal communication between these two men is severely restricted by their aphasic difficulties. The speech of both patients is characterized by pauses and limited sentence structure. M uses gesture to assist understanding of his speech. B seeks clarification (line 4) of M's reply to his question, but then appears to accept a repetition without further clarification. B attempts no clarification of the response 'buts' which is the trouble source, either in speech or by the use of an alternative means of communication such as writing or gesture. At lines 7 and 8 both participants seem to accept that they have reached an impasse. B develops the topic at line 9, but M rapidly returns the burden of maintaining the conversation to B, selecting him as next speaker by formulating a question which offers a paraphrase of 'sums' as 'maths'. M's attempt to develop this theme in line 14 seems to be ambiguous; he could for example be asking whether maths is good or whether B is good at maths or even possibly (assuming a tense error) whether B was good at maths at school. However, B this time seeks no clarification, but settles for a minimal expression of agreement, which M repeats.

In the next sample an aphasic woman, E, retired after a stroke a year before, is conversing at home with a visiting student, L, about the need to travel in a black taxi (i.e. one which has more space for a handicapped person).

(2) (Perkins, in progress)

```
 1. E and I [dada] er er that got home
 2.    you see we couldn't get (.) the car and I thought we
 3.    were going to (3.00) got up (6.00 drumming fingers)
 4.    [blə brak] taxi
 5. L o::h you might be able to get it in a black taxi
 6. E                                    yea an yes I
 7.    got a black taxi [təfəst] get one out and
 8. L                                            right
 9. E I rang it up and I [wə] man come and he said er [gin]
10.    been in it nobody had [wigəd] and wanted one
11.    and I was just er (0.8)
12. L so they wouldn't take you in the black taxi
13. E                                    no:: 'nd there was
14.    an ordinary taxi that came eee::
15. L oh:: no::
16. E eee it was terrible
17. L I bet you weren't very pleased
18. E 'nd er I [s] well I just (.) had to get out [sət] one it was
19.    terrible
```

This patient has less difficulty communicating than M and B in the first sample, and she shows an ability to produce more complex syntax. She has word-finding difficulties, however, which result in pauses and incomplete sentences and apparently frustrate her (line 3, drumming fingers). These difficulties may be related to phonological problems, for example her attempt at 'black' in line 4, her correction of [gin] in line 9 and the uninterpretable [dada] in line 1 and [wigəd] in line 10. Her conversation imposes additional work on the listener. For example, in line 4 L offers an interpretation of 'got up black taxi' as 'get it in a black taxi', which E subsequently rejects. E has in fact confused L by initially stating (lines 6 and 7) that she got a black taxi, though it subsequently emerges that she did not succeed in getting one (lines 12–14). In view of this outcome we can interpret [təfəst] in line 7 as an attempted self-repair. By the end of the conversation it is still uncertain whether E travelled in the ordinary taxi (as opposed to the black one) and L's contributions provide no clear evidence of understanding.

These samples illustrate a few of the difficulties which occur in spoken language in aphasia. It is in the essence of aphasia that it is not just speech which is impaired, however. In the majority of cases (indeed according to some definitions in all), aphasia impairs all media for the use of language – speech, auditory comprehension, reading comprehension, writing, signing. There has also been extended discussion of whether the impairment in true aphasia extends beyond the linguistic, to affect, for example, the use of non-verbal communication. The impairment is often not so much that these aphasic individuals fail to produce speech, or fail to comprehend, but that they produce speech which does not seem to reflect their intentions and which the listener has difficulty comprehending. Add to this (to name but a few components of communication) the aphasic person's own problems in comprehension, difficulties with formulating conversational contributions in accordance with the split-second time-scale which characterizes dialogue, referring to entities in such a way as to pick them out adequately for the needs of a specific hearer, and it is clear why conversations between patient and and even an unimpaired partner can be replete with difficulty, and why aphasia is a disorder which can have significant repercussions on an individual's lifestyle and social interactions.

Attempts have been made to sift out commonalities amongst aphasic individuals and to classify them into syndrome groups. The linguistic approaches described in this book use a more individualistic approach, and align themselves with the criticisms which have been made of the inadequacies of grouping patients together into polythetic syndromes on the basis of behavioural symptoms which may reflect differing underlying dysfunctions (see for example, Caramazza, 1984). Nevertheless the aphasiology literature at present remains dominated by a neurological classification of the aphasias, and most studies still feel it necessary to identify their cases with these clinically conventional labels. We shall not describe them in detail here , but give a brief account of the main features of what has become known as the 'Boston classification' (see also Geschwind, 1965).

This categorizes non-fluent and generally agrammatic patients whose auditory comprehension is relatively good, but who have articulatory difficulties, as Broca's aphasics. Wernicke's aphasics show the reverse pattern, that is fluent, well-articulated (though sometimes 'paragrammatic') speech, but marked auditory comprehension difficulties. (The terms 'agrammatism' and 'paragrammatism' are discussed in Chapter 5.) Patients who have good comprehension and reasonably fluent spontaneous speech, but nevertheless find it difficult to echo back speech which they have just heard, are labelled as Conduction aphasics. Again the opposite phenomenon occurs, in Transcortical aphasias, in which patients have preserved echoic abilities despite either poor comprehension (in Transcortical Sensory aphasia) or restricted spontaneous speech (in Transcortical Motor aphasia). A fifth common type of aphasia is described as Anomic aphasia or Anomia; it is characterized by word-finding difficulties in spontaneous speech and in naming. Wenicke's aphasia and Conduction aphasia may resolve over time into Anomia. Patients with severe problems in all aspects of language are classed as Global aphasics.

These labels appear frequently in research studies of aphasia, and serve to alert the reader to a rough expectation of the type of individuals who are later described in more detail. These detailed specifications not infrequently then demonstrate that the individual's disorder did not conform to the expectations of the syndrome, and had features shared by members of other syndromes. The viability of distinctions between agrammatism and paragrammatism is a case in point, and is discussed in Chapter 5.

RECOVERY FROM APHASIA

What kind of remediation is possible for such a heterogeneous and complex disorder? A theory of therapeutic intervention must be based on a theory of recovery. It is, therefore, necessary first to consider what recovery may be expected to take place without any deliberate attempts at remediation by professionals. Fortunately, there is often a good degree of recovery which occurs without any direct intervention by a therapist. The basis for this is physiological, aided perhaps by the language stimulation which surrounds the patient, often at first on the hospital ward, then later amongst the family. It is one of the aphasia therapist's early functions to ensure that the family understands the nature of the disorder, maintains this stimulation and involves the patient in communication, despite the conversational stresses.

In the case of stroke (the most common cause of aphasia) this spontaneous recovery occurs principally in the first three months (Sarno and Levita, 1971). In some cases recovery is more rapid, and is sufficient to change the patient's classification from one syndrome to a milder one. Two-fifths of the patients studied over a year post stroke by Pashek and Holland (1988) were initially classified as having a global aphasia, but three-fifths of the cohort showed changes during recovery which were so great that they involved reclassification to a milder syndrome or to normal use of language. The majority of these changes occurred by the end of the second week post-onset (and mostly in the second week rather than the first). The prognosis for recovery during the first six months (in association with help from therapy) has been found to be better in those who are younger, in better general health, and who started with a less severe aphasia with good auditory comprehension and fluent speech (Marshall and Phillips, 1983). Other researchers have confirmed the association of better recovery during the first three months with younger age and with less need for prolonged hospitalization after the stroke (Holland, et al., 1989). The prognosis for recovery, however, does seem to depend on the aetiology of the aphasia (Fazzini, et al., 1986), and has been related to the degree of temporarily swollen and nonfunctioning (but potentially viable) tissue around the source of the damage to the brain. People suffering from traumatic head-injury generally recover better than those with stroke, and those who have survived a haemorrhagic stroke recover from aphasia better than those whose stroke was thrombo-embolic in nature.

Following a sudden focal brain lesion, there is thought to be a state of neural shock, or diaschisis, which may affect metabolic activity not only in adjacent areas but also in areas anatomically removed from the actual site, but which are functionally linked with it. It is recovery from this diaschisis and oedema which may account for the rapid improvements which can occur within the first two weeks after injury, although suppression of metabolism within the damaged hemisphere may persist over several years (Metter, 1987). Fazzini, et al. (1986) suggest that altered neurotransmitter levels in the brain due to neural shock may lead to another series of events which in due course effect some degree of recovery of function. Of these the slowest is the sprouting of injured neurones. Fairly rapid improvement (usually within about a month) may be due to recovery from metabolic suppression in the hemisphere contralateral to the damage due to restabilization of catecholamine levels. The most rapid is the activation or 'deblocking' of synapses which were previously latent due to inhibition from the now damaged tissues. Due to the decrease in neurotransmitter levels from the injury, surviving neurones become supersensitive. Fazzini, et al. suggest that this can be the cause of a number of phenomena: perseverative behaviour, the restriction of speech to stereotypes, depression, and epilepsy. We see already that the study of aphasic individuals involves taking into consideration many other factors than their language disorder.

There is a considerable amount of evidence that recovery from aphasia due to left cerebral damage may be partly mediated through the right hemisphere (see Code, 1987, for a review). Knopman, et al., (1984), for example, examined regional blood flow and computed tomographic (CT) scan data in aphasic patients who showed different degrees of recovery; they demonstrated that those who made a good recovery of auditory comprehension had a significant increase in right hemisphere blood flow within 100 days after their strokes.

These observations underlie various approaches which have been used over the last half century towards therapy for aphasia.

APPROACHES TO THERAPY

Given that an indeterminate degree of spontaneous recovery is to be expected within a few weeks and months of the brain damage, there has been discussion of at what stage active intervention by an aphasia therapist is appropriate. In the early stages the aphasia therapist's role is likely to be twofold. First, there is a need to identify the patient's particular disorders, and the monitoring of the evolution of symptoms is a part of this; thus therapist and patient can come to terms in understanding the effects of the injury. Secondly, the patient's family and other carers need the therapist's supportive advice and counsel. At a later stage, active intervention may be considered to be appropriate. The issues which arise in effecting changes in the settings in which the patient communicates will be discussed later, in the context of the implications of pragmatics. Here we will discuss the main approaches which have been used in direct therapy when aphasia is no longer acute.

The three main approaches to direct therapy may be characterized as being directed at reactivation, reorganization and substitution (Lesser, 1985). Basso (1989) interprets these as, first, assisted recovery of the anatomical 'hardware' of the brain itself, secondly, the adoption of new algorithms by compensating brain areas, and, thirdly, the achievement of previous goals by different means. For clarity here, we divide this last category, substitution, into three subdivisions (cognitive relay, use of external prostheses, and compensatory functional strategies), making five approaches in all.

Reactivation

Reactivation of function is consistent with the claim that neuronal sprouting occurs through stimulation, and with an expectation that the original behaviour should be restored in its original form. It should be noted, however, that the extent of neuronal sprouting is probably limited to a few micrometres, and that compensation may be restricted to adjacent tissue only (Ferry, 1989). Recovery through reactivation is perhaps better accounted for by the notion of redundancy of neurones in a brain system, so that small lesions can be compensated for by other undamaged neurones within the same system. Whatever the underlying physiology, the expectation is that the recovered function will be identical to that which has been lost. This can account for complete recovery after small lesions, but it is not so easy to apply when the destruction has been extensive. Nor does it account for the qualitatively different evolution of symptoms over a period of time, such that a patient may be classified into different syndromes during the path to recovery (Pashek and Holland, 1988).

Reactivation is a more plausible avenue to recovery for an aspect of language which seems to be widely represented in the brain like lexical semantics, where even substantial left-hemisphere damage may leave sufficient neural tissue to provide a basis for recovery of the original function. Thus auditory comprehension at the lexical-semantic level seems to recover early and well in patients who do not have extensive bilateral damage. Stimulation by comprehension tasks such as category sorting and semantic exercises may assist this process of recovery. One of the earliest systematic programmes of therapy was based on the premise that intensive repetitive auditory stimulation, using object names, was the foundation of recovery (Schuell, et al., 1964). The stimulation approach is based on the belief that the patient has not lost language abilities, but rather that the language system now operates with reduced efficiency, and needs exercising to improve its functioning. Indeed some speech pathologists suggest that increased cortical activity through problem solving, learning and thinking (convergent, divergent and evaluative) may be the basis of recovery from aphasia through stimulation (Chapey, 1983).

Although lexical comprehension improves the most rapidly of all language functions after brain damage (as is consistent with this theory of reactivation), we may note in passing that an impairment in the ability to name objects and to retrieve exact words in conversation is the most ubiquitous and tenacious of disorders. This difficulty draws attention to the analysis of naming and word-retrieval as implicating several other components besides lexical semantics, a theme we amplify later.

Related to the reactivation approach was the work in aphasia done by some psychologists in the 1960s and early 1970s applying behavioural techniques. This was based on the premise that aphasic patients' difficulties were compounded by anxiety, and that release from this would allow the better functioning of language to be revealed (Ince, 1968; Damon, et al., 1979). Operant conditioning techniques were also used at this time, in which patients were given instructions to improve speech, verbal approval for responding correctly and feedback on results, with reported success (Goodkin, 1969; Ince, 1973; Goldfarb, 1981). The implication was that language functions were retained, and could be used again provided that the appropriate encouragement was given to reduce the non-linguistic factors which were concealing those aspects of language which had recovered spontaneously and were in fact usable by the patient. Indeed it may be more appropriate to label this aspect of aphasia therapy as 'revelation' rather than reactivation.

A direct reactivation approach is the aim of the pharmacological treatment of certain types of aphasic disorder which is now being explored (Albert, 1988: Bachman and Morgan, 1988; Bachman and Albert, 1990). Bachman and Morgan report the effect of bromocriptine treatment on three aphasic patients, described as having, respectively, transcortical motor aphasia, mixed anterior aphasia and severe aphasia of the Broca type (all of these aphasias being ones in which speech fluency is compromised). These investigators suggest that the drug assists speech initiation in particular, through sub-cortical activity.

Reorganization

In contrast to reactivation, reorganization implies that language functions need to be taken over by brain areas which were previously not actively involved, perhaps because they were inhibited by the neurones which have now been put out of action. In adults the recovered function in this case may not be totally identical to that which has been lost.

In reorganization in aphasic adults the newly engaged neurones, with their latent synapses unmasked, may be in other areas in the left hemisphere. Based on the presumption that the neural substrate of the *syntactic* production of language is lateralized to the left hemisphere (a presumption originally derived from association of the left hemisphere with sequencing activities), programmes which use syntactic drills for patients with long-standing restrictions on syntactic output are applying this notion of left hemisphere reorganization through exercise.An example of this notion is the use of syntax stimulation programmes for patients with non-fluent agrammatic speech (Helm-Estabrooks, et al., 1981; Doyle, et al., 1987). The Helm Elicited Language Program for Syntax Stimulation (HELPSS) consists of a series of sentences which follow an empirically established gradient of difficulty, with several examples at each level. They range from imperative intransitive and transitive

('Wake up', 'Drink your milk') to embedded clauses and the use of auxiliaries to express future time ('She wanted him to be rich', 'He will walk'). The example sentences (illustrated by drawings) are modelled by the therapist for repetition by the patient after a delay, and then elicited from the patient without a direct model. Success with this programme with some patients has been reported, with some limited generalization from the example sentences to similar ones which had not been incorporated into the therapy, but without generalisation across sentence types (other than, in one subject, generalization from intransitive to transitive imperatives) (Doyle, et al., 1987). Moreover the trained sentences are not usually produced fluently and at normal speed, raising the question as to whether new strategies of production are being applied. The reorganization underlying such improvement therefore seems to be specific to exercised types of items rather than generalizing to new structures, and to be a vicarious functioning rather than a reactivation of inhibited capabilities.

Another kind of reorganization, for which there is more physiological evidence, is the adoption by the right hemisphere of language functions for which the left hemisphere was previously dominant. Such anatomical reorganization is presumably the basis of much recovery in those young children who appear to be able to compensate even when the left hemicortex has been removed; consistent with the notion that in reorganization the recovered function is not identical to the lost function, recent studies suggest that the recovered language is inferior in some respects to that of their cerebrally intact peers (Cooper and Flowers, 1987). Several studies have shown that language in recovered aphasic adults who were previously left-hemisphere dominant for language (in that aphasia resulted from left-sided damage) is now supported by the right hemisphere. This evidence comes from studies which have temporarily inactivated a hemisphere with sodium amytal injection (Kinsbourne, 1971; Czopf, 1972, cited by Basso, 1989), or examined hemispheric blood flow as an indication of function (Yamaguchi, et al., 1980; Knopman, et al., 1984; Demeurisse and Capon, 1989). The substrate for some facets of language seems to be shared by both hemispheres in normal brains, and there is some indirect evidence from people with right brain damage that the right cerebral hemisphere may even be dominant for some aspects of language. Right brain damaged people can be more impaired than left brain damaged people on some tasks which involve prosody (Bryan, 1989) and awareness of metaphoric meaning (Winner and Gardner, 1977). The right hemisphere seems to have a substantial role in lexical semantic processing, (Lesser, 1974; Zaidel, 1977; Gainotti, et al., 1983). It seems that the normal systems of language processing involve synergistic activity in both hemispheres, with the left hemisphere perhaps playing a more important role in the semantics of abstract words, syntax, phonology and rhythm and the right hemisphere playing a more important role in intonation, affective, non-literal and some social aspects of language.

Fazzini, et al. (1986) have pointed out that a suppression of metabolic activity in the right hemisphere following onset of aphasia due to left-hemisphere damage may last for about one month. What we see therefore in the early days following the sudden onset of aphasia may reflect the malfunctioning of both hemispheres, and what early recovery occurs may be due to the reactivation of function in the right hemisphere ('right hemisphere language'), before the more limited and slower recovery of function in the more extensively damaged left hemisphere. The brain therefore becomes reorganized, with a greater participation of the right hemisphere in language. The capacity for the right hemisphere to support language varies in individuals, and may be associated with handedness, age, gender and anatomical asymmetry.

Consequently, some systems of therapy are directed at stimulation of the right hemisphere in an attempt to accelerate the reorganization process. Three example programmes illustrate this for, respectively, lexical semantics, intonation and gestured concepts. The first, 'Brain Function Therapy' (Buffery and Burton, 1982), aims at stimulating the right hemisphere to make lexical semantic decisions, by asking for a response as to which is the odd-one-out amongst inputs to the left ear, left visual field and left hand (all of which are assumed to be processed first by the right hemisphere). The decision, for example, could be as to which of the words 'boy','lad','toy' has a disparate meaning. The left hemisphere's involvement in this task is supposedly minimized by introducing masking activities to occupy the right ear, right visual field and right hand.

Our second example is Melodic Intonation Therapy (MIT), which has been used as a formal programme since the early 1970s

(Albert, et al., 1973), though based on much earlier observations that aphasic patients could sometimes sing what they could not speak. Multisyllabic words and short functional phrases are first intoned musically and tapped out syllable by syllable. When the patient is able to repeat these satisfactorily and produce them on request (after several programmed sessions), longer phrases are introduced, and the musical pattern is replaced with exaggerated speech prosody and then normal prosody. MIT has been reported to be successful with a number of patients (Sparks, et al., 1974; Dunham and Newhoff, 1979; Van Éeckhout, et al., 1979; Buttet and Aubert, 1980; Helm-Estabrooks, 1983).

For our third example we refer to the visual and gestural systems of therapy which have also been used in order to draw on abilities for which dominance of the right hemisphere has been claimed: visual and visuo-spatial abilities. Gesturing, using only the left hand (a necessary restriction in many patients who have a right-sided hemiplegia) is also exercising the right hemisphere, as pathways of motor control cross in the brain. Initially the non-preferred left hand may be clumsy, and the patients may show signs of motor or ideational apraxia (difficulty in the deliberative execution of planned movements, which may be imitative or expressive of ideas). Bailey (1989) describes the use of a visual system of signs, Blissymbolics, with a man with a severe aphasia, although other studies have not been so encouraging (Funnell and Allport, 1989). Training in the pro-duction of symbolic gestures for unseen objects is the basis of Visual Action Therapy (Helm-Estabrooks, et al., 1982). This is recommended for severely aphasic patients, and one of its attractions for them may be that, since it is conducted in silence, it puts no pressure on them to attempt to produce speech. The programme begins with simple tracing around the patient's hand, to demonstrate how line drawings can represent real objects, and progresses to the patient's producing a pantomime gesture to indicate a small hidden drawing of an object. Interestingly, the programme is claimed to improve the ability not only to produce representational gestures but also auditory comprehension. This may be due to improved attention to stimuli, but it seems likely that there is also a reintegration of the total capacity for attending, performing a mental operation and acting on the output. Fazzini, et al. (1986) suggest that 'this non-linguistically based therapy seemed to stimulate functions of the right hemisphere and in the process increase access to latent pathways subserving language' (p. 35). Reorganization involving the right hemisphere therefore seems a good candidate for accounting for some recovery (spontaneous or assisted) from aphasia.

Cognitive-relay substitution

The third approach to therapy is based on the notion of substitution. This is based on a less optimistic expectation that the brain is capable of recovering its original function, either through reactivating the original ability or achieving it through reorganization. The substitution theory is that the original ability cannot be restored in its original form, but that alternative means can be found to achieve a communicative goal, using intact brain structures which also serve other purposes. These are sometimes known as cognitive *relay* strategies (although Luria, 1963, includes them within reorganization).

One of the clearest illustrations of this approach is in the use of lip-reading by those who have an acquired deafness. Another is in the reteaching of reading to patients who have become 'alexic without agraphia' after a stroke, that is who can write but not read. This occurs with vascular damage to part of the occipital lobe of the left hemisphere, and possibly to the posterior part of the band of fibres which connects the two hemispheres, the corpus callosum. Such damage disconnects the visual input in reading from the more central and anterior zones which participate in the comprehension and production of language. Patients with this condition can therefore write but not read. Writing, however, may be able to act as a relay route to reading. In such cases the therapist is often able to assist the patient's recovery of the ability to read by getting him or her to gesture the writing movements required for each letter while reading. Such patients can often learn to read again in a functionally useful way, passing through a stage of being 'letter-by-letter readers'. The writing gestures can then become internalized, and neither patient nor therapist may be aware that they are being used. Reading, however, continues to be slow and effortful by this route, which has been substituted for the original direct reading system. Behrmann, et al. (1990) showed that, although a case, MB, whose recovery they monitored over 12 months improved in reading (particularly in the first 20 weeks post onset), the improvement was due to increased efficiency in the serial processing of letters rather than to recovered automaticity in access to semantics. This indicates the continuing use of a cognitive relay method in reading rather than reactivation or reorganization. Beauvois and Derouesné (1982) have described an even more elaborate cognitive-relay method, taught in therapy, based on substituting an indirect route for a patient with alexia without agraphia who did not respond to the strategy of learning to read again through internalization of writing gestures. They diagnosed this patient as having a disconnection between verbal semantics and visual semantics. In this case a gestural code distinct from letter shapes was first taught, and later linked with visual letter names.

Teaching of mnemonic strategies to help recall word and sentence lists is another method which uses substitution by a cognitive relay. Gasparrini and Satz (1979) have described how 15 left-brain-damaged aphasic patients were taught the use of a visual imagery technique to help them learn paired associates and remember sentences, for example 'The doctor said to take two red pills after breakfast'. Van der Linden and Van der Kaa (1989) describe a similar programme using imagery mnemonics devised by Branle for mildly impaired aphasic patients.

The slow, although complete, responses made by patients who have been assisted in the ability to produce sentences by learning colour coded identities of parts of sentence structure also indicate the use of substitutions by deliberate cognitive-relay strategies rather than recovery through reactivation or reorganization.

Substitution by prostheses

The most obvious use of substitutory techniques externalizes the prosthesis. Computers have provided a means of communication for many cerebrally palsied people and adults with acquired dysarthria, but, like other visual communication systems such as Blissymbols (Funnell and Allport, 1989) and visual communication cards (VIC, see Gardner, Zurif, et al., 1976), they have also had some limited use as communicatory media in aphasia, if the ability to handle symbols is not too impaired. Weinrich's development of the C-VIC system is an example (Weinrich, 1991).

An example of the use of computers to externalize a relay strategy such as those described above is the use of computer cuing by initial sound to assist in naming, where the patient learns to cue himself or herself through prompting the computer to give a phonemic cue (Bruce and Howard, 1988). Interestingly, one of the patients described in this study (of which we give more details in Chapter 10) learned to internalize this relay after practice with the computer, thus adopting a cognitive relay strategy.

Functional communication strategies

There are other adaptations which aphasic patients make without external prostheses, which cannot be identified as cognitive relays, but are apparently pragmatic strategies to achieve communication. The use of gesture (pointing, simple mime) does not come as easily to aphasic adults as might be presumed from a simple interpretation of their disorder as being one of language, and many studies have been devoted to examination of aphasic patients' disabilities in non-verbal communication (see Peterson and Kirshner, 1981, for a review). Some linguistic strategies, however, have been reported in agrammatic patients who adopt compensatory strategies in an attempt to achieve effective communication, albeit in an abnormal way. One such case is described by Hand, et al., (1979). This 42 year old ex-teacher four years after her stroke had acquired the habit of using dummy elements ('This is' 'It was') to circumvent her difficulty in encoding subject and verb in the same utterance; this resulted in sentences like 'This is Eddie the telephone' (presumably for 'Eddie worked for the telephone company') or 'Well this is bad the cookies'. It may be that this was a carry over from some naming drill in speech therapy ('This is a . . .') which had been overgeneralized by this patient. Other agrammatic patients can be more successful in their substitutory strategies, which may include non-verbal, or stereotypic verbal, turn-holding gestures, production of sentence fragments or word repetitions to sub-stitute for intensifying adverbs, or of adverbs as substitutes for tense markers, use of direct for indirect discourse, or use of stressed words as sentence initiators (Goodglass, 1976). Sometimes compensatory strategies have consequences which are not at first sight obvious; for example, the compulsive talking of the patient studied by Edwards and Garman (1989) seemed to be a strategy to avoid yielding the floor to a conversational partner and so revealing his comprehension problems. Adoption of compensatory strategies has also been documented in another type of aphasia, severe jargonaphasia, where speech is fluent but unintelligible due to uninterpretable neologisms. Panzeri, et al., (1987) found that the apparent recovery in linguistic abilities of patient PZ over three years was best explained as not due to improved lexical access or improved self-monitoring of speech, but as due to an increased use of stereotypical expressions as a way of avoiding difficulties. This at least makes the speaker appear socially as a better conversational partner, whether or not it improves his ability to communicate the intended message.

SUMMARY

This review of clinical aspects of aphasia and theories of direct intervention has been aimed at providing some necessary background to the survey of linguistic aspects of aphasia which follows. We have briefly reviewed the nature and aetiology of aphasia, and outlined the currently dominant neurological classification of the aphasias by the Boston school, knowledge of which is assumed in many of the research studies we shall be reporting. We have also emphasized the individual nature of patients' disorders, and referred to reservations about classification systems other than for pragmatic clinical purposes. In our review of theories of recovery, spontaneous and assisted, we have distinguished five ways in which some recovery of communicatory abilities is thought to be achieved: the neural theories of reactivation and reorganization, the psychological theory of cognitive relays and the pragmatic use of prostheses and functional strategies. All of these are based on speculative notions about what happens in spontaneous recovery and assisted restoration of function, and the divisions we have made are somewhat arbitrary – consider for example the conversion of a prosthetic strategy into a cognitive relay strategy described above. Nevertheless, in broad terms, the majority of psycholinguistically based interventions can be classed as drawing on reactivation or cognitive relay theories, and the majority of pragmatic interventions on compensatory strategies. We shall attempt to make these relationships more explicit in Part III.

PART II:
MODELS AND METHODS

Part II reviews the theoretical basis and orientation of psycho-linguistics and pragmatics, with respect to their applications in aphasia studies. The review is therefore selective, the basis for selection of particular topics being either that applications to assessment and intervention in aphasia have already been developed, or that they seem to have a significant potential for such an application.

The review begins with a general assessment of the role of linguistics in language pathology, and a cautionary note on the limitations of idealized linguistic theories with regard to their applications either to psycholinguistics or pragmatics. The following two chapters (4 and 5) describe psycholinguistic models respectively at the lexical and sentence level, which are becoming extensively applied to the interpretation of language processing in aphasia. These are already influential in some parts of the world on the planning of direct intervention in clinical practice. Chapters 6 and 7 address a broad range of theoretical issues which are particularly relevant to pragmatic dimensions of aphasia. The concluding chapters of Part II (8 and 9) focus on conversational analysis, a pragmatic approach which, while having considerable potential for direct application in assessment and intervention, is as yet underused in clinical practice.

THREE

Applying linguistics in aphasia research and therapy

There used to be a view that all linguistic theories functioned at a level of abstraction which allowed them to idealise away from actual performance and language use. From such a perspective, it was not clear how the gross imperfections of the language of people who had become aphasic after brain injury could contribute to linguistic theory, or indeed how linguistic theory could help them in suggesting ways of remediating their disorders. The last two decades have seen a transformation of this view. It has happened largely through the development of two hybrid sub-disciplines of linguistics, psycholinguistics and pragmatics. Both of them are heavily indebted to adjacent disciplines – psychology in the case of psycholinguistics, and philosophy and sociology (chiefly) in the case of pragmatics.

PSYCHOLINGUISTICS AND PRAGMATICS

Broadly speaking, psycholinguistics is concerned with language as mental processes, pragmatics with the use and interpretation of specific utterances by speakers and hearers in particular situational contexts. Both have been applied to the study of aphasia in ways which are transforming not only our understanding of the nature of this phenomenon, but also therapists' approaches to helping aphasic patients.

Although this brief summary presents psycholinguistics and pragmatics as two distinctive sub-disciplines, it is important to emphasize that from the point of view of their application to aphasiology they are not entirely dissociated. As Seron and Deloche (1989) stress, aphasia will benefit best, not from any opposition of the laboratory work that characterizes psycholinguistics to the naturalistic observation that characterizes many pragmatic perspectives, but from an approach which develops 'a unitary theoretical framework for both kinds of data' (p. 11). In truth, such a framework is as yet unformulated, and the characteristic methods, goals and assumptions of the two disciplines are frequently quite sharply opposed to each other. Particularly, observational and naturalistic approaches to the structure of conversation contrast dramatically with the various procedures such as control of variables, coding and quantification which characterize psycholinguistic work. Nor do researchers always view such a difference in orientation as beneficial, each side sometimes questioning the validity of the approach of the other (see, for example, Roger and Bull, 1989). Nevertheless, there are within the broad conception of pragmatics which we shall adopt a number of different approaches to utterances in context (as discussed in Chapter 6) and the conflict between the experimental and the observational is not always so extreme. Furthermore, some researchers have united the two traditions; for example Clark and his associates have developed an interesting approach to the formal modelling of discourse which combines the insights of naturalistic methods of conversation analysis described in Chapter 8 with the rigour of controlled experimentation of the kinds described in Chapters 4 and 5 (Clark and Wilkes-Gibbs, 1986; Clark and Schaefer, 1989; Isaacs and Clark, 1987). Therefore, despite a certain tension between the two approaches, we hope in this book, after describing them separately, to show the aspects in which they may enmesh, particularly in their practical applications to the remediation of aphasia. However, our goal here is a good deal less ambitious than the development of a unitary theoretical framework as recommended by Seron and Deloche.

THE ROLE OF LINGUISTICS IN APHASIA STUDIES

Linguistics as a discipline has contributed to aphasiology in a number of rather different ways. For example, the influence of Chomsky's (1965) 'mentalist' linguistic theories on psycholinguistic model-building is of a rather different kind from that of the Quirk grammar (Quirk, et al., 1972) which has provided a basis for much descriptive work in aphasic syntax. On the other hand, the various procedures for pragmatic assessment and remediation which have been developed in recent years seem to stem from a rather different kind of descriptive linguistic activity. Yet we cannot easily impose subdivisions on our descriptions of language use. Pragmatic and syntactic abilities are more often presented in the literature as opposed than as interconnected, but some of the topics frequently dealt with under the heading of pragmatics have a clearly syntactic dimension; examples are the use of definite pronouns and of direct and indirect articles. Since this piecemeal and disparate character of applied linguistics in the context of aphasia studies presents a rather confusing overall picture, we shall devote some space in the following sections to separating out a number of different but interrelated issues.

A useful initial distinction is between relatively direct applications at the level of *theory*, with particular reference to experimental psycholinguistic research, and applications at the level of *description and analysis* which are characteristic of a more observational style of research and are often designed to inform clinical practice quite directly.

Commentators on the role of linguistics in aphasiology do not always distinguish theoretical and descriptive types of application, and indeed, where linguistic analysis is sophisticated and associated with a complex and rather abstract theory such as Chomsky's recent Government and Binding model (1981), the distinction between theory and description is far from straightforward, as we shall see. Even so, it is notable that applications at the level of theory did not begin to play a major part in aphasiology until a decade ago. As Hatfield (1972) noted in her paper 'Looking for help from linguistics', most speech therapists looked primarily to the neurological and psychological literature to inform them as to the nature of aphasia. Hatfield contrasted the linguistic and psychological approach to language, in that linguists see it as a system of relations, while psychologists see it as an aggregate of discrete phenomema, 'to be dissected out and experimented with, some might say' (p. 65). Hatfield showed how a patient's recovered ability to produce speech sounds supported the linguist Jakobson's contention that it should follow the acquisition of phonemic contrasts by children. She also described two other patients with disorders at other levels than the phonological, that is the morphological and the syntactic, interpreting them in Jakobsonian terms as paradigmatic and syntagmatic disorders respectively. These patients, she wrote 'show again the searching questions which the clinician, scratching away in his own *ad hoc* way at fragments and very often not going beyond surface phenomena, but deeply conscious of the need for an underlying, unifying theory, would like to put to the linguists' (p. 75).

Reviewing progress in applying linguistics to the treatment of aphasia seven years later, Ulatowska (1979) noted that speech therapists often had an unrealistic expectation of linguistics' current ability to supply the necessary descriptions and data on both normal and disordered language. She proposed that linguistics could contribute only indirectly to aphasia treatment by enhancing the therapist's understanding of language structure and function. What could be singled out as significant in this understanding is threefold. First, the disruption of language in aphasia is a rule-governed phenomenon with error types and error directions being systematic in all types of aphasia. Secondly, there are biological constraints on the disruption of language which account for similarities across languages. Thirdly, aphasic language is on a continuum with normal language. Ulatowska also notes the role of linguistics in clarifying what utterances are disordered and which are characteristic of speakers of non-standard English. She concludes, however, that, although linguistics attempts to provide facts, techniques and explanations for aphasic language 'there is a gulf of complexity, obscurity and sheer ignorance' which separates the linguistic and clinical levels of operation, 'so we should proceed with patience and humility' (p. 322).

Ulatowska is certainly right in her contention that aphasiologists (and in fact psycholinguistic researchers generally) have a rather over-optimistic view of the potential contribution of linguistics. However, it may be the widespread tendency, evident in her comments, to conflate theoretical with different kinds of descriptive contributions, which is partly responsible for confusing the issues and giving rise to this over-optimism. She alludes to the role of universalist theories in accounting for cross-language similarities in patterns of breakdown, and also to that of careful descriptive work at the level of speaker's underlying linguistic system. The application of sociolinguistics in clarifying precisely what utterances may reasonably be seen as genuinely 'disordered' is a different matter again, overlapping in fact with an important concern of applied pragmatics with the nature of 'normal' conversation. Green (1984) has pointed out the relevance of this issue for aphasia therapy.

We shall start distinguishing the various contributions of linguistics by considering the role of *linguistic theory* in psycholinguistics and aphasiology. This will involve some attention to the question of how far linguistic theories can be said to be 'psychologically real', an important issue which affects the relationship between linguistic and psycholinguistic theories, and has remained contentious both for researchers and for those who interpret and implement their findings. Subsequent sections of this chapter will concentrate on the various applications of linguistics (including pragmatics) which are more clearly *analytic* and *descriptive*. However, it is important to remember that even apparently straightforward description and analysis is always the product of a particular underlying theoretical orientation. Pragmatics itself is a cover term inclusive of a very disparate set of approaches, not all of which originate from within linguistics. Later in the chapter we shall try to identify these orientations, and to motivate the approach to pragmatic analysis developed in Chapters 6 to 9.

LINGUISTIC THEORY AND APHASIA

As in so many other areas the application of linguistics to aphasiology has since the 1960s been greatly stimulated by the universalist, mentalist linguistics pioneered by Chomsky, as well as various developments from and reactions to Chomsky's proposals (see for example Caplan, 1987; Hildebrandt, et al., 1987; Lesser, 1989; Byng and Black, 1989). After a dip in popularity in the late 1970s and early 1980s, this type of generative linguistics has recently re-emerged as extremely attractive and suggestive to psycholinguists at the level of model building and theory construction. Essentially, it has a psychological orientation, conceptualizing a grammar as a detailed specification of the abstract knowledge which a speaker has of his or her language rather than an account of the structure inherent in language which may be checked against systematically collected spoken or written texts. Generative grammar is thus quite different from, for example, Halliday's functional grammar, which is socially rather than psychologically orientated, presents a coherent, multilevel theory of language, and attempts to relate each feature of a text to the overall language system. Halliday has remarked that although the two traditions borrow insights from each other, 'they are ideologically fairly different and it is often difficult to maintain a dialogue' (Halliday, 1985: xxviii). A generative grammar is also very different in its goals and orientation from the corpus-based reference grammar of Quirk, et al., (1972).

Recently, generative linguists have been more concerned with specifying the universal properties of (mental) grammars than, as in earlier versions of the theory, writing grammars of particular languages. Consequently, although such abstract grammars are attractive to psycholinguistic theorists and experimenters, they are a great deal more theoretically contentious than for example, a Hallidayan grammar, and of much less value in providing a coherent account of the various morphological, syntactic and semantic subsystems of a language. Our reason for concentrating on generative grammars here is not that they possess any particular overall superiority, but simply because of their wide currency in psycholinguistic research. Their attraction to psycholinguists is illustrated by the extract below from one recent introductory text, which describes Chomsky's recent universalist theories as follows:

> UG [Universal Grammar] theory holds that the speaker knows a set of
> principles that apply to all languages, and parameters that vary
> within clearly defined limits from one language to another. Acquiring
> language means learning how these principles apply to a particular
> language and which value is appropriate for each parameter. Each
> principle of language that is proposed is a substantive claim about
> the mind of the speaker and the nature of acquisition
>
> (Cook, 1988: 2).

THE QUESTION OF PSYCHOLOGICAL REALITY

The mentalist orientation evident in the language of Cook's summarizing paragraph has created a number of problems.

Perhaps the most pervasive of these is a misunderstanding of the kind of *psychological reality* which is being claimed in relation to 'the mind of the speaker'; arguably, this misunderstanding has been largely responsible for the over-optimistic expectations of linguistics to which Ulatowska alludes. Black and Chiat (1981) have suggested that an ill-conceived notion of the psychological reality of a linguistic theory has laid the basis for the relationship between psycholinguistics and theoretical linguistics. It has had the effect of stunting the development of a powerful psycholinguistic theory while at the same time being irrelevant to the actual practice of theoretical linguistics. Chomskyan claims of psychological reality of the kind described by Cook belong to the domain of *metatheory* in that they set out the fundamentally mentalistic and deductive (as opposed to socially oriented and inductive) character of the theory. But the actual process of constructing linguistic theories and linguistic argumentation follows quite different principles, such as consistency, economy and the general aesthetics of the discipline. Some generative linguists in fact have adopted Chomsky's descriptive system, but see their goal as being the construction of a grammar which most elegantly describes the language rather than one which a native speaker might in some sense be said to have in his head (for further discussion see Matthews, 1979; Katz, 1981; Spencer, 1988). Psycholinguists have frequently differed from theoretical linguists in interpreting the claim of psychological reality to mean that linguistic theory can provide psycholinguistic explanations which can in turn be translated directly into experimentally testable hypotheses. The chief consequence of this misunderstanding is that distinctions made in linguistics are sometimes interpreted as corresponding directly with real-time comprehension and production processes. We can illustrate this with two examples which have cropped up frequently in the literature.

The first of these is the *competence/performance* distinction which has sometimes given rise to a general assumption of parallelism between linguistic and psycholinguistic concepts. This was applied, for example, in hypothesizing a correspondence between the processing involved in different types of *passive* construction and the linguistic theoretical devices known as transformations. The much-discussed distinction between competence (a speaker's knowledge of his or her language) and performance (use of it in an actual situation) was originally introduced by Chomsky (1965: 4) chiefly as a means of abstracting away from a large number of factors involved in language use. These ranged from sociocultural conventions such as style and politeness (now the domain of sociolinguistics and pragmatics) through to processing phenomena such as slips of the tongue (the foundation of much psycholinguistic modelling) and memory limitations on production. The competence/performance distinction is a highly contentious one which has provoked much criticism over the years. For example the phenomena mentioned above from which it abstracts the underlying language system are highly relevant to psycholinguistic and aphasiological research. Nor is the distinction general to linguistic theory, since it simply does not emerge as an issue in a socially oriented Hallidayan functional analysis. Although Chomsky's original purpose in making the distinction was evidently to narrow down and make manageable the legitimate domain of enquiry for grammatical theory, *competence* has sometimes been interpreted psycholinguistically or neurolinguistically as corresponding to a general linguistic capacity, and *performance* as corresponding to the ability to *access* linguistic information (see Lesser, 1989: 48ff. for further discussion).

Sometimes hypotheses which conflated theoretical linguistic and psycholinguistic concepts are more specific than this. We take, as our second example, the *derivational theory of complexity*, which held that transformational complexity would correlate with real-time processing difficulty and/or order of acquisition by children. Consider (1)–(3) below:

(1) The toy was broken by the boy.
(2) The toy was broken.
(3) The boy broke the toy.

The version of transformational theory current in the 1960s would have handled structural relationships between sentences of these types by deriving both (1) and (2) from an underlying active sentence, corresponding to (3), so that the so-called 'agentless passive' (2) would be more derivationally complex than (1), requiring the application of an additional transformation to delete the prepositional phrase *by the boy*. But transformations are devices for capturing generalizations about grammatical structure with no direct psycholinguistic correlates, and in fact experimental investigation revealed that (2) was both easier for adults to process and earlier acquired by children (see further Fodor and Garrett, 1966; Black and Chiat, 1981; Aitchison, 1989). Although proponents of the derivational theory of complexity may with hindsight be judged to have been somewhat naive, the hypothesis seemed to be a sensible one at the time and still stands as a clear demonstration of the essential independence of psycholinguistic and linguistic theory; quite simply, linguistic constructs are neither intended to be interpreted in psycholinguistic terms, nor do linguists necessarily think it desirable that they should be. Chomsky himself has always denied a direct relationship between abstract *knowledge* and actual *use* of language, and Spencer (1988) typifies orthodox linguistic thinking in specifically rejecting the idea of modifying linguistic theory to align it with the results of psycholinguistic investigations.

Many psycholinguists have come therefore to realize that they cannot expect too much of linguistic theory. Caramazza and Berndt, for example, suggest that the real time processes of psycholinguistic theory 'will bear some relationship to the formal, linguistic descriptions of a language (the grammar)' but add cautiously that they 'are not isomorphic with such descriptions' (1985: 28). Byng and Black are careful to point out that the syntactic framework which they use to examine aphasic sentence production has been used for independent psycholinguistic investigation and is based on naturalistic data from the speech errors of normal subjects (1989: 245). But despite this tendency to a more judicious use of syntactic theory, two contributors to a recent book entitled *Theoretical Linguistics and Disordered Language* felt constrained to repeat the point that 'linguistic concepts are part of a theory about language systems in the abstract, and not about realtime language processing' (Chiat and Jones, 1988: 38).

All this does not mean that linguistic theory is irrelevant to psycholinguistics. First and most obviously it provides a vocabulary for the precise and principled description of linguistic phenomena and the formulation of important psycholinguistic questions, as illustrated by Byng and Black. Here, they conceive of syntactic constituents such as noun phrases and preposition phrases as realizations of an underlying conceptual and semantic structure. This leads them to formulate a psycholinguistic question concerning aphasic speakers' ability to produce so-called *predicate-argument* structures, distinguishing throughout, however, between underlying semantic structure and its syntactic realization. Consider for example the following:

(4) John kicks Tim.
(5) Tim is kicked by John.
(6) John gave Tim a prize.
(7) John presented Tim with a prize.

Sentences (4) and (5) have an identical basic predicate-argument structure, in that in each case the verb *kick* requires an Agent (John) and a Patient (Tim). Yet, the syntactic realization of this structure, as evidenced both by constituent structure and linear ordering, is different in each case. Similarly, although (6) is effectively a paraphrase of (7), sharing the same underlying semantic structure, the items *give* and *present* 'drag along' with them rather different syntactic structures. Although Byng and Black do not confuse linguistic and psycholinguistic dimensions of analysis, they are able to draw on recent theoretical work to describe linguistic phenomena in a detailed and sophisticated way, distinguishing carefully between structural, functional and semantic levels. It is only thus that they are able to articulate a precise and principled formulation of the psycholinguistic issues. Such work shows that the potentially useful distinctions made by linguistic theories have developed far beyond the commonplace distinctions of earlier years – such as the distinction between morphology and syntax. But in a parallel way this once clarified the thinking of aphasiologists, without entailing a strong claim of psychological reality.

There is another important but rather less straightforward psycholinguistic application of linguistic theory, which tends to blur the distinction between the two disciplines. As a consequence of its concern with specifying universal properties of language and properties of individual languages, a linguistic theory can suggest constraints on the construction and evaluation of plausible language-processing models. One example (amongst many others) of this kind of application is provided by Grodzinsky (1988) who sees *trace theory* as accounting for certain selective deficits characteristic of agrammatism. Traces are abstract constructs, postulated in order to mark the places from which elements, originally present in underlying structure but not present on the surface, have been moved (Cook, 1988: 3). In distinguishing different types of trace, linguistic theory provides a precise account of linguistic structure which is also biologically feasible; 'theories are used as descriptive frameworks of language deficits' (p. 28). However, Grodzinsky suggests that to be empirically helpful linguistic theories need to be used in conjunction with other kinds of theory – in this case, neuro-psychological theory. Hildebrandt, et al. (1987) also use trace theory to account for the selective difficulty of an agrammatic patient in assigning antecedents to different types of empty Noun Phrases, as in the following examples:

(8) John seems to Bill to be shaving.
(9) John promised/persuaded Bill to shave.

The aphasic subject apparently experienced more difficulty in specifying in (8) than in (9) whether Bill or John was shaving, this pattern of deficit reflecting distinctions between different types of trace on purely linguistic grounds. The work of these researchers and of others who apply linguistic theory in this way is discussed further in Chapter 5.

Researchers such as Grodzinsky and Hildebrandt are interested in modern linguistic theories in so far as they are able to make insightful generalizations about increasingly abstract properties of the language, as in providing a motivated distinction between different types of empty category. One theory is selected in preference to another to the extent that it can make insightful generalizations which potentially predict patterns of grammatical deficit. There may indeed be some correspondence between psycholinguistic processes and formal linguistic categories, and with recent developments in generative theory this correspondence seems to be closer than it once was. However, acknowledging as much does not amount to a direct claim for the psychological reality of those categories.

LINGUISTIC DESCRIPTION AND APHASIA

Rather different from the theoretical applications reviewed in the last two sections is the use of descriptive linguistic techniques to uncover structure in bodies of recorded data. Linguistic description is also used quite directly for routine clinical work, offering a clear vocabulary for making well-motivated distinctions at phonological, morphological, syntactic and semantic levels. But in making this convenient distinction between theory and description, we need to bear in mind that *theoretically coherent description* has an important role in developing psycholinguistic models of the kind discussed by Hildebrandt and her colleagues, and conversely that even apparently straightforward descriptions reflect some underlying theory. For example, as Garman has pointed out, Crystal, et al.'s (1976) treatment of negation as a phrase structure phenomenon is actually quite controversial (Garman, 1989: 33).

The development by these authors of the Language Assessment, Remediation and Screening Procedure (LARSP) is a well-known application of descriptive linguistic techniques, which has been used in aphasia studies as well as with children. Derived quite straightforwardly from the Quirk reference grammar of English (Quirk, et al., 1972), LARSP has enabled many clinicians to describe the characteristics of their patients' language and specify quite accurately their syntactic strengths and weaknesses: 'Instead of the data being a sizeable, and daunting, porridge of words, it became a much more manageable sequencing of various phrase- and clause-structure patterns, many of them frequently recurring, under various lexical guises' (Garman, 1989: 32).

In his re-evaluation of the clinical role of descriptive linguistics, Garman has suggested that its applications are chiefly in assessment and interpretation. Assessment is taken rather straightforwardly to mean the identification of linguistic strengths and weaknesses, at an appropriate level of accuracy and detail. Interpretation is the activity of relating patterns of impairment to models of language structure; thus for example a particular aphasic symptom-complex might be related to specific patterns of linguistic impairment. Remediation is more problematic, since remediation strategies need to be based not only on assessment and interpretation but also on a large number of other factors, social and linguistic. Amongst the latter are, first, a proper psycholinguistic theory of reacquisition which takes into account information about processing as well as linguistic structure and, secondly, the neurolinguistic theories of recovery which have been described in Chapter 2.

The LARSP procedure is generally less widely used with adults than with children in describing patterns of impairment, probably because it is organized according to developmental principles which do not facilitate coherent linguistic classification of different aphasic symptom-complexes. However, Penn (1988) has used the framework to describe the language of 14 aphasic speakers in terms of a number of different profile types (see also Penn and Behrmann, 1986). At the time of writing, Garman and his colleagues are engaged in collecting a systematic body of data with the purpose of describing the characteristics of aphasic syntax in relation to normal language behaviour. An alternative method of grammatical analysis, which was devised specifically to examine aphasic patients' use of sentence structure and verb arguments in particular, is that of Saffran, et al. (1989) and its adaptation by Byng and Black (1989). The use of this has, however, so far only been reported with elicited narrative speech (the Cinderella story) rather than the spontaneous speech to which LARSP is usually applied.

Spontaneous language of the kind typically analysed by means of LARSP can be approached not only *formally* in terms of structural categories such as noun phrase (NP), verb phrase (VP), post-modifying clause and so on, but also in terms of the *function* and *use* of these and other categories in a given context. In other words, one can relate a given utterance not only to the structure that underlies it but to what goes before and after it – to its place in discourse. Scholars who work directly with speakers in specifiable situational contexts (and so with sizeable bodies of intractable data) have often found attractive the emphasis of functional linguistics on social rather than psychological aspects of language. For example, Wells (1985) has developed from Halliday's functional grammar an elaborate analysis of the textual and interpersonal function of utterances. This framework is capable of characterizing both relationships to preceding utterances and the kind of 'act' accomplished by the speaker.

'Functionalism' is an imprecise umbrella term, covering a very wide range of approaches which focus in some way on meaningful communication in context rather than on an abstract, decontextualized structure. Broadly interpreted, a functional perspective can refer to relationships between language and such characteristics of the wider social context as setting, topic and participants. We shall see that these situational factors affect linguistic patterns in a number of ways. Reflecting a certain looseness of definition, Grunwell and James (1989) include a wide and rather disparate range of contributions in a volume on functional approaches to disordered language.

WHAT DO WE MEAN BY PRAGMATICS?

Since the range of phenomena referred to by this term is itself contentious, we shall try in this section to indicate our own orientation in relation to the contributions of others. Some scholars, like Quirk, et al. (1972) and preeminently Halliday (1985), have developed *functional models of grammatical description* which do not separate language structure and language use. Others, such as Leech (1983), view *grammar* (the abstract formal system of language) and *pragmatics* (the principles of language use) as complementary fields of enquiry. This general model of grammar and pragmatics as separate but at various points interdependent seems, for various reasons, to embody the most practicable approach to aphasic language, and it is the one which will be assumed in this book. However, at various points it is the interdependence rather than the fragmentation of syntactic and pragmatic dimensions of language behaviour which needs to be emphasized (cf. a similar emphasis by Fletcher and Garman, 1988), and at first sight this emphasis might seem to align well with an integrated theoretical model of language structure and language use such as Halliday's. In fact, although we shall make reference in later chapters to Halliday's work, systematic adoption of his model as a theoretical and descriptive framework for aphasic language seems at present to create more problems than it can solve. This will become apparent when a range of relevant pragmatic issues is reviewed in later chapters, but we shall mention one particularly important problem here.

Analysts of aphasic spoken language (and it is spoken language with which we are chiefly concerned) often stress the salience of psycholinguistically significant production phenomena such as pauses, and repetitions, non-verbal signals, minimal responses and backchannels such as *yeah* and *uhuh*. Since these phenomena also represent an important meeting point between psycholinguistic and pragmatic investigation, we need an analytic framework which interprets them, rather than idealizing away from them. Of the various pragmatic approaches discussed in Levinson's now standard text (Levinson, 1983), it is that of *conversation analysis* which addresses them most systematically. At present, it is hard to see how this approach, or indeed detailed consideration of such conversational phenomena, could be accommodated within an integrated linguistic theory. While all linguistic theories idealise away from the data to some extent, conversation analysis explicitly rejects prior idealization of the minutiae of conversational interaction. Indeed, Halliday's own account of his integrated theory emphasizes that it does not offer a dynamic model of speech, and that many detailed features of the spoken language lie outside its scope (Halliday, 1985: xxvii).

Some linguists, like Leech (1983), explicitly interpret the term *pragmatics* in such a way as to exclude a social interactional dimension of language use. Others, notably Levinson (see particularly Levinson, 1988), view such a dimension as an essential component of any meaningful account of language use in context. Levinson provides a useful characterization of narrower and broader conceptions of pragmatics (1983: 27ff.), and it is a broader, sociolinguistically orientated conception (similar to Levinson's own) which we shall adopt. Clinicians like Green (1984) and Penn (1988) who have developed pragmatic approaches to aphasic language characteristically take this wider, more eclectic, essentially sociolinguistic approach. Although it embodies a less theoretically 'tidy' conception of pragmatics, it seems to be the more useful for their purposes. Its essence is a concern with *situated speech*, the kind of everyday spoken language which is generally collaboratively produced and is embedded in a web of surrounding contextual constraints and supports.

LANGUAGE PATHOLOGY AND PRAGMATICS

The term 'pragmatics' covers a very wide range of behaviours, if this social dimension is admitted. Much of Levinson's text reflects the resultant complexity, being taken up either with definition of terms or with a (critical) account of disparate and sometimes incompatible traditions of pragmatic theory and analysis drawn from many disciplines. The chief of these are philosophy, psychology, ethnography of speaking, anthropology, linguistics and sociology. As a consequence of this mixed heritage, pragmatics lacks an agreed terminology and descriptive framework to an extent which creates considerable difficulty in delimiting precisely the range of phenomena which might be described as pragmatic. Coulthard (1985: 5) has reviewed the confusingly varied applications of even such basic terms as *discourse, pragmatics* and *text*. Interestingly, the same history of inter- and intradisciplinary terminological confusion was bewailed by McMahon in 1972 as plaguing the study of aphasia, a complaint that is still to some extent valid today.

Clinicians such as Green (1984) Prutting and Kirchner (1987) and Penn (1985) have grappled with the task of extracting from the variegated knowledge base of pragmatics those elements most appropriate to the analysis of aphasic (usually spoken) language. Their task is made even more difficult by the highly controversial status of pragmatic and sociolinguistic concepts within linguistics. Levinson has warned against 'premature acceptance and application of untested concepts and theories' of the kind which vitiated early attempts to apply sociolinguistic ideas to educational practice (Levinson, 1983: 378), and indeed problems springing from such premature acceptance and application are quite evident in language pathology. McTear (1985a) suggests that much published work which attempts to measure pragmatic ability suffers from poor definition of categories and insufficient consideration of the theoretical assumptions underlying the analysis. Six years later, at the time of writing this book, the situation has not greatly improved. Clinicians who seek to apply pragmatic and sociolinguistic analysis need to be aware that the theoretical and descriptive frameworks for examining these dimensions of language performance are nowhere near as well-defined as the psycholinguistic frameworks discussed in Chapters 4 and 5 – and, as we shall see, these are themselves underspecified and controversial. Yet, the latter have been developed over several decades from experimental investigations of the production and comprehension of words and sentences in isolation, without reference to textual, situational or social context. They have not therefore had to tackle some of the complexities of spontaneous language in its social contexts with which pragmatics is currently attempting to grapple.

In recent years, there has been a move to systematize the intuitive and empirical approaches to assessment and therapy in aphasia which have been the mainstay of clinical practice for many years. Clinicians have for a long time used approaches which are sensitive to communicative context and social needs, and which focus on an overall ability to communicate. These approaches, like the complementary ones which focus directly on language forms in the restricted context of a clinical setting, have recently become more structured. We do not claim that the application of pragmatic theories has effected a sea-change in practice in aphasia therapy; in fact the application of psycholinguistics could make a better claim for this in respect both of assessment and therapy. Nevertheless, we hope to show in Chapter 12, that much more is involved in the systematic application of pragmatics than that 'A new label is simply being given to old methods' (Davis, 1986: 251).

An example of the recent trend towards systematic application of pragmatics in aphasia therapy is the PACE procedure (Promoting Aphasics' Communicative Effectiveness), devised and evaluated by Davis and Wilcox (1985), which utilizes a broad pragmatic and interactive framework (although Howard and Hatfield, 1987, have pointed out that its application results in a far from naturalistic situation). Penn (1985, 1988), Skinner, et al. (1984) and Prutting and Kirchner (1987) have proposed similar frameworks for constructing communicative profiles which might be used to provide a principled basis for clinical intervention. Pragmatic concepts such as 'conversational repair' and 'indirect request' have also found a place in recent years in experimental investigations (Chapman and Ulatowska 1989; Weylman, et al., 1989; Schlenk, et al., 1987). Although the range and scope of this work is considerable, the absence of an agreed descriptive and theoretical framework makes the task of pragmatic analysis difficult and contentious. However, we shall conclude this section on a positive note by picking out some reasons for the interest of language pathologists in pragmatics, despite the difficulties.

First, advances in linguistics, however piecemeal, have reflected a concern with various aspects of language use. As has happened with parallel advances in previous years (in the areas of phonetics, phonology, and syntax) the groundwork has been laid for developments in language pathology. Many language pathologists feel in any case that descriptions of formal systems need to be allied to some clear account of language use if they are to be clinically useful. It has often been feared that remedial strategies which focus on formal syntactic categories like preposition phrases or verb phrases may be rendered ineffective unless therapists take account of how the patient uses these items in everyday contexts.

Secondly, some disorders have been seen as pragmatic in type. For instance, Hawkins (1989) presents case studies of two patients whose problems he analyses as discoursal rather than syntactic or semantic, the term *discourse* referring to a linguistic unit larger than the sentence. Brain-damaged patients whose lesion is in the right cerebral hemisphere, or who have widespread bilateral changes (as in dementia), have frequently had their difficulties with language described as pragmatic, in the sense that some of their problems are attributed to a reduced sensitivity to their conversational partners' nonliteral meaning. Pragmatic abilities in the right-brain-damaged and demented are currently being extensively investigated (see, for example Molloy, et al., 1990, and Frederiksen, et al., 1990, on the right-brain-damaged, and Glosser and Deser, 1990, on a comparison of Alzheimer patients with fluent aphasic and head-injured patients). However, a review of this application of pragmatics to the study of impaired language is beyond the scope of this book.

There has been a tendency to assume that pragmatic skills are retained in aphasia (see Holland, 1991, for a review). However, difficulties with syntactic structure or lexical access are likely also to have pragmatic consequences – for example in so far as they affect conversational pause and timing phenomena, or the ability to effect successful clarifications (cf. p. 9f. above). As we shall see in Chapter 9, the interactional effects of such irregularities can be quite far-reaching. An interesting example of such a 'knock-on' effect may be found in Edwards and Garman's (1989) account of a subject whose strategies for dealing with lexical retrieval problems apparently affected his conversational style. Therefore, although it may indeed be possible to isolate a primarily 'pragmatic' type of disorder, the conversational abilities of almost all aphasic patients are likely to be affected in some way which will repay closer examination.

Finally, it may be appropriate in the case of some severely impaired patients to teach communicative strategies which maximize existing ability, however limited that might be; in Green's terms, 'Communication therapy aims primarily to enable the aphasic to function in the community regardless of the residual aphasia' (Green, 1984: 41). Thus, even if the ability to produce and interpret semantically and syntactically well-formed sentences is impaired, alternative communicative strategies may be taught in a principled way, and it is the pragmatics literature from which the relevant principles are likely to derive.

PRAGMATICS, SOCIOLINGUISTICS AND APHASIA

Within the context of developments in linguistics, we have attempted to outline the scope and application of a sociolinguistically oriented pragmatic approach. We shall conclude this chapter with a short review of the theoretical and methodological stance more specifically characteristic of *sociolinguistics*, to which the conception of pragmatics developed by clinicians like Green and Penn is related.

Over the last 25 years or so sociolinguists and conversation analysts have examined language in its social and situational context from several different perspectives. Their work is primarily empirical and naturalistic, their conclusions based on inductions drawn from observable bodies of data, and the end product a socially realistic but principled account of various aspects of contemporary language use. One clinically relevant development from such work is a more liberal conception of the nature of 'normal' language.

Labov (1966) led the way with a data-based study of language variation in several speech styles amongst 88 New Yorkers of various ages and social groups and both sexes. He hoped to develop a more realistic model than was currently available (in Chomskyan linguistics, for example) of the inevitably *variable* language behaviour of real speakers. One important implication for language pathology of the enormous amount of work carried out since 1966 according to Labovian principles has been an appreciation that normal language needs to be defined in terms of patterns of use observable in the community, rather than taken for granted as previously given (see further Milroy, 1987: 208ff.).

The field of *interactional sociolinguistics* as developed by Gumperz (1982) provides a link between work like Labov's which deals with large-scale community patterns and the work of the conversation analysts which falls within the scope of a socially oriented pragmatics. Unlike Labov, Gumperz focuses on *interactions between speakers* rather than on variable and socially constrained elements in a linguistic system. Using a *post hoc* interpretative method (sometimes asking participants themselves for interpretations of their behaviour) he examines the use to which various available linguistic resources are put and the inferences which interlocutors are able to draw from these 'discourse strategies'. An important piece of work in the interactional sociolinguistic tradition to which we will later refer is Brown and Levinson's (1987) extensive cross-linguistic study of *politeness phenomena*, where much of the vagueness and indirectness characteristic of normal conversation is attributed to rational strategic behaviour of interlocutors. Brown and Levinson account for a great deal of apparently routine and pointless linguistic behaviour in terms of the standard desire of conversationalists to avoid threats to their own *face* or the face of others.

Socially sensitive approaches have also been adopted to very detailed studies of the nature of *conversational* behaviour in naturalistic settings; conversation can be minimally defined as a type of interactive discourse produced by more than one speaker. As with the sociolinguistic approaches of Labov and Gumperz, recent developments in the analysis of conversation have resulted in a more liberal conception of *normal* language especially informal spoken language. Most people have a very hazy idea of the characteristics of such language. For example, conversation is frequently described rather pejoratively as ambiguous, unstructured, inexplicit, incomplete and repetitive, but we shall see in Chapter 8 that these very characteristics are important aspects of its organization.

There are several reasons for this knowledge gap, which frequently extends even to the various professions working directly with spoken language data. First, present-day linguistic theory has evolved in a continuous line from traditional Greek and Latin grammars, which are essentially grammars of the written language, and it is only since the invention of the tape-recorder that natural conversation has become amenable to systematic study (Halliday, 1985: xxviii). We might also add that only very recently have small, inconspicuous, relatively inexpensive tape-recorders become available which produce good quality sound and are also easy to transport and operate in everyday conversational settings. However, despite these technological developments, the influential linguistic model developed by Chomsky has actually intensified the long-standing tendency of linguistic theory to idealize away from the data of everyday speech; critiques inspired by the findings of conversation analysis such as that offered by Givon (1979) have had little effect on current generative linguistic thinking. The influential pragmatic approaches which we shall consider in Chapters 6 and 7 also stem from a classical tradition and focus on isolated, usually invented, utterances. It is not surprising that traditional linguistic classifications of aphasia from Jakobson onwards reflect current linguistic practice in ignoring most aspects of naturally occurring conversation. They generally focus on linguistic description at the level of the sentence while abstracting away from the discourse and situational context (see Hawkins, 1989).

Secondly, the dominant research tradition in psychology favours laboratory work where variables can systematically be controlled, manipulated and quantified. For this reason, several papers in Roger and Bull's (1989) collection see psychological approaches to naturally occurring speech as inappropriate and even inimical to worthwhile progress. The tension between psychological and conversation-analytic models (of which the nature of an appropriate data base is just one aspect) is revealed here and elsewhere as a live and controversial issue.

It is probably reasonable to suggest that the somewhat hazy perception by professionals of the character of interactive discourse in everyday situations is largely due to these powerful linguistic and psychological research traditions, the methods, findings and assumptions of which have filtered through to dominate textbooks and professional practice in applied areas like language pathology and education. Yet, the empirical work which we shall review in Chapters 8 and 9 has shown that the richness of real conversational data is such that it cannot conceivably be matched by invented or idealized data of the kind usually found in textbooks: 'Data of this [invented] sort can always be viewed as the implausible products of selective processes involving recollection, attention and imagination' (Atkinson and Heritage, 1984: 3).

Finally, this widespread ignorance of conversation reflects widespread and deeply entrenched sociolinguistic norms. The general public are much inclined to impose written norms on speech, even in making such commonplace comments as, for example, 'he never really speaks in proper sentences'. This tendency is highly resistant to conscious reflection and appears to be a social consequence of literacy and a high level of language standardization in our culture (see further Milroy and Milroy, 1991). But in fact, the repetitions and incomplete utterances characteristic of conversation are not plausibly describable as 'errors' unless conversation is judged from the normative standpoint of written language or speech events based upon written language. In a paper which anticipates the preoccupations of researchers such as Atkinson and Heritage, Abercrombie (1965) pointed out that conversation was not the same thing as either monologue or spoken prose.

The relatively recent development of a more liberal conception of the normal is highly relevant to language pathology, since clinicians with an unrealistic model of normal interaction are likely also to have difficulty in specifying accurately what is *disordered*, and may demand of their patients strange and unnatural skills which do not form part of the repertoire of normal conversationalists. Green (1984) draws a further distinction, arguing that after establishing what is normal, the clinician must next decide whether *normal* or *effective* communication is the focus of therapy. She argues that in order to draw up a realistic programme of assessment and therapy more information is needed on how aphasics actually communicate. We shall explore this question in Chapter 11.

SUMMARY

We have attempted in this chapter to give an overall survey of the relevance of modern linguistics to aphasia research and therapy, with a particular emphasis both on the limits of theoretical linguistics as a foundation for the study of the mental processing of language in psycholinguistics and on the developing field of pragmatics. We suggested that two important contributions of linguistics to aphasiology derived from its capacity to generalize insightfully about abstract properties of language, and to offer a coherent descriptive framework.

However, until recently, linguistic descriptions have frequently idealized away from details of everyday spoken language such as pauses, repetitions, incomplete utterances and so on.

These essentially conversational phenomena are highly relevant both to the description and to the analysis and interpretation of aphasic language. Finally, it is important to recognize the wide variety of spoken language which may be considered to be normal rather than pathological as shown by sociolinguistic and interactional research, and this more liberal conception of normality is critically important to the aphasia researcher and therapist.

It is against this background that the psycholinguistic and pragmatic approaches to intervention in aphasia have been developed. In the next two chapters we look at the interpretations of language offered by psycholinguists which have been applied to aphasia. Some of these originate from cognitive psychology, and use relatively simple linguistic concepts. Others seek insights from highly elaborative theories of grammar. Taken together they are contributing to the transformation of clinical practice in using assessment as a basis for direct work on language structures at the word and sentence level.

FOUR

Psycholinguistic models: lexical processing

Current psycholinguistic models have been applied extensively over the last few years to the study of disordered language, and in particular to difficulties in the reading and writing of single words. As we demonstrated in the last chapter their derivation owes more to psychology than to linguistic theory, since early attempts to translate generative theories into psychologically real mental processes proved ingenuous and abortive. The source of these models has therefore been primarily the work of cognitive psychologists, who initially approached language from a some-what simple perspective. The empirical parameters of language in which they have been interested have been such variables as the frequency with which words occur in language (generally in written texts), the age at which they are acquired, and subjective ratings of the extent to which the referents of the words can be imaged. The focus has been on the mental operations underlying the processing of these words in various cross-modality tasks, such as matching words to pictures or reading words aloud. Models of these processes have been constructed originally on the basis of laboratory experiments with psychology students.

COGNITIVE NEUROPSYCHOLOGY

The study of language-disordered patients has offered cognitive psychologists the opportunity to test the viability of these models against the behaviour of people who, it is proposed, have some of the processes malfunctioning. In fact this interest extends well beyond language (just as applications of pragmatics to aphasia need to extend to non-linguistic aspects of social interaction). From this a new discipline of *cognitive neuropsychology* has arisen, which incorporates within its field not only the study of how language breaks down in aphasia but also the many other aspects of cognition which brain damage affects, notably memory, attention, planning and perception. For aphasiology, cognitive neuropsychology has the potential advantage of expanding the study of the aphasic individual from a narrow focus on language to considerations of the wider cognitive deficits which follow brain-damage – an attractive prospect for aphasia therapists, who of necessity are concerned with the individual as a whole.

In practice, however, this extension of aphasiology has not been as great as might have been expected, due to a tenet of cognitive neuropsychology. That is that the mind is modular in its organization, i.e. is comprised of potentially autonomous components, which brain damage can disturb selectively. To some extent this has been taken as a justification for examining linguistic processing independently from other aspects of cognition – an approach which has inherent limitations. *Modularity* is currently a very powerful notion in several disciplines. In linguistics, Chomsky's Universal Grammar treats language as organized into autonomous components; we shall have more to say about this in Chapter 5. In neurophysiology specificity of processing has been taken down to the neuronal level in, for example, single-cell responses to line orientation and the control of leg movements in walking. In psychology, modularity has been used by Marr (1982) in his influential exposition of visual processing (in which, for example, depth perception is a separate module), and by Johnson-Laird (1988: 259) in explaining why singers may not automatically be able to write in musical notation. In psycholinguistics the modules which have been proposed include auditory, visual, phonological, orthographic, lexical, syntactic, semantic and pragmatic.

Consequent to this emphasis on modularity, cognitive neuropsychology tends to pull the aphasiologist towards a reductionist rather than an integrative study of the whole individual. It can be argued, however, that a reductionist approach is not disadvantageous at this stage of our understanding of language disorders after brain damage, since it reduces the questions to be asked to more delimited and manageable topics. In discussing the implications of cognitive neuropsychology for therapy in particular, Seron and Deloche (1989) use the metaphor of pointillism, after the impressionist painters' technique of building up pictures from small discrete dots. The implication is that, if we stand far enough back in the future, we may yet be able to see the whole picture, even though we may still need to interpret it at different levels of abstraction. Moreover, the development of modularity into a 'functional architecture' of language processing does not preclude the interactive employment of these modules (provided that a strong interpretation of modules as informationally encapsulated and innately wired is not used, as by Fodor, 1983).

One currently applied adaptation of a weak interpretation of modularity, which has attractive implications for aphasiology, is known as the 'multiple representation hypothesis' (Townsend and Bever, 1991). This equates modules with levels of structure and allows for simultaneous processing at several of these levels, from auditory to pragmatic. At each level Townsend and Bever propose that distinct procedures are used in order to produce different types of representations, for example lexical processes apply principles of phonological and lexical organization to auditory input to produce words, and words can then be operated on to produce semantic representations. Interactions therefore occur between adjacent levels. Of particular relevance to aphasia is that the multiple representations hypothesis contrasts with a stricter model of architectural modularity 'in claiming that processes at different levels of structure may share processing resources' (Townsend and Bever, 1991: 53). If processing resources are pathologically limited, comprehension and production difficulties may be due, not so much to impaired levels of representations themselves, but to the need for a trade-off between them in actual processing. This idea has been applied to one interpretation of agrammatism, as difficulty in coping simultaneously with the requirements of syntactic and semantic processing, as we discuss in Chapter 5.

Some psychologists see cognitive neuropsychology as a sub-discipline of cognitive science (e.g. Caramazza, 1989). Cognitive science 'tries to elucidate the workings of the mind by treating them as computations' (Johnson-Laird, 1988: 9), with the ultimate aim of mapping these onto neurophysiological processes. Psycholinguistic models are not yet so well specified that their computer modelling can make any real claim to representing brain function, although parallel processing 'neural' networks are able to mimic some aspects of human performance like learning a vocabulary or parsing sentences (Arbib, et al., 1982; Schneider, 1987).

We must also remember that, just as linguistic theories operate at a different level of abstraction from psychological reality (as discussed in Chapter 3), so the psycholinguistic theories applied in cognitive neuropsychology also operate at a different level from neurological reality. Just as extrapolations have been made from linguistics to psycholinguistics, similar attempts have been made to extrapolate from psycholinguistic theory to the neurological, using the new technology of brain imaging. Petersen and his colleagues (Petersen, et al., 1988) have used Positron Emission Tomography with normal subjects to trace the extent to which some of the autonomous modules postulated by cognitive neuropsychological models involve activation of differently located brain areas. So far they have claimed to find evidence that semantic processing does indeed activate different regions from those activated by lexical processing, and that visual and auditory lexical inputs stimulate different areas of the brain. Despite such claims the relationship between mind and brain remains a fertile area of philosophical dispute (see, for example, Blakemore and Greenfield, 1987). For the present, as Hatfield (1988) argues, knowledge of brain function in respect of language is currently so limited that psycholinguistic theory does not yet need to take into consideration any possible *neurological*, as distinct from cognitive neuropsychological, constraints. Thus we have a similar gap between cognitive neuropsychological theory and neurophysiology as between linguistic theory and psycholinguistics; each operates at a different level of abstraction.

The evidence we obtain from aphasia raises other questions. Is disordered language literally just normal language which has become disordered, or does it operate with new rules, that is has it become a new language from which we can only indirectly make inferences about the computations which occur in normal language? What, for example, about the 'agrammatic' patient who has difficulty in producing auxiliary verbs to mark aspectual and tense distinctions, and who has learned to say 'Soon I come' instead of 'I'll come'? Psycholinguistic models generally do not yet take into sufficient consideration the adoption of compensatory strategies to circumvent deficiencies (as documented for example by Kolk and Van Grunsven, 1985, in Broca's aphasia), although, as we discussed in Chapter 2, they form a substantial element in some recovery of behavioural function. Nor do analyses of disordered language sufficiently distinguish between the acute stage of recovery (when the language system may be particularly obscured by other difficulties such as lowered efficiency reducing attentional capacity) and the chronic stage (when learned compensatory strategies may equally be obscuring the essence of the disorder).

Given the difficulty of formulating the theory and the even greater difficulty in translating it into a meaningful analysis of an individual patient's disorder, when confronted with its complexity in the clinic, it is gratifying that a number of studies have already applied some aspects of psycholinguistic theory to aphasia remediation. We shall consider these in Chapter 11. In this chapter we shall outline the models of the mental processing of single words which underlie these specific attempts. In the following chapter we shall attempt this for the processing of sentences.

A MODEL OF THE PROCESSING OF WORDS

A current model of cross-modal processing was proposed by Patterson and Shewell (1987) and has been elaborated by Ellis and Young (1988). An adaptation of this model is shown in Fig. 4.1. We shall discuss aspects of this model in some detail shortly, but first make some general comments concerning its validity for aphasia. A claimed strength of such models is that their original specification was based on experimental data from normal subjects, although now many refinements have been built in to account for the behaviour of brain-damaged people. Such models use labels like 'lexicon' and 'system' which imply that there are static elements in the mental representation of language, which are linked by processing mechanisms. This is a convenient visual mnemonic rather than necessarily being a direct record of what we may suppose to be the actuality of processing language. For instance, what is the mental phonological input lexicon? Does the mind have a *store* of phonologically represented word shapes divorced from meaning? In what sense can an entity exist in a store in the mind, when continuous activity is required? Is this store a recurrent dynamic patterning which has to be in constant activity for it to exist? And in this case how does it differ from

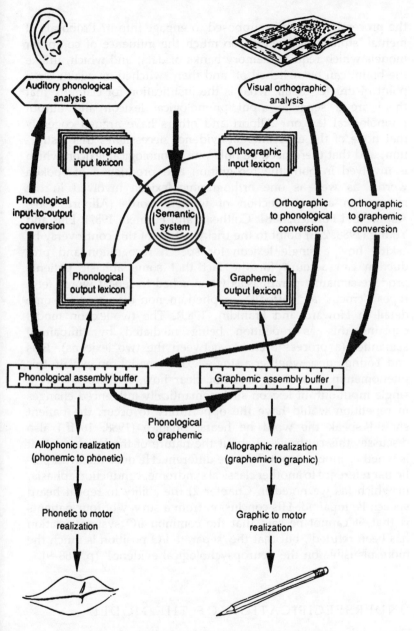

Figure 4.1: Cross-modality model of single word processing

the processing which is supposed to engage into it? Proposals of mental 'stores' may reflect too much the influence of computer models which require memory banks of data, and which, unlike the brain, can be switched off and then switched on again. On a point of greater detail, what is the justification for claiming that there are a separate input phonological lexicon and output phonological lexicon? Allport and others have argued cogently that none of the experimental evidence necessitates this distinction, and that there need be only one phonological lexicon which is involved in both the recognition and production of spoken words, as well as one orthographic lexicon involved in the recognition and production of written words (Allport, 1984; Allport and Funnell, 1981; Coltheart and Funnell, 1987). Ellis and Young (1988: 236) point to the tricky nature of this controversy by asking how a single lexicon for speech recognition and production can account for the fact that some aphasic patients produce semantic paraphasias when asked to repeat words (e.g. repeat 'crocus' as 'daffodil' – a phenomenon discussed in some detail in Howard and Franklin, 1989). The two-lexicon model explains this as repetition being mediated by (impaired) semantics (a process occuring between the two lexicons). Ellis and Young query whether a single-lexicon model can explain this phenomenon so neatly. It is not clear how, if there is only a single input/output lexicon such semantically influenced changes in repetition would have the opportunity to occur: the patient should speak the word he hears. Shallice (1988: 164ff.) also discusses this controversy about the nature of the lexicon/s, that is whether input-output (I/O) are different. He does this with particular reference to another classical syndrome, conduction aphasia, in which (as we noted in Chapter 2) the ability to repeat heard speech is impaired. His conclusion from a survey of four patients is that 'it cannot be said that the common I/O system position has been refuted', but that the 'separate I/O position is much the more plausible on the neuropsychological evidence' (p. 168–9).

UNDERSPECIFICATION OF THE MODEL

Despite the uncertainty of claims for independent processors, and their lack of specification at this stage of the model's development the modules run the danger of becoming reified.

Ellis and Young, for example, in respect of repetition write that 'it can proceed *straight through* the phonological lexicon' (1988: 236) (our emphasis), as if the phonological lexicon/s were indeed mental entities, and repetition a mental process. In fact, virtually every component in these models awaits further clarification, and indeed an agreed label which reflects such clarification. The *graphemic output buffer*, for example, is variously referred to as 'graphemic buffer' (e.g. Carlomagno and Parlato, 1989), 'graphemic level' (e.g. Ellis and Young, 1988) and 'orthographic string' (e.g. Kohn, 1989), reflecting considerable uncertainty as to its nature. Caramazza, who is to date probably the researcher who has investigated in most detail the nature of this postulated buffer, writes (1989: 388) that

> the notion 'graphemic buffer' remains woefully underspecified. Our present understanding of the graphemic buffer is that it is a fast-decaying, capacity-limited component for the temporary storage of graphemic representations. However we have neither estimates of the time course of information decay nor of the capacity of the proposed working memory system. Worse still, we have very little understanding of the type of information stored in the buffer.

It is such lack of specification that allows the suggestion, on the evidence of different abilities in oral and written spelling in a dysgraphic patient, that there may be different graphemic output buffers for the production of letter names in speech and orthographic symbols in writing (Lesser, 1990). Other elaborations of the modules involved in spelling have been proposed. Black, et al. (1989), for example, carry the distinction between store and output buffer to more peripheral aspects of the output of spelling, that is they propose an allographic long-term store and allographic buffer, a graphic motor pattern store and a graphic motor pattern buffer. They locate their patient's dysfunction to the stage where the allographic code is transferred from the allographic buffer to the graphic motor pattern store, since frequency of occurrence of letters in the English language significantly influenced success in his written spelling.

As the controversy about the distinction between input and output modules illustrates, the model presented in Fig. 4.1 minimizes the interactions which must occur in language processing. The multiple representations hypothesis allows for interactions between adjacent levels and for sharing of resources, but studies of the brain-damaged raise further questions about the interdependence of even grosser domains of language, such as speaking and writing. Kohn (1989) has illustrated this in her demonstration of how spelling to dictation reflects the same difficulties as repeating words orally in a patient diagnosed as having conduction aphasia (i.e. good comprehension, but with phonemic pharaphasic errors in speech, particularly marked in repetition tasks). Kohn proposes that this patient's writing and spelling difficulty were primarily a by-product of his speech deficit. She proposes that one source of difficulty could be in clearing information from the phonemic output buffer, resulting in perseveration. A similar dependence of writing on speech is also proposed by Howard and Franklin (1989) in their comprehensive examination of a patient whose conventional classification would be as a Wernicke's aphasic. They maintain a strictly modular interpretation of his disorder, however, by proposing use of a routine for writing to dictation 'which depends on subword level phonological-to-orthographic conversion' (p. 81).

In the present state of the art, a number of speculations may be offered to account for these observations of similarities amongst patients' difficulties. An alternative, physiologically based interpretation of the perseveration in Kohn's patient would be that a common initiatory difficulty was also independently affecting the graphemic output system as well as the speech output system. Rapp and Caramazza (1989) offer a different explanation to account for symmetrical deficits which affect two modalities in the same way. In their patient it was not speaking and writing which showed the same influences but the reading and writing of letters. Rapp and Caramazza's reconciliation of this with a modular model is that processes which perform distinct computations may share certain computational resources. Like the multiple representations hypothesis, this shows an explanatory shift from specification of components to the control of resources used in employing them. Green (1986) has applied a similar notion of inadequate regulation to account for differential patterns of recovery of the different languages of aphasic bilinguals.

We raise these queries, not to diminish the potential value of such models for intervention in aphasia, but in order to set them in a realistic perspective (as we later attempt in our review of developments in pragmatics). Models of language processing are still at an early stage of development (Ellis and Young date the basis of the growth of cognitive neuropsychology to around 1970). Their empirical validity is constantly being tested by evidence from brain-damaged patients. The speech-language therapist applying cognitive neuropsychological models in aphasia therapy needs therefore to be aware of these limitations. The models do, however, suggest a rationale for analysing an individual patient's disorders, as a basis for devising a method of intervention. They provide a framework for perception of the nature of the individual's language, which is relatively simple and easily visualized. Different disciplines have different needs. For the neurologist a framework which uses the classical syndromes may be sufficient at this point of time to meet the needs of informed discussion about the neuroanatomical localisation of functions (and indeed of pharmacological treatment, as Albert, 1988, has proposed). For the aphasia therapist cognitive neuropsychological models, even in their present underspecified form, provide an additional dimension in planning therapy. The detailed evaluation of specific therapies targeted at hypothesized deficits in individual patients may even be one means of specifying the models more exactly or exposing their limitations.

With all these caveats, let us now look at how psycholinguistic models have been used to interpret language disorders as a basis for the remediation studies described in Chapter 11.

AUDITORY COMPREHENSION DISORDERS

The extrapolation shown in Fig. 4.2 from the model which was presented in Fig. 4.1 has been used to account for disorders in auditory comprehension, naming and repetition. We shall discuss these first, in our exposition of the application of psycholinguistics to the interpretation of aphasia.

In an anatomical study, Varney, et al. (1989) reported that, of 30 aphasic people with scores below the lst percentile on comprehension tests, 37 per cent performed normally on recognition of non-verbal sounds such as a dog barking or a telephone ringing. There were no patients with defective sound recognition and intact aural comprehension. This is consistent with the proposed model: acoustic/auditory analysis is a necessary but not

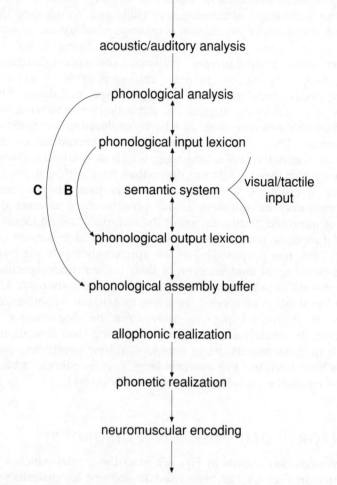

Figure 4.2: Hearing, repeating and naming words

sufficient preliminary to auditory verbal comprehension, and there are later stages in the process which may be impaired independently of auditory analysis. We may note in passing that the claim that acoustic/auditory analysis is necessary prior to comprehension rests on a lack of specification in the model of what this analysis consists of; there is evidence from normal subjects that words can be recognized at speeds which indicate that all the word has not yet been heard (Aitchinson, 1989). A complete word-by-word auditory analysis is therefore not a necessary precursor to access to the phonological output lexicon. Indeed when context restricts the plausible interpretation of an utterance, minimal acoustic processing may be required.

Discrimination and recognition also dissociate, as van Lancker, et al. (1988) have shown through evidence from brain-damaged patients. In this case the evidence is neurological: recognition of familiar voices may be impaired by right parietal brain damage, whereas difficulty in discriminating between voices can follow either unilateral right or left brain damage.

In the verbal domain Franklin (1989) distinguishes five levels of impairment in auditory comprehension. In her proposal a disorder at the level of phonetic/phonemic analysis results in the symptom of *word-sound deafness*. This will affect all auditory verbal comprehension, although not necessarily the ability to discriminate between and recognize nonverbal sounds. Franklin allows for variable degrees of impairment at this level, such that with a mild disorder the patient may be able to comprehend by using contextual information. Such patients will be expected to make errors on tasks of phonemic discrimination between minimal pairs. They will also be unable to repeat words out of context or non-words.

In contrast to word-sound deafness, the symptom of *word-form deafness* is accounted for in Franklin's proposal by an impairment in the phonological input lexicon. Such patients might be expected to confuse similar sounding words when they hear them, and to rely heavily on text for auditory comprehension. This should not in itself affect the ability to repeat words and non-words, if the direct phonemic input to phonemic output conversion routine is available (identified as C in Fig. 4.2).

Another symptom has been described by Franklin as *word-meaning deafness*. This is considered to be due to difficulty in accessing the semantic system from the phonological input lexicon. Again this need not necessarily impair repetition, provided that either the lexicon-to-lexicon bypass routine (identified as B in Fig. 4.2) or routine C remain unaffected. Indeed repetition may often be remarkably preserved, as has frequently been described in the syndrome of transcortical sensory aphasia (Lesser, 1989b).

These three symptoms can occur in independence from each other, it is claimed, though it should be noted that the published literature only attests to the *relative* prominence of one symptom rather than another. None of the three postulated deficits should affect other routes to meaning, e.g. through reading or comprehension of sign language. The other two disorders described by Franklin, however, necessarily do this: they are *central semantic disorders* which detract from all processing of meaning regardless of input. Franklin suggests that these two can be distinguished according to whether the disorder is specific to abstract words and words of low imageability (the two are not synonymous). Though this occurs in some individuals, in others all verbal semantics is affected in a more diffuse way. A necessary consequence of a central semantic disorder (whether restricted to abstract words or not) is that the production of names (whether in response to objects or to written words in reading) will be impaired, as well as their comprehension.

NAMING DISORDERS

Naming and comprehension deficits have also suggested other characteristics of the verbal semantic system. A dissociation between high and low-imageability words is plausibly accounted for by the greater participation of the right cerebral hemispheres of aphasic patients in verbal semantics which have a high imagery quality. As we discussed in Chapter 2 when describing theories of recovery, since the right hemisphere is thought to be dominant for visual processing, a superior retention of words whose referents can be easily visualized has some plausibility if this hemisphere has become more actively involved in lexical processing.

There is also accumulating evidence that semantic systems may be organized categorically. The categories which have been described as being selectively impaired by brain damage include household objects, flowers, animals, colours, letters, numbers, fruits, foods, plants, occupations, tools, clothing and cloth materials (Warrington and McCarthy, 1984, 1987). Such a disorder is not necessarily one which implies loss or even degradation of a specific category or categories. If the impairment is not consistent, or is alleviated when more time is allowed for retrieval, it is interpreted as being a disorder of *access* to that category (Shallice, 1988: 279ff.).

It should be noted that there are problems in concluding that the semantic system is deficient, rather than that access to the system is the source of the difficulty. The technique of priming the recognition of a word by preceding it with a semantically associated word has been applied to patients with supposedly semantic disorders, such as Wernicke's aphasics and sufferers from the type of dementia which characterizes Huntington's disease (Blumstein, et al., 1982: Smith, et al., 1988). Such semantic priming speeds up patients' reaction times to deciding whether a letter string they see is a real word or not (a 'lexical decision' task); this supports the claim that these patients have not lost the meanings of words, but that their difficulty is in accessing semantics as a deliberative act. They remain unable to make judgements of semantic relatedness or select the correct picture for a word from semantic distractors, although in some sense the automatic knowledge of the word's meaning is retained, as indicated by the priming effect.

The model predicts that other disorders besides semantic ones will also affect naming. These include difficulty in accessing this phonological output lexicon from semantics and difficulty in output from the lexicon to the phonological output buffer, as well as impairments of the phonological lexicon or output buffers themselves. None of these processes have so far been well enough specified for access-output problems to be unambiguously distinguished from impairment of the modules themselves. Naming will also be affected, of course, by disorders of phonetic realization or neuromuscular encoding. These are more easily recognized as attributable to the phonetic sound-searching difficulties of verbal apraxia or the neuromuscular disorders of dysarthria (either of which may occur without a concurrent aphasia).

Lesser (1989a) has suggested that both naming and spontaneous speech may act as guidelines in determining the locus of the word-retrieval dysfunction in aphasia. When patients are struggling to find a name, if the difficulty is only in *accessing* the appropriate item in the phonological output lexicon from an intact semantic system they should be helped by hearing phonemic cues as to the initial sounds or syllables of the word. This is similar to the 'tip-of-the-tongue' phenomenon for very low frequency words in normal subjects. It also follows that such patients should have no problems in echoic repetition, since they can access the lexicon from auditory processing even though they have difficulty in access from the semantic system.

A disorder which primarily affects the *phonological output lexicon* itself may result in retrieval of word fragments, with circumlocutions and exploratory searchings. These may take the form of searchings based on the partially retrieved sound pattern of the word sought (phonemic paraphasias). This is consistent with the notion that the phonological output lexicon is at least partly organized by phonological shapes. But these patients seem often to be influenced by semantic relatedness as well in their exploratory searchings. This observation raises a number of questions about the nature of these modules. Is there a separate *semantic lexicon* (as distinct from verbal semantic system)? Or is there continuous spreading (cascading) or even recursive activity between the phonological lexicon and the semantic system? Or do such observations support the notion of an editing device which gives preference to semantically and phonologically acceptable words, unless deliberate strategies are employed to override it? Detailed analyses of the naming behaviour of aphasic patients may in due course be able to throw some light on these questions.

Since norms of word frequency are based on word-form productions (albeit generally written ones rather than spoken), in a lexical disorder there are reasons to expect a significant influence of word frequency on the ability to retrieve words. Extract (1) below is from a patient whose severe naming difficulties seem to be due to either a problem of accessing the phonological output lexicon from the semantic system or to a dysfunction in this lexicon itself. Since his naming shows a significant effect of word frequency, and cuing by initial phonemes often does not assist his word search, the preferred explanation may be that his difficulty lies in the phonological output lexicon itself; this uncertainty of explanation is a further example of the underspecification of the model. The patient is a 62 year old former engineer, S, six years after an operation to remove a left-parietal brain tumour, and the extract is from a clinical session where the therapist, T, had asked him to describe the picnic scene drawing from the Western Aphasia Battery. The two features he is attempting to describe at this point are a kite held in the air by a boy standing near a tree, and a flag. His 'asides' to the therapist are indicated by dashes.

(1)T: what else can you see in the picture
 S: a tree, a tree er (1.0) a lad on the right (3.0)[POINTS TO KITE] – and this is the sort of thing that I have trouble – (.) it's on the right, it's (.) blowing, on the right, and er there's four letters in it, and I think it begins with C (.) goes (.) when you start it and then goes up in the right in the air (.) I would I would have to keep racking my brain how would I spell that word (.) that flies, that that doesn't fly, you pull it round, it goes up with the air (1.0) and I can't (1.0) I can't just tell you what it is but I know more or less there'd be four I would think there'd be four letters and it's a (1.0)
 T: begins with K
 S: K oh [ka] kite (.) kite
 T: good
 S: kite (.) that's better(.) I kept thinking there was a C in kite, yes and there's not four letters in it (.) there's (.) kite (.) no there are four (.) that's right (.) [POINTS TO FLAG] on the left (.) on the left I should know this because I have (.) when when you go in the when you go in the army or when you go in the (.) boat or (2.00) this is flying over you if you go in a boat, this is (.) flying over the (.) the boat and it's a (.)I (.) again I would have to try and keep to spelling the letters in that and keep coming round (1.0) there are, each different country each different country has different (.) colours on that bit of (1.0) it's not paper, bit of (1.0) different, different countries have their own, have their own (.) bit of this stuff wrapped on – it's not wrapped on, I have to use words like that that
 T: it begins with F
 S: F (1.0) it's oh it's a a fly, flight, not a flight, a flea, not a flea, a fly, a flea [WHISPERS] a [fla] (.) a [fla] [NORMAL VOICE] again there's four letters in it, it begins with F and it's a (.) it's not a [tr]
 T: a [flə]
 S: er [flə]
 T: flag
 S: flag, yeah, a flag, a different flag
 T: OK

From this extract it is clear that S has all the necessary semantic information about the two items he is seeking to name.

He also appears to have some orthographic information, particularly as to the length of the written item, and in fact to be able to access an orthographic lexicon more easily than the phonological output lexicon. This orthographic information, however, does not seem to assist him in oral name retrieval, an observation which is consistent with the dissociation between orthographic and phonological representations in the psycholinguistic model. S also indicates to the therapist the strategies he has learned to use in order to try to retrieve items from his phonological lexicon. As well as recalling the spelling, he attempts to cue himself by starting sentences for him to complete with the unavailable word (e.g. 'different colours on that bit of . . . [cloth]'), and he allows himself to produce semantic paraphasias ('wrapped on' [for, presumably, 'attached']) in his search for the word form, while making clear to the listener that he knows they are incorrect ('it's not paper'). S's naming difficulties result in frequent circumlocutions, often with further word-finding difficulties in turn embedded within these circumlocutions. He also produces phonemic paraphasias where he tests out various related possibilities in his phonological output lexicon, for example in his search for 'flag' *fly, flea, flight*. The phonemic paraphasias are predominantly real words, and when he produces part-words or neologisms it is clear from his change of voice that this is an attempt at a self-cuing strategy. Such part-word cuing is often ineffective, even when the part-word has been supplied to him as a prompt by the therapist; this again favours an interpretation of his disorder as being in retrieval processing within the phonological output lexicon rather than in the access from the semantic system to an intact phonological output lexicon. Some of the phonemic paraphasias share semantic links with the target word, as well as phonological – a not atypical feature of this type of naming difficulty, as we noted above. Once the target word is achieved, either spontaneously or by a complete prompt, S has no difficulty in recognizing it as correct, and in repeating it.

With a disorder beyond the level of the lexicon, that is in which the lexicon is intact but there is difficulty in *transmitting* items from it into the phonological output buffer, frequency should not be influential (unless frequency is considered to be related to processes concerned with ease of articulation, another interactive possibility discussed by Seidenberg, 1988). With difficulties at this level Lesser suggests that the phonemic paraphasias should be more closely related to the word-form target than to its meaning, with circumlocutions only used as a strategy to convey the intended communication rather than as a device to assist word retrieval itself. Extract (2) illustrates a patient whose disorder may be at this level. In this example the patient, B, a 63 year old ex-miner two months after a stroke, is describing the Cookie Theft drawing from the Boston Diagnostic Aphasia Examination to a student, C. His attention is drawn to part of the picture which shows a mother absent-mindedly drying a plate while water overflows from the kitchen sink. In the extract we have inserted in brackets the probable intended words for phonological paraphasias which result in either the uttering of real, but semantically inappropriate words, or neologisms.

(2)B: she's (.) walking (washing) the (.) [dzinən] (.) the [dzinən] (.) [uus] [AS AN ASIDE] what will I do [us] on that, you know

(2.0)

B: [POINTS TO PLATE] [eipəl] (.) *[eipəl]*
C: *[plə]*
B: the [eipəl]
C: plate
B: the [pənəl] (.) the [pənəl]
C: plate
B: yes the [pənəl]

(2.0)

C: watch me (.) the plate
B: the (.) blaze
C: very close
B: the blaze
C: plate (.) and what's she doing to it?
B: er cleaning
C: right

(2.0)

C: and (1.0) what do you think about the water?
B: it is closing, it is [tum] too [hər] too [wad] too (1.0) you see I'm not [panausʌn] (pronouncing) anything what I should (1.0) from the [grant] (.) from the [asspərəl]
C: which bit are you trying to say? point to –
B: the [aspəl]
C: right, from there?

B: [spəl]
C: from the tap (.) yes
B: from the gas (.) from the gas (.) from the gas (.) from the gas
C: tap
B: [gat] (.) not er (.) you see I'm not promising (pronouncing) them what I should
C: you're getting some of them
(two turns omitted here)
B: what'll I pronounce that again? say that again?
C: plate
B: pencil
C: you've got the first sound but not the last (1.0) watch me (.) the plate
B: the pate
C: plate
B: the pate
C: very close
B: the pate
C: you're just missing out one sound in the middle
B: the pate (1.0) the pate
C: plate
B: pate
C: plate
B: pate (MOVES TO ANOTHER PART OF THE PICTURE)

This patient's naming difficulties are very different from those of S in (1.0). Again he generally appears to have both the necessary semantic information, and a specific target word in mind. There may be some exceptions to this, in that some of his (uncorrected) lexical retrievals could be semantic paraphasias ('cleaning' is a little odd to describe the drying of the plate, and 'closing' is not apt for the water overspilling at the sink). Frequently, however, the evidence is that he has in fact accessed an appropriate item in his phonological output lexicon, but has difficulty progressing further. Lexical access as such cannot be the problem, since, even when the word is provided in its entirety by someone else for repetition, his speech shows the same difficulties. Sometimes the word is spontaneously produced as a real word which has phonological but not semantic links with the target (e.g. 'walking' (washing), 'promising' (pronouncing), 'pencil' (plate)). Although B seems to be aware of his mispronunciations he is unable to correct them, despite a large number of models being given to him for repetition, with lip-read support, and a splitting of the [pl] cluster into a syllable in [pəleit]. B's first spontaneous attempt at 'plate' in fact suggests that he has some knowledge of the necessary sounds, but is unable to arrange them in the correct order, resulting in [eipəl]. His attempts at repeating 'plate' are inconsistent, but persevera-tive, that is *blaze* on the first series of attempts, *pate* on the second. A significant problem for him therefore appears to be located in processes somewhere after the stage of lexical retrieval from the phonological output lexicon. It is uncertain whether this should be interpreted as a difficulty in accessing the *phonological output buffer* or in the buffer itself. If the difficulty lies only in the phonological output buffer itself, word length should be a critical factor, with multi-syllabic words resulting in more phonemic paraphasias than mono-syllabic. This will apply whether speech is spontaneous or performed as a repetition task. In the case of patient B in extract (2) he makes errors even on monosyllabic words in both repetition and spontaneous speech, while producing some polysyllabic words spontaneously (and repeat-ing 'plate' as *pencil*). A simple explanation in terms of a disorder in the phonological buffer itself is not fully consistent with the data; a preferred account could be a variable difficulty in the input to the buffer.

Again this example, like the one in extract (1) shows how underspecified the model is. Both, however, support its general structure in respect of word-retrieval for naming and its at least temporary utility in the analysis of individual patients' difficult-ies. The examples also show that clinical descriptions of paraphasias as semantic or phonemic are not in themselves sufficient to assist in the interpretation of processing disorders. Both S and B produce both phonemic and semantic paraphasias in the samples of spontaneous speech cited, but the motivation for each of them in each patient is quite different. For S, semantic paraphasias are acknowledged as part of a self-cuing strategy, and phonemic paraphasias are part of a searching procedure. For B semantic paraphasias are uncorrected, and his phonemic paraphasias are neither corrected nor do they function as controllable search ploys. They are in fact a devastating handicap to communication in a task such as the one he was presented with. Interestingly enough, later in the same conversation B goes on to describe how earlier that day he had had a visit from the gasman to read the meter, during which his speech had been so good that he felt the gasman had not noticed any problems. Like many similar patients, B can cope quite well with conventional social greetings, which use high frequency phrases which may be more readily accessible to automatic processing than picture naming or repetition. If our analysis of B's disorder is correct, this suggests an influence of automaticity on input to the phonological output buffer.

All the patients we have described would perform poorly on standard tests of naming ability. A psycholinguistic model, as we have tried to show, gives an account of how the underlying processing dysfunctions behind this common aphasic behaviour may be very different. As we shall discuss in Chapter 10, an analysis of this kind results in very different inferences as to the appropriate therapy to use for individual 'anomic' patients.

LEXICAL READING DISORDERS

Figure 4.3 extracts the part of the psycholinguistic model which accounts for reading comprehension and reading aloud. Again there is some evidence for a three-operation system in reading aloud. These comprise one which includes meaning, one (B) which uses lexical information while by-passing semantics and a third (C) which acts through conversion of sub-word orthographic units to units which can be used by the phonological output buffer. The most suggestive evidence for a distinction amongst these three operations comes from brain-damaged patients. For example, McCarthy and Warrington (1986) describe a patient with very poor comprehension of words (deficient semantic operation), who made errors on reading aloud irregular words (deficient lexical operation B), but who could nevertheless read out nonsense words with as much skill as university students (intact conversion operation C). Another patient, described by Lytton and Brust (1989) as having *direct dyslexia*, also had poor comprehension of what he read aloud. However, this individual could not read orthographically simple non-words (deficient C operation) although he made only a few errors in reading aloud real words, whether simple or orthographically complex (relatively intact operation B).

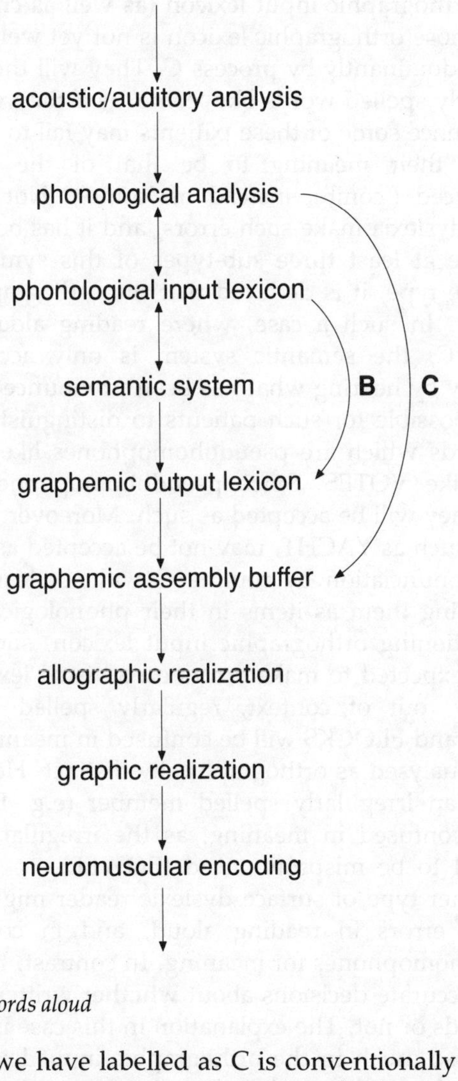

acoustic/auditory analysis

phonological analysis

phonological input lexicon

semantic system   B   C

graphemic output lexicon

graphemic assembly buffer

allographic realization

graphic realization

neuromuscular encoding

Figure 4.3: Reading words aloud

The operation we have labelled as C is conventionally referred to as 'grapheme-phoneme-conversion', though there is in fact reason to question whether the elements in it are indeed graphemes rather than larger word-fragments. Some such routine must obviously be postulated to account for the fact that it is possible to pronounce novel words (including unfamiliar people's names) and invented non-words. Patients with the symptom-complex of *surface dyslexia*, who appear to have some impairment of the orthographic input lexicon (as well as children learning to read, whose orthographic lexicon is not yet well established) may read predominantly by process C. They will therefore pronounce irregularly spelled words like 'come' as if they were regular. As a consequence some of these patients may fail to understand them, or take their meaning to be that of the word they have pronounced ('comb', instead of 'come'). Not all patients with surface dyslexia make such errors, and it has been suggested that there are at least three sub-types of this symptom-complex.

In one type, it is deduced that the orthographic input lexicon is faulty. In such a case, where reading aloud is achieved by routine C, the semantic system is only accessed in reading indirectly by hearing what has been pronounced. It will therefore not be possible for such patients to distinguish between written non-words which are pseudohomophones like VOATS and real words like VOTES. Since pseudohomophones *sound* like real words they will be accepted as such. Moreover irregularly spelled words, such as YACHT, may not be accepted as real words, since their pronunciation by routine C will not lead to the patient's recognizing them as items in their phonological lexicon. With a malfunctioning orthographic input lexicon, such patients would also be expected to make errors on a visual lexical decision task. Similarly, out of context, regularly spelled homophones like PHLOX and FLOCKS will be confused in meaning, although they can be analysed as orthographically distinct. Homophones which include an irregularly spelled member (e.g. BOWL/BOLE) will not be confused in meaning, as the irregular member may be expected to be mispronounced (BOWEL).

Another type of surface dyslexic reader might show the same kind of errors in reading aloud, and in confusing regularly spelled homophones for meaning. In contrast, however, this type makes accurate decisions about whether written letter strings are real words or not. The explanation in this case is that the problem lies not so much in the orthographic input lexicon itself, but in outputs from this lexicon to the semantic system and the phonological output lexicon; it is this which throws the patient back onto the use of routine C.

In a third type, it is deduced that the errors typical of surface dyslexia (regularizations of irregularly spelled words, such as reading HAVE as [heiv]) are due to damage to the phonological output lexicon instead of the orthographic input system. In such a case the patient will *not* misinterpret the mispronounced word, since its meaning will have been understood through the input lexicon. This type of surface dyslexic reader will also be able to disambiguate homophones like PHLOX and FLOCKS through their distinction in the orthographic input lexicon. Distinguishing between real and non-words without speaking (i.e. lexical decision) should be performed accurately. Such a patient would of course be expected to have naming difficulties as well, due to impairment of this part of the speech output system (Kay and Patterson, 1986).

Whatever the underlying difficulty, in the symptom-complex of surface dyslexia the ability to read non-words, however, is not impaired, since this can be achieved by routine C. In order to differentiate the proposed underlying dysfunctions, however, an assessment of an individual patient would need to include a lexical decision task, which includes pseudohomophones, as well as examination of whether homophones are confused for meaning and the influence of regularity of spelling on such possible confusions.

We have so far discussed what happens when readers have to fall back on the use of routine C in this model. Now we turn to the contrasting difficulty, an impairment in routine C. This will evidence itself in an inability to read novel words or non-words. Two forms of acquired reading disorders in which this occurs have been called 'phonological dyslexia' and 'deep dyslexia'.

Unlike other forms of acquired dyslexia, the phenomenon of *phonological dyslexia* has been reported in at least one case as an absolute difficulty, with total failure on all non-words, rather than a relative problem (Funnell, 1983). It is, however more common to find this inability to read non-words associated with additional semantic difficulties, giving rise to *deep dyslexia*. This is characterized by the production of semantic paralexias (e.g. CITY read as 'town'), and greater difficulty with abstract than concrete words. In deep dyslexia, reading aloud therefore evidently employs the semantic route, but either the semantic system or access to or from it is deficient. Deep dyslexia often occurs in association with agrammatic speech, which may account for greater difficulty in reading aloud function words than content words. This depends on one's interpretation of grammatical disorders, as we shall discuss in the next chapter. There are other features associated with deep dyslexia which exceed the explanatory power of the model in Fig. 4.3, that is the occurrence of visual errors ('single' for SIGNAL)) and errors of derivational morphology ('editor' for EDITION) in reading aloud. Some researchers have proposed that deep dyslexia does not in fact reflect a disruption of the normal reading system, but use of the right hemisphere's alternative reading system when the left hemisphere is malfunctioning (see Ellis and Young, 1988, for a discussion).

Other forms of acquired reading difficulty have been observed, which the model is not clearly enough specified to enlighten us about, that is the *letter-by-letter reading* we have already mentioned in Chapter 2 in alexia without agraphia, *neglect dyslexia* (Ellis, et al., 1987) and *attentional dyslexia* (Shallice and Warrington, 1977). Reviews of these can be found in Ellis and Young (1988). However, we shall not elaborate on them here, both because some of them are rare and because therapy for them has not been closely related to a psycholinguistic model.

Of all the aspects of language investigated by psycholinguists and cognitive neuropsychologists, it will be noted that reading aloud is one of the most uncommon activities in everyday life, other than in certain occupations like broadcasting and infant education – but even here it is rarely lists of single words that are read aloud. Since it is on the basis of reading words aloud that psycholinguistic models of language processing were initially developed, it is not too surprising that many linguists (and in particular the pragmatically oriented sociolinguists described in Chapter 2) see little relevance in them. We shall try to show in Part III of this book how a psycholinguistic model of reading aloud has at least an empirical value as a guide to intervention for acquired disorders of reading. In the next section we turn to an activity which has a little more claim to be part of many people's lives, that of writing.

LEXICAL WRITING DISORDERS

Again, cognitive neuropsychological investigations of writing have largely concentrated on single words, particularly spelling errors, as have remediation attempts based on such models. By now it will not be too surprising that Fig. 4.4, which models the writing of words to dictation, shows a close similarity to Figs 4.2

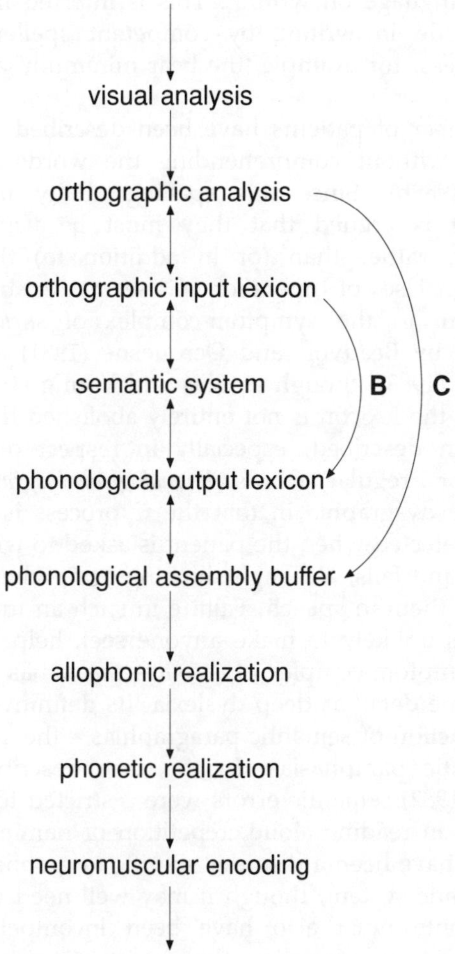

visual analysis

orthographic analysis

orthographic input lexicon

semantic system   B   C

phonological output lexicon

phonological assembly buffer

allophonic realization

phonetic realization

neuromuscular encoding

Figure 4.4: Writing words to dictation

and 4.3. Again this is not due to paucity of the imagination but to experimental and neuropsychological evidence. The potential independence of the writing and speaking systems in educated adults is attested to by the ability of some brain-damaged patients to produce language through writing which they cannot do through speech (despite intact articulatory mechanisms), for example Bub and Kertesz's anomic patient (1982). The model of writing used here, however, acknowledges an influence of spoken language on writing. This is inferred from homophonic errors made in writing by competent spellers when writing under stress, for example 'the bear minimum' and 'maid up her mind'.

A number of patients have been described who can spell to dictation without comprehending the words (Patterson, 1986; Lesser, 1989b). Since this spelling ability includes irregular words, it is argued that they must be using the lexical B operation, rather than (or in addition to) the conversion C operation. Use of operation C seems to be the dominant mechanism in the symptom-complex of *surface dysgraphia* as described by Beauvois and Derouesné (1981) and Hatfield and Patterson (1983), though as Ellis and Young (1988) note spelling by use of the lexicon is not entirely abolished in the cases which have been described, especially in respect of high frequency (regular or irregular) words. *Phonological dysgraphia*, the obverse of surface dysgraphia in that the C process is inoperative, can only be detected when the patient is asked to write non-words to dictation and fails, although showing comprehension of them by repeating them in speech. Failure in such an unusual activity on its own is unlikely to make anyone seek help from a therapist.

The symptom-complex of *deep dysgraphia* has not been studied in the same detail as deep dyslexia. Its definitive characteristic is the production of semantic paragraphias – the analogy in writing of semantic paraphasias. In the case described by Bub and Kertesz (1982) semantic errors were restricted to writing and did not occur in reading aloud, repetition or naming. This therefore seems to have been a disorder specific to graphemic output from the semantic system, though it may well need to be argued that the C route must also have been incompetent, or at least unemployed, in correcting these semantic errors in writing to dictation.

Peripheral dysgraphias have also been reported, which are 'pure' in the sense that other central language processes involved in speech and reading are intact. A disorder affecting the graphemic output buffer results in spelling errors of additions, deletions, and substitutions, which it is claimed will intrude on any spelling output (written, oral, by typewriter, etc.). However, Lesser (1990) has offered some neuropsychological evidence from different patterns of error in oral and written spelling which is better explained by there being different buffers for these two outputs. Spelling errors attributed to dysfunction of the graphemic output buffer increase with the length of the word but are unaffected by frequency, imageability or grammatical class (Caramazza, 1989). Uncontroversially, difficulties in allographic realization will affect writing but not oral spelling; these affect the assignment of the appropriate visual shape for the letters (e.g. upper or lower case, or substitutions across letters such as D and P). Apraxic difficulties, by analogy with verbal apraxia in the spoken medium, can impair the selection of graphic motor patterns, and result in errors like the fusion of two letters. In addition there can be paretic problems at a more peripheral level, the analogy of dysarthria in speech. An additional dimension enters into writing, however, and that is the spatial. Impairment of the spatial aspects of the written production of language, generally showing only for larger units of script than single words, is often associated with right brain damage: this spatial disorder results in neglect of the left-hand side of the page, slanting writing and letters which have perseverative strokes in them. Ellis and Young (1988) suggest also that afferent feedback difficulties contribute to peripheral writing disorders in some patients. They point out that normal subjects make similar perseverative errors and misplace strokes when visual and afferent motor feedback is interfered with by asking them to write with eyes closed while tapping sequentially the fingers of the left hand.

SUMMARY

In this chapter we have described, and pointed out some of the limitations of, psycholinguistic models of single-word processing across the modalities of listening, speaking, reading and writing. These limitations include both underspecification of the proposed processing modules of which they are comprised and their interactions, as well as uncertainty as to the role played in such models by systems of control and allocation of resources. We have indicated in places the role which neuropsychological evidence has played in developing one of these models of cross-modal processing of single words, and specified different types of disorders of verbal comprehension, naming, reading and writing which can be interpreted in terms of this model. We have also attempted to show which behaviours must be incorporated into the assessment of aphasic individuals in order to establish the location of their dysfunctions in terms of such a model.

One of the obvious limitations of such a model is its restriction to single words. For some patients this does not necessarily limit its relevance for remediation of the disorder (as we hope to show in Chapter 10). But for others it is a serious disadvantage. Indeed Howard and Franklin (1989), two aphasia therapists whose case study, *Missing the Meaning*, describes an extensive and scholarly analysis of a patient's difficulties in processing single words, come to a sad conclusion:

> Over the years that we have been seeing him, we have tried a
> number of different treatment approaches . . . None have been
> conspicuously successful and so no results seem worth reporting . . .
> The difficulty is that the greatest impediment to communication is
> probably his severe problem in sentence comprehension
>
> (Howard and Franklin, 1989: 145)

This comment reminds us that the processing of words is only one element in the complex activity of language, and aphasia therapists may only wish to use decontextualized words in their remediation programmes as one limited aspect of intervention in certain cases. We need now to consider other levels of language processing and language use, beginning with the level of the sentence.

FIVE

Psycholinguistic models: sentence processing

If we have had to acknowledge the underspecified nature of the single-word processing models used as a basis for aphasia therapy, we have to admit an even less clear state of affairs in the processing of sentences, whether for the production of speech or its comprehension. We shall attempt to show in this chapter how, on the one hand, psycholinguistic models of speech production, applied in both 'off-line' and 'on-line' tasks, and, on the other hand, a linguistic theory, have been applied in attempts to elucidate the nature of the problems which some aphasic speakers experience in stringing words together at the sentence level. Again this is not a comprehensive review of psycholinguistic models or linguistic theories, but a selective survey of some which have been applied to illuminate understanding of aphasic difficulties in sentence production and comprehension.

The main psycholinguistic model of speech production at the sentence level which we shall describe is one developed by Garrett (1982) and expanded by Schwartz (1987). This model is derived from data from the errors of speech made by normal subjects, and is therefore empirically based rather than an application of a pre-existing theory. It is of particular interest because it has been directly applied in aphasia therapy. It has also lent itself to explanation of the different types of disorders which occur in difficulties in producing sentences after brain damage, in the continuum from *agrammatism* (characterized classically by limited syntactic structure and omitted grammatical morphemes) to *paragrammatism* (characterized classically by ill-formed sentences and substitution of morphemes).

A PSYCHOLINGUISTIC MODEL OF SENTENCE PRODUCTION

Schwartz's adaptation of Garrett's model proposes five levels of representation involved in constructing sentences:

> *message* (pre-linguistic conceptual and inferential), which initiates a search for the appropriate words;
> *functional* (creation of the predicate) which assembles, without ordering, the argument structure of the proposition, generally based on the verb;
> *positional*, with creation of an ordered syntactic planning frame, and insertion of the lexical items into appropriate slots and phonological encoding of first the content words and then minor syntactic elements (grammatical morphemes, whether bound, like inflections, or free, like prepositions);
> *phonetic*, with realization of the phonological into its phonetic structure;
> *articulatory*, with realization of the phonetic into neuromuscular coding.

The processes which mediate between these levels are, respectively: logical/syntactic between message and functional; syntactic and phonological between functional and positional; phonological between positional and phonetic; and neuromuscular encoding between phonetic and articulatory.

Speech errors have been used in order to justify both claims about the serial nature of sentence production and the elements proposed in this model, particularly in specifying the elaborative stage of transition from functional to positional level and the positional level itself. For example it has been asserted that affixes are inserted later than content word stems. This is on the basis of errors where the affixes have become transposed, as in Garrett's (1980) example:

(1) I've got a load of cooken chicked (. . . cooked chicken).

At the positional stage, Shattuck-Hufnagel (1983) uses the analogy of a scan-copier, and suggests that lexical items are inserted phoneme by phoneme into the planning frame. The phonetic specification of inflections must come later, since speech errors show appropriate phonetic realizations of inflections for the uttered error rather than the intended word. In the example below, the transposition of /t/ to the first word results in the realization of the plural affix as /s/ rather than /z/.

(2) tie boats (. . . tight bows).

'Agrammatism' and the model

Theories of aphasic disorders of sentence production have selectively invoked all the different stages of production specified in such a model. Rather than classifying patients globally as 'agrammatic' or 'paragrammatic', if we wish to target therapy around a specific disorder, it is desirable to specify more exactly the semantic/ syntactic/ morphological/ phonological disorder which is most impaired in that individual patient. It should be noted that this is not a view taken by every aphasiologist. Many researchers have sought for a unitary explanation of all the phenomena which occur in this syndrome (e.g. Villiard, 1990; Caplan, 1991). Here we take the psycholinguistic orientation which seems more applicable to the analysis of an individual patient's language abilities prior to therapy. We view agrammatism, not so much as a coherent syndrome, but as a convenient label for certain surface behaviours which may have different causes in different individuals. The various proposals about the nature of agrammatism are therefore seen as possible distinctions which may be applied to differentiate individual patients. At the same time, however, it is readily acknowledged that, as with applying the single word models described in the last chapter, many patients are likely to have impairment with more than one component.

Early accounts of agrammatism, observing that it occurred principally in association with the 'articulation difficulties' of Broca's aphasia, associated it with a disturbance at what, in Garrett's model, would be at the phonetic level of representation. Some accounts went even further than this and described telegrammatic speech as being due to economy of articulatory effort, an interpretation which would place the disorder at the articulatory level of representation. A more recent explanation of agrammatism (Kean, 1977; Nespoulous and Dordain, 1990) accounted for it in phonological/prosodic terms, from the observation that the grammatical morphemes which are omitted do not normally carry stress, but that performance can improve when attention is directed to them (an encouraging observation for therapy).

More discussion has centred on disorders of the syntactic and morphological processes which Garrett's model places between functional and positional levels of representation. Historically, difficulties with grammatical morphemes ('closed-class items') have received most attention, since omission of these featured as an essential component in the classical definition of agrammatism. Zurif (1980) proposed that 'the relative inability of Broca's aphasics either to produce closed-class items or to make use of them in comprehension is tied to a disruption of the specialized mechanism for retrieving closed-class items, foreclosing the ability to use these items as syntactic placeholders' (p. 310). For some patients these morphological problems seem to predominate, but for others the essential difficulty seems to lie in the planning frame itself (Berndt, 1987; de Bleser, et al., 1988).

This analysis is potentially important in aphasiology for its implications for the more exact assessment and differential treatments of disorders of grammatical production.

SYNTACTIC PRODUCTION AS INDEPENDENT OF COMPREHENSION

The Garrett–Schwartz model is essentially of sentence *production* and makes no claims about comprehension (though, as we shall see in Chapter 10, extrapolations have been made from it about using comprehension tasks as a medium for therapy). It would be consistent with a claim that sentence comprehension and sentence production can be impaired independently by aphasia. A number of case studies have reported that this does indeed occur and we will describe one as an illustration of this point of view.

The case ML described by Caramazza and Hillis (1989) had severely agrammatic speech but almost intact sentence comprehension. ML made word order errors in writing and (probably) in speech, had a mean length of utterance of about two words, and omitted 62.4 per cent of free grammatical morphemes, 18.5 per cent of grammatical inflections and no derivational suffixes. In terms of Garrett's model, Caramazza and Hillis put the locus of the lesion 'at the positional level (or some aspect of the processes that generate this level of representation)' (p. 640). They acknowledge the lack of specification of just what computations might be entailed at this level, and the extent to which any such computations might dissociate. Some candidates for such dissociations are: the construction of the sentence frame (possibly from ready-made fragments as suggested by Dell, 1986), and its temporal ordering; phonological specification of the content words to be inserted into it; phonological specification of grammatical inflections on these content words; selection and phonological specification of free grammatical morphemes. ML's sentence productions showed severe errors of construction, including word order particularly in writing, and omissions of free grammatical morphemes. They showed less impairment of bound morphemes and very little (3.8 per cent) of content word production (omissions). The distinction between free and bound grammatical morphemes in ML's productions is striking, but difficult to account for in view of the fact that the functions served by both are represented only in the form of inflections in many languages. Also difficult to accommodate to linguistic analytic principles is the observation that ML's omission of free grammatical morphemes was fairly consistent across this hetero-geneous class, which serves a variety of linguistic functions, that is articles were omitted about 63 per cent of the time, pronouns 72 per cent, conjunctions 71 per cent, auxiliary verbs 82 per cent, prepositions 38 per cent, have/be full verbs 58 per cent and here/ there adverbs 100 per cent. The analysis of ML's disorder, therefore, although it endorses the empirical separation of sentence production and comprehension disorders, provokes more questions than it answers about the processes which contribute to sentence production.

Other analyses have proposed selective disturbances of syntactic frame construction and morphological processes (Berndt, 1987; Nespoulous, et al., 1988). Aphasia is a productive medium through which possible dissociations of speech production mechanisms can be explored but it is obvious that many more analyses need to be made of the grammar of aphasic speech before such issues can be clarified, and Garrett's (or any other) model expanded further. Certain 'on-line' experiments of the syntactic comprehension of agrammatic patients have thrown some light on the relationship between speech and comprehen-sion, and we shall return to these later in this chapter.

PROBLEMS WITH VERBS

The Garrett–Schwartz model has been used to inform therapy for grammatical disorders, particularly in respect of two notions which concern interpretation of the disorders as affecting transition. By this is meant transition between the message and functional levels, not transition between the functional level of representation and the positional with which the above studies have been concerned. These notions address first, problems related specifically to verbs and their arguments, and, second, difficulty in the mapping of semantic representations onto syntactic structures. Both of these have been suggested to be supramodal, in that at this high level of sentence organization where syntax and semantics enmesh they affect both comprehension and production.

A number of studies have reported that verbs present particular difficulties for some patients. Miceli, et al., (1984) suggest that a difficulty in the processing of verbs is a common feature of agrammatism. Kohn, et al., (1989) used a synonym and sentence generation task to detect verb-finding difficulties in a group of nine aphasic patients. They found one patient, classed as a transcortical motor aphasic, who had difficulties particularly with referentially vague verbs like 'make' 'have' 'get', although she was not impaired on nouns. They suggest that she was unable to choose amongst the variety of roles into which such verbs can enter in sentence planning.

In another study McCarthy and Warrington (1985) also claimed that the underlying disorder in an agrammatic man was secondary to impaired representation of verbs. Grammatical morphemes, both free and bound, were relatively preserved in the speech of this patient, a former accountant, but he omitted main verbs frequently, as in (3) and (4) below, or substituted nouns with an-ing inflection for the verb, as in (5) and (6) below:

(3) The woman is [drinking] a cup of tea.
(4) The child was [pulling] the trailer.
(5) The child was laddering [climbing].
(6) The daughter was chairing [sitting].

This observation, incidentally, suggests that simple subject-verb (SV) or subject-verb-object (SVO) sentence frames can be created without the dependency on verb retrieval implied in Garrett's model, though it should be noted that these examples were drawn from a formalized test of picture description where the SV or SVO structures were repetitive. This behaviour may often be observed in therapy interactions with agrammatic speakers. When both the structure and the lexical items are prompted by use of repetitive syntactic frame and pictures, sentence production can be markedly superior to spontaneous speech. In the case of McCarthy and Warrington's patient comprehension was also more severely impaired for verbs than nouns and these researchers interpret their findings as a disturbance of a selective 'semantic' category, that is verbs. It should be noted, however, that the distinction they draw is in fact a grammatical one between lexical categories, and not a semantic one, although it gives substance to a claim that the lexicon is organized grammatically as well as semantically. McCarthy and Warrington's observations of their agrammatic patient speak to the centrality of his disorder with verbs, since he was equally impaired on speech and comprehension.

Commenting on McCarthy and Warrington's findings, Berndt (1988) notes that it has been claimed that verbs are more complex than nouns, as 'they are harder to remember, more broadly defined, more prone to alteration in meaning when conflict of meaning occurs, less stable in translation between languages, and slower to be acquired by children than nouns' (p. 239). To this we may add a further complexity already mentioned in Chapter 1 in relation to the work of Byng and Black. Verbs vary functionally with respect to predicate-argument structure sometimes in an apparently arbitrary way, in that permissible and obligatory thematic roles of NPs vary even between near synonymous lexical verbs. Consider, for example, (7) and (9) below, where the choice of 'devoured' as the verb specifies that an object NP must be realized with the thematic role of Patient or Theme:

(7) He ate slowly.
(8) He ate the steak.
(9) *He devoured slowly.
(10) He devoured the steak.

Shapiro, et al. (1987) claim that there is a processing device which temporarily activates all the argument structures of a verb during comprehension of a sentence. Evidence, however, that it is not just a postulated greater difficulty with verbs than nouns for normal subjects that makes them harder to use by certain patients comes from the study of an anomic patient who was better able to produce verbs than nouns (Zingeser and Berndt, 1988). For those patients who do have specific difficulties with verbs and the verb phrase, it seems that this may not be simply due to a greater inherent difficulty which lies in verbs as such, but that the patients have specific difficulties in the operations which verb processing requires.

THE 'MAPPING HYPOTHESIS'

The second notion deriving from the psycholinguistic model of Garrett and Schwartz which has been used as a basis for therapy for agrammatic patients is the 'mapping hypothesis' (Schwartz, et al., 1985). This attempts to account for the difficulty many patients have with comprehending plausibly reversible sentences in test situations where they are asked to choose a picture for a sentence. As we noted above in the discussion of Caramazza and Hillis' (1989) patient, word-order difficulties which affect sentence production but not comprehension have also been attributed to difficulty in the transition from functional to positional level in Garrett's model. Schwartz (1987) has suggested that they may reflect a problem in assembling fragments, since information comes from the functional level unspecified for order, for example a passive or active realization is equally consistent with the functional argument specification. If word-order confusions occur in comprehension as well as in production, it is hypothesized that the location of the difficulty may be the supramodal one of mapping sentence meaning onto sentence form, or in other words mapping thematic roles onto syntactic functions (Byng, 1988). This mapping is heavily dependent on the lexical-grammatical information associated with specific verbs. For example, as we described in Chapter 3, in

(11) Sandra buys the puppy from Jack.
(12) Sandra sells the puppy to Jack.

the semantics of the verb indicate the different thematic roles for 'Sandra' – recipient/goal in (11), agent/source in (12) – although Sandra is the grammatical subject of the sentence in both examples. (Contrasts of sentences which include verb pairs of this type are, in fact, difficult for some aphasic people to interpret.) In English such mapping is also heavily dependent on word order in plausibly reversible sentences like those in (13) and (14) below:

(13) John was following the dog.
(14) The dog was following John.

Byng has tested her version of the Garrett model along with the claim that mapping deficits may be supramodal, by examining the response of patients to therapy. She has tested in particular whether therapy aimed at improving comprehension resulted in an improvement in sentence production (see further Chapter 10).

CONTROL PROCESSES IN SENTENCE PRODUCTION

Garrett's model is not the only psycholinguistic model of sentence production which has been used to account for aphasic phenonema. A proposal distinguishing representations from control mechanisms has been applied to sentence production similar to the one we referred to in the context of single words in Chapter 4. Butterworth and Howard's (1987) model – see Fig. 5.1. – was derived from observations of 'paragrammatism' in aphasia, as well as speech errors in normal subjects. Paragrammatism is operationally defined, in order to distinguish it from agrammatism, as incorporating ungrammatical sentences in which the errors are typically of morphological selection rather than omission. In fact detailed analyses of aphasic speech suggest a continuum between paragrammatism and agrammatism, with errors of morphological selection occurring in both types of aphasic speech. Butterworth and Howard (1987), through use of the notion of control processes (illustrated as ovals in the figure), have offered a model which accommodates both this continuum and speech errors from normal subjects. It is, however, more restricted than Garrett's model in its specification of what 'syntactic' processing is. Butterworth and Howard suggest that, not only are the modular systems independent in speech production, but also the control mechanisms for each module. This model therefore differs from the multiple representations hypothesis of Townsend and Bever (1991) in which common resources may be shared. A sentence production deficit may be

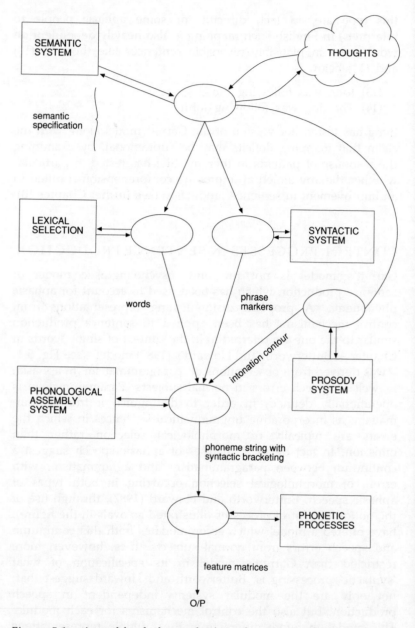

Figure 5.1: A model of the production of sentences (Butterworth and Howard, 1987), reprinted from Cognition, *Vol 26, pp 1–37, by permission of Elsevier Science Publishers BV, Amsterdam.*

secondary, therefore, to a malfunction of any of these systems, or to a malfunction of the control of any of them. The control apparatus initiates the operation of the module, coordinates it with the input from the other modules, checks on the output for the module and terminates its operation as appropriate. This model therefore incorporates the notion that language processors as such may be intact in aphasia, but that defective control systems impede the smooth operation of production. As all the researchers into syntactic disorders in aphasia acknowledge, however, models such as this are consistent with some of the data obtained from aphasic speech, but they are not necessarily the only explanations possible. Butterworth and Howard conclude that a 'much more detailed analysis of syntactic errors is needed, in the context of a more detailed and explicit theory of syntactic production' (p. 35).

Before we move to consideration of the comprehension of sentences, in contrast to their production, we will mention one further theory of grammatical disorders which is of relevance to the question of control resources and to therapy. This is Kolk's (1987) *adaptation theory*. Kolk argues that we should look at the positive rather than the negative symptoms of aphasic speech. He suggests that 'whereas paragrammatic speakers are the ones who keep trying to produce fully elaborated sentences as they used to before the illness, agrammatics make a strategic choice in favor of abbreviated forms, which leads to telegraphic speech' (p. 377). Kolk argues against the notion that there is a loss of grammatical competence in agrammatism, but proposes that grammatical disorders in speech are due to a specific resource limitation. This affects the short-term memory buffer concerned with sentence representations; it may take the form of slower activation or faster decay of elements in these representations. Consequently agrammatic speakers have to deal with a reduced 'temporal window' for sentence production. They adapt their speech from complex to simple and from complete to elliptical forms. This is a *preventive* adaptation. Kolk also accounts for a possible *corrective* adaptation or overt or covert self-repair, which results in the pausing, effortfulness and reduced rate of speech associated with Broca's aphasia (at, it should be noted, the level of sentence production rather than articulation as in the classical model).

The implications for intervention of such a model are various. Since this short-term memory or working buffer for sentence representations is clearly different from that used for single lexical items as in digit span tests (see for example Shallice and Butterworth's, 1977, demonstration that a severely reduced memory span need not affect the production of speech), there is no justification for recommending memory training exercises as such. Assistance with speeding up sentence production by rehearsal of syntactic frames and/or lexical items may be worth considering. In pragmatic terms, strategies for holding the listener's attention during pauses, or for attuning the speaker's partner to the contrastive significance of this type of pausing with others may be the preferred form of management.

LINGUISTIC MODELS

In contrast to psycholinguistic models, linguistic theories operate at a level of abstraction (as we discussed in Chapter 3) at which the distinctions between comprehension and production are not material. Before we discuss some psycholinguistic investigations of sentence comprehension in aphasia, therefore, we shall refer to some linguistic investigations which have used production or comprehension tasks indiscriminately as an avenue to exploring the nature of the grammatical disorder in aphasia as a supra-modal disorder. As we described in Chapter 3, these have employed linguistic postulates in order to ascertain whether they provide a principled analysis of the problems which occur.

As we have already discussed in the context of modular theories of language, Chomskyan linguistics argues that language is organized into relatively distinct components, which allows (for example) morphology to be discussed separately from thematic roles or pragmatic functions. It is on this general premise that the linguistic theory whose applications in aphasiology we describe below is based.

Chomsky's most recent and to date most comprehensive generative model, Government and Binding (GB) theory, has been invoked as an account of syntactic comprehension disorders (Caplan, 1987; Caplan and Hildebrandt, 1988). Since this is one of the most detailed recent expositions of aphasic syntax, and a marriage of this with a computer parsing model gives it some claim to a form of psychological validity, we will describe it in some detail.

ASPECTS OF GB THEORY

In their application of parts of the GB model, Caplan and Hildebrandt maintain a clear distinction between syntactic and semantic representations, which is also maintained in the application of the model to the processing required in the parser. GB theory describes a grammar as having several modules or components, which interact according to certain principles and parameters. It is this interaction between modules which produces differences between grammars of different languages. Theta theory deals with semantic dimensions of sentence structure, namely the assignment of thematic roles (theta roles) such as *agent* or *recipient* to NPs in the sentence. Theta theory is also used to handle, for example, transitivity. GB theory, moreover, postulates two levels of syntactic representation, related by *movement* rules; a D (or deep) structure where elements such as agent and recipient are in their original position before movement takes place, and S structure in which elements have been moved (see Cook, 1988; 28ff.). This movement leaves behind empty place-holders or traces, and a further set of bounding rules specifies what movement is possible without making a sentence ungrammatical. Empty traces may be of four kinds:

1. WH-traces (as in WH questions, or in sentences with relative clauses);
2. NP-traces in 'NP raising', where an NP has moved into a grammatical position which can potentially receive a grammatical role, but does not receive one because the verb does not have one to assign;
3. other kinds of NP-traces due to passivization or clefting of the sentence;
4. (in some languages, but not in English) 'pro' gaps where pronouns have been omitted.

Examples of sentences which illustrate the first three types (and in which the trace is represented by t with a subscript$_i$ to identify what the trace is linked to) are:

(15) Who$_i$ did John see t_i?
(16) John$_i$ seems t_i to be dancing.
(17) It was John$_i$ that t_i was dancing.

There are also other gaps which do not need to be identified by traces, since they occur in the D-structure itself rather than being due to movement at S-structure level. These are labeled as PRO, as in (18):

(18) John$_i$ promised PRO$_i$ to dance.

where the D-structure itself assigns theta roles both to John (in relation to 'promise') and PRO (in relation to 'dance').

The link between a moved NP and its empty trace is known as its *referential dependency*. Another type of referential dependency is between a reflexive such as 'himself' or a pronoun and its antecedent: these are overt referential dependencies in contrast to the covert ones of empty traces with their moved NPs. As well as distinguishing overt and empty categories, binding theory distinguishes between *anaphors* and *pronominals* according to the syntactic domains to which referentially dependent NPs are bound. Reflexives, like 'himself', and reciprocals, like 'each other', are anaphoric, and must be coindexed with a constituent-commanding NP within the same domain. Multiplying these four permutations of ±anaphoric and ± pronominal by the orthogonal feature of overt/empty, GB theory derives a complex eight-fold typology for the description of referential dependencies in sentences. These linguistic representations are essentially of underlying linguistic knowledge, and are neutral with regard to modality. Grodzinsky (cited by Shankweiler, et al., 1989) has proposed that the failure of some agrammatic speakers to produce grammatical morphemes is due to a selective impairment at the level of S-structure; this also affects comprehension of these grammatical morphemes.

To apply the insights offered by such linguistic representations to the study of syntactic *comprehension* as such, however, requires a model of how they may be related to the processing involved in understanding sentences. Berwick and Weinberg's (1985) computational model has been used for this purpose by Caplan and Hildebrandt (1988). In this computer model of sentence comprehension a parser is seen as performing specifically syntactic operations with semantic aspects being referred to a 'propositional list'. The parser may consult this list in order to prepare its output of an interpretable semantic representation and complete its job of assigning theta roles. Since many sentences include empty traces (according to GB theory), it also needs to have a gap-hunting procedure, and a means of searching for antecedents for co-indexed items (which would include overt reflexives as well as traces). It therefore requires an input buffer or working memory (provided in the working model with cells for three words) to enable it to hold sufficient information to assign a thematic role. It also requires a 'push-down stack' in which it can keep completed constituents and the ones on which it is currently working. It is assumed that the parser is supplied with knowledge of the grammatical form of words and permissible constituents. The parallel between this and the 'temporal window' proposed by Kolk (1987) for sentence production is obvious (cf. p. 91 above).

APPLYING GB THEORY TO APHASIA

Applying this parsing model and in conjunction with the categories of GB, Caplan and Hildebrandt devised sets of sentences which aimed to test aphasic comprehension of various referential dependencies and compare them with baseline measures. Sentences like those in (16) to (18) and (19) to (24) and others were given to the patients to act out, using toy animals and dolls, although in some instances picture choice was also used.

(19) The elephant was hit by the monkey.
(20) It was the elephant that hit the monkey.
(21) It was the elephant that the monkey hit.
(22) The elephant gave the monkey to the rabbit.
(23) The elephant was given to the monkey by the rabbit.
(24) The elephant that the monkey hit hugged the rabbit.

Caplan and Hildebrandt (1988) report the results on various groups of English- and French-speaking patients, selected as having adequate comprehension of single words, together with a finer analysis of nine individual cases. Their general conclusion was as follows: 97 per cent of aphasic patients (when those with motor speech disorders are excluded) have a disorder of syntactic comprehension detectable by their measures. It should be noted that their subjects were not restricted to those with agrammatic speech.

The researchers claim that the disorder was indeed of syntactic comprehension rather than semantic-syntactic comprehension (as reflected in the title of their book as *Disorders of Syntactic Comprehension*), since it was not specific to the meaning of individual sentences, but conformed to patterns which are consistent with syntactic parsing and syntactic representations as such. They cautiously state that 'the results are at least suggestive that aphasic patients have specific difficulties with assigning and interpreting specific aspects of syntactic form' (Caplan and Hildebrandt, 1988: 271). They conclude that there is an overriding common factor in all aphasic patients (whether 'agrammatic' or not), which is interpreted as a reduction in the computational resources needed for syntactic comprehension, that is of parsing workspace. The disorder can be specifically in parsing, and not in the post-parsing interpretation of the sentences.

Caplan and Hildebrandt note that a number of patients develop compensatory heuristics in attempting to understand sentences, the most common being that thematic roles are assigned in the order Agent, Theme and Goal to sequential NPs regardless of the syntactic structure, and that antecedents are sought locally. For example in:

(25) John promised Bill to shave.

the characteristic error was to show Bill shaving. Despite the free format of the doll manipulation task (in contrast to a picture selection task where options are restricted), the errors which patients made were of similar types, suggesting that there is a common tendency to use the same heuristics.

From the point of view of linguistic and psycholinguistic theory, however, the most interesting finding in the Caplan and Hildebrandt study is of selective impairments, some of which correspond to the predictions of GB theory. Against the general background of reduction in parsing workspace, both the group studies and the individual case studies indicated specific patterns of impairment, which fell outside the common rank order of difficulty. In some tests (particularly the picture-choice test) these accounted for 35 to 50 per cent of the variance. These specific impairments include difficulties related to:

1. the functional argument structure of the verb;
2. the number of verbs in the sentence;

3. the assignment of lexical grammatical categories to category-ambiguous lexical items;
4. the presence of pronouns and possessive determiners requiring coindexation;
5. the presence of noncanonical orders of NP constituents (as in passives).

Two double dissociations were found. One patient was unable to perform correctly when sentences included PRO empty categories (a D-structure level of operation) (see example 18 in this chapter), but succeeded with NP traces (an S-structure level of operation) (see example 16). Another patient showed the reverse pattern. Again a different patient was impaired on sentences which included reflexives (+anaphoric −pronominal) but not on those which included pronouns (−anaphoric +pronominal), while another showed the reverse. Caplan and Hildebrandt conclude that primary deficits such as these interact with the general capacity limitation found in aphasia, such that the processor becomes overloaded when the level of complexity for an individual patient is reached.

A word of caution needs to be introduced in interpreting these results as characterizing aphasic disorders only. Davis and Ball's (1989) studies of normal elderly subjects show that accuracy in comprehending sentences declines after about age 60 in many subjects (close to the average age of many group studies of aphasia). Using a task in which subjects were asked to indicate the thematic roles in plausible, implausible and reversible embedded or right-branching sentences, Davis and Ball note that it is the syntactic component rather than semantic structure which presents difficulties; they consider it is the *processing* of syntax rather than syntactic *knowledge* as such which is affected in ageing: 'A component may operate well in one circumstance but not in another due to either the manner in which cognitive components normally interact or the overcrowding of working memory' (p. 149). This similarity between disorders of sentence comprehension in aphasia and in the elderly may provide some support for a claim made by Frazier and Friederici (1991) that 'several of the commonly assumed properties of agrammatism are shown by normals when processing under capacity limitations' (pp. 60, 61).

There are other difficulties of interpretation in Caplan and

Hildebrandt's finding that almost all of the patients they examined had a specifically syntactic disorder. We have already referred, in Chapter 3, to the problems of taking a linguistic theory as a psychologically real model of the way language is mentally processed. Despite Caplan and Hildebrandt's insistence that their sentences were testing only syntactic knowledge, it seems self-evident that any sentences using real lexical items in order to test comprehension, particularly in a non-anomalous way, must require semantic processing as well as syntactic. It is therefore arguable that some patients, such as those with Wernicke's aphasia, might be expected to fail on sentence comprehension tasks due to their lexical-semantic difficulties rather than to syntactic difficulties, as a number of researchers have proposed (e.g. von Stockert and Bader, 1976).

Another explanation is that those patients who fail in the sentence comprehension task do so because of a general overloading of computational resources through simultaneous semantic, syntactic, working memory and executive processing. This may apply particularly when the response required is one which is elaborate and requires the manipulation of objects (Lesser, 1976). Linebarger, et al. (1983) reported that some agrammatic patients succeed in judging whether sentences are grammatical (an analogy to a lexical decision task at the single-word level) although they fail in picture-choice tasks of sentence comprehension. Linebarger and her colleagues therefore propose a trade-off between syntax and semantics in comprehension.

Before such conclusions are reached, however, it is necessary to analyse the performance components in the tasks in which 'syntactic comprehension' deficits occur (Parisi, 1983). The details of the procedures used in these tasks may be critical. For instance, in picture-choice tasks there may be different consequences depending on whether the pictures are shown first or the sentences heard first. Where pictures are shown first, to illustrate plausibly reversible sentences, the patient may need to employ what Caplan and Hildebrandt (1988: 67) would call a post-parsing operation in order to adjudicate between two pictorially aroused sentences. In contrast, when the sentence is heard before the pictures are seen, the linguistic input may affect the perception of the pictures (Black, et al., 1991). Black and her colleagues propose five linguistic stages before a representation is achieved which can be related to the picture. These are:

1. identification of phonological words in the input string, with consequent lexical access;
2. construction of a syntactic representation based on this initial process of segmentation and recognition;
3. selection of thematic roles by reference to the semantic representation of the verb;
4. the mapping of these thematic roles onto structural positions;
5. the integration of the semantic content of the phrases in the sentence to form a full semantic representation.

These stages also apply before other kinds of tasks which have been used in order to examine sentence comprehension, such as judgement of anomaly, comprehension of instructions or acting out the sentences through manipulation of figures. Like picture-choice, the acting out of sentences using toy figures is also compounded by non-linguistic factors, such as praxis and visual perception, and has been reported to correlate significantly with gesture apraxia (Lesser, 1976a). 'Trade-off' between different levels of processing due to computational overload is one area of investigation which may also be fruitfully undertaken at higher levels of language than sentences, that is in discourse and conversation.

ON-LINE PROCESSING

All the tasks described above are 'off-line' ones, in that what is measured is a response after completion of the processing, an assessment of 'linguistic knowledge' as available to deliberative judgement (Sproat, 1986) (the question of the automatic or attention-free access to linguistic knowledge is a different matter in the examination of aphasia). If we wish to test actual performance (processing) some investigators (Tyler, 1987; Shankweiler, et al., 1989) have suggested that we need to use 'on-line' probes. This approach is likely to be more informative in the investigation of any problems of trade-off and overload.

Examining on-line processing uses a technique of measuring the time it takes to react to a probe heard during a sentence. In early experiments with normal subjects the probe used was generally a click. The position of the click in the sentence could be varied, and it was shown that it took less time to react to a click when it occurred at a major constituent boundary than when it occurred within a phrase. In the examples below, for example, a click occurring after 'Anna' would be located more quickly in (26) than in (27), and would be perceived as occurring earlier:

(26) Your hope of marrying Anna was surely impractical.
(27) In her hope of marrying Anna was surely impractical.
                                              (from Garrett, et al. 1966)

Click experiments also showed that reaction times were shorter near the end of a clause than near the beginning. This suggests that a structure is assigned to a sentence as soon as it begins to be heard and information is provided, without waiting for all its words or constituents to be received. When the processing of a clause is syntactically and semantically complete, information from it is generally thought to be maintained in an abstract semantic form (the gist) without its specific syntactic form being retained for any considerable length of time, unless attention has been specifically directed to this.

Experimenters have used other kinds of probes besides clicks, for example listening for a particular word, listening for a rhyme to a given word, listening for a semantic category, changing the ear in which the sentence was heard, or visual lexical decision while listening to a sentence. These studies also support the claim that the interpretation of a sentence begins as soon as the listener hears the first part; prior contextual information speeds up the recognition of words near the beginning of an utterance. It seems that the listener is constructing a semantic and syntactic interpretation of the sentence as each word is heard, although syntactic processing of each clause cannot be completed until its end. It is in this way that sentence comprehension therefore makes demands on working memory, or computational space; this is not simply a matter of the number of words which have to be coped with, as in digit span, but concerns the syntactic units which have to be processed and held over until the sentence is complete. As Saffran and Martin (1990) have pointed out, although there has been much investigation of the role played by a phonological buffer in memory for sentences, very little is known about the nature of the representations that are constructed at the deeper levels of sentence processing which involve the alignment of noun phrases with verb argument structures as a basis for semantic interpretation in terms of thematic roles.

There is still some controversy as to the extent to which syntactic processing is obligatory in sentences which could be interpreted from pragmatic knowledge, as in 'The girl carries the plate', which could be understood from the meaning of the three words *girl, plate, carry*. Bates, et al. (1982), for example, propose that sentence comprehension is achieved by means of such a lexico-pragmatic, or functional, route through probabilistic interpretation and cues such as word order, case marking, stress. Others, such as Caplan and Hildebrandt (1988), argue that use of syntax (as an independent language system) is obligatory in comprehending sentences. Studies of on-line processing in comprehension in fact support this latter interpretation.

ON-LINE STUDIES OF APHASIA

In aphasic studies, Tyler (1985, 1987) has reported use of the probe technique principally to investigate the sentence comprehension of agrammatic speakers. She has distinguished between syntactic and semantic processing through monitoring reaction times to probe words in contextually set sentences which are anomalous (semantically incoherent) (as in (28)) or scrambled (syntactically incoherent) (as in (29)) or normal (as in (30)) (probe word underlined).

(28) *The power was located in great water. No buns puzzle some in the <u>lead</u> off the roof.

(29) *In was power water the great located. Some the no puzzle buns in <u>lead</u> text the off.

(30) The church was broken into last night. Some thieves stole most of the <u>lead</u> off the roof.

Tyler also varied the position of the probe word in the sentences, to test whether, as in normal listeners, agrammatic patients react more quickly to probe words occurring later in sentences which retain syntactic structure but not in scrambled sentences. The results reported for one agrammatic patient, DE, were that latencies decreased only when the sentences were normal, but not when they were anomalous, despite the fact that syntactic structure is retained in this condition. DE therefore seemed to be able to use syntactic structure in normal sentences, since he responded like normal subjects in distinguishing normal and scrambled sentences. In contrast to normal subjects, however, he did not seem able to use syntactic structure in sentences which were semantically anomalous. One interpretation of this could be that DE needed both semantic and syntactic knowledge in order to process a sentence. Tyler interpreted the result as indicating that DE may be able to use syntactic knowledge in processing local phrases but not in construing a global representation of the sentence (Tyler, 1989).

Shankweiler, et al.'s (1989) use of on-line techniques in examining six Broca-type aphasic patients was directed at exploring whether they had a *loss* of syntactic knowledge or a difficulty in *processing* it, with particular reference to grammatical functors. The ungrammatical sentences in this experiment contained a single grammatical violation involving agreement between a determiner and a noun, or a preposition, particle or verbal element, as illustrated in (31) to (34).

(31) *The banker noticed that two *customer* deposited the checks late.
(32) *The milkman was speaking *out* a man who needed advice.
(33) *The wife of the owner took the new hobby *down*.
(34) *Peter *have* planning to see a new movie Saturday night.

The position of the violation in the sentence varied, as did the nature of the substituted word, which was sometimes within-class (as in the above examples) or from a different grammatical class. The patients were asked to press a response key as soon as they detected that a sentence was ungrammatical. All were better able to reject between-class substitutions than within-class substitutions. Like Tyler's patient they also showed the normal word position effect, that is faster response times for words nearer the end of the sentence than the beginning. These results are compatible with the claim that agrammatic speakers retain syntactic knowledge in respect of the use of functors, despite the restrictions they show on their use in speech.

Both Tyler's and Shankweiler, et al.'s on-line studies suggest that any equation between syntactic difficulties in speech and comprehension in aphasia is likely to be too simple. DE seems to employ syntax in comprehending meaningful sentences, but not in anomalous ones; he seems, however, to have a limited capacity for syntax which makes its employment in construing the whole sentence limited. This is analagous to the account of agrammatic speech given by Gleason, et al. (1975), in their report of results of a story-completion test designed to elicit specific phrases and sentences; Broca-type aphasics proved capable of responding with appropriate and varied sentence fragments, but found difficulty in constructing the whole sentence. Shankweiler's results also suggest retention of the morphological building bricks of grammar, despite restrictions on their use under pressures of real-time processing in speech production.

Measuring on-line processing of sentences in aphasia is therefore one promising technique in exploring comprehension, particularly as it seems to access automatic processes rather than conscious judgements. Discrepancies have been found in aphasia between automatic processes and deliberative ones in lexical semantics (Blumstein, et al., 1982), as well as forming an essential distinction in the clinical symptom of verbal apraxia. It is also a documented phenomenon in other fields of cognitive neuro-psychology such as 'blind-sight' (see Schacter, et al., 1988, for a review). Unfortunately, as used so far in aphasiology, like any technique which relies on measuring reaction times in brain-damaged patients the use of on-line probes runs into some practical problems. It is generally not feasible to employ it with severely damaged patients, whose reaction times are slow and variable for reasons which do not correspond with the stimuli, and, even with milder impaired patients, much data from aberrant responses may have to be disregarded, making conclusions questionable. It requires substantial lists of sentences and may be as much a test of attention as of linguistic processing. It also requires laboratory equipment, which may make its use for routine clinical assessments impossible.

PRAGMATICS AND SENTENCES

We conclude with a note which links sentence processing with the topic of the next chapters, pragmatics. There is well-attested evidence that aphasic people comprehend sentences which cannot plausibly be reversed (see example (35) below) better than those which can (see example (36) (Schwartz, et al. 1980; Lesser, 1984; Jones, 1984). This suggests a fall-back on contextual and

(35) The man is patting the dog
(36) The man is watching the dog

real-world knowledge, the domain of pragmatics, when syntactic parsing fails.Tyler's (1987, 1989) on-line processing experiments in aphasia have also examined the effect of pragmatic factors through the inclusion of sentences with violations of pragmatic expectancies set up by a preceding context such as (37):

(37) The crowd was waiting eagerly. The young man *buried* his guitar . . .
(38) The crowd was waiting eagerly. *The young man *drank* his guitar . . .
(39) The crowd was waiting eagerly. *The young man *slept* his guitar . . .

Aphasic subjects seem to be particularly sensitive to such violations in that, in comparison with normal subjects, they show an abnormally large disruptive effect of such a contextual anomaly as opposed to anomalies in selection restrictions (as in (38)) or theta role restrictions (as in (39)).

Black, et al. (1991) have also shown that some passive sentences may owe their difficulties of processing (in the sense of resulting in more errors when normal or aphasic subjects hear them in sentence-picture matching tasks) to the pragmatic properties of passives described by Pinker (1990). Pinker identifies one of these as an 'agency effect', that is the use of a passive construction presumes the existence of an agent-like party responsible for the circumstance expressed. The semantic specification of some verbs includes an inherent causality, in that one party in the relationship which they express is seen as more causally weighted than the other. Passives are pragmatically more acceptable where this causality is reflected, as can be illustrated by a comparison between the intuitively perceived 'naturalness' of the two sentences below:

(40) The meal was served by the cook himself.
(41) The meal was seen by the cook himself.

Much psycholinguistic modelling at the sentence level has

ignored this question of the 'naturalness' of the materials used, in contrast to some of the pragmatic approaches which we shall discuss in the next four chapters.

SUMMARY

In this chapter we have outlined the version of Garrett's model of sentence production used by Schwartz in her analysis of aphasic disorders. We have discussed whether a model like this can be used to differentiate processing disorders in individuals in two different ways. These are first in distinguishing people who have disorders only in production and not in comprehension, and secondly in distinguishing people with problems at the positional level from those with problems at other levels. At the positional level the disorder may affect the construction of the sentence frame and/or the phonological specification of the grammatical morphemes for insertion into these frames. Other possible causes of agrammatism which have been suggested are difficulties in the operations which verb processing requires, or difficulty in mapping sentence meaning onto sentence form. A theory that the disorder may be one of control of processes (shown more clearly in paragrammatism than in agrammatism) was outlined.

We showed how one linguistic theory which has been applied to the analysis of sentence comprehension in aphasia, Government and Binding Theory, has been claimed to account for some aspects of sentence difficulty which influence not only aphasic but normal comprehenders. The notions of a restricted 'time window' and computational overload in comprehension (especially when allied to the need to make a response) were discussed. Some on-line studies of aphasia were reported as an attempt to analyse what the computations are which are required in sentence comprehension.

SIX

Pragmatics: theoretical issues

The experimental, model-based approaches to aphasia described in Chapters 4 and 5 attempt to locate and describe as precisely as possible the nature of a linguistic breakdown. They attempt a comprehensive examination of all modalities of language, written as well as spoken, comprehension as well as production. Pragmatic approaches, which focus chiefly on communication through spoken language, are best seen as complementing rather than competing with this laboratory or clinic based psycholinguistic work, being attractive chiefly for their 'high ecological validity' (Holland, 1991). Their emphasis on social and situational context seems to offer opportunities for capitalizing on the impaired individual's capacity to use contextual information and knowledge to enhance his or her everyday communicative potential. However, pragmatics is an even more diffuse and contentious subject area than psycholinguistics, and it is not at all clear which pragmatic concepts are most amenable to application or how they can most fruitfully be applied. We shall try in the remaining chapters of Part II to clarify the situation a little, as we selectively describe and evaluate topics and approaches which have emerged recurrently in the aphasia literature, or which seem to be particularly pertinent to the management of aphasia.

In Chapter 3 we noted that the scope and definition of many key terms in pragmatics was controversial, but offered fairly uncontentious working definitions of *discourse* as a linguistic unit larger than the sentence, and of *conversation* as a type of interactive discourse produced by more than one person. A broad coverage of pragmatics from several perspectives can be found in key texts such as Coulthard (1985), Leech (1983), Brown and Yule (1983) and Stubbs (1983), Levinson (1983) being particularly recommended. Their approaches vary; for example Brown and Yule devote a good deal of space to the contrasting features of spoken and written discourse. But all are interested in conversational structure, in explaining how speakers and hearers interact meaningfully and in searching for principles of *coherence* in discourse. We do not attempt in these chapters to duplicate such texts or to provide a comprehensive coverage of the subject area.

This chapter and the following three are intended to complement each other. Chapters 6 and 7 concentrate on principles underlying discourse and conversational structure, rather than offering a template for analysing 'real world' discourse or conversation. Chapters 8 and 9 on the other hand describe the mechanisms of negotiating a conversation and suggest procedures for approaching real and (particularly from aphasic conversationalists) therefore intractable data. This division corresponds roughly to two major approaches to conversation, the 'top-down' linguistics/philosophy-of-language approach and the 'bottom-up' ethnomethodology/conversational analysis approach.

Top-down approaches are older and more traditional; Austin's seminal work on speech acts for example, which has been influential in the aphasiological literature (see further Chapter 12), dates from 1962. They employ a deductive type of reasoning, in which an abstract competence is modelled by idealized speakers in idealized situations, and speaker intention is often invoked to explain features of isolated utterances. Organizational principles of some kind are posited, such as conversational maxims (Grice, 1975), relevance (Sperber and Wilson, 1986), speech acts (Searle, 1979), and an attempt is made to fit these to data, which in the philosophical tradition are generally constructed rather than naturalistic. Exceptions to this last practice are Brown and Levinson's (1987) account of politeness phenomena using a combination of naturally occurring and invented data, and Labov and Fanshel's (1977) 'speech-act' style of analysis of a therapeutic interview.

It is important for clinicians who attempt applications of these top-down approaches to understand that they originated and were subsequently developed from the abstractions of philosophy rather than the descriptive needs of linguistics. Characteristically, they do not draw on the insights of the socially orientated approaches to conversation which we briefly introduced in Chapter 3. Leech and Thomas (1990) suggest that their philosophical orientation accounts for difficulties in application to naturally occurring discourse, and the same difficulties arise in applying them to the description and assessment of aphasic discourse. However, several groups of discourse analysts have developed top-down approaches which are primarily linguistic rather than philosophical. Of these we shall be concerned in Chapter 8 chiefly with the Birmingham group (Coulthard, 1985; Coulthard and Montgomery, 1981; Stubbs, 1983) who use naturally occurring rather than invented data, building up an analytic system based on a limited number of categories. These categories then provide an analytic framework which follows Hallidayan principles of linguistic analysis.

The conversation analysis tradition offers a contrasting 'bottom-up' approach in positing initially no such set of analytic or organizational principles but inductively seeking patterns and structures in bodies of naturally occurring data (see Atkinson and Heritage, 1984, for examples). Such analysts as Schegloff, Sacks and Jefferson confine themselves strictly to descriptions of the observable behaviour of conversationalists, drawing conclusions from repeated details of such behaviour. Some recent work which falls most clearly into this strongly empirical and inductive camp forms a bridge with the linguistic and philosophical traditions by developing discourse models which are designed to be modified and applied to other bodies of data. An example of this is Schiffrin's (1987) study of discourse markers, and McTear (1985a) offers an analytic framework which derives from a number of approaches. The 'bottom-up' tradition seems recently to have been gaining ground to the extent that some researchers such as Levinson (1983), Clark and Wilkes-Gibbs (1986) and Schegloff (1988) have offered alternative accounts of phenomena which have routinely been the province of 'top-down' analyses (see further p. 178ff. below). Furthermore, Sperber and Wilson's (1986)) philosophically oriented account of communication has been subject to sustained criticism by (amongst others) the cognitive psychologist Gibbs (1987, 1988 et al.), who argues that it is socially unrealistic in not accounting for the manner in which speakers *collaborate* in creating coherent conversations. We shall explore the implications of this important point for our understanding of both normal and aphasic conversations, in Chapters 8, 9, and 12.

Mey and Talbot (1988) have also criticized Sperber and Wilson's work fiercely, describing it as 'irremediably asocial and therefore relevant to neither communication nor cognition'. Cicourel (1987) has commented on Searle's recent work in a similar fashion.

Since clinicians need to approach the task of examining the pragmatic abilities of their patients open-mindedly and eclectically, we shall suggest that a bottom-up type of analysis is particularly helpful and appropriate. Therapists are routinely faced with the task of seeking patterns in bodies of intransigent spoken language data which are intolerant of prior theoretical assumptions at the pragmatic level (although, as we have shown in the last two chapters, providing fertile material for theories at other levels). Furthermore, clinicians require a framework which allows them to characterize the interactional behaviour of aphasic conversationalists without prior assumptions of how this may relate to 'normal' interactional behaviour.

We pointed out in Chapters 3 and 5 that it is not always useful to consider pragmatic, semantic and grammatical dimensions of language behaviour independently, and in fact several concepts central to the analysis of interactive discourse, such as *deixis* and *definiteness*, straddle all three areas. Both are pertinent to an account of speakers' use of language to *refer* to entities in the immediate context or the wider universe of discourse in such a way as to identify them adequately enough to be understood by their hearers. What Caplan (1987: 159) describes as 'this ability to utter a simple sound and thereby designate an item or class of items' is a prerequisite of successful communication which is characteristically impaired in aphasia. We begin with a general account of deixis and definiteness in relation to aspects of normal language behaviour, and conclude the chapter by examining their relevance to a pragmatic analysis of aphasic language.

DEIXIS

Deictic expressions are variable in form, comprising items from many different grammatical classes. Certain lexical verbs, tenses, adverbial expressions of time and place, pronouns and determiners are salient in grammatical and semantic descriptions but are all analysable in some contexts as having a deictic function. The Greek root of the word, which means 'pointing' or 'indicating', suggests the relevance of deixis to any treatment of language in context. In fact deictic expressions by definition take an essential part of their meaning from the context of the utterance in which they occur; quite simply, as we can demonstrate with straightforward examples, they are not inter-pretable unless participants in the discourse share certain kinds of extra-linguistic contextual knowledge. Thus, a 'back in 10 minutes' notice on a corner shop cannot be located in calendric time unless the time of writing is supplied; the date on a letterhead provides this kind of temporal anchorage. A similar point is made by Levinson's example of a message found in the sea in a bottle (1983: 55):

(1) Meet me here a week from now with a stick about this long.

The uncertain location of the message deprives the reader of crucial contextual information, ensuring that s/he cannot identify the referent of *me*, does not know where or when to meet him or her, nor what size of stick to bring along. However, (1) also demonstrates that deictic expressions can pick out referents *compactly*, if communicatively inadequately. More explicit speci-fication of time, place and speaker requires much more linguistic structure – more noun phrases, prepositional phrases and so on. This is a point to which we shall return later in this chapter, as overuse of *proforms* such as the pronouns *it, that* and the pro-adverbials *here, there* (often in a deictic function) is a well-documented feature of some types of aphasic language (Wepman and Jones, 1966; Crystal, 1987: 121; Edwards and Garman, 1989; Armstrong, 1991). The most basic features of context necessary for interpreting deictic expressions are *speaker*, *place* and *time* of utterance, so we shall look briefly at person, place and time deixis, before distinguishing between *gestural* and *symbolic* deixis.

Personal deictic reference is relatively straightforward; *I* is always the speaker, *you* the addressee and *he, she, it* the third person referent. As participant and discourse roles change, different terms are systematically employed to pick out the same referent – Paul, in the example below:

(2) Paul: *I* got a nasty letter from the bank manager yesterday.
   Mother: *You* should be more careful with your money.
   Father: *He's* a good boy.

Children at a relatively early stage of language acquisition find this system of deictic reference difficult. Chiat (1982: 366) cites the example of two and a half year old Matthew who can select the appropriate pronoun for self-reference but has difficulty with addressee reference:

(3) Shula: What will happen if you cut my hair?
    Matthew: I'll cry
    Shula: Who'll cry?
    Matthew: Shula.

Although problems similar to Matthew's are frequently associated with certain disorders (such as Down's and autistic syndromes) aphasic speakers seem only rarely to encounter specifically deictic difficulties in relating personal pronouns to alternating participant roles. However, the response in 4(a) of a severely impaired aphasic to a question about his holiday plans seems to indicate such a difficulty; it is later clear from the unfolding discourse that the third person singular pronoun *him* is being used self-referentially. But it is important not to lump together all kinds of confusions of pronominal reference, since those which are much more frequently reported in both paragrammatism and mild agrammatism are generally *he/she* confusions within the third person form. They are usually attributed to semantic paraphasia, and are better described as morphological or semantic than as deictic, in that speakers fail to mark pronouns correctly for features of number or gender. Thus, all that is wrong with the pronoun *she* in (4b) is that it needs to agree in gender with its male antecedent *Norman*. Unlike (4a) the relationship between pronoun choice and participant role is not a problem:

(4a) T. is it just you and Lily going?
     P. no/Gosforth [P's home suburb]/him and Lily/him and Lily/but Hazelrigg ah/the bungalows stick/it's Margaret no/Fenwick yeah/oh dear me
(4b) Cos Norman (.) *she's* very for working late

Time and place deixis are less easily described than person deixis, being complicated both by the cognitive complexities associated with the concepts of space and time and by the way languages encode these concepts (Wales, 1986: 427; Lyons, 1977,

Ch. 15). As Wales points out, cognitive issues are not usually treated in the deixis literature (but see Joshi, et al., 1981; Fillmore, 1982), and we can therefore say very little about them here. Here are some deictic expressions of place:

(5) *This* part of the country is beautiful.
That part of the country is beautiful.
(6) *This* is *here* in front of me.
That is *there* in front of you.

In (5) the demonstrative determiners *this* and *that* encode a contrast in the noun phrase position. This contrast allows the referent to be specified as relatively near to or distant from the speaker, who is the point of anchorage or *deictic centre*. Equally, the demonstrative pronouns *this* and *that* in (5) and the adverbial proforms *here* and *there* in (6) encode the same proximal/distal distinction, always with the assumption that referents in the environment can be readily identified.

Some lexical items expressing *movement* or *orientation* in space have a deictic component; for example pairs such as *bring/take*; *come/go* seem to be distinguished chiefly by a feature of directional orientation to the speaker. The prepositions *behind* and *in front of* are deictic if they are used in relation to objects like trees, stools or tables, which (unlike sun-houses, cars or television sets) have no intrinsic backs or fronts. In (7) *behind* is used deictically, since it specifies location from the speaker's point of view. However, as Levinson (1983: 82) points out, utterances like (8) are ambiguously deictic or non-deictic, in that the dog might be either at the intrinsic rear of the car or at some other point near to the car, when the car intervenes between the speaker and the dog.

(7) I saw your dog a moment ago behind that tree.
(8) I saw your dog a moment ago behind that car.

The same ambiguity between deictic and non-deictic reference is notoriously inherent in expressions like 'David is the boy on the left of Andrew', where the direction can (but need not) be understood from the speaker's point of view. Such ambiguities as are inherent in these prepositions present particular difficulties in the design of tests of comprehension in aphasia – see for example the liberal interpretation which has to be used in the Revised Token Test (McNeil and Prescott, 1978).

Time deixis is more complex still, being encoded in English in various ways. Deictic time differs clearly from calendric time, in being expressed from the point of view of the speaker; compare *last August*, which is interpretable only if the time of utterance is known, with *August 1988* where time is measured absolutely from an agreed point of origin. Here are some relatively straightforward examples of deictic time reference, where the underlined expressions need to be interpreted in relation to the time of utterance:

(9) He had a celebratory drink *yesterday/last week/a minute ago/at two o'clock*.

(10) He intends to have a celebratory drink/*tomorrow/next week/in a minute/at two o'clock*.

It is perhaps less immediately obvious that in contexts where *tense* contrasts encode temporal distinctions, tense is a deictic phenomenon (but see Huddleston, 1984: 143ff. for an account of non-temporal uses of tense). Consider the following pair of examples:

(11) The Vikings are sacking Lindisfarne.

(12) The Vikings sacked Lindisfarne.

(11) would be true if the time of utterance was around 793 AD, at the time when the sacking of Lindisfarne took place, while for (12) to be true the sacking would need to have taken place at some unspecified time prior to the time of utterance. Thus, tense expresses temporal meanings in (11) and (12) in a way which is entirely dependent upon time of utterance.

We can now consider deictic expressions in *reported speech* (see Coulmas, 1986), where the *deictic centre* shifts from the original to the current speaker (the reporter), the coding time from the time of the original utterance to the time of the report. Since the place of utterance may change too, we find a corresponding shift in all deictic expressions, including tense (Levinson, 1983: 64; Lyons, 1977: 579).

Utterances (13) and (14) show how this works, while (15) gives some idea of the difficulties of an aphasic speaker, JH, in handling deictic shifts.

(13) William: *I will* cut *your* hair *here* in *this* salon *tomorrow*.

(14) Mary: William said that *he would* cut *my* hair *there* in *that* salon *the following day*.

(15) Denise says everyone should clear up your mess.

(16) You should all clear up your (own) mess.

(17) Denise said that everyone should clear up their (own) mess.

(18) The captain says 'You've got an eye for it'.

Presumably Denise's words were something like (16) while a corresponding reported utterance might be expected to shift in the absence of the original addressees to something along the lines of (17). The difficulty apparently experienced by JH is likely to be particularly clear in any kind of narrative discourse which reports on the comments of individuals and may explain the evident preference of aphasics for reporting direct speech, as exemplified by JH in (18) (see also Hand, et al., 1979). This preference might be interpreted as a strategy for avoiding the complex shifting which reported speech requires.

Another aspect of deixis is the contrast between gestural and symbolic deixis. Compare the following pairs:

(19a) I'll have *this, this, this,* and *this* (spoken by a customer in a cakeshop, as she points to four items).

(19b) *This* country is still one of the wealthiest in the world.

(20a) Take the television from *there* and move it to *there*. Get *him* and *him* to help you.

(20b) I know that John will be *there*.

All the hearer needs to know to interpret symbolic uses of deictic terms (exemplified as (19b) and (20b), the type we have discussed so far) is the spatial or temporal context of the utterance. Thus, the expression *this country* is the country in which the speaker is currently situated and *there* is an unspecified place relatively distant from the place of utterance, presumably known to both speaker and addressee. However, to interpret gestural uses as shown in (19a) and (20a), close physical monitoring of the speech event is required; and as its name implies gestural deixis is usually interpreted along with the appropriate gesture (see Levinson, 1983: 66).

Many characteristically deictic items have non-deictic functions also, that is their interpretation is not context-dependent in the precise way we have specified. For example, none of the italicized items below is deictic, but they have a variety of other syntactic and discourse functions. Thus, the reference of the pronouns in (21) and (22) is vague and non-specific and is not clarified by the context of utterance; *this* in (23) marks an indefinite noun phrase, and can be described as an alternative to the indefinite article *a* which is characteristic of certain spoken language styles; *there* in (24) is not a locative expression but a semantically empty item which fills the subject slot in the sentence; *now* in (25) is not a temporal expression but is what Schiffrin (1987) describes as a *discourse marker*, functioning supra-sententially to mark out units of spoken interactive discourse:

(21) *You* can never tell these days what *they*'ll get up to next.
(22) A. What are you doing now?
    B. Oh, *this* and *that*.
(23) I saw *this* man getting on the train and he told me . . .
(24) *There* are ghosts in the sun-house.
(25) *Now* this is what I'd call real tea.

DEIXIS AND ANAPHORA

In this section we adopt Huddleston's (1984) relatively straight-forward distinction between deictic and anaphoric functions of pronouns and other proforms. Anaphora is an important relationship associated with *textual cohesion* which can function across clauses, sentences and conversational turns. Consider (26), (27) and (28):

(26) *He* looks very fit for a man of 86 (spoken while watching an 86 year old man digging his garden).
(27) The Home Secretary appeared on television; *he* made a statement about the Guildford Four.
(28) Look at *her*! *She's* driving a bit close to the side!

In (26) *he* refers deictically to a person in the immediate context of utterance shared by interlocutors. In (27) however *he* refers to no such person but is co-referential with *The Home Secretary*, so that the referent of *he* is identified not from the context of utterance but from previous mention in the text. *Anaphora* is the name given to the relationship between the noun phrase *The Home Secretary* and the pronoun *he* (see further Huddleston, 1984: 272ff.) (Note that anaphor is used here in a different sense from its use in GB theory, where it contrasts with pronominal – see page 94). Deictic and anaphoric pronouns are distinct in that deixis involves a direct relationship with a *referent* (a relationship sometimes described also as *exophoric*, as by Halliday and Hasan, 1976) while anaphora involves a relationship with a *linguistic form*. Thus, the first pronoun in (28) functions deictically, picking out a referent in the context of utterance, while the second is anaphoric with the first. Pronouns are not, however, the only kind of proforms which can function anaphorically, nor are deixis and anaphora mutually exclusive. We shall cite just one example, taken from Huddleston (1984: 283) to illustrate these points:

(29) Max came to Australia when he was five and has lived *here* ever since.

Here is deictic in that it locates the place of utterance as Australia, but is simultaneously anaphoric with *Australia*.

DEFINITENESS

We turn now to the related topic of definiteness which, like deixis, is closely associated with the use of language to *refer* to entities in the environment and straddles grammatical, semantic and pragmatic dimensions of language. Both topics are subsequently considered together in the next sections of this chapter in relation to aphasic discourse, particularly the difficulties experienced by aphasic speakers in achieving successful reference.

The distribution of definite and indefinite expressions in discourse is associated in a complicated way with the extent to which interlocutors can assume mutual knowledge of referents (Clark and Marshall, 1981). The ability to manipulate the system of alternating definite and indefinite expressions is also associated with the ability to structure 'given' and 'new' information intelligibly. Since the way in which such structuring is accomplished is complex and still disputed, we can only touch on the major issues here, but we shall attempt to review some problems associated with standard accounts. Useful discussions are provided by Clark and Wilkes-Gibbs (1986); Brown and Yule (1983: 169–89); Lyons (1977: 177–97); Brown, et al. (1987).

Brown and Yule (1983: 169) summarize the generally accepted view that 'in English, new information is characteristically introduced by indefinite expressions and subsequently referred to by definite expressions'. Thus, in selecting definite expressions, a speaker is conveying an assumption that the hearer can identify the referent of that expression: 'Very roughly, he must believe that the referent is mutually identifiable to him and his addressee from their common ground' (Clark and Wilkes-Gibbs, 1986: 28).

Definite reference is generally said to be realized linguistically by one of three types of noun phrase: a definite description like *the man in the grey suit, this book,* a proper noun like *Haymarket, John* or a pronoun like *he, they, this* (Lyons, 1977: 179). This widely accepted idealization is described by Clark and Wilkes-Gibbs (1986: 3) as an aspect of 'the literary model of definite reference', and indeed, as we shall see in Chapter 8, may well be more appropriate to written text than to spoken conversation. We should also note that the semantics of the definite and indefinite articles are further complicated by their associated functions in expressing specificity and genericity (see further Huddleston, 1984: 248–55).

Generally speaking there are two obvious reasons for a speaker to assume that a referent is mutually identifiable to him and his addressee: either it has already been introduced recently or at some earlier point into the context (sometimes implicitly), or it is the only entity of its kind in the context. Here are some examples.

(30a) *The queen* is visiting Northumberland today.
(30b) *A Forestry Commission official* is visiting Northumberland today.
(31a) It's standing on *the cooker.*
(31b) It's standing on *a stool.*
(32) I found *a stray dog* yesterday: today I took *it/the dog* to the RSPCA
(33) I took *a bus* to work yesterday. *The driver* was rather reckless.
(34) *John's* favourite meal is chilli beans.
(35) *John* bought *some oranges* at the market. *The oranges* were delicious.
(36a) *It* belongs to my uncle.
(36b) *The car* belongs to my uncle.
(36c) *The grey car with the red trim and the sunroof* belongs to my uncle.

In (30a) a definite NP is selected because in the context of a

British conversation there is only one queen. There are, however, many Forestry Commission officials, so that the choice of an indefinite NP in (30b) conveys no assumption that the referent of the NP can be identified either by virtue of uniqueness or following prior mention. The contrast in (31a) and (31b) follows from a different kind of uniqueness; although there are many cookers, most households have only one, making the cooker (but not a stool) unique in the context. In (32), (33) and (35) we see the use of an indefinite NP for the first mention of a referent. Subsequently, some type of definite NP is appropriate, an anaphoric pronoun being a likely choice in (32). The definite NP *the driver* in (33) is a little different. What seems to be involved here is a combination of two factors. These are:

1. the kind of inferential reasoning which is characteristic of everyday discourse links the driver to the bus which has already been introduced into the discourse; we shall have more to say about such reasoning in Chapter 7;
2. the uniqueness of the referent in the context of utterance; buses have only one driver.

In both (34) and (35) the speaker assumes by selection of the definite expression *John* mutual knowledge of the referent of that expression. The same assumption is of course expressed in the selection of deictic pronouns as exemplified in (31); in each case *it* refers to some item in the context which, if the pronoun is selected appropriately, both interlocutors can identify. Examples (36a,b,c) demonstrate a rather different but important point, which is particularly relevant to aphasic discourse.

When a speaker uses a definite NP to pick out some entity which he or she wishes to say something about, the amount of syntactic structure needed for adequate reference will vary according to the number of such entities in the context. Thus, for example, if the speaker wishes to refer to a particular car, the pronoun *it*, possibly supplemented by gaze or gesture is sometimes adequate. If there are several objects (say a car, a motor-bike, and a van) to which *it* might refer, then the NP *the car* will be adequate. If, however, there are several grey cars in the context a more elaborate NP along the lines of 36c is required. Post-modifying phrases and clauses have an important function in identifying referents where there are several similar entities in the context. This factor is discussed by Brown (1989: 100) as an obvious source of cognitive difficulty for any speaker not only in adequately referring but in constructing a narrative:

> it is easier to tell or to understand an account of a traffic accident involving a bus, a lorry and an ambulance than one involving three cars. However it is easier with three cars if the cars are of different colours: an accident involving three cars, each coloured grey, produces a conceptually difficult problem for speaker and hearer.

It is not always clear whether the substantial body of research by, for example, Ulatowska and her colleagues which focuses on the narrative and procedural discourse abilities of aphasic speakers (see further p. 130 below) takes account of this 'trade-off' relationship between syntactic elaboration and uniqueness of a given entity in the context of the discourse. The study of narrative discourse by Ulatowska, et al. (1983a) simply required patients to relate a memorable experience, tell a story about a cat elicited from a sequence of drawings, and recall an Aesop fable, while procedural discourse was tested by Ulatowska, et al. (1983) by asking patients to describe how to change a light bulb, make a sandwich, scramble eggs or shop in a supermarket.

Definiteness and cohesion

One consequence of the simple principle that the indefinite article is used for first mention and the definite article for subsequent mention of a referent, is the role of the articles in constructing *cohesive discourse*. Cohesion is the property derived from the use of specifiable textual procedures which enables a stretch of discourse to be perceived as connected text, rather than a collection of unconnected sentences. Compare (39) and (40), which demonstrate straightforwardly this cohesive function of indefinite and definite articles:

(37) *A* car speeded up to the cross-roads. *The* car shot through two sets of lights.

(38) *A* car speeded up to the cross-roads. *A* car shot through two sets of lights.

Since both the subject NPs in (37) might reasonably be assumed to refer to the same car, we have here a small piece of connected text and the alternation of definite and indefinite articles serves as a *cohesive device* (Halliday and Hasan, 1976). In contrast, (38) reads oddly and disconnectedly, and the two NPs are not readily understood as referring to the same car. The following fragment of text, taken from a set of instructions to participants in a treasure hunt, shows how the principles governing the use of definite and indefinite articles are associated with the progressive development of a context into which entities such as huts, bags of food and maps are gradually incorporated. In this way cohesive text is constructed.

(39) You will see *a hut* by the side of *the road*. If you go into *the hut* you will find *a map* and *a bag of food* on the table. Pick up *the map* and *the food*, making sure that you leave *a clear space* on *the table*. Then *the space* will be available . . .

Investigating reference in conversation; a methodological problem

The ability to *refer* or signal '"something" in the world in such a way that the listener is able to understand what is being talked about' is frequently disrupted in aphasia (Chapman and Ulatowska, 1989: 653). Investigators such as Ulatowska and her colleagues (1983) have picked out abnormal distributions of, and comprehension of the referents of, pronouns, nouns, and definite and indefinite articles as characteristic of such a pattern of impairment, and this pattern is generally explored within the framework presented in this chapter.

However, the framework itself is problematic, although it is now widely accepted as standard in both the aphasiological and the descriptive linguistic literature. It is, for example, the framework which is assumed in experimental studies of pragmatic ability by Bates, et al. (1983). The difficulty arises because most linguistic analyses of both definiteness and deixis are top-down in the sense that generalizations are constructed and then tested out on isolated and usually manufactured examples. Seldom do we find empirical studies of the way 'normal' conversationalists spontaneously alternate definite and indefinite reference or use deictic expressions to refer to 'something' in the world. Therefore, our knowledge of the everyday language use against which patterns of aphasic language use are measured is shaky (cf. p. 48ff. above). Chapman and Ulatowska have commented on the difficulty of designing appropriate methodologies for investigations of reference abilities in aphasia, and noted the artificiality of the tasks they used and their disparity with everyday conversations. The routine examination of the 'conversational and expository' speech of aphasic patients in standard aphasia tests such as the Boston Diagnostic Aphasia Examination (Goodglass and Kaplan, 1983) throws no light on this question. The recommended routine is an interview situation in which a series of questions are used in order to elicit responses, followed by a conversation about the patient's occupation and illness and a description of a picture illustrating a composite scene (e.g. the Cookie Theft). The recommended analysis is restricted to a severity rating of communicatory ability, and ratings of intonational contours, phrase length, articulatory agility, paraphasia, grammatical form and word-finding.

We shall examine the methods and findings of some of the specific work on aphasic reference in the following section, moving on in Chapters 8 and 9 to tackle the methodological problems which seem to have restricted them in the way Chapman and Ulatowska suggest. But we conclude this section by showing how the small amount of systematic investigation into actual language use of normal speakers suggests that the framework presented so far does not model 'real world' reference entirely accurately. Therefore, more empirically accountable studies such as the two described below may provide a sounder methodological basis for investigating the referring abilities and strategies of aphasic individuals.

Brown (1989) provides a useful summary of her own recent work and that of her colleagues. In one experiment which attempted to model the variations in shared knowledge between interlocutors which might be supposed to influence choice of definite or indefinite article, she asked pairs of adolescents to play a board game where one participant helped the other to find a route across an island (Brown, n.d.). Although both of the participants A and B had maps, B's map was incomplete, giving rise to the need for A to check on the information available to B before assuming mutual knowledge of a referent. These conditions gave rise to exchanges like the following:

(40) A. Have you got a waterfall
     B. yes
     A. Go up beside the waterfall. (p. 5)

While this exchange seems to fit the accepted principles of

definite/indefinite article choice, Brown finds that this is not always so:

(41) A. Now you go up to the windmill. have you got a windmill?
      B. got the windmill. aye. done it. (p. 6)

What seems to be happening here is a little more complicated, with A presupposing the existence of the windmill and *then* checking it. Speaker role appears also to be important, with the authoritative speaker A generally preferring definite NPs, and to account for such behaviour, Brown constructs generalizations which differ somewhat from the idealizations of the standard model of reference.

Clark and Wilkes-Gibbs (1986) also present pairs of subjects with a task in which mutual knowledge cannot be assumed. One of the participants (the matcher) has to place a set of abstract drawings in an order known to and to be specified by the other (the director). The director's role is to provide instructions to help the matcher identify and order the drawings. Much as Brown finds, the predicted alternation between indefinite and definite NPs on first and subsequent mention does not materialize; rather, several different patterns of first mention form a basis for progressive *collaborative* achievement of successful reference. Clark and Wilkes-Gibbs propose an alternative to what they describe as the 'standard literary model' of definite reference, which is based on the principle of conversation analysis that conversation is always jointly and progressively constructed. Findings like these suggest that the standard model may be more appropriate to written texts than to spontaneous conversation (cf. p. 117 above).

DEIXIS, DEFINITENESS AND APHASIA

In this section we shall review some issues associated with deixis and definiteness in the aphasiological research literature, looking also at examples of aphasic discourse which illustrate difficulties with successful reference commonly encountered by aphasic conversationalists. Some of the complexities which plague attempts to investigate this area systematically spring from problems of narrowing and controlling the scope of the investigation and the variables involved. Thus, for example, deixis and definiteness are central topics in pragmatics, associated both with the integration of cohesive discourse and with the accurate assessment of the amount of mutual knowledge shared by interlocutors. However, they also interface in various ways with central aspects of grammar and semantics, such as tense, pronoun and determiner systems.

Utterances such as (15) and (18) above suggest that inability to alternate deictic terms as the deictic centre shifts in reported speech may account for difficulties with tense and a preference for direct speech; both are widely reported characteristics of aphasic discourse. Yet it is difficult to know how data of this sort should be interpreted. It is possible (and this is Ulatowska's explanation) that they reflect a purely *linguistic* difficulty with the rules for alternating pronominal, temporal and spatial expressions, as exemplified in (13) and (14). But Wales's account of the (deictic) acquisition process suggests that more general *cognitive* abilities of the kind associated with temporal or spatial organization might also be implicated (Wales, 1986: 417). If this is so the use of deictic terms would presumably be impaired in (non-aphasic) right-brain-damaged patients, in whom the occurrence of spatial disorders which affect language tasks is well documented (for example, Delis, et al. 1983), but to our knowledge this has not been reported.

Apparent inability to use deictic terms appropriately with due attention to the information available to the hearer may also be interpreted more positively as the manifestation of a compensatory *communicative strategy* of the kind discussed by Miller (1990: 103; and see also p. 110 above). Crystal (1987) has remarked that the replacement of a deictic term by a referentially more explicit expression like a noun phrase or an adverbial phrase is likely to place considerable demands on the patient's syntactic abilities. We might expect to find a high incidence of deictic terms in the discourse of relatively fluent aphasic speakers, simply because they offer the speaker a means of producing relatively intelligible well-formed utterances with reduced processing 'costs'. However, non-fluent aphasics appear to prefer nouns to pronouns (Wepman and Jones, 1966), and pronouns are classed with the grammatical morphemes which are frequently omitted in agrammatic speech, which seems to suggest that the use of pronouns may impose a greater syntactic processing cost (see Kolk's adaptation theory of agrammatism, described in Chapter 5, p. 91). Edwards and Garman (1989) report on a fluent aphasic individual, who uses more pronouns but fewer nouns than a comparable normal speaker. Commenting that 'Mr V's conversational abilities may founder chiefly on the problem of retrieving concrete-noun word forms' (p. 175) they suggest that his use of proforms may be a strategic response to the difficulties of noun selection.

Further light is thrown on this strategic use of pronouns by an interesting experimental study of the effect of focal brain damage on pragmatic expression, carried out by Bates, et al. (1983). The authors report a high level of pronoun use by Wernicke's but not by Broca's aphasics. Further, they attribute 'bizarre' patterns of use by Wernicke's aphasics to a general strategy for wordfinding, whereby utterance beginnings like 'uh, this one here, he . . .' serve as alternative referring expressions pending the successful outcome of a lexical search. Highly relevant here is the connection illustrated in (36) above between the syntax and lexical content of the NP, the uniqueness of the referent, and the adequacy of the referring expression. The less distinctive an entity is in its context, the more post-modifying and premodifying structure is needed. It is this association which is likely to make adequate reference difficult in some circumstances more than others for a fluent aphasic with lexical-retrieval difficulties and to give rise to the 'semantically empty' and context dependent mode of discourse described by Crystal (1987: 121):

> It is a familiar clinical experience to have a conversation proceeding relatively smoothly as long as the subject-matter relates to the 'here and now', but as soon as topics outside the room are introduced the smoothness disappears.

This perception of reduced smoothness seems to be largely attributable to excessive use of proforms in the absence of contextual support, which seems at least partly to be a strategic response to lexical retrieval problems. However, Chapman and Ulatowska (1989) suggest it might also reflect an impairment of the *pragmatic* ability needed to judge the amount of information shared by interlocutors, and the issue of how far such pragmatic sensitivity might be said to be spared but masked by other kinds of linguistic disability is one which Bates, et al. (1983) attempt to address in some detail. Their comparison of the behaviour of

Broca's and Wernicke's aphasics suggests that the latter but not the former group reveal pragmatic sensitivity in their choice of definite versus indefinite articles, although the results with regard to pronoun use are unclear.

Although the frameworks used to investigate reference abilities in aphasia are usually rather artificial, there appears to be universal agreement on the importance of *conversational* data as a basis for deriving a reasonable assessment (Edwards and Garman, 1989: 166). For this reason, Perkins (1989) carried out a pilot study in Newcastle upon Tyne which compares the referring strategies of one normal with two relatively fluent aphasic speakers in a somewhat more naturalistic way. The performance of the three subjects was investigated under three conditions – a route direction task, an adapted version of Brown's map game (see p. 121 above) and free conversation. Perkins found that both aphasic subjects experienced considerable difficulty in achieving adequate reference, judged in terms of the addressee's ability to pick out the referents of referring expressions. Overall, they used many more pronouns and other proforms than the normal speaker, but apparently employed some interrelated strategies to deal with difficulties in both syntactic structuring and lexical retrieval:

(42) I used to use it with *my things* before and er . . .
(43) with one of these things that er/she had *these things she asked before* you see
(44) erm/I've got *these things* [shows an exercise book]
(45) just the sea *there* you know/and the flat *here*
(46) is to go from the RVI er *Thomas*/go straight off er (.) Marks Marks and [spans] . . .

Examples (42)–(44) illustrate a reliance for successful reference on a semantically non-specific noun (*things*) supplemented in (43) by a post-modifying relative clause and in (44) by gestural indication of the intended referent. The underlying problem here is, as Perkins suggests, probably one of lexical retrieval. In (45), however, the speaker seems to be using the deictic proforms *here* and *there* gesturally, to compensate for a syntactic impairment which makes it difficult for the speaker to structure the sentence. Perkins paraphrases his intended meaning as 'the flat is very close to the sea'.

A rather different referring strategy is illustrated by (46).

Relative to the normal subject, a very high proportion of the definite noun phrases in the discourse of both aphasic subjects are realized as *proper nouns*. To interpret this pattern, we need to remember that proper nouns resemble pronouns in that both categories regularly function as one word NPs and do not normally require a determiner. Thus, a proper noun like *John* or *Haymarket* or a pronoun like *he* or *that* fills the same syntactic 'slot' as much more syntactically elaborate NPs like *the road which leads to the motorway* or *my younger brother*. Recognition of personal names also seems to be remarkably preserved even in global aphasia (van Lancker and Klein, 1990); these authors offer the neurolinguistic explanation that they are mediated by the right cerebral hemisphere. There would therefore appear to be less 'cost' in retrieving a proper noun, in situations where a trade-off between syntactic processing and lexical retrieval is required. In (46), however, the proper nouns to be retrieved are not single words (St Thomas Street, Marks and Spencer) and still present problems to the patient with some disruption of sentence structure. The preference of Perkins' aphasic speakers for proper nouns was of course particularly evident in the route directions task.

The interactional consequences of excessive pronoun use are evident in the short piece of conversation transcribed below, which reflects a problem both with anaphoric and deictic reference:

> **(47)** P: I/and of course *she* was saying today/well eventually/I says no no no I says *they* won't/I says
>
> LP: who's this/Dierdre was saying this today was she?
>
> P: yes yes/half past ten on a Friday.

Here, P evidently intends *she* to refer anaphorically to the NP expression *Dierdre* the name of P's therapist who been mentioned some 60 turns previously in the conversation and is known to LP. But this previous mention is too distant to enable the interlocutor to identify the co-referential NP without requesting clarification. The referent of *they* is entirely unclear, since there is no NP in the text with which it might be associated and no entity in the context to which it might refer deictically. It is worth noting that the temporal deictic expression *today* seems also to present difficulties, since P prefers the non-deictic formulation *on a Friday* (the day of utterance was Friday). Meyerson and Goodglass

(1972) reported, however, that adverbial temporal expressions (apparently both deictic and non-deictic) such as 'once a week' and 'five years ago' were relatively well retained in the agrammatic patients they studied. Using a story completion format, Herzog, et al. (1982) found that errors of tense marking by 14 aphasic patients were not affected by the presence or absence of adverbs of time like 'yesterday'. Despite these occasional studies, as far as we know, temporal expressions have not been systematically investigated in aphasic language, although time is one of the semantic fields which Crystal (1982) indicates should be used in profiling linguistic disability. Certainly adverbial expressions of time, both deictic and non-deictic, appear to be critical in *developmental* language disorders (Fletcher and Garman, 1988).

DEFINITE AND INDEFINITE REFERENCE IN APHASIA

A more specific question associated with aphasic discourse which has attracted the attention of researchers is the distribution and use of definite and indefinite articles. We have seen that, like pronouns, articles might function as *cohesive devices* in connected discourse, and that they can mark out given and new information in discourse (cf. (32) above). Early and VanDemark (1985: 250) report that aphasic speakers use the indefinite article considerably less than normal speakers to mark 'newness' of information. This pattern is generally reported in the literature with specific reference to agrammatic patients, but may also occur in the paragrammatisms associated with fluent speech (cf. Chapter 5, p. 81). Bates, et al. (1983) report a clear distinction between Broca's and Wernicke's aphasics. Broca's aphasics used mainly definite articles, regardless of contextual requirements, while for Wernicke's the proportion of definite versus indefinite pronouns was much more balanced and the choice seemed to display pragmatic sensitivity. The interactional consequences of difficulty with the definite/indefinite article distinction were explored by Perkins in her adaptation of Brown's map-game task:

(48) I/it's er/well it's in *the island* but it's in *the bridge there*

In fact both italicised NPs introduce information which the

speaker has been instructed to assume is new to the addressee. The selection of the definite article therefore appears to be inappropriate, but it is not clear whether the problem is one of retrieval of an item from a set of choices, or one of memory span where the speaker has difficulty in recalling what has been introduced to the context. Alternatively, the difficulty might be more clearly pragmatic, reflecting an insensitivity to the extent of shared knowledge (Early and VanDemark, 1985: 252). Such confusing interrelationships between grammatical, semantic, and pragmatic dimensions seem to be inherent in investigations of spoken language issues associated with deixis and definiteness. Bates, et al. attempt to disentangle these interrelationships, and it is likely that advances in our knowledge will take place if we combine experimental studies like theirs with observational studies utilising frameworks which more accurately reflect everyday patterns of reference. Perkins' work (1989), although exploratory and limited in scope, investigates a dimension of communicative behaviour which cannot be handled within the rather artificial frameworks used in most clinical studies.

SUMMARY

In this chapter we have focused on deixis (including anaphora) and definiteness, two central pragmatic topics which interface also with central grammatical and semantic dimensions of language. We examined deictic expressions of various kinds, and different noun phrase realizations of the definite/indefinite distinction. Because of their central importance in acts of adequate reference, mastery of the semantic and grammatical complexities associated with deixis and definiteness are crucial to successful communication. Ability to handle these complexities – for example, tense, pronoun and article systems – is often impaired in aphasia, with far-reaching communicative conse-quences. Researchers have tended to suggest that while prag-matic ability in aphasia is spared, it is masked by a range of grammatical, semantic and lexical retrieval difficulties. The validity of this view is not entirely clear, however, and more systematic investigation is needed.

We pointed to the benefits of developing 'bottom-up' pro-cedures for analysing normal and aphasic speech, to supplement the 'top-down' investigations which have hitherto predominated, and which impose theories and descriptive frameworks which may not be supported by data derived from more naturalistic studies of both aphasic and normal speech. The issue of how far current research procedures are adequate was discussed in respect of both deictic expressions and expressions of definiteness. We concluded that patterns of use by normal speakers are not well understood, and that most clinical studies utilize rather artificial frameworks which may not yield reliable information on pragmatic dimensions of language use by aphasic speakers.

SEVEN

Coherence in discourse

In Chapter 6 we touched on the cohesive function of pronouns and other types of definite noun phrase in the creation of *connected discourse*. The precise specification of how connected discourse achieves *coherence* in being distinguishable from any random set of consecutive utterances is an important goal in pragmatics, but it is difficult to achieve since coherence needs to be understood as an abstract property of connected discourse going far beyond surface cohesiveness. The nature of coherence has been examined from many different perspectives; for example van Dijk (1977) and van Dijk and Kintsch (1983) have developed a complex scheme for text analysis which has been used by Ulatowska and her colleagues (1983 and 1983a) in their work on the narrative and procedural discourse of aphasic speakers. One of the points here is that to be comprehensible narratives require in addition to surface cohesiveness certain structural components such as an outline of the setting, a specfication of the complicating action and the resolution. Joanette and Brownell (1990) describe applications of the Kintsch and van Dijk framework in the development of neuropsychological and psycholinguistic discourse processing models used to investigate the discourse abilities of aphasics. They also provide an overview of other recent approaches to the relationship between discourse ability and brain damage.

The abstract nature of coherence is reflected also in everyday conversational exchanges, and the approach to pragmatic abilities in aphasia which we are developing in this book focuses chiefly upon such everyday interactive discourse rather than on procedural or narrative discourse. We need, for example, to try to account for the remarkable ability of conversationalists to make sense of consecutive utterances which are unlike those discussed so far, in that they are apparently *semantically* unrelated. Language pathologists generally seem to be appealing to some notion of coherence when they refer to the *appropriacy* or otherwise of the conversational behaviour of aphasic speakers (Penn, 1985), but since the character of this central property of discourse remains elusive, it is difficult to articulate a rational and principled basis for judgements of appropriacy. However, since such judgements are in practice often made, we shall examine the pragmatic principles which might underlie them, concentrating in this chapter on attempts to model discourse coherence from various perspectives.

Two important topics related to coherence are reviewed in some detail, each addressing different aspects of *speaker meaning* in that they go beyond the semantic structure of utterances to take into account speakers' evident communicative intent. The notion of *conversational implicature* was developed by Grice (1975) to account for the sometimes large discrepancy between what is said and what is meant. *Speech act theory* (Austin, 1962; Searle, 1975, 1979) developed an explicitly *action-based* model of speaker meaning, rather than one based on the truth or falsehood of an utterance. Both of these central pragmatic topics have become prominent in a number of applied areas, including language pathology. As we shall see in Chapter 10, speech act theory in particular provides the basis of several procedures in aphasia assessment, while Gricean theory is central to Penn's (1985) Profile of Communicative Appropriateness. Although they have been criticized or modified in various ways, both these theories continue to be influential and to act as catalysts for new developments.

CONVERSATIONAL IMPLICATURES

Consider the following unremarkable (and real-life) exchange between a mother and her son where the son's utterance was accepted as a negative response to the mother's *yes/no* question:

(1) Mother: Are you going out?
    Son: (who is wearing pyjamas) I'm not getting dressed.

An inference of the kind made by the mother is known as an *implicature*. Implicatures orientate to what is meant rather than what is explicitly said and do not follow logically from any given premises. In making her inference the mother seems to have drawn on contextual (non-linguistic) facts and assumptions accessible to both speakers, and by locating these facts and assumptions we can try to express a little more explicitly what was communicated, as follows:

(2) Mother: I need to know whether you are going out, and I am framing my question in such a way that I will interpret any response you make as either positive or negative.

Son: I know that since you are not visually impaired you can see that I am wearing pyjamas. We both know that persons do not customarily go out still wearing pyjamas, but need to change into day clothes. I am therefore providing some information from which you can infer that my answer to your question is negative.

The reasoning used here in deriving the implicature contrasts with the reasoning used in deriving an *entailment*, which is an inference following inevitably from logical reasoning, given the truth of a set of premises such as (i) and (ii) in (3) below:

(3) A. (i) All cats like milk
(ii) Hamish is a cat.
B. Hamish likes milk.

The premises in A are said to *entail* the conclusion B: given the truth of A, B cannot be false, nor can the truth of B be affected by the addition of further premises. One important way in which implicatures differ from entailments is that only implicatures are *defeasible*, or cancellable; they can be altered by the addition of further information. Thus, the son could have cancelled the implicature 'I am not going out' by saying to his mother:

(4) I'm not getting dressed but I suppose no-one would see me if I just popped out into the garden and dead-headed a few roses before I have my shower.

In fact, logical reasoning of the kind illustrated by (3) is not at all characteristic of conversation, such a sequence being rather uninformative in terms of our expectations of routine communication. Much more characteristic is the type used by the mother and son, which Grice explicates in terms of some sort of general principle of providing relevant and helpful information. Here are some further examples of implicatures, which illustrate this everyday kind of reasoning:

(5) A: Have you emptied the dishwasher and locked up?
   B: I've emptied the dishwasher.

Implicature: I've not locked up.

(6) A: Do you know where today's paper is?
   B. I wonder if Linda threw it out

Implicature: I don't know (but I'm making a helpful suggestion).

(7) A: Is there some cake in the tin?
   B: There are three boys in this house

Implicature: There is likely to be none.

To account for the inferencing procedures used in deriving such implicatures, Grice (1975) proposed that conversationalists were normally guided by a *co-operative principle*, and engaged in everyday conversational activity on the general assumption that their partners' contributions were intended to be relevant and generally helpful even when they appeared on the surface not to be. So faced with a response as in (7), a speaker searches for relevance, drawing on a stock of (often culture-specific) background knowledge and assumptions – in this case the well-known tendency of boys to have large appetites and to enjoy cake. This underlying assumption of co-operative behaviour often involves much more inferencing activity than these examples illustrate. Consider for example (8) where A has recently arrived to visit B:

(8) A: I couldn't get to the bank this morning and I need a fair bit of cash for this evening.
   B: There are several cashpoints at Tesco.

It is likely that A will interpret B's response not only as suggesting how he might solve his liquidity problems but as providing reasonably helpful and practical information, in that (for example) Tesco is located nearby, the cashpoints are likely to function, and that at least one of them will be usable by A. This assumption of co-operation is apparently so binding that a co-operative response is often preferred to a more direct response to a question:

(9) A: Is Mike there?
    B: Try the computer room, and if he's not there he might be in the tea-room.

More direct response: No [and I don't really know where he is].

The co-operative principle also seems to ensure that on the whole ambiguous public notices, such as the following on the door of a department store, are not wilfully interpreted literally as prohibiting human beings from entering the store:

(10) Guide dogs only

The cooperative principle is elaborated in terms of the four *maxims* of quantity, quality, manner and relation, which are expressed by Grice as general instructions for competent conversationalists (see Levinson, 1983: 101). *Quantity* is concerned with not giving too much or too little information; *quality* with being truthful; *manner* with clarity and orderliness; *relation* with relevance. To illustrate these maxims and to clarify the contrast between co-operative and merely truthful utterances, we can look at possible consequences of breaching the maxims:

(11) A: Do you have two cats?
    B: (who actually has two cats) I have one cat.

Although B is not strictly speaking being untruthful, his reply is unhelpful and breaches the maxim of quantity in giving too little information. Consider also (12):

(12) A: Did you spend much money today?
    B: I bought a skirt.

If it transpires that B also bought two jerseys, a fur coat and a hat, it is reasonable to accuse her of being misleading; being co-operative involves much more than telling the truth, even though truthfulness is part of being co-operative. Truthful but unco-operative responses are, however, characteristic of much discourse which takes place in *legal* settings, and a good cross-examination needs to take account of the distinction. It has been observed that speakers' expectations of the extent to which the maxims will be observed vary in accordance with the type of interaction they are engaged in (Levinson, 1979; Holdcroft, 1979), and we shall see shortly the importance of this observation when a Grice-style analysis is applied to *clinical* discourse. Sometimes, however, a deliberate flouting of the maxims can itself give rise to an implicature:

(13) Politicians are machines.

Being palpably false, (13) breaches the maxim of *quality*. But on the assumption that at some deeper level the co-operative principle is being observed, conversationalists seek an alternative interpretation. While interpretations of (13) may vary with context, they are likely to be along the general lines that politicians share with machines certain non-human characteristics such as automatic responses, lack of emotion or ethical fastidiousness, or insensitivity. Thus, Gricean theory provides a framework for explicating *metaphor* and *irony*.

If the maxim of *quantity* is flouted as in (14), which is a lengthy and obscure version of the apparently more co-operative (15), again a further implicature is triggered; most probably a hearer (or reader) would interpret (14) as hinting that the thesis had little to recommend it apart from its physical characteristics:

(14) Mr Joseph made a series of marks on 283 pages of A4 paper, bound them and submitted them for the degree of M.Phil.
(15) Mr Joseph submitted a 283 page M.Phil. thesis.

By virtue of its requirement that contributions be orderly, the same maxim has been invoked to explain why utterances like (16) and (17) are heard as expressing events in the same order as the order of mention. However, (17) is more complicated than (16), implicating additionally (by the maxim of relation) that Keegan and not someone else scored the goal. The temporal relationship between the two events indicated in these examples is difficult to explain in purely semantic terms, as the notion of sequentiality is not inherent in the sense of *and*:

(16) Peter cried and Mark ran off (cf. Mark ran off and Peter cried).
(17) Keegan kicks the ball and it's a goal.

Finally, here is a case where the maxim of relation is flouted:

(18) A: Is it true that you have quadrupled your salary since you changed your job?
B: I do so like your delicious dessert.

The irrelevant response implicates that B may not want to supply the information requested by A or may have some other reason (such as the presence of an eavesdropper) for not pursuing the topic.

Grice did not view the co-operative principle as specific to conversation, but as fundamental also to other types of socially organized behaviour. Thus, if Jack and Jill are co-operating in making a Christmas pudding and Jack is passing implements and ingredients to Jill, he does not hand her eight eggs when she asks for five or offer to fetch the hair-dryer when she wants the mixer, nor does he conceal the pudding bowl. We thus have an overall picture of conversation as a subset of co-operative behaviour generally, of conversationalists *assuming* in accordance with a more general social contract which applies also to other kinds of everyday behaviour that maxims are not being violated, and so working hard to make sense out of responses which at first sight appear to be irrelevant. But Grice should not be understood as implying that human nature is particularly benevolent or co-operative. Conversationalists can 'opt out' of the co-operative principle ('No comment!'), tell lies, obfuscate, and deliberately produce tedious, lengthy and unintelligible utterances. The point is that if the assumptions of co-operation and relevance are not routinely made, many perfectly normal utterances in context are hard to follow.

In fact people do apparently make extraordinary attempts to extract relevance from the remarks of drunk, demented or rambling conversationalists; consider for example the experience of trying for some time to make sense of the remarks of a drunken party-guest before finally abandoning the attempt. Sometimes the reasoning needed to make sense of responses of even sane and sober interlocutors is extremely elaborate and highly context-dependent, as in the following (attested) example cited by Sperber and Wilson (1986: 121):

(19) Flag-seller: Would you like to buy a flag for the Royal National Lifeboat Institution?

Passerby: No thanks, I always spend my holidays with my sister in Birmingham.

The authors point out that to understand this as a relevant response the flag-seller must be able to supply the following highly culture- and context-specific information: that Birmingham is inland, that the Royal National Lifeboat Institution is a charity; that buying a flag is a way of subscribing to a charity; that a person who spends holidays inland has no need of the services of that particular charity and so cannot be expected to subscribe to it. All this, in conjunction with the passer-by's reply, must be understood to implicate that this particular passerby cannot reasonably be expected to buy a flag.

What this amounts to is that the reasoning used in everyday conversation is different from logical or scientific reasoning although in fact Grice's main interest was in underlying similarities between conversational logic and formal logic upon which we have not dwelt here. It is particularly important for therapists to be aware of distinctive characteristics of conversational reasoning such as vagueness, indeterminacy, and defeasibility (of implicatures). Thus, if a speaker makes a statement which is true but apparently irrelevant like (20), the hearer is likely to try and 'sniff out' its possible relevance on the assumption that people do not make such remarks for no reason:

(20) The sun will rise today.

Similarly, if the same speaker makes a remark like (21) he does not expect a response such as (22):

(21) I wonder what time the sun goes down today.
(22) Well actually, it is the earth that moves, not the sun.

GRICEAN THEORY AND APHASIA

We have devoted some space to this selective review of Grice's ideas because of their considerable scope and their implications for aphasia studies. One obvious point is that therapists need to be wary of labelling conversational contributions as 'irrelevant' or 'inappropriate'. The characteristics of everyday conversational reasoning highlighted by Grice are such that the notion of a conversational norm against which aphasic performance can be assessed is problematic (cf. Green, 1984). In particular, the ability to extract meaning from written and spoken discourse cannot reliably be assessed on the assumption that the everyday reasoning used by conversationalists is similar to logical reasoning. Furthermore, the notion of a *comprehension* problem in aphasia is sometimes vague. We have described in Chapters 4 and 5 how psycholinguistics is attempting to differentiate different types of comprehension problems at the word and sentence level. The need to do this also at the level of pragmatics is also evident. Present assessment procedures, however, do not distinguish between comprehension difficulties which can be explicated in terms of a failure of routine conversational inferencing and those which emerge from difficulties in computing sense relationships between lexical items or sense properties of sentences. For example, one part of the auditory comprehension section of the Boston Diagnostic Aphasia Examination (Complex Ideational Material) (Goodglass and Kaplan, 1983) attempts to test comprehension in a rather undifferentiated way by requiring the patient to respond to questions on the content of short paragraphs read aloud by the examiner. Some questions seem to test an ability to derive implicatures (e.g. that a hotel guest carrying his own fire escape might leave without paying his bill), but vary a great deal in the amount of background knowledge required to arrive at the implicature. Others seem to test a more clearly linguistic knowledge of relations between vocabulary items or underlying propositional structure. Others still can be answered correctly from general knowledge. Yet, it is surely important for assessment procedures to distinguish between difficulties with 'linguistic meaning' and difficulties with 'speaker meaning', since the latter involve inferencing activity, as opposed to more clearly linguistic processing abilities. In fact, we shall see shortly that recent research links different types of deficit to difficulties with these two kinds of meaning.

Hawkins (1989) is critical of the intrinsic vagueness of the notion of a comprehension problem, as exemplified by the conversational behaviour of a patient who appears to have difficulty in working out the *appropriate* (or more accurately perhaps *relevant*) response. He argues that the primitive notion of appropriacy which so frequently figures in pragmatic assessment procedures can usefully be elucidated in terms of relevance.

He gives an example of a patient whose 'comprehension problem' seems to be at the level of speaker meaning dealt with by Grice's work:

(23) 1. T. is it raining today
      2. P. er (cough) it's quite (cough) pardon / no it never
            put me off (uhuh) no I was quite happy (right)
            even if it was raining and then I'd see it would
            cloud away and would be blue (OK) and you're
            happy (yes) all over again I always used to feel
            good about things
      3. T. OK and the last one /is it Monday today
      4. P. Monday/ that's the beginning (right) it is *the*
            beginning
      5. T. is it Monday today
      6. P. it's a Monday
      7. T. is it Monday today
      8. P. oh this one you mean
      9. T. Today
     10. P. oh now this is fourth fifth February/ its about the
            fourth fifth is it now . . .

(Thirteen more turns follow on the topic of days of the week.)

We need to be a little careful in interpreting this example, since the patient appears to be responding to a series of *yes/no* test questions, and the kind of responses given and judged acceptable in test situations do not always correspond to acceptable conversational responses (compare (36) and (37) below). The therapist's goal is to obtain clear evidence of the patient's understanding of particular questions rather than simply to conduct a coherent conversation, so that some of the indeterminacy and vagueness characteristic of conversation is not allowed to pass, as is shown by the therapist's rejection of the patient's apparently relevant reply on turn (6). Nevertheless, we can agree with Hawkins that the patient's first response, while addressing the general topic of the weather, is not quite co-operative in the Gricean sense. More specifically, the maxim of quantity seems to be violated, since the patient answers the next question at quite unreasonable length, possibly understanding the word *Monday* but not the rest of the utterance: 'His reply is therefore of the "tell him everything you know about Monday" variety' (p. 196). What Hawkins does not point out, however, is that this could be considered an appropriate responding strategy, given the underlying goal of the questioning in a clinical setting. There is also some indication (a possibility not discussed by Hawkins) that the temporal deictic expression *today* is a particular source of difficulty (cf. (47) above). Although a comprehensive characterization of this patient's problem is beyond the scope of this chapter, and indeed beyond what has yet been achieved by pragmatic research, it is reasonable to suggest that Hawkins' perception of 'inappropriacy' in the patient's conversational contributions derives to a considerable extent from the latter's failure to converse with due regard to the co-operative principle:

> Make your contribution such as is required, at the stage at which it occurs, by the accepted purpose of direction of the talk exchange in which you are engaged.

Descriptions of logorrheic speech in Wernicke's aphasia suggest that the co-operative principle may frequently be violated in this syndrome. Goodglass and Kaplan (1983) describe these patients as frequently having 'press of speech' of which they are unaware. Lecours, et al. (1981: 20) point out 'the main characteristic of logorrhea is rather that the speaker tends to keep talking for long periods in response to minimal stimulation (or no stimulation at all)'. However, the situation is considerably complicated by the clinical setting; we have already remarked that speakers' expectations of the extent to which the maxims will be observed vary in accordance with the type of interaction they are engaged in.

GRICE'S THEORIES: LATER DEVELOPMENTS

Grice's work is extremely powerful in illuminating important aspects of *meaning* in both spoken and written discourse, and particularly in suggesting the nature of the everyday reasoning used by communicators to extract such meaning. However, it is important to recall that Grice's mode of argumentation and use of exemplificatory data are rooted in the abstractions of philosophy. It is the concerns of philosophers rather than descriptive or applied linguists which are addressed by his preoccupation with distinguishing meaning in everyday discourse from meaning in the more precise truth-conditional sense. Consequently, although Gricean principles to some extent illuminate the nature of the problem in (23), they are not adapted to describing and analysing stretches of spontaneous (or clinical) discourse, and it is hard to see how they can be applied to data like these in an any more precise way than we have suggested. This is not a problem peculiar to aphasic discourse, since attempts to apply Grice's work to various types of naturally occurring discourse reveal a certain looseness in the concept of the co-operative principle and an arbitrariness in the number and definition of the maxims which have led to some modification of his original work. For example, Leech (1983) proposes a *tact* maxim and a *politeness* principle, and there has been some debate as to how the culture-dependency of conversational behaviour might affect the universality of the maxims (Keenan, 1976). The resultant confusing picture reflects a general feeling that Gricean theory needs to be tightened up.

In our discussion of the maxims, we have appealed frequently to the the maxim of relation, particularly the notion of *relevance*. This focus reflects the primacy assigned to the maxim of relation by several commentators, particularly Sperber and Wilson (1986) who propose that the co-operative principle be replaced by a single redefined *principle of relevance*. Relevance, the property sought by all conversationalists, is effectively defined in terms of the interplay between the information available (or 'manifest') to speakers, and the effort needed to process that information; the relevance principle is said to operate without exception, in that it is never deliberately violated by a rational speaker. The theory is ambitious and complex, intended to supersede Grice's work as a general theory of communication. In claiming to be a cognitive theory and to take into account constraints on human cognitive abilities, it contrasts with Grice's rather vague notion of a social contract, embodied in the co-operative principle. This claim has, however, proved controversial, and the potential of relevance theory to provide a psychologically real model of human communicative behaviour has been questioned. Particularly, it has been subjected to sustained criticism for its disregard of the advances achieved by the more socially sensitive approaches to pragmatics which we shall outline in Chapter 8. Currently, a number of psycholinguists are attempting to incorporate these approaches (explicitly preferring them to relevance theory) into cognitive theory as part of a *collaborative* model of communication (Gibbs, 1987; Gibbs, et al., 1988; Clark and Schaefer, 1989). While it is too early to offer a reasoned evaluation of relevance theory, it seems to be useful chiefly in offering a rigorous account of a general organizing principle underlying coherent conversation rather than any kind of usable blueprint for analysing samples of discourse. We shall return later to the tension between social and psychological accounts of conversation which we have touched upon here.

SPEECH ACTS

Along with implicature, speech act theory is widely regarded as central to pragmatics, having originally been developed by the philosopher Austin (1962) in response to what he saw as an excessively narrow concentration on the purely *informative* function of language. It has appealed to researchers in related disciplines such as social anthropology, sociology and psychology, and been widely applied not only in language pathology but in such areas as the analysis of cross-cultural communication and second-language acquisition. Although to some extent the concerns of speech act theory with speaker meaning overlap with those of Grice, a speech act approach to discourse is distinctive for its emphasis on the *act* accomplished by an utterance, and with the problem of how speakers (and hearers) manage to relate acts such as warning, requesting, apologizing to the semantic and syntactic form of utterances. Consider (24) (25) and (26) below:

(24) This plate is hot.
(25) Do you have a match/tissue? (uttered for example by one passer-by to another).
(26) Do you have £10?

Although (24) can be analysed in terms of linguistic (truth conditional) semantics as a proposition concerning a plate which might be either true or false, with the assumption that its function is purely to make an assertion, such an analysis does not explain why in an appropriate context (say, addressed by a cook to an assistant in the kitchen), (24) is likely to be interpreted and intended as a warning. To grasp the speaker's meaning (intention), the addressee needs to be capable not only of accessing propositional meaning, but also of making a number of assumptions about the motives of the speaker, and his likely purpose in speaking at all. To interpret (25) when uttered by a stranger as a request for a match, a hearer additionally requires the *social* knowledge that matches are free goods, for in the same situation (26) would probably not be interpreted as a request. It is possible that some aphasic individuals rated as having poor comprehension may have problems in an experimental task with this dimension of speaker meaning, particularly if the request is a negative one (Wilcox, et al., 1978).

What follows here is a simplified and selective account of speech act theory, which is dealt with extensively and critically by Levinson and others (see also Bach and Harnish, 1979; Searle, 1979; Leech and Thomas, 1990). Three interdependent issues of some importance to language pathologists are prominent in the literature. The first concerns the 'mapping' of speech act types on to utterances, the second considers *how* speakers and hearers assign a particular meaning to ambiguous utterances such as (24)–(26), and the third *why* they should communicate in such an indirect fashion as this.

Distinguishing form and function

Starting relatively straightforwardly with the mapping of speech acts on to utterances, we can make a distinction between the semantic and syntactic form of an utterance on the one hand, and its communicative (speech act) function on the other. Some procedures for analysing aphasic discourse which make use of speech act theory fail to draw this essential distinction, using for example the terms 'interrogative' and 'request' interchangeably. This is the kind of thing McTear (1985) has in mind in his comments on the 'terminological confusion' in the language pathology/pragmatics literature. Below are set out in the left hand column the three major sentence types of English. These are sometimes assumed to correspond to the functions (or illocutionary forces) traditionally associated with each type which are set out on the right hand side. These functions actually refer to the 'speech act' intended or achieved by the actual utterance, rather than to formal sentence types:

(27) DECLARATIVE   ASSERTING
INTERROGATIVE ASKING/REQUESTING
IMPERATIVE   COMMANDING/ORDERING

The speech-act concept allows such functions to be described, regardless of whether utterances are tokens of declarative, interrogative or imperative sentence types. For example, a request for lunch may take a number of syntactic forms, not necessarily interrogative; nor need its semantic form encode an underlying proposition which mentions lunch:

(28) get me my lunch
(29) are you getting lunch?
(30) can you get lunch?
(31) would you mind very much if we had lunch?
(32) is lunch ready?
(33) I get pretty hungry around 1 pm.

These formally diverse utterances might all be described as *speech acts* which fulfil an identical communicative function, differences between them being accounted for chiefly in terms of a range of contextual and social factors. Some utterances have both a *literal* and an *indirect* reading; for example the direct reading of (30) would be a query about the hearer's ability to get lunch, and the indirect reading a request for lunch. Leech (1980) approaches such ambiguities by drawing a useful distinction between the *sense* (literal meaning) and the *force* ('speech-act' meaning) of an utterance. Thus, (30) is interrogative in sense but directive in force. Emphasizing the overlapping concerns of speech act and Gricean theory, Leech links speech act theory with implicatures, pointing out that utterances might be indirect to varying degrees, in that different amounts of inferencing activity are required to interpret them. He connects degree of indirectness with politeness, a general rule of thumb being that the greater the indirectness the greater the politeness, so that utterances like (28)–(31) can plausibly be ranked in a roughly ascending order of politeness. This suggests a rational and interactionally strategic *motivation* for the apparently dysfunctional tortuousness and indirectness of an utterance like (31), which is expounded in detail by Brown and Levinson (1987).

While these examples show that a given function such as 'request' can be realized in a number of ways, the converse is also true in that a single sentence type such as an interrogative has functions other than 'requesting'. In the example below, B's utterance, which is interrogative in sense, is understood by A as *asserting* that the jam-jars are kept on the shelf:

(34) A. Where do you keep empty jam-jars?
   B. Do you see that shelf above the fridge?
   [A places empty jam-jar on shelf]

This conceptual distinction between sense and force, literal and indirect interpretation, is a fundamental one for clinicians; interrogatives are not always questions and statements are not always assertions.

One salient preoccupation of speech act theorists has been to group together related speech acts, in order to delimit and restrict the possible range of speech act types. For example, Searle compositely classifies as *directives* acts like requests or orders which attempt to get the hearer to do something, so that one may speak of utterances such as (28–33) as having the force (or *illocutionary force*) of a directive without considering further whether they are requests, appeals or commands. The chief function of the discourse particle *please* seems to be to mark this particular illocutionary force, as in the following utterance addressed by a lecturer to a group of students. Without the particle (35) appears to be interpretable as an assertion without any directive force:

(35) The projector really ought to be put there, please.

How do hearers interpret ambiguous utterances?

This question, which has been the subject of extensive psycho-linguistic experimentation at the sentence level, has also been considered at the pragmatic level, in respect of how conversationalists manage to relate *function* to *form* (or, in Leech's terms, *force* to *sense*). For example, how does a hearer interpret an utterance like (30) as a request to get lunch rather than a question about ability, adopting the indirect rather than the direct interpretation? Furthermore how is a single function related to a diverse range of forms? Following Austin, the notion of *felicity conditions* of a speech act has been used to account for these abilities. These are conditions which must be fulfilled in the situation in which the act is carried out if it is to be carried out felicitously (or appropriately), felicity conditions being devices which explain how hearers interpret speech acts when the linguistic form of the utterance gives them so little help. Thus the act of *enquiring* may be said to be felicitous (i.e. a genuine enquiry) only if the speaker does not know the answer to the question, and believes that the hearer does. Note that by this definition *test questions* of the kind often used in classrooms and clinics do not have this condition attached to them. Compare (36) and (37):

(36) Passer-by to policeman: Where is the nearest chemist, please?

(37) Therapist to patient: What do you do when you make a cup of tea?

In addition to a Gricean analysis, we can thus use the notion of felicity condition to explicate (23.6) above, where the therapist rejects the patient's response to a test question.

Since requests have received a great deal of attention in the aphasiological literature, it is worth noting a major felicity condition on such acts – the belief of the speaker that the hearer is able to carry out the request. Therefore, utterances like (38) and (39) are generally interpreted as requests, the direct reading (an enquiry about the hearer's ability) being infelicitous if the ability of the hearer to fulfil the request is obvious or already known. However, the direct reading of (38) is felicitous if, for example, the hearer is physically handicapped, and of (39) if the hearer is aphasic:

(38) Can you pass the salt?

(39) Can you tell me how to make an omelette?

At this point the overlap between speech act theory and Gricean theory is clear, and Levinson (1983: 241) has made the point that felicity conditions on major illocutionary acts like requesting and enquiring are predictable from general principles of rationality and co-operation. Sperber and Wilson have taken this line of criticism further, arguing that speech act theory as a whole can be subsumed within relevance theory (1986: 243).

When the felicity condition notion was originally developed to explain how listeners assigned particular speech act interpretations to ambiguous utterances, it was assumed that the plausibility of a literal interpretation was evaluated before being discarded in favour of an indirect interpretation. However, this assumption, which is effectively a *psycholinguistic* claim (such as has been experimentally investigated in respect of ambiguous lexical items) has not always been born out by the results of experimental research into speaker behaviour. Gibbs (1983) shows that listeners can use contextual information to arrive at indirect interpretations without previously rejecting direct readings, and Clark's (1979) examination of the effect of *conventionality of wording* suggests that 'high conventionality' question forms such as 'Can you . . .' tend to be responded to as requests, while 'low conventionality' forms ('Are you able to . . .') encourage a literal interpretation. Abbeduto, et al. (1989) provide a convenient summary of the experimental psychological literature on speech acts, the goal of which is generally to specify the kind of contextual information utilized by listeners in assigning interpretations to ambiguous utterances. Their own experiment yields no firm conclusion, but confirms that listeners use a wide range of contextual cues, following a broad 'answer obviousness rule' in evaluating the plausibility of alternative interpretations. This process need not, however, involve prior rejection of an implausible direct reading, as speech act theory assumes.

SPEECH ACT THEORY AND APHASIA

Speech act theory has recently been evaluated as offering a useful 'shorthand way of discussing speaker meaning; a helpful means of abstraction whose terminology lingers on because it is such common currency and useful for that reason alone' (Leech and Thomas, 1990: 196). Most pragmatists would probably agree, but Leech and Thomas's comment rather underestimates the useful insights supplied to speech-language therapists by the theory. Although we shall see that it hardly holds water as a theoretical model, some of its basic distinctions and concepts are quite fundamentally relevant to clinical practice, and this is probably why it has been so attractive as a basis for the applications which we shall consider in Chapter 12. Davis and Wilcox (1985) have emphasized the need for therapists to be alert to potential ambiguities between direct and indirect readings of utterances like (38) and (39) when directing patients during assessment and therapy sessions.

Because of its attention to the mismatch between linguistic form and communicative function, speech act theory has attracted attention from researchers investigating *functional communication* in aphasia. Prinz's experimental work (discussed by Lesser, 1989: 201) suggests that even global aphasics can *use* requesting acts appropriately. With regard to *interpretation*, an investigation by Davis, et al. (1978) suggests that aphasic speakers retain the ability to respond to indirect speech acts, although there is some indication that acts of the form 'Must you . . ., should you . . .' which request the hearer *not to* perform an action present some problems. It is, however, quite possible that the complex semantics of the modal verbs are the source of difficulty here (in interpreting *sense* as opposed to *force*) rather than the inferencing ability needed to interpret indirect speech acts.

More recently, Weylman, et al. (1989) have followed Clark (see p. 147 above) in investigating the effects of both context and conventionality of wording on the interpretation of ambiguous indirect requests (such as 'Can you open the door?) by left- and right-brain-damaged patients. Like the experimental work on normal speakers reviewed above, the results are somewhat unclear, but suggest that both groups resemble normal speakers in being sensitive to conventionality of wording and in tending to use this as a guide to interpretation. However, the two groups seem to be differentially impaired with regard to their ability to utilize *contextual cues* (such as the presence of an open door) as a guide to interpretation. Weylman, et al. interpret their rather inconclusive resulΩts as linking impairment of inferential and integrative (as opposed to general linguistic processing) capacities with *right* brain damage. Unlike aphasics, the central semantic, syntactic and phonological abilities of the right-brain-damaged group seem to be unimpaired, although the generality of this conclusion is open to question in view of the association of prosodic and semantic impairment with right brain damage (see Code, 1987, for a review). Foldi (1987) reports similar conclusions to those of Weylman, et al. One of the chief interests of work in this area is such differential performance of right-brain-damaged and left-brain-damaged patients. The latter group seem to be impaired in their ability to link social and previous textual information in such a way as to derive inferences, and both the major issues in pragmatics discussed in this chapter are relevant to any attempt to elucidate this difficulty. However, despite the substantial amount of experimental work in this area , the picture is far from clear. The inconclusiveness which characterizes systematic investigations of both normal and language-impaired speakers may well spring from the flaws underlying a speech-act model of dialogue, to which we now turn.

INDETERMINACY OF MEANING AND MULTIPLICITY OF MEANING: SOME PROBLEMS FOR SPEECH-ACT THEORY

An important and quite specific aim of speech act theory is to map acts on to utterances, a prerequisite being the specification both of a set of utterance types and a set of speech act types (cf. (27) above). In fact, it has proved difficult to specify comprehensively a finite and principled set of speech-act types (even within the aphasia literature we find a proliferation) or to specify a set of utterance types independently of function.

Indeterminacy and multiplicity of meaning have plagued attempts to apply a speech-act framework to *situated speech*, the kind of discourse which is embedded both in sequential conversational context and in a web of surrounding contextual and situational constraints. But from the point of view of the practical analyst, perhaps the most serious problem is that meanings seem to be jointly negotiated as conversation proceeds, interpretation consequently changing as the discourse unfolds. Cicourel (1987) has criticized Searle's most recent substantial work on speaker intention (1983) for its failure to handle simple instances of jointly negotiated interpretations. The following two comparable pieces of real-life situated discourse (both involving members of the same family) illustrate these problems:

(40) A. Is lunch ready?
     B. Would you stop nagging me!
     A. I was only asking!

                              (Milroy and McTear, 1983: 64)

(41) A. Are you eating at 6.30 tonight?
     B. We can do if you want to go out
     A. Don't bother/ I'll just get a pizza in town/ oh maybe I will eat with you actually.

The force of A's first utterance in (40) is evidently interpreted by B as directive, and while we may surmise that such an interpretation would have been allowed to stand had B's response been compliant, a directive intent is subsequently disclaimed in the face of B's hostile reaction. The problem is that there is no set of rules or conditions which enables us to predict A's intention, which is likely to have changed in response to the contribution of his conversational partner and seems in any case to be quite indeterminate. The best we can do is use the addressee's response and A's subsequent contribution to justify a *post-hoc* assignment of illocutionary force to 'Is lunch ready?'

The unpredictable nature of the outcome of such exchanges is evident if we compare (41) with (40). Here, B seems to interpret A's first utterance as an indirect request to prepare the evening meal early, an intention which A seems first to disclaim but then to acknowledge in the face of B's compliant response (compare B's non-compliant response in (40) and A's subsequent disclaimer, which on that occasion is allowed to stand). But in (41) even more than in (40) A's intention seems quite indeterminate and a speech act function hard to assign to his first utterance. It is difficult to apply to even such mundane stretches of situated discourse an analysis which presents interpretations as somehow previously given and aligned with a pre-existing set of felicity conditions, rather than negotiated in a sequential context in a sometimes changing response to a previous conversational contribution. In general, conversationalists vary in their reponses to ambiguous utterances. Sometime they appear to misunderstand the communicative intent of the speaker, while at other times the multiplicity of meaning of utterances in context seems to be strategically exploited, as in both these examples. Such an exploitation offers a rational motivation for the indeterminacy and ambivalence (or 'multivalence') so prominent in everyday discourse, which is commonly accounted for in terms of politeness, as elucidated by Brown and Levinson (1987).

Labov and Fanshel's (1977) extended speech-act type of analysis of a stretch of psychotherapeutic discourse highlights the difficulties which seem to beset any 'top-down' attempt to specify *rules* for producing and interpreting utterances in context. The fact is that no-one has yet managed to work out a set of predictions which have held up in the face of everyday conversational behaviour, but perhaps this is not surprising as

Searle himself has remarked that the speech-act approach to dialogue is designed to deal with isolated pairs of utterances and has not yet been developed to handle conversation (Searle, 1986: 7).

In view of the evident popularity of speech-act theory amongst therapists who are developing pragmatically orientated assessment and therapy procedures (see further Chapter 12), it has seemed appropriate to spell out some of the associated practical and conceptual problems. However, our intention is not entirely negative, since we consider in Chapter 8 an analytic procedure which, while not claiming to offer a rigorous model of dialogue, sidesteps some of the difficulties. The changing and negotiable character of utterance interpretation is assumed, and utterance function is elucidated not in terms of constructs like felicity conditions, but with reference to sequential placement in conversational structure. We shall see that the fundamental problem addressed by speech-act theory, of how indirect speech-acts are interpreted by hearers, can be articulated quite differently and at least partially resolved when relevant instances of actual (as opposed to invented) conversation are exposed to a detailed 'bottom-up' empirical analysis with a minimum of prior theoretical constraint.

WHAT DO WE MEAN BY 'COHERENT DISCOURSE'?

We began this chapter by commenting on Penn's (1985) description of coherence as a central feature of discourse, the property which makes it more than a collection of unrelated sentences. Coherence also seems to be the property which language pathologists like Penn (and see also Prutting and Kirchner, 1987) are attempting to evaluate by means of procedures for rating the *appropriateness* of conversational contributions. This chapter and Chapter 6 have drawn together a number of rather varied topics all of which in some way contribute to specifying those properties which make a sequence of utterances coherent, but the jigsaw is incomplete in that no-one has yet succeeded in adequately describing the properties which differentiate coherent and incoherent discourse. Bearing in mind the centrality of this distinction for assessments of functional communication ability such as those described in Chapter 12, we conclude this chapter with some comments on why it is proving difficult to make.

Speakers often claim an intuitive ability to recognize a piece of dialogue as incoherent in the sense that while it is unproblematic at the level of syntax or semantics it nevertheless appears in some way not to 'hang together'. Here are some candidate dialogue fragments:

(42) A: Those skin grains leave your face lovely and smooth.
     B: I wouldn't mind. *Mississipi's Burning*'s on at the Tyneside.
(43) A: I feel quite queasy.
     B: No.
(44) A: Hi.
     B: Thank you.

(Schiffrin, 1988: 258)

(45) Doctor: What's your name?
     Patient: Well, let's say you thought you had something from it before but you haven't got it any more.
     Doctor: I'm going to call you Dean

(Labov and Fanshel, 1977: 2)

One obvious way of specifying what is odd about these examples (assuming that readers will judge at least some of them to be odd) is to construct rules of coherent discourse which are then applied to data, rather like a piece of litmus paper to a mixture of substances. The distinction between well-formedness and ill-formedness yielded by such a procedure is central to *syntactic* and *semantic* analysis, and it is tempting to extend the model to discourse. Although in fact Labov and Fanshel tried, with only limited success, to model speech act production and interpretation in this way, a quick look at our limited data suggests that we might be able to make some progress in specifying oddity. For example, while B's response in (42) seems to be to an offer it is hard to interpret A's utterance as having such a force. Labov and Fanshel have accounted for the oddity of utterances like (43) in terms of their *AB event* framework, which distinguishes between mutual and private knowledge of participants. According to this analysis, B cannot coherently disagree with a proposition of A's which is known only to A (Labov and

Fanshel, 1977: 62). Example (44) also seems at first sight to be ill-formed in an easily specifiable way; greetings like A's utterance are routine forms of reciprocal conversational behaviour, and B's utterance does not constitute a reciprocal greeting. But unfortunately for our endeavour, (44) actually occurred, under the following circumstances. After receiving the message that B had telephoned her, A returned the call within five minutes. Hence, B's utterance simultaneously indicates recognition of A's voice and appreciation of the speedy return of the call.

This example illustrates the chief problem inherent in an approach to modelling discourse coherence which extends syntactic analytic methods, appealing to intuitive judgements without fully specifying the central and quite particularistic role of context. Furthermore, despite feeling intuitively that some discourse *is* distinctly incoherent, speakers who are presented with examples such as (42–5) often struggle to make sense of them, arguing for example that (45), a piece of schizophrenic discourse cited by Labov and Fanshel as a clear example of incoherence, is not in fact as totally incoherent as they claim. The function of prefatory *well* as a 'hedge on relevance', discussed by Levinson (1983: 162), may be one reason for this feeling that some sense can be made of (45). Similar comments might be made about the conversation discussed by Hawkins (1989; see (23) above). While we are able to comment in a general way that this patient is not conversing 'co-operatively' (in Grice's sense) an accurate specification of his discourse problem is quite another matter.

Both the pragmatics literature and the real world abound with examples of conversational fragments like (46) which make perfect sense to participants but seem quite incoherent when quoted out of context. Consider the following piece of dialogue originally introduced by Sacks and cited by Levinson (1983: 292):

(46) A: I have a 14 year old son.
    B: Well, that's all right.
    A: I also have a dog.
    B: I'm sorry.

In isolation this is puzzling, but all becomes clear once it is explained that B is a landlord from whom A is seeking accommodation.

Certain principles of conversational structure which have been discussed in this chapter are likely to undermine any top-down attempts to determine the properties of coherent discourse. First, conversations rely on infinitely varying *context* and the equally variable *shared knowledge* of interlocutors to the extent that many central linguistic phenomena such as deixis and definiteness cannot adequately be explicated except with reference to these factors (see Chapter 6 for a discussion of deixis and definiteness in these terms). Nor can either context or shared knowledge be adequately modelled as static phenomena, simply because in a real conversation each person's contribution changes the context in which a subsequent contribution is understood.

Secondly, a general co-operative principle appears to underlie conversational interaction with the consequence that participants carry out a great deal of inferential work in a search for relevance in even rather puzzling utterances (see for example (19) above). Thus, coherence might be seen less as a property of conversations or of texts than as a strategy of participants; they create coherence by searching for relevance or by responding to utterances in a relevant and co-operative way. If they fail to do this, communication breaks down.

The situation is further complicated by the stereotypical knowledge which speakers progressively acquire of appropriate responses in different situations. This discourse knowledge is part of their broader knowledge of *scripts*, mental representations of event sequences for situations in daily life which are learnt on the basis of experience. Thus, many adults have scripts for situations like visiting a pub or restaurant, responding to questions in a job interview and so on. They can know how to approach or respond to specific questions from the barman or waiter or potential employer only by reference to these scripts, and if they lack the experience they are likely to lack the knowledge. For example, an applicant for a job would be very unwise to respond to a question about his motives in applying by admitting that he was tired of living on social security benefits or found his current employer uncongenial. Generally speaking this type of question (in British culture at least) seems to require a statement of commitment to the prospective employer. This response needs to be learnt experientially, although the potential pool of relevant responses is very large (see further Blakemore, 1988: 236; Levinson, 1983: 281). A recent investigation of aphasics' knowledge of such scripts, which required non-brain damaged and aphasic subjects to select and order phrases descriptive of particular sequences of events (eating in a restaurant, taking a bus ride), suggests that this experiential knowledge is unimpaired (Armus, et al., 1989). We should note in passing that Holland (1991) in her 'conversational coaching' procedure seems to have a rather different understanding of the notion of 'script' from the generally accepted one we have described here. Her use of six- to eight-word scripts (parallel perhaps to Armus et al.'s phrases which describe single events in a script) is discussed in Chapter 12.

The importance of context and previously acquired 'script' knowledge in determining the appropriacy of responses and the perception of coherence of discourse supports Johnson-Laird's argument that a theoretically adequate explication of coherence needs to go beyond language. He offers such an explication in terms of *mental models* of a cognitive and experiential kind which represent a plausible state of affairs in the real world. While including scripts, these mental models include also other cognitive frameworks of a temporal, causal, spatial and intentional kind upon which perceptions of plausibility depend (Johnson-Laird 1988: 345). This emphasis on the importance of experience and cognition for the building of discourse models embodies a much more abstract notion of coherence than constructs such as implicatures which link linguistic units like utterances (or, in the case of Sperber and Wilson's theory, underlying propositions).

Top-down models like those of Johnson-Laird and of Sperber and Wilson are fundamentally designed as computer-testable models of discourse. As such, they are serious attempts to embody principles underlying conversational coherence, our knowledge of which is as yet incomplete. While they can certainly suggest directions for research into aphasic discourse abilities (such as Armus et al.'s work on scripts) their more general applicability in clinical contexts (or indeed to the analysis of any stretch of naturally occurring discourse) is far from clear. We shall see in Chapter 9 that it is possible to view coherence in a way more directly translatable to situated aphasic or non-aphasic discourse, as being *jointly constructed* through interactional procedures of various kinds as interlocutors nudge each other towards a mutual understanding. A conversation *becomes* incoherent (coherence not being viewed as an independently establishable property) if this joint work is unsuccessful and interactive procedures break down. In the meantime we should note that an understanding of the inherent difficulties of specifying coherent discourse is central to any attempt to construct a profile of pragmatic or conversational ability such as those considered in Chapter 12.

Despite these difficulties in specifying coherence, it is perverse to deny that some utterances are tenuously connected to prior text for reasons which are best elucidated in clearly linguistic terms, and we can conclude this chapter on a more positive and optimistic note by looking at some examples. Responses to WH-questions are revealing here, since this type of question characteristically restricts the possible range of responses by specifying the type of information sought. Thus, (47) seems to require some kind of information about time:

(47) When did Ted have that brilliant idea for a short story?

Consider now some likely and unlikely responses:

(48)   (i) In the pub.
       (ii) He didn't.
      (iii) I've no idea.
       (iv) What's that got to do with it?
        (v) His name isn't Ted.
       (vi) Better ask Bessie.
      (vii) *Oh, this and that.
     (viii) *Because I hate salami.

None of these responses actually contain a temporal expression, but while not all are equally informative, only the last two seem incoherent. The first seems to depend on the hearer's ability to implicate a time of day from the information provided; the second and fifth to query the presuppositions (effectively assumptions) underlying the original question; the fourth apparently queries the speaker's right to ask the question while the sixth seems to reroute it and so on. All these and many more responses are possible and likely, and the reasons for the oddity of (vii) and (viii) appear to be that both are responses to a different type of WH-question which, unlike (i) cannot be interpreted as implicating a time of day. Additionally, (viii) is topically unconnected to the question. Yet, however clear-cut

(viii) may seem as an example of an incoherent response, we have to be careful of making *topic* a general yardstick of coherence in dialogue. Quite apart from the difficulties associated with analysing topic (see further Chapter 9) we encounter the recurrent problem of the particularistic effect of context, since in some situations 'licensed' topic shifts are common. At mealtimes for example talk about food takes priority:

(49) A: She's in real trouble now don't you think what with the money markets and the National Health Service and all that.
B: Try that red cabbage it really is good with pork.

Finally, we need to draw a clear distinction, which is implicit in much of the foregoing discussion, between *cohesion* and *coherence*. The term 'cohesion' generally describes the resources available in the language for creating text, and as such cohesion can be studied as an extension of syntax and semantics. A number of *cohesive devices* (Halliday and Hasan, 1976) have already been identified in our earlier discussion of the definite and indefinite articles and of the use of proforms in anaphoric and deictic expressions (see (27), (28), and (39) in Chapter 6). Another cohesive device is the kind of *ellipsis* which is very common in response speech:

(50) A: Where do you want to go for lunch.
B: The Wooden Doll.

The point here is that the frame into which this response fits (I want to go to ———— for lunch) is precisely recoverable from the previous utterance, with the result that utterances A and B are bound to each other in a clear and specifiable way. Various types of conjunction and adverbial expression such as *but, so, however, nevertheless, yet, frankly* also have a cohesive function, as does discourse intonation. Readers are refered to Halliday and Hasan (1976), Johns-Lewis (1986), Crystal, et al. (1981: 81) for a full account of these and other devices. Armstrong (1991) summarizes the framework of Halliday and Hasan, and provides a useful account of the applications of cohesion analysis to the analysis and treatment of aphasic discourse. Our chief intention here is not to replicate these accounts, but to stress that cohesion is not the only property of coherent dialogue. We have seen that this elusive property is much more abstract than surface features of text such as pronouns, articles and conjunctions. As Hawkins (1989) points out, any attempt to account for the inadequacy of discourse such as that of his patient in terms of an analysis of these surface features of the text is unlikely to be successful.

SUMMARY

Coherence is generally viewed as a central property of discourse, and the task of discriminating between coherent and incoherent discourse has been approached from a number of different directions. The notion of *appropriacy* which frequently appears in clinical assessments of pragmatic ability seems to refer to the property of coherence. The two concepts which we have concentrated on in this chapter as particularly relevant to coherence in everyday conversational discourse (as opposed for example to narrative or procedural discourse) are Gricean principles of conversational logic and co-operation and speech acts. These have been discussed in some detail not only because they are referred to and applied extensively in aphasia studies, but because each illustrates some of the difficulties in establishing the nature of coherence in discourse. Conversation is not only highly context dependent (as we emphasized in Chapter 6), but is actively and collaboratively constructed by interlocutors. The evidently changing and negotiable nature of speaker intention as revealed in conversation produces problems for speech act theory as a model of dialogue, and provides a further illustration of the limitations of top-down approaches to the analysis of everyday interactive discourse. Cohesion, a surface feature of texts, is distinguished from coherence, a more abstract property of discourse, and a number of approaches to the specification of coherence are briefly reviewed.

EIGHT

The structure of conversation

In Chapter 3 we offered a broad definition of conversation as discourse produced by at least two persons. To point up the contrast between different types of interactive discourse, we shall now define conversation more restrictively as the kind of everyday discourse which takes place between persons with equal rights to speak, where no participant overtly controls the proceedings. Conversation in this sense is the commonest type of interactive discourse, and as such is a basic site for the study of spoken interaction. Yet, until relatively recently little has been known of the way people converse in everyday contexts when they are not using language self-consciously or transactionally – that is, to attain some independently specified goal. Recall also that we relied very little on naturalistic data in our account in Chapters 6 and 7 of the 'underpinnings' of coherent conversation. Even less is known about *aphasic* discourse outside the clinic, despite the high premium placed by clinicians on the everyday interactions of patients with family, friends and acquaintances. Most current research utilizes material collected in clinical contexts with the investigator firmly in control of the proceedings, and we saw in Chapter 6 (p. 120f. above) that Chapman and Ulatowska were critical of these rather artificial frameworks. The purpose of this chapter and Chapter 9 is to explore other frameworks which might grant some insight into the everyday conversational behaviour of both normal and aphasic speakers.

We shall focus in these chapters not on the relatively abstract aspects of discourse organization considered up to this point, but on the directly observable sequential structure of conversation. This can usefully be approached from two perspectives, the first of which, in a fairly general way, distinguishes conversation from more institutional and publicly visible types of discourse of the kind used in committees, clinics, classrooms, medical consulting rooms and law courts. Most people are intuitively aware that these interactions are structured rather differently from the conversation which is the normal medium of interaction in the social world.

The second perspective involves examining details of such everyday conversational organization without reference to any comparator, and this is the one on which the bulk of this chapter and Chapter 9 will focus. Conversation, traditionally viewed as unplanned and lacking overt structure, will be treated as an interactive achievement resulting from the co-ordinated work of at least two speakers, accomplished by means of specific management procedures. This approach deals with such questions as how conversations are initiated, sustained and closed down, and how the identification and repair of misunderstandings and other interactional trouble spots is routinely handled. In the final section of this chapter, some of the insights into conversational organization provided by such an analysis will be compared with those provided by some of the top-down approaches previously discussed.

The balance between 'normal' and 'aphasic' material in these chapters requires some comment here. We shall refer frequently (particularly in Chapter 9) to aphasic conversation – that is conversation where one or more participants is an aphasic speaker. However, fairly extensive stretches of text will focus more generally, without necessarily referring to aphasia, on the explication of analytic principles and procedures. This is simply because it is the principles and procedures themselves which are important and, if they are to be useful, need to be carefully described. Most importantly, since they deal with relatively small fragments of talk and do not encompass any notion of a conversational norm, they are capable of granting useful insights into the structure of even irregular and non-standard types of material such as aphasic conversational sequences.

CONVERSATIONAL VERSUS INSTITUTIONAL DISCOURSE

Sequences (1) and (2) below are taken from a large body of data collected in 1975 from working-class communities in Belfast in such a way as to bring out the differences between the kind of speech characteristic of *interviews* and the kind characteristic of conversations between peers. The goals and methods of this work are described in detail by Milroy (1987). The first extract is taken from the beginning of a fairly informal interview where the fieldworker (LM) is questioning a middle-aged man, George, about his life in the city. The second is part of a long multi-participant conversation which had already been underway for more than an hour, where the fieldworker as a participant observer played only a marginal role in the proceedings. The other participants are Dick, his wife Maggie, and his brother Eddie (all in their mid 40s). Also present in the room, but offering no verbal contribution at this point is Ted, an 18 year old friend of Dick and Maggie's son. Even a cursory glance at these data reveals sharp structural contrasts between (1) and (2); most obviously perhaps the interview can easily be analysed as having a clear *two* or *three* part exchange structure.

(1) 1. LM: well could you tell me/ first of all you say you   I
were born here/ could you tell me where you
were born?

2. G: (1.00) uh (1.00) Parker Street in East Belfast   R

3. LM: (0.5) a wee bit across the road/ and when did
you come to live here?   F/I

4. G: here/ uh (0.5) just about three years ago (1.00)   R

5. LM: yeah (.25) and have you ever lived outside East
Belfast?   F/I

6. G: uh (.) for a period   R

7. LM: (.) when?   I

8. G: (0.5) a couple of year in Ballybeen (.) it's
actually Ardcairn/ Ballybeen was an extension
from that you know (2.00)   R

9. LM: oh yeah/ how long for?   F/I

10. G: (1.00) just a few year   R

(2) 1. M: . . . and she said/ I'll bring all youse girls out for
chicken suppers/ but we [LM LAUGHS] we all sat
and ate chicken suppers till Nellie comes for her
club money/ (3.00) Sarah squealed like a pig /my
purse my purse/ [HIGH PITCHED VOICE] (2.00)/
I said/ Blondie stole it/ she bought us all fish
suppers uh chicken suppers/ Sarah was *going to*

2. D: *at least* she was half decent about it
             [ALL LAUGH]
3. M: (.) bloody well (1.00) she says/ my bloody money
             bought it=
4. E: =they were good but
5. LM: (.) good suppers?
6. E: (.) good at their job
7. LM: what was their job?=
8. E: =stealing
             [ALL LAUGH]
9. M: I was only out of the hospital and she bought me
             over a dozen eggs/ she says/I stole them from a
             farm-house/ and some man had been beating his
             carpet and threw it over a hedge/ Eileen passed
             and stopped the car and took the carpet
             [ALL LAUGH]
10. D: every so often they used to invite you over for a
             drink/ all the drink you wanted/ you heard the
             next day such and such some place was done
             [ALL LAUGH]
11. M: do you see when you look back on the troubles
             you get a queer laugh/ look at Lizzie that day/ his
             mother-in-law /[POINTING TO E]/ she asked me
             over/ she'd a wee pub up here you know/ chased
             her out you see . . .

Sinclair and Coulthard's description of *classroom* discourse is
appropriate to the interview style of (1):

> A more simple type of spoken discourse, one which has much more
> overt structure, where one participant has acknowledged
> responsibility for the direction of the discourse, for deciding who
> shall speak and for introducing and ending topics.
>
>   (Sinclair and Coulthard, 1975: 6)

Working at first chiefly with such overtly structured types of
discourse, Sinclair and Coulthard developed in the early 1970s an
influential procedure for analysing interactive discourse within
the specifically *linguistic* framework provided by Halliday's
grammatical theory. Discourse was conceptualized as a further
level of linguistic organization, where elements were realized by
items at the level of grammar. The *exchange* is an important unit
of interaction within this system, consisting at least of an

initiating move by one speaker and a *responding* move by another. Initiating moves are prospective, setting up constraints on possible types of response, while responses are retrospective in that they are analysable only in relation to what has gone before. A third type of move is a *follow-up* which differs from either. Unlike an initiation it does not predict a response, and unlike a response it is an optional element of structure in the sense that its absence does not leave such an obvious 'gap' in the discourse. Thus in (1) some exchanges can be coded according to this system as (I)nitiation/ (R)esponse, some as I/R/(F)ollow-up.

This type of underlying two or optionally three-part discourse structure seems to be characteristic of interviews. A three-part structure is, however, particularly common in instructional contexts, where the teacher initiates, the pupil responds and the teacher follows up with feedback. Here is an example taken from a recent study of classroom discourse in South Africa:

(3) T: Is the reaction exo- or endothermic, Theresa?   I
    S: Exothermic   R
    T: It's exothermic . . .   F

(Adapted from Muller, 1989: 321)

Since absence of feedback is often a sign that the student has not produced the answer the teacher wants, educational or clinical assessment procedures which instruct the tester silently to withhold feedback do not ensure tester neutrality, and we shall see shortly that powerful inferences are regularly triggered by short periods of *silence* in certain predictable sequential contexts. Participants in any kind of discourse are caught in a web of such inferences, and indeed persons responsible for controlling discourse of the type of (3) often feel constrained to provide a follow-up move.

A similar underlying structure may be found in doctor–patient interaction and in some therapeutic contexts. Here are two examples, (4) being an extract from a speech therapy session and (5) a piece of doctor-patient talk, cited by Stubbs (1983:29).

(4) T: did you get the van out of the garage?   I
    P: no(.) no (.) because we had seen em . . . hhh . . . it
       was like a (.) um . . . a . . . two . . . oh dear me=   R
    T: =you're doing well/ you really are   F

(5) Doctor: you've only had one attack?   I

Patient: well(.) as far as I know   R
Doctor: yeah   F

It is clear from even such short pieces of institutional discourse as (1), (3), (4) and (5) that there is very much more to be said about their sequential structure. However, although there are obviously other types of exchange structure possible within this situation, the IRF analysis provides a useful way of characterizing the interactional reflexes and of formalizing the mechanism by which interviewer, doctor, teacher or therapist retains the interactive initiative. Fairclough (1989) explores broader issues associated with the manifestation of power and role asymmetries in discourse, which we shall touch on only peripherally here. We can begin by trying to specify, fairly broadly, some of the organizational features which mark out (2) from the kind of institutional discourse discussed so far.

First and perhaps most obviously many of the speakers' turns at talk in (2) are longer, reflecting both a general (clinician's) assumption and a well-attested sociolinguistic finding that conversation provides more data for research or assessment purposes than speech collected in therapeutic sessions, classrooms or interviews. Secondly, there is no overt obligation on any participant in (2) parallel to the obligation resting upon interviewers, teachers, therapists and doctors to control the discourse. This is not to say that all contributions or conversational contributors are equal; plainly Maggie says much more than anyone else and Ted nothing. But conversationalists characteristically *negotiate* such rights to speak, while the essence of institutional discourse is that the rights of teachers, interviewers and clinicians are accepted in advance. What appears to be happening in (2) is that Maggie is narrating a series of humorous stories, the chief theme in this sequence being the activities of some dishonest neighbours. By virtue of her role as narrator, which may (and in fact later in the conversation does) pass to another participant, she currently has the right to initiate and end topics or stories free from the danger of interruption. The role of the others is to support her in various ways – for example by adding short amplifying remarks or by laughter. They may also seek clarification if necessary, as the fieldworker LM does, about what or who is 'good'.

A third characteristic of (2) is that direct speech and various voice effects are used for dramatic purposes. Certain stylistic effects are evident, such as the alternation between past tense and the so-called historic present which is characteristic of narratives (see also Wolfson, 1982). Finally, we do not find in (2) the linear 'chaining' structure, realized in (1) as a series of IR(F) exchanges. For example the exchange between LM and E is nested within the main structure of the discourse and within that sequence we find a further embedded sequence seeking clarification of 'their job'. In the course of this *side-sequence* (Jefferson, 1972), problems of interpretation and understanding are sorted out without disrupting the progression of the main narrative.

Even from such a brief comparison it is evident that conversation is likely to provide a structurally richer and more varied data base for the analysis of interactive discourse than an interview such as (1), and it is this variety and complexity which makes it such a rich source of information on the language abilities of speakers. Experimentally generated or role-play language of the kind criticized by Chapman and Ulatowska (1989) is similarly impoverished in comparison with naturally occurring data, as is clear to anyone who has had an opportunity for comparison (Heritage, 1989: 38). In much the same way, aphasic clinical discourse seems impoverished in comparison with aphasic conversation. Edwards and Garman for example comment of Mr V, a fluent aphasic, that 'spontaneous speech . . . was his most accurate speech' (1989: 176), and he himself expresses vividly his awareness of his superior performance in conversation with his wife:

(6) talking with [pi:θ] (people)/ it's alright like my, my old wife at home [θ]/ when he say to me [θ] about it and I could talk beautiful/ . . . y'know/ it's funny, init/ y'can't talk with everybody – this is , this is what it's about [θ]

Conversely, Mr V's worst performance is in response to therapeutic tasks designed to elicit expressive speech, and some of the conversational data presented in Chapter 9 shows that even severely impaired aphasic speakers achieve a great deal when thrown upon their own conversational resources, in terms both of the effectiveness of their conversation and the *amount* of speech produced. We shall describe in Chapter 12, how this interactional dynamic has been used as a basis for pragmatic intervention in aphasia.

Stubbs (1983, especially ch. 7) has discussed the question of extending the Sinclair and Coulthard exchange structure analysis to casual conversation. However, although the latter have developed a more elaborate framework than that described above (see, for example, Coulthard, 1985: 120ff.), the issue is not whether it can or cannot be extended, but on whether such a top-down model which so aptly characterizes the structure of classroom and other institutional discourse types *should* be used as the basis for analysing casual conversation. It is not immediately obvious how such a framework can grant useful insights into the structure of multi-participant conversation such as (2); indeed, it cannot easily deal even with some types of *dyadic* conversation where neither party exercises overt control over the discourse. The alternative approach outlined at the beginning of Chapter 6 is to work inductively, fitting linguistic forms directly accessible to observation into more abstract structures and categories only *after* their use and distribution have been observed. We shall look shortly at such a procedure, which offers a means of approaching not only everyday conversation, but non-standard, irregular kinds of conversation, like those of aphasic or bilingual speakers. It is data such as these which pragmatic and discourse theorists have traditionally shied away from, viewing them as too idiosyncratic to be handled by predictive models.

INTERVIEWS AS A SOURCE OF DATA

Language pathologists seem generally to be aware that data collected in clinics under test conditions or as a product of therapist–patient discourse might reflect only very indirectly everyday communicative behaviour and potential. Since clinical discourse has been shown to have structural affinities with both classroom and interview discourse, we shall use the generic label of 'interview' in considering briefly, from a broader sociolinguistic perspective, some of the consequences of using as a source of linguistic information the type of two-party speech event where one participant has acknowledged responsibility for controlling the discourse.

It is evident that in Western society an interview is a clearly defined and quite recognizable event to which a formal style and slowish tempo is appropriate. Participants are often either strangers or relatively socially distant persons with clearly defined asymmetrical roles; the control exercised by the interviewer is instantiated in topic selection and choice of question form. The interviewee, on the other hand, in accepting that role has contracted to provide *co-operative* responses. From his or her point of view these may well be maximally brief and relevant, and response speech is likely to be further curtailed by the normal and predictable patterns of ellipsis which frequently plague clinicians' attempts to collect large volumes of data.

Having elicited a response, the obligation (and so the onus of continuing the conversation) rests upon the interviewer to follow up with a further question, sometimes first providing feedback. While some interviewees are more talkative than others and may not confine their contributions to responses, our discussion so far has suggested good sociolinguistic reasons why interviews are likely to yield scantier data and exemplify a narrower range of linguistic structures and communicative functions than conversations. If the interviewee is aphasic the data are likely to be even scantier. But this is not entirely a consequence of linguistic impairment, since a relatively good conversational level can often be achieved when relatives collaborate with the aphasic conversationalist in pursuit of joint interactional goals (see p. 214 below). If the therapist withholds such collaboration in attempting to elicit expressive speech for a particular assessment or clinical purpose, a poorer performance may result, as happened with Mr V. It is notable that standard aphasic tests which incorporate elicited speech (such as the Boston Diagnostic Examination and the Western Aphasia Battery) give no guidance on what collaboration the interviewer may give in encouraging the patient to continue speaking.

One recent pilot study in Newcastle which used interview-style data to compare the discourse profiles of ten aphasic and two normal speakers offers some support to these suggestions, in that a higher proportion of all the aphasic patients' turns were responses (as opposed to initiations), and of those responses a higher proportion were *minimal* responses (Watson, 1989). This pattern is not a natural and obvious consequence of the aphasic speakers' linguistic (and perhaps conversational) incompetence; on the contrary, they could be said to be using their limited linguistic resources quite rationally, exploiting the interviewer's role as the controlling participant in such a way as to maintain interactive discourse with minimal linguistic input from them-selves. Conversations, however, are unlike interviews in that they do not offer this automatic support system for any given participant; discourse roles in peer conversations are negotiated rather than institutionally specified. In most Western societies conversationalists seem to be uncomfortable with silence and sensitive to a general obligation to maintain a flow of talk, unless they are intimate enough to engage in what Goffman (1981) has called a 'state of open talk', where they have the right but not the obligation to speak. We shall see that even quite severely impaired aphasics are able to communicate effectively, producing a surprising amount of situated speech in contexts where they feel an obligation to maintain the flow of talk. The sensitivity of such patients to the same kind of psycho-social constraints as normal conversationalists needs to be taken into account in assessment and therapy.

SOME CHARACTERISTICS OF CONVERSATION

The perspective on interactive discourse offered by the conversa-tion analysts, which views it primarily as a *co-operative achievement* rather than the sum of two or more independent contributions, has important implications for the analysis of aphasic conversation. This is because utterances are examined not in isolation as the product of an impaired speaker, but systematically as part of a co-operatively constructed conversa-tion. Such a perspective is radically different from that presup-posed by, for example, speech-act theory, where isolated utterances are first assigned a speech-act description and the building of utterances into sequences is viewed as a different and later analytic task. Although research in the conversation analysis tradition over the last twenty years has shown that many of the structural characteristics of conversation are related to its co-operative mode of production, the implications of this work are only slowly being taken on board by professionals who work directly with language, including speech-language therapists. When the structure of conversational speech is discussed at all, it is generally assumed to be ambiguous, unstructured, inexplicit, incomplete, repetitive, sloppy and the like. But in fact the original conversation analysts (Sacks, Jefferson, Schegloff) and those following their procedures (e.g. Atkinson and Heritage, 1984; Button, 1987; Roger and Bull, 1989) have shown quite conclusively that such characteristics are important aspects of the organization of conversation. They constitute strategies for monitoring the reactions of conversational partners, and for clarifying and repairing misunderstandings and mistakes as interlocutors follow the various cues which accompany interaction. Schegloff concludes an investigation of recycled (i.e. repeated) turn beginnings with the following comment:

> . . . such partial repetitions or recycles are frequently treated as sloppiness, as inarticulateness, as not having thought about what one was going to say, as evidence of the disorderliness of single occurrences in passing conversation. I hope it can now be seen that precisely the opposite of each of these is the case. We should thereby be encouraged to investigate other apparently unorganised 'sloppy' materials in the natural world.
>
> (Schegloff, 1987: 84)

Quite clear here is the conversation analysts' central concern with aspects of conversation which are generally ignored by researchers, and which theoretical linguists explicitly exclude from analysis (this follows particularly from the competence/performance distinction of generative theory).

The following samples of conversation (7) and (8) are transcribed in such a way as to reveal some of their underlying orderliness. Extract (7) is a fragment recorded in a classroom during a lesson break where three children, S, A, and J are competing for the teacher's (T's) attention. It provides an interesting contrast with the kind of classroom discourse discussed in the previous section; since the context is not instructional the teacher does not control the discourse by selecting topics and speakers. Rights to speak are here more equally distributed in that the teacher asks questions emerging from a pupil-initiated topic, and otherwise responds to initiations and summons of her pupils. Extract (8) is part of a conversation between two close friends, both young women, about car-parking problems in Manchester city centre.

(7) 1. J: I give I give Pepper er a plate full of dog food
     2. T: what sort does he like?
     3. J: (.) er meat

4. T: proper meat/ (.) *or meat* out of a tin?
5. J: *yeah*
6. J: mea/ dog meat
7. T: yeah
8. T: what does your Jack Russell eat?=
9. S: =she doesn't eat dog food/
10. T: (.) no
11. S: she only eats *chicken* turkey/ er heart (.)
12. J: *er*
13. S: *erm (0.5) er/ don't know what all* rest is
14. J: *.hh our Rebel doesn't eat dog food/ he eats all left overs/*
15. J: Miss?=
16. T: =mmm
17. J: our dog doesn't eat dog food/ he eats all left overs
18. T: yeah/ that's good it's good having a *dog like that/ isn't
    it?/*
19. S: *she's just*
20. S: she's fussy our dog because (.) she won't she won't
21. T: (.) yeah
22. S: sometime she even turns her nose up at chicken or
    turkey=
23. T: =really?/ good heavens I bet she costs you a fortune

(8) 1. S: They wanted to go to this posh shopping centre car
    park/ takes you an hour an half to park up/ whereas
    if you keep to back streets and just go and park/ you
    know/ (.) gets in this one behind Hills/ this multi-
    storey thing/ *oh God*
2. B: *oh that one/* the one behind the
    Arndale Centre=
3. S: =I don't know what the hell it were/ (.) but it went
    up and up and up/ and oh God/ aren't they arent
    they law (?)/ I would never dream of *parking in* a
    place like that
4. B: *wouldn't you?*
5. B: I don't mind them
6. S: you know where I used to park?/ I don't know if it's
    still (.)/ behind the Oyster Bar/ (.) you know *that*
7. B: *that* little one?=
8. S: =yeah
9. B: =that little multi-storey one?=
10. S: =yeah/ I always park there

We shall look again at many of the features displayed in (7) and (8) as we systematically consider details of conversational organization. For the moment we can take note of some prominent features such as the so-called discourse markers *yeah*, *you know* and *oh* which are characteristic of interactive discourse and have a clear organizational function in indicating various kinds of participation and acknowledgement (Schiffrin, 1987). In S's first contribution in (8) for example *you know* appears to function as an attention-checking device. Another feature of conversation, particularly evident in (8), is that there do not seem to be consistently recurring units corresponding to the *sentence* of the written language and of more formal spoken language. Although clauses and phrases are evident, sentences are in general extremely elusive in conversational speech (Miller, 1990).

We can also see such characteristics of conversation as overlapping speech (italicised in (7) and (8) above); repetition; pauses which might be unfilled or filled by items such as in or out breaths, or the vocalisation *er*; false starts and self-corrections (all particularly evident in (7)). These phenomena have been examined by psycholinguists as an indication of cognitive processing at various levels – planning topic, structuring sentences or searching for words. Butterworth (1979) and Schlenk, et al. (1987) have particularly associated unfilled pauses with cognitive processing and word-finding difficulties by aphasic speakers, and the aphasiological literature contains many terms relevant to the description of this range of conversational phenomena. However, there is seldom any clear analysis of the role of these behaviours in interaction, 'fluency' for example often being viewed as a dimension of pragmatic behaviour and globally assessed as appropriate or inappropriate (see for example Penn, 1985). Yet, as we can see from (7), although repetitions have an important function in normal turn-taking, there is as far as we are aware no principled way of delineating the boundaries of such normally dysfluent conversational behaviour. Similarly, the term 'press of speech' seems to refer to a number of turntaking, pausing, timing and conversational content characteristics (see Edwards and Garman, 1989: 168). We would support Garman and Edwards' view that these characteristics are best considered separately, and may in fact be viewed as heterogeneously functioning strategies which fulfil a range of conversational goals. Terms like 'paraphasia', 'paragrammatisms' and 'jargon', which are generally only clinically or psycholinguistically defined in the literature, may similarly be more systematically discussed by examining the sequential placement of utterances in conversation.

TRANSCRIPTION: A COMMENT ON PROCEDURE

The familiar punctuation conventions which are routinely used to organize written language cannot easily be adapted to show these spoken language features in either normal or aphasic conversation, and indeed such features are usually edited out of institutional transcriptions of law-court proceedings, parliamentary sessions, meetings and the like. A set of transcription conventions originally developed by Jefferson is widely used in conversation analysis to show such features *at whatever level of detail is necessary for the current analysis*, and a modified set of these conventions is provided at the beginning of this book (for further details see Levinson, 1983: 369–70; Atkinson and Heritage, 1984: ix). Linguists have often been critical of the notational conventions used in conversation analysis, particularly of the lack of consistency and systematic detail in the presentation of intonation. A useful and constructive recent discussion of issues in the transcription of conversation, including the use of phonetic notations, is provided by Kelly and Local (1989).

The problem is not, however, simply one of consistently representing surface features of talk; transcription is always a selective process, reflecting underlying (though sometimes unacknowledged) goals and assumptions (Ochs, 1979: 44). There is no such thing as an absolutely complete or correct transcription, and a system such as Halliday's (1985) cannot be adopted 'off the peg' without also importing the theoretical framework within which Halliday analyses discourse. Our general strategy here is to select and show in our transcriptions the types of features which are of interest *at any given point in the discussion*, although we have not attempted to interfere with the transcriptions of scholars whose work is cited. This means that we do not offer completely consistent or equally detailed transcriptions at all points, but attempt to strike a balance between reasonably systematic presentation on the one hand and visual clarity on the other. It is in fact for reasons of clarity that phonetic transcription of conversational materials is generally avoided, although phonetic details are certainly relevant to many aspects of conversational organization. Conversational transcriptions can often look very cluttered, and even (7) and (8), which contain relatively little detail, may look a little daunting at first to readers who are not used to dealing with such data. They do, however, give some idea of the kind of details handled by conversation analytic procedures, and will serve as a useful reference point as we proceed to consider some principles and assumptions characteristic of this approach.

CONVERSATION ANALYSIS: APPROACH AND ORIENTATION

Unlike other scholars whose contribution to pragmatics we have discussed, Sacks, Schegloff, and Jefferson are not linguists or philosophers, but were originally associated with an innovatory group of sociologists. These latter scholars (the best known of whom are probably Goffman and Garfinkel) described themselves as *ethnomethodologists* to reflect their preoccupation with analysing data according to categories demonstrably oriented to by *participants*, rather than superimposing the *analyst's* categories (cf. the analyst-oriented categories employed by the exchange structure analysis of Coulthard and his colleagues (Coulthard, 1985; Coulthard and Montgomery, 1981)). They adopted a rigorously empirical and inductive 'bottom-up' approach, rejecting preliminary theorizing of the kind characteristic of all the styles of pragmatic and discourse analysis considered so far. The *orderliness* of natural conversations is repeatedly emphasized, the goal of the analysis being

> to explicate the ways in which the materials [natural conversations]
> are produced by members [of a society] in orderly ways that exhibit
> their orderliness and have their orderliness appreciated and used.
> (Schegloff and Sacks, 1973: 290)

Ethnomethodologists have examined repeatedly and in great detail small samples of naturally occurring conversation, seeking to develop analytic categories and higher level theories only in so far as they could be seen to emerge from, and be justified by, direct reference to these data. Analyst intuition of 'what is going on' is therefore not viewed as a valid source of evidence, such evidence being sought chiefly in the behaviour of *recipients* (i.e. hearers or addressees) who reveal directly by their responses an analysis of the preceding speaker's turn. While it is difficult to maintain this stance, it is methodologically important to attempt to do so, since it provides the chief means of achieving a reliable and valid analysis of a single piece of data of which the analyst has no intuitive or situational knowledge. The use of a recipient's next turn to validate interpretative conclusions about a previous speaker's turn is particularly clearly demonstrated by Atkinson and Heritage (1984: 8), and will be evident in our own discussion of conversational data. Schegloff and Sacks summarize these various strands of their analytic orientation vividly (if rather tortuously) in their classic account of conversational closings:

> In the ensuing discussion, therefore, it should be clearly understood that the 'closing problem' we are discussing is proposed as a problem for conversationalists; we are not interested in it as a problem for analysts except in so far, and in the ways, it is a problem for participants. (By problem . . . we mean that closings are to be seen as achievements, as solutions to certain problems of conversational organisation.)
>
> (Sacks and Schegloff, 1973: 290)

Analyses in this tradition characteristically take shape as pieces of inductive reasoning structured round small pieces of data. These fragments are repeatedly scanned for evidence of how participants are accomplishing a task such as closing a conversation (as above) or disagreeing (Pomeranz, 1984). The conversation analysts shy away from a concentration on particular linguistic items considered out of sequential context. This is because of the assumption intrinsic to such a procedure that a given item will in different sequences have the same interactional implications (Atkinson and Heritage, 1984: 298).

Focusing on participant accomplishments rather than on linguistic items entails also a rejection of *quantitative analysis*, a method considered to be doubly flawed in that it is not faithful to everyday styles of reasoning employed by participants. Schegloff (1988: 136) cites two separate exemplars 'of the single occasion as the locus of order'. The first concerns his celebrated (1968) study of 500 openings of telephone conversations, where he arrived initially at a generalization which adequately accounted for 499 –

a satisfactory result for most statistical analysts. Schegloff's response, however, was to wonder how the participants in the one remaining case achieved the desired outcome, that is of getting the conversation underway. In response to this evident problem (for participants, if not for a quantitative analyst) he constructed an entirely different generalization which adequately accounted for all 500 cases. His second example humorously asks the audience of his colloquium paper (1988), to consider their response should he, poised on the podium, begin to produce some bizarre behaviour; he suggests that they would not be likely to set it aside as a statistical anomaly which, by the law of probability, was bound to occur sooner or later:

> Rather, you would find yourself making some sense or other of what was going on, and finding some way of conducting yourself that would deal with this situation. On reflection of course that is what you have done in each of the ordinary occasions in which you have participated in the past; you have found on each singular occasion whether and when to laugh, when to knit the brow, whether and when to applaud, when and how to leave early if it was a bore or you were not feeling well or both, and how to indicate which of these was the case.

(Schegloff, 1988: 137)

It is clear from this that the analytic machinery of conversation analysis is intended to explicate the orderly procedures of participants in such a way as to deal illuminatingly with repeated *single* episodes of naturally occurring talk. Phenomena such as overlaps and pauses are seen as embedded in a sequential context which changes with each conversational contribution. Thus, counting the incidence of behaviours such as filled or unfilled pauses and comparing frequencies between speakers is seen by conversation analysts as problematic (see for example Schlenk, et al. 1987 for an example of a standard quantitative approach to these phenomena in disordered discourse). This is because pauses generate different types of conversational inference, depending upon their sequential placement (as we shall see in Chapter 9). However, the emphasis upon sequential context means that it is difficult to describe conversation analytic methods independently of demonstrating them on specific examples, and for this reason we shall in Chapter 9 follow this account of the theoretical framework with detailed discussion of single examples.

The issue of quantitative analysis shows up a methodological and theoretical chasm between the way in which the conversation analysts on the one hand and experimental psychologists on the other characteristically treat questions of reliability and validity. This is a major discrepancy between approaches, of which both ethnomethodologically and experimentally orientated readers need to be aware and to which we shall return (see Beattie, 1989); it is one example of the partly complementary and partly conflicting approaches used in aphasiology.

Heritage (1989) provides a useful discussion of assumptions underlying the theoretical orientation of conversation analysis. He explains in detail the view that interaction is structurally organized according to certain *social conventions*, which means that it can be studied independently of psychological or other attributes of participants. The kind of conventional organization and autonomy assumed is similar in some respects to the conception of pre-Chomskyan structural linguists who used 'a slot and filler' heuristic, that is they investigated how sequential (or *syntagmatic*) considerations restrict the class of items that might be expect to follow, and of how items in that class contrast with each other, that is stand in *paradigmatic* relationship (Levinson, 1983: 367). We shall see shortly that there is gathering evidence that many central but not immediately obvious features of conversational organization fit in with the predictions of *politeness theory* (Brown and Levinson, 1987), so lending plausibility to the view that conversation is structured according to social convention.

A further assumption, touched on earlier in this section, is that any conversational contribution is *context-shaped*, in that it can be understood only with reference to the context in which it participates, particularly the preceding context. It is also *context-renewing* in that it creates a context for what follows. One far-reaching consequence of this insistence on the primacy of context, which is viewed as dynamic rather than static, is that the meaning of an utterance (or perhaps more accurately what an utterance *comes* to mean) is the product of *interactional work*, a concept of speaker meaning which contrasts sharply with the relatively static analyses we examined in Chapters 6 and 7. Thus, for example in developing speech-act theory Searle gives primacy to the isolated utterance, which is analysed in terms of syntactic and semantic features. Searle and Grice both deal separately with the speaker's meaning and the listener's understanding. Speakers are seen as performing certain illocutionary acts like requesting, enquiring and asserting; and, provided certain felicity conditions are fulfilled and the co-operative principle is operative, these intentions are recognized by hearers, who are thus in a position to go beyond what is said to what is implicated. We saw in Chapter 7 that this orientation makes speech-act theory extremely difficult to apply to even relatively short stretches of situated speech such as (40) and (41) in Chapter 7, where indeterminacy and multiplicity of meaning are commonplace.

Examples such as these do not, however, present any particular problem to conversation analysts, who by focusing on the dynamics of joint interactional work conceptualize conversational organization rather differently and have been consistently critical of speech act theory. Schegloff (1987) points out that utterances are *primarily* understood by reference to their sequential placement, so that the basic units of analysis are not utterances but *sequences*, and the relevant question is how people *together* direct the course of a conversation and sort out problems as they emerge. Thus, the question of 'who talks when' is managed through a system of turn-taking; when one person speaks, the other not only listens but indicates acceptance and understanding in various ways, sometimes quite minimally with *yeah, uhuh*, head nods and so on. Absence of these *tokens of recipiency* is itself an indication of problems – which perhaps explains why persons unaccustomed to telephone answering machines find them such disconcerting conversational partners. It may also be a cause of misunderstandings in some dysarthric speakers as in Parkinsonism where automaticity of head and facial movement may be lost. There are also orderly and structured mechanisms for repair and clarification when things go wrong, and equally structured ways of opening and closing conversations and the topics within them to the mutual satisfaction of interlocutors. Within this interactional framework, a much more dynamic analysis of speaker meaning than that offered by the traditions of Searle and Grice becomes feasible:

An utterance does not necessarily mean what it might mean or what it seems to mean at the moment when it is uttered. Its meaning is defined in part by what follows. A silence might seem to mean, at the moment of its occurrence, that the speaker is for some reason unwilling to produce a preferred response, but if the speaker then goes on to produce such a response the meaning of the pause may be reassessed.

(Bilmes, 1988: 174)

Conversation analytic research on tiny segments of talk each considered as single episodes, on the pauses, discourse markers and repetitions which figure so prominently in conversation, seems at first sight to be fragmentary with little theoretical power or capacity to generalize. The same criticism has been levelled at the current predominance of single case studies in cognitive neuropsychology (Fitz-Gibbon, 1986). However, in the case of conversational analysis, large numbers of these detailed analyses of single and sometimes fragmentory episodes of talk have been placed together, like pieces of a jigsaw, to reveal that ordinary conversation has a detailed and specifiable multi-level structure. Despite (or perhaps because of) its freedom from initial hypotheses this inductive procedure can be shown to have yielded many more detailed insights than any of the approaches considered so far. To try to give an idea of how a conversation analytic style of analysis contrasts with the top-down type of approach to conversational organization with which readers are likely to be more familiar, we shall re-examine from this perspective *definite reference* and *indirect speech acts*. Both topics have figured prominently in the aphasiological literature where the standard theoretical and descriptive frameworks, described in Chapters 6 and 7, have generally been adopted.

ANOTHER LOOK AT DEFINITE REFERENCE

In a vivid demonstration of the potential of conversation analytic methods, Clark and Wilkes-Gibbs (1986) have proposed that successful acts of *reference* are, like utterance meaning, collabora-tively achieved. This runs contrary to the generally accepted (or 'literary') model of reference outlined in Chapter 6 according to which, Clark and Wilkes-Gibbs suggest, speakers are said to refer much as if they were writing to distant readers:

> When Elizabeth selects the noun phrase *the clown with the red nose* in talking to Sam, the assumption is that she intends it to enable him to identify the clown uniquely. She satisfies her intentions by issuing the noun phrase . . . she retains complete responsibility and control over the course of this process. Sam hears the definite description as

if he were reading it and, if successful, infers the identity of the referent. But his actions have no bearing on hers in this reference.

(Clark and Wilkes-Gibbs, 1986: 3)

Although we have seen that this is the general model used in studies of the abilities of aphasic speakers to integrate reference appropriately into discourse, such as those of Early and VanDemark (1985), or Chapman and Ulatowska (1989), for a number of reasons it is an unconvincing account of what happens in everyday conversational referring. Most obviously, speech is unlike writing in that speakers have limited time and are pressured into making their contribution quickly. Furthermore, they are likely to alter their contributions in response to signals of various kinds from recipients, and indeed, data from actual conversations show that successful referring is responsive to these constraints and incentives. Thus for example speakers *expand* on a noun phrase until understanding is signalled as in (9); or use *trial* noun phrases, which are noun phrases uttered with a rising intonation as in (10);

(9) S: Take the spout – the little one that looks like the end of an oil-can –
    J: Okay.
    S: – and put that on the opening on the other large tube. With the round top.

(10) S: Okay now, the small blue cap we talked about before?
    J: Yeah.
    S: Put that over the hole on the side of the tube.

(Clark and Wilkes-Gibbs, 1986: 4–5)

The hearer routinely indicates understanding as soon as the referent is identified. This may be done in several ways, apart from the use of assent tokens *yeah* and *okay* as in (9) and (10). For example in (11) mutual understanding of the referent of the noun phrase *the governor* is signalled by what Schegloff (1982) has called a *continuer*. Not only does B signal continuous attention and assent, but with the second *mh hm* indicates that she is passing up the chance of querying A's utterance and so by implication claiming understanding:

(11) A: Now I wanna ask you something, I wrote a letter
    B: Mh hm
    A: T'the governor
    B: Mh hm

(Adapted from Schegloff, 1982: 82)

Understanding may also be indicated by interruption; for example in (8) (p. 170 above) S struggles to identify two car parks. B twice interrupts to signal that she has identified referents of *this multi-storey thing, behind the Oyster bar*. B goes on to check with a trial noun phrase that mutual understanding has actually been achieved.

It seems clear from these examples that conversationalists view adequate identification of a referent as a mutual responsibility; the hearer not only indicates understanding but assists in the identification. This happens also with conversations between aphasic speakers and their non-aphasic interlocutors. Although the unimpaired partner is likely to accept greater responsibility in maintaining the conversation (de Bleser and Weisman, 1986), the mechanism is similar to that identified in a sequence such as (8) and, as a result of this *collaborative* effort, the aphasic partner succeeds in achieving his or her interactional goals. In (12) for example (already cited in Chapter 6 but reprinted here for convenience) the referent of *she* in the first turn is jointly identified, and in (13) the NP expression *air traffic controller* is jointly located:

(12) APHASIC: I /and of course she was saying today/ well eventually/ I says no no no I says they won't/ I says

NON-APHASIC: who's this/ Deirdre was saying this today was she?

APHASIC: yes yes/ half past ten on a Friday

(13) APHASIC: and er Joan/ she was erm/ he was a what was it/ come on

NON-APHASIC: she was an air hostess?

APHASIC: yes/ a what

NON-APHASIC: an air hostess

APHASIC: yes but in the airforce

NON-APHASIC: oh/ was she an air traffic controller

APHASIC: that's right

The critical question is therefore not the extent to which the aphasic patient achieves 'normal' reference as defined by the so-called literary model, but whether, in collaboration with a conversational partner who may offer additional support, he or she is able to utilize a range of conversational management procedures to achieve successful reference. The amount of such additional support might be a reasonable basis for any assessment of referential ability. Note that in each of our two examples the aphasic speaker clearly indicates in her final turn the successful outcome of the joint act of referring.

To account for the evidently systematic patterns revealed in such conversational data, Clark and Wilkes-Gibbs suggest a collaborative *process* model of reference comprising three stages; initiating a reference, refashioning it and accepting it. The process usually begins with some sort of noun phrase, but initiating NPs are much more varied than the three types proposed by the literary model, and, as is implied by their descriptive label, they do no more than initiate the process.

The achievement of mutual understanding of a referent is an excellent example of the collaborative nature of conversation. In recent years, collaborative models of discourse such as this one, also based on the insights of the conversation analysts, have been further developed by cognitive psychologists and psycholinguists. Their claim to offer realistic models of human communicative behaviour has received experimental support (Clark and Schaefer, 1987; Gibbs, 1987; Gibbs, et al. 1988; Resnick, et al., 1991), and such approaches can equally well be adapted to analysing aphasic discourse. In their treatment of collaboration and co-operation as central rather than peripheral, they accommodate the common perception of clinicians that the role of the aphasic patient's conversational partner is crucial in maintaining effective everyday communication. The interactional behaviour of non-aphasic partners is examined in Chapter 9 and Chapter 12.

ANOTHER LOOK AT INDIRECT SPEECH ACTS

In a parallel way, the problem of how speakers handle the ambiguity inherent in indirect speech acts can be explored using conversation analytic methods. Recall, however, that ambiguity is of interest to conversation analysts only if it is actual rather than theoretical, a participant rather than an analyst category. Thus, more than one meaning of a given utterance must be shown to be processed by participants. Schegloff (1988a) has contrasted the analysis offered by speech act theory of utterances which have the form *Do you know* + *[embedded WH-question]* with the analysis which participants in real conversations actually arrive at. One of the example utterances discussed by Schegloff is 'Do you know who's going to that meeting?' in its context in the following fragment of conversation at a family dinner table:

(14) MOTHER: . . . I wanna talk to you about where I'm going tonight
RUSS: mm hmm
GARY: Is it about us?
MOTHER: uh huh
RUSS: *I* know where you're going
MOTHER: where
RUSS: To the uh eighth grade=
MOTHER: =yeah. Right
MOTHER: Do you know who's going to that meeting? T1
RUSS: Who   T2
MOTHER: I don't kno:w   T3
RUSS: Oh:: Prob'ly Mrs McOwen ('n detsa) en prob'ly Mrs Cadry   T4

The point at issue here is that in the four labelled turns we find evidence of two interpretations of the T1 question. In T2, Russ seems first to have interpreted the question as a *presequence* – a prelude to some later announcement of a type more clearly exemplified by an utterance such as 'do you know who I met in town today?'. The response to this is also likely to be 'Who?'. Presequences are very familiar types of utterance which we shall describe in more detail in Chapter 9. When they are in the form of questions they do not seek information, but rather project forward to a following sequence. Thus the response to 'do you know who I met in town today?' signals readiness to receive further information. This is exactly what Russ does in T2, but mother reveals in her T3 response that this is not what she intended. Russ repairs the misunderstanding in T4, reinterpreting the utterance as a request for information. As he does so he reveals that he actually knows who is going to the meeting.

There are several points of interest here to researchers who are considering speech-act theory as a serious discourse model (see p. 147f. above for a review of such work on aphasic discourse). First of all, this sequence does not seem to be particularly rare or atypical; we could cite several sequences, observed without difficulty, which are structurally identical to T1–T4. However, if (14) is indeed typical of participant responses to ambiguous utterances, serious doubt is cast on the likelihood of widespread ambiguities occurring precisely as predicted by speech-act theory. Recall the difficulty of applying a speech-act analysis to real examples of situated speech, which means that the empirical validity of speech-act theory remains an open question. When misunderstandings do occur in 'normal' conversations they seem to be rapidly and collaboratively *repaired*, as in T4. If, as Schegloff suggests, speech-act theory does indeed offer a fundamentally misconceived account of how speakers and hearers handle ambiguity, it is perhaps not surprising that the experimental work on responses to ambiguous utterances by both normal and aphasic patients has yielded inconclusive results (see p. 149 above).

Arguably, T1 is an example of an ambiguous question of the type handled by speech-act theory and demonstrably subject to two interpretations. The problem is that the literal interpretation (i.e. an enquiry about the state of Russ's knowledge) does not figure at all in this sequence, so that the two interpretations are not those suggested by speech act theory. Rather, the observable ambiguity needs to be explicated in structural and sequential terms, rather than in terms of a previously established set of felicity conditions which may be fulfilled or violated to permit one or another interpretation. Presequences by definition come before other sequences, and it is the placement of T1 in a potential presequential slot which allows Russ's first interpretation. Only after this has been tried and failed does Russ attempt a second interpretation, and it is this T4 interpretation which speech-act theory would consider to be the 'normal' one. The puzzle of how speakers and hearers resolve the ambiguity inherent in indirect questions dissolves when we see that Russ actually reanalyses mother's T1 utterance as soon as her response shows him that his first analysis is incorrect.

CONCLUDING REMARKS

These two reanalyses demonstrate how, unlike the approaches discussed in Chapter 7, a conversation analysis is validated in terms of patterns in the data, since each turn offers a participant's analysis of the prior turn. Speech-act theory can thus be shown to be inaccurate in so far as it claims to provide an account of how *participants* assign interpretations to utterances. Schegloff's discussion of the distinction between *theoretical* and *empirical* ambiguity suggests that ambiguity is an overhearer's rather than a participant's problem, as only a limited number of theoretically possible ambiguities actually seem to arise in the course of conversations (1984a: 51). Levinson (1983: 356) has generalized the type of reasoning used by Schegloff in his exposition of (14). Drawing on the work of a number of researchers, he has shown that participants' interpretation of indirect questions can be explicated much more easily with reference to their placing in conversational sequence and to the collaborative work of conversationalists, than by tortuous attempts to analyse them at the level of isolated sentence syntax and semantics (see further (17) in Chapter 9).

Although speech-act theory grants important insights into speaker meaning, the theoretical and empirical problems associated with it cast doubt on its capacity to provide a basis for sound empirical research and on its practical utility for clinicians. Prutting and Kirchner (1987) report an unsuccessful attempt to construct their Pragmatic Protocol in line with a speech act model of dialogue, diagnosing the problem as one of 'drawing a line between intentionality and the necessary presuppositions, propositional knowledge and social rules of discourse needed to carry out the intentions' (p. 106). One of the frequently repeated criticisms of speech-act theory is in fact precisely that it forces unverifiable speculation about speaker intentions. Conversely, a major advantage of the conversation analysis approach is that it removes such a necessity.

We turn in the following chapter to look at some details of the structure of conversation which a conversation analysis approach has revealed, concentrating on topics which seem to be of particular importance in analysing aphasic communication.

SUMMARY

In this chapter we described and contrasted two approaches to the analysis of interactive discourse. The first was the 'top-down' exchange analysis of the Birmingham group, and the second the 'bottom-up' procedures of the conversation analysts. The Birmingham group initially developed their linguistically oriented approach in response to the structural patterns observable in teacher/pupil discourse, and we suggested that its chief value lies in its capacity to capture the mechanisms by which the conversational initiative is retained in situations where an asymmetrical relationship holds between interlocutors. However, it seems less successful as a procedure for analysing everyday peer conversations.

Such conversations are often said to be sloppy, inarticulate, ambiguous and unstructured, replete with such features as overlapping speech, repetition, filled and unfilled pauses and self-correction. Conversation analysis, developed originally by a group of micro-sociologists, does not idealize away from such features, but rather sees them as an important part of the organization of conversation and as evidence of its collaborative and skilful mode of production. Speaker meaning is seen as unfolding with each new contribution, rather than as previously given, and we suggested that this inductive mode of analysis was capable of granting important insights into the structure of everyday conversation.

We described the application of this approach to two pragmatic phenomena previously described in terms of 'top-down' frameworks; the first was the analysis of reference in conversation, and the second the analysis of how ambiguous utterances (of the kind handled by speech-act theory) are understood and ambiguities resolved. The means by which understanding is progressively achieved by the collaborative efforts of interlocutors is highlighted by conversation analysis, and we suggested that such an analysis provides more insights and has greater real-life validity than approaches which superimpose theories on isolated utterances, and do not provide for turn by turn changes in the contextual information available to speakers. In the next chapter we show the relevance of this conversation analytic approach to the understanding of aphasic communication.

NINE

Conversation as a collaborative achievement: some conversational management procedures

We turn now to look in detail at samples of conversation, some of which involve at least one aphasic participant. Discussion of these is organized round several topics, each being viewed as a *procedure* by means of which participants jointly achieve orderliness along a particular dimension of conversational structure. Several relevant questions for aphasiologists are suggested by this approach. We can ask first whether orderliness is achieved at all by aphasic patients – that is whether their conversations can be said to have structure. If they do, we can then ask whether it is of the same kind as is revealed by conversation analytic methods in non-aphasic conversations. If it is not, we can try to find out how aphasic speakers and their partners succeed in achieving order, a key question being whether they routinely use particular strategies in a different way from non-aphasic conversationalists in pursuit of particular interactional goals. We can also ask whether (and why) any of the management procedures outlined in this chapter are likely to present particular difficulty for aphasic conversationalists and their partners.

The topics discussed are selected partly for their general salience and importance – it is hard for example to conceive of an exposition of conversation analysis which does not look at turn-taking – but chiefly for their particular relevance to the problems and strategies which can be observed in aphasic conversation. We begin with *turntaking* and move on to consider *adjacency pairs*, *preferred* and *dispreferred* second parts of pairs and various structures which do not fit into a pairs schema. We then look at the structure of conversational *openings* and *closings*, various types of presequences, and repair procedures. We conclude with a discussion of discourse markers and a brief comment on non-verbal behaviour. The approach developed in this chapter focuses on the mechanisms of conversational management, rather than on issues associated with power and role differentials. As we have already suggested in Chapter 8, the procedures developed by Sinclair and Coulthard are better suited to this latter type of analysis.

TURNTAKING

This term refers to the orderly sharing of time and sequencing of contributions evident in any conversation, a turn being roughly a conversational contribution by one speaker followed either by silence or by a contribution by another. The basic question investigated by Sacks, Schegloff and Jefferson (1974) is how interlocutors manage to co-ordinate contributions so that for the most part turn transitions are smooth, with relatively little gap or overlap. It cannot be the case that intending speakers wait for a previous speaker to finish; otherwise we would find gaps between turns of the kind which are sometimes evident in amateur dramatic productions. In real life, gaps between turns can usually be measured in microseconds, a miracle of split-second timing which tends to be taken for granted but which is in fact a considerable collaborative achievement. In conversation, as opposed to institutional settings like debates, parliament, press-conferences, courtrooms and so on this turn-taking system operates without a specified set of rules, even where the number of speakers is large. A current speaker may select a next speaker in a number of ways such as with vocatives (*What do you think, Sam?*) and with items like *pardon?* which select the prior speaker as next. But this right to select operates on a strictly turn-by-turn or *local* basis, as there is no way of selecting (for example) the next speaker but one. The basic turn-taking system operates in telephone conversations also, where there is no possibility of visual monitoring. Yet, the difficulty experienced by amateur actors suggests that despite its apparent simplicity it must be vulnerable to breakdown, and it seems likely that aphasic speakers, who often need to take extra time for cognitive processing, will find this split-second timing difficult to achieve. It is important to explore the details of aphasic turn-taking behaviour with these potential (and predictable) problems in mind, as some investigators have reported that 'conversational turn-taking behaviour remains intact in aphasia' (Schienberg and Holland, 1980: 110). We shall look shortly at the kind of turn-taking problems which aphasic conversationalists encounter and the coping strategies which they adopt.

Sacks, et al. (1974) tackle the problem of accounting for smooth turn transitions within this 'local management system' by suggesting that turns are made up of *turn constructional units*. Speakers may (but need not) change at a *transition relevance place*, located at the end of the first such unit and then at the end of each subsequent unit. The character of these units is not particularly well understood; they may be words or phrases or sentences, or intonational units. Referring to Sperber and Wilson's relevance theory, Power and Dal Martello (1985) have suggested that they are *semantic* units sufficiently large for the speaker to establish the relevance of what s/he is saying, and Owen (1989: 253) demonstrates an example of how this might work. Plainly, however, the character of turn construction units will vary in accordance with sequential constraints. For example a response to a greeting is potentially complete as soon as the greeting has been returned, but a speaker may continue his turn beyond this first TCU (marked # in (1) below). Note in this same example that there is a further possible completion point before the end of A's first turn. However, C's second turn, a response to A's tag question, consists initially of a single unit:

(1) 1. C: Hello Lynn=
    2. A: =Hi(.)# she doesn't get any quieter(.)# does she?
    3. C: (.)you're telling me
                          (0.5 sec)
    4. C: What can I do for you?

Patterns of overlap between the *simultaneous speech* of conversationalists may be cited as evidence for the existence of turn constructional units. *Accidental overlap* tends to occur at the end of such a unit which marks a possible turn completion point. In (2) for example *actually* is, syntactically speaking, an optional extra and is overlapped by M's utterance. M appears here simply to have *misprojected* P's turn, and speakers do seem to perceive a distinction between such accidental overlap and *interruption* where overlap does not begin at a transition relevance place, as in (3). These two different patterns of simultaneous speech are not simply convenient categories imposed by the analyst but have different interactional consequences and are identifiable from different patterns of participant behaviour. In (3) MK recycles that part of his turn which has been impaired by the overlap, while in (2) P does not:

(2) 1. D: What do you think of the Fulham By-election?
               (5.00 sec)
    2. P: I watched it *actually*
    3. M: *no wonder* the SDP candidate didn't
       get in/ did you see him?

(3) 1. MK: did you *see*
    2. P: *he* was saying about last year's election
    3. MK: did you see that guy who actually got in?

Since simultaneous speech accompanies speaker transition relatively infrequently, the question arises of how conversationalists manage for the most part accurately to distinguish ends of turns from non-turn final TCUs. In a recent study of turn-taking in Tyneside English, Local et al. (1986) identified a number of phonetic features ranging through pitch, tempo, loudness, vowel quality and duration phenomena which seem to cluster at turn-endings and are apparently 'read' by recipients as indications of turn completion. Local (1986) has further identified a range of prosodic phenomena. However, as Ellis and Beattie point out (1986: 181) non-verbal cues such as posture, gesture and gaze appear also to play an important role. They argue that such cues are critical in explaining why interlocutors do not self-select at possible transition relevance points, a problem to which conversation analytic (as opposed to psycholinguistic) research until recently has provided no satisfactory solution. However, Kelly and Local (1989) have identified various phonetic cues which they suggest are indeed supplemented by a range of non-verbal behaviours to mark turn completion. It seems likely that non-verbal turn-completion cues will be particularly prominent in aphasic conversation (see for example (5) below).

Particularly in adversarial arguments or in multi-party conversation, turntaking can be seen as a competitive activity, where speakers employ various techniques to both seize and retain the floor (see French and Local, 1983 for details). We can see the evidence of this competitive activity particularly clearly in (7) in Chapter 8 where repetition, false starts and filled pauses occur regularly at or near the start of turns as speakers compete for the floor, rushing to speak without taking time to pre-plan an utterance. There are also various ways of holding turns while cognitive processing is taking place (or for other reasons); pauses might be filled with items such as *you know* or *um* or by marking them prosodically or syntactically as incomplete. Political interviewees are often particularly adept at retaining the floor, while at the opposite extreme young children need to learn these skills. One analysis of simultaneous speech during a short mealtime conversation with two child participants, aged 6 and 9, and three adult relatives suggests that both children are interrupted frequently, but interrupt the adults very little. What is more, the younger child has greater difficulty than her sister in taking the floor at all (Fenwick, 1989; Gallagher and Craig, 1982).

How do speakers resolve turn *overlap*, which might occur following accidental misprojection of a turn-ending, violative interruption, or when two speakers start up together at the completion of a previous speaker's turn? One of them may drop out, but if this happens s/he may take the turn later repeating the part that was impaired by the overlap. Hence, self-repetition is predictably associated not only with turn-beginnings (see (7) in Chapter 8) but with the resolution of overlap as with MK's two turns in (3) above. Sometimes however overlap is resolved by one speaker *upgrading* to shout down a competitor, who then drops out. This is shown in the third, fourth and fifth turns below, a fragment of a conversation where four Tyneside (dialect-speaking) participants are discussing the cost of bar meals:

(4) 1. R: His starter was about two pound fifty
         (0.7)
      2. H: He would have a heart attack=
      3. F: =I would *wash the dishes*
      4. R: AND HE DIDN'T HAVE ANY WINE y'know (.) cos they divvent (i.e. don't) drink=
      5. F: =I would wash the dishes for that

Despite the split-second timing of turntaking in normal interaction, aphasic speakers seem on the whole to handle turn-taking remarkably well, although we shall qualify this remark later. They appear to exploit some turn-taking management mechanisms particularly extensively since, other things being equal, both filled and unfilled pauses fairly obviously crop up more frequently in aphasic than in non-aphasic conversations. The unfilled pauses generate a large number of transition relevance places, increasing opportunities for overlap and speaker transition. The filled pauses, however, perform an important turn-holding function, as does a further strategy noted by Ahlsen (1985) in her study of aphasic discourse in Göteborg, Sweden. She suggests that a raised hand may be widely used as a turn-holding signal to avert interruption, the hand being dropped to signify completion of the turn. One patient studied by Conway (1990) altered her body posture to mark periods of 'speakership', sitting forward in her chair for the duration of her own turns and relaxing this posture to mark turn completion. The following extract of conversation (recorded on videotape) between herself (P), her husband (H) and the student therapist (T), illustrates the frequency of pauses (particularly within her turn) which, if unfilled by an item such as *er* leaves her vulnerable to interruption. But her ability to take an extended turn provided she remains uninterrupted is also evident:

(5) 1. H: anybody can give in you know (1.00) easy to give in
       (.) you've got to find a little fight in yourself you
       know (.)

    2. P: [sits forward] there's one comes to the club (1.00) er
       [kom] come er on (1.00) one two (1.00) she come on
       twice [holds up two fingers] to the club [leans back]
       (1.00)

    3. T: uhuh

The work which we have discussed here suggests that such floor holding strategies as filled pauses, body posture and hand movement are an important means of maintaining orderly turn-taking patterns. Hand movement seems to function in a similar but probably more limited way in marking out turn completion points in non-aphasic conversation; Ellis and Beattie (1986) and Duncan (1972) have discussed both the attempt suppression signal (that is the use of continuous hand movements to suppress any attempts to take the floor) and the turn yielding signal which is the termination of hand movement to indicate that the current turn is finished.

It would be wrong, however, to imply that turntaking in aphasic conversation always proceeds so smoothly. Mr V., the fluent aphasic studied by Edwards and Garman (see p. 46

above) apparently tried to mask his lexical retrieval problems by contributing excessively long and semantically opaque turns, frequently running on until interrupted. His conversational problems (which are probably best analysed mostly as turn-taking problems) thus seem to spring from a strategy adopted to cope with a different level of impairment. Difficulties seem sometimes also to emerge when an aphasic speaker rushes to take the floor, much as a normal speaker does, before adequately planning the current utterance. However, unlike the precipitant conversationalists in (7) in Chapter 8, aphasic speakers are generally unable to accomplish the rapid repairs which so frequently characterize turn beginnings. The following extract is part of an extremely confused conversation between a student therapist and an aphasic patient with severe lexical retrieval problems. Pauses within turns are generally longer than pauses between turns, probably because T, in the grip of the no gap/no overlap turn-taking principle, rushes to start speaking without allowing sufficient time for cognitive planning:

(6)   1. T: Did you stay in this country=
     2. P: =no *no*
     3. T: *you went* abroad=
     4. P: = *no no* no we (7.1) [teriz] (2.4)
     5. T: is it [teteri] terrors
     6. P: (.) no (2.0) um (6.4) [4 syll] (3.1) ah (4.0)
     7. T: are you trying to tell me the name of a country=
     8. P: =no no=
     9. T: =no=
    10. P: =no I've (4.1)

In fact the tendency of P to 'latch' turns to one another and sometimes even to overlap the preceding utterance is arguably the behaviour which gives rise to a prolonged communicative breakdown from which the participants became disentangled only with great difficulty. It emerged later from the conversation that the intended answer to T's first question was *yes* and the resultant misunderstanding was not actually put right for another fifty turns. We shall return to this speaker in the following section.

PAIRED TURNS AND PREFERENCE ORGANIZATION

The concept of the *exchange* developed by Sinclair and Coulthard (see p. 162f. above) formalizes the tendency of speaker turns in interactive discourse to be grouped in more or less closely related pairs, examples being question-answer, offer-acceptance, assessment-agreement, greeting-greeting. The equivalent concept developed by the conversation analysts to describe these sequentially constrained pairs of turns is the *adjacency pair* (see Schegloff and Sacks, 1973) where the occurrence of a first pair part creates a slot for the appropriate second pair part. By constraining the type of second pair part which follows – for example, a greeting is routinely followed by a further greeting – a first pair part sets up an expectation which the second speaker's contribution is interpreted as fulfilling. This sequential property of discourse is described as *conditional relevance*. It effectively enables the 'slot' which follows a first part of a pair to generate powerful inferences and constraints on the interpretation of anything occupying that slot. A failure to fulfil conditionally relevant expectations by producing something which can be interpreted as a second pair part results in a 'noticeable absence', and speakers' orientation to this pairs structure is indicated by their reactions to such absences. Hence we find comments such as 'I offered him a coffee and he didn't even answer me' or 'I said hello and she looked straight past me'. Questions which do not receive an answer are regularly repeated, thus providing clear evidence of speaker expectations:

(7) 1. A: Is there something bothering you or not?

       (1.0)

   2. A: Yes or no

       (1.5)

   3. A: Eh?

   4. B: No

(Atkinson and Drew, 1979: 52)

Pairs structure permeates conversation, being particularly prominent in openings and closings where *Hellos* and *Goodbyes* are routinely twinned. It is also a component of the turn-taking system in that it enables a current speaker to select a next speaker (as A does in his first turn in (7)), and the failure of a selected speaker to take his turn results in silence which is attributable to a specific individual (Sacks, et al., 1974). We may contrast the silences in (7), both attributable to B, with the half second silence in (1) which is attributable to neither speaker, but occurs at the end of a minimal turn. Here, according to the rules of turn-taking set out by Sacks, et al. (1974) (see also Levinson, 1983: 296ff.) the current speaker has the option of continuing to speak. C initially passes up this option, and the silence provides a slot where A can but does not take the floor. Thus, both speakers have effectively passed up opportunities for contributing, and the half second 'lapse' following C's second turn effectively allows her to initiate a new topic, where she begins by explicitly selecting A as next speaker. The important point illustrated by a comparison of (1) and (7) is that silence in conversation is in no sense neutral but may be assigned in accordance with sequential constraints to one or another participant, or to neither.

Following these insights, much work has been done on what has become known as *preference* organization (Levinson, 1983; Pomeranz, 1984; Davidson, 1984; Bilmes, 1988). The concept of preference is a structural one, referring not to a psychological, affective, or socially determined disposition, but fundamentally to the observably *different* ways in which alternative second pair parts (such as granting or refusing a request, agreeing or disagreeing with an assessment) are routinely accomplished. Thus for example the preferred response to an invitation is an acceptance, to a request a granting, although people obviously do not always want invitations to be accepted and requests granted. The corresponding dispreferred second parts are rejection and refusal. Preferred second parts seem to be structurally simpler in that they latch smoothly on to first parts without intervening filled or unfilled pauses or any particular complexity. But dispreferred second parts are commonly marked in various ways with accountings, apologies, filled and unfilled pauses, with a *well* preface (see Levinson, 1983: 334 for a comprehensive list of such markers). These characteristic differences in realization are illustrated by the contrast between (8) and (9), two comparable service encounters on consecutive days which supply something close to a controlled naturalistic experiment. In a more complex sequence, (10), the barman's dispreferred response points up the distinction between *structural* and *affective* dispreference. Here, the customer actually ends up with paying less for his drink as a result of the barman's dispreferred response to his request:

(8) 1. Customer: could I have a *Journal* please?=
    2. Shopkeeper: =a *Journal*(.) yes (.) twenty please=
    3. Customer: =thanks

(9) 1. Customer: could I have a *Journal* please?
    2. Shopkeeper: (.) um sorry pet (.) they're all gone (.) Journals go very fast you know early on.
    3. Customer: (.) OK thanks

(10) 1. Customer: a pitcher of margarita and some corn-chips please
    2. Barman: (.) um (.) is it for the two of you
    3. Customer: (.) yes
    4. Barman: (.) well there's the same in these [indicating menu] a pitcher's just two big ones (.) you'll save yourself 95p (.) it's happy hour=
    5. Customer: =oh (.) great (.) two jumbo margaritas then (.) thanks (barman goes to get)

Conversation analysis often focuses attention on the communicative importance of apparently trivial phenomena such as the short periods of silence and *ums* which speakers seem to take for granted in sequences such as (9) and (10) where preferred second parts do not slot smoothly into place. We can now see how, as a consequence of their sequential placement, inferences are triggered by such semantically empty tokens; any delay after a first part is itself heard as a signal that some complexity is coming up. Hence, regardless of the addressee's actual intention, which only the subsequent discourse can illuminate, C interprets a two-second pause following a request as a negative (dispreferred) response:

(11) 1. C: So I was wondering, would you be in your office on Monday (.) by any chance?
                              (2.0)
    2. C: Probably not
                     (cited by Levinson, 1983: 320)

Coulthard directly compares the insights of conversation analysis with those provided by Grice's analysis of conversational implicatures in his comment on this example:

The strength of the conversational analysts' approach is that the structures they have isolated do not, like Grice's maxims, predict simply that inferencing will take place but also predict the *result* of that inferencing. Thus to spell out the steps in the interpretation of the example above: by the rules of the turn-taking system C has validly selected the next speaker and thus the pause is assigned to the addressee; the adjacency pair system makes a yes/no answer transitionally [sic] relevant and the preference system isolates delay as one of the markers of dispreferred seconds, in this case 'no'. Thus the system predicts, rather than simply accounts for the fact that silence will be interpreted as implicating 'no'.

(Coulthard, 1985: 74)

It is important to spell out the significance of this analysis in making explicit some of the conversational problems likely to be encountered by aphasic speakers, whose discourse is characterized by frequent filled and unfilled pauses. The following example, being part of the same confusing conversation excerpted as (6) above, illustrates inferencing processes similar to those described by Coulthard. Here, because of its sequential placement, a one second pause after the therapist's first question implicates a dispreferred response, much as in (11):

(12) 1. P: (1.0) we (.) ma ma ma (2.4) married (8.0) pre-war=
  2. T: =mhm
  3. P: (.) we got married=
  4. T: =yeh mhm did you go away for the war
  5.   (1.0)
  6. T: no (.) you didn't=
  7. P: =no no no no (1.0) er (2.5) um (13) [4 syll] (7.0) [3 syll] married=
  8. T: =mhm
  9. P: (2.5) [5 syll]=
  10. T: =mhm

It emerged after 120 subsequent turns and considerable confusion that T had misinterpreted the pause, since the date of P's marriage was not pre-war as he had indicated. Retrospective interpretation of this extended sequence shows that his last two utterances in (12) were just the beginning of a lengthy attempt to repair the prolonged misunderstanding precipitated by his selection of the wrong lexical item *pre-war*.

This example gives an idea of how a conversation analytic

perspective might be applied to aphasic discourse. First, it raises the issue of *intentionality* which Prutting and Kirchner (1987) found so problematic in their attempts to apply a speech-act model of dialogue to aphasic discourse. It is evident here that the patient's intention becomes apparent only gradually, which means that the analyst needs to examine a very long conversational sequence, in order to work out that he was attempting a repair following T's misunderstanding. This raises a second point, often made by conversation analysts, namely that the relatively short examples commonly cited in both pragmatics and language pathology literatures to support particular analyses may be misleading if they are not contextualized within much longer stretches of conversation. Thirdly, the central importance of a *collaborative* model of discourse is particularly evident here. The 'error' is not simply P's. Both T and P are implicated in the misunderstanding, P because of the original lexical retrieval error and T because of what turned out to be her incorrect interpretation of the one second pause. It is also clear that since the meaning of pauses varies with their sequential placement, we must be careful of a research design which involves counting pauses and interpreting the quantitative results without due attention to their conversational context.

Clinicians are aware in a generalized way of the need to develop a tolerance of gaps and pauses in their conversations with aphasic patients. However, this example illustrates the reason for taking this awareness further, recognizing that likely interactional effects of pauses will vary with sequential context. For example, pauses within turns do not have the same capacity for the generation of inferences about interaction as do pauses between turns. In addition the latter will vary in their potential effects, depending on which speaker the pause is assigned to. Particularly, it would have been helpful here if T had been explicitly aware of the sequential implications of a brief pause following the first part of a pair, and able to monitor her unconscious but quite predictable inference. Since an aphasic conversationalist such as P needs time to formulate his turn, a pause clearly cannot be interpreted as prefacing a dispreferred second part. Conversely, P's tendency to respond rapidly and sometimes misleadingly (see (12) above) may spring from his sensitivity to the split second timing by which the turn-taking system operates. It may be sensible to encourage him to inhibit his tendency to take his turn as soon as the other has finished speaking, since the long pauses *within* turns suggest that he needs a great deal of time for cognitive processing.

The pauses, apologies and accountings associated with dispreferred second parts are an aspect of conversational organization which can be linked with Brown and Levinson's politeness theory, which was touched on briefly in Chapter 3. Data such as (8)–(11) above would be interpreted as showing that speakers avoid dispreferred second parts if they can, and if they are unavoidable signal them in advance to minimize potential threat to face. We shall see shortly that conversationalists routinely prefer speakers to *repair* their own errors, corrections by the other being marked as dispreferred in a parallel way to dispreferred second parts of adjacency pairs. This evidence of preference for self-correction can be encompassed within the preference system described here, and accounted for in terms of politeness theory.

EMBEDDED SEQUENCES

Although conversations are pervaded by a pairs structure, they are clearly not comprehensively analysable as sequences of chained pairs (but cf. the structure of *interviews*, discussed in Chapter 8). An example like (10) illustrates how a second pair part may be delayed in various ways, so that although the first part still sets up the expectation that the second will occur, various pieces of structure can intervene. Thus the first part is followed first by a question/answer sequence (T2, T3) and then by an explanation and suggestion (T4) which, in turn, is followed by an acknowledgement and acceptance (T5) before the original request is finally (non-verbally) granted. *Insertion sequence* is the name given to a sequence such as T2–T5 which comes in place of a second pair part and is in effect an independent structure embedded between the two halves of the pair (Schegloff, 1968). Participants do however orient themselves to the second part of the pair, the assumption in (10) for example being that the T2 is conditionally relevant, in that the granting is in some way dependent on a response to T2. As Goffman (1981) has pointed out, question/answer sequences sometimes have an extremely complex *nested* structure, as in the following insertion sequence where Q/A^3 is nested in Q/A^2 which in turn is nested in Q/A^1:

(13) 1. Q^1: Where's the railway station please?
2. Q^2: Victoria or Piccadilly?
3. Q^3: Where do I get a train for Sheffield?
4. A^3: Piccadilly.
5. A^2: OK. Piccadilly then.
6. A^1: First street on the right/ you'll see it as you go in.

Such elaborate non-linear structures are in no way unusual, and are indicative of the remarkable capacity of conversationalists to keep track of several levels of embedding simultaneously. Perhaps significantly, in many hours of aphasic conversation we have not come across any sequences of a structure similar to (13), although they crop up regularly in everyday conversation. While this might simply reflect an accidental gap in our sample, we should perhaps consider the possibility that some aphasic speakers prefer a linear chaining structure in conversation, finding 'nested' or 'embedded' conversational structures difficult much as they find embedding in syntax difficult (Goodglass, et al., 1979). It is tempting to associate this also with a reduction in 'computational space', although here an explanation in terms of short-term memory may be equally plausible. Embedding may therefore be another structural characteristic of conversation which therapists need to be explicitly aware of in their own conversational contributions, since aphasic speakers may lose track of structural relationships in sequences such as (13).

Another kind of embedded structure has been referred to as a *side sequence* (Jefferson, 1972). Side-sequences are distinct from insertion sequences chiefly in that they do not occur in second part slots but at unpredictable points in the conversation where it is halted, often by the need for *clarification*; it then picks up where it left off as is illustrated in the side-sequence between the fieldworker LM and Eddie in (2) in Chapter 8. Again, participants appear to have no trouble in keeping track of the main conversation, which restarts without apparent disruption.

Embedded sequences are not the only structures which defy a pairs analysis. Some kinds of first parts such as *summonses* and *presequences* set up expectations of a further contribution by the first speaker. Summonses are minimally three-part sequences; summons – response – reason for summons:

(14) 1. Mother: Alex
2. Alex: yes
3. Mother: it's bed-time now

The orientation of participants to the third part is routinely indicated by a minimal second part contribution, creating a slot which 'belongs' to the first speaker. The same orientation is indicated by Alex's response on a different occasion, when he replied to mother's summons with silence, thus forestalling the expected and unwelcome third part. Summonses may in fact be seen as a type of *presequence* of which there are various sorts, such as the familiar *pre-invitation*, recognised as such by Alex in (15), as his response reveals:

(15) 1. Mother: Are the pair of you doing anything tomorrow night?
2. Alex: (.) we were thinking of staying in and working (.) what have you got in mind?

Pre-announcements often take forms such as *Guess what/who . . . you know NP/what/who; r'member NP/what /who . . .* Often they are characterized by a phonological reduction, which makes them readily identifiable, and like summonses they are usually followed by a minimal second part leaving a third part slot for the first speaker. Here is an example of an aphasic speaker's pre-announcement in the course of an elaborate explanation to a post-graduate student of stock market fluctuations. The student (who is Australian) fills the second slot with the particle *right*, uttered with a fall-rise tone. *Right* does not seem generally to be used in this sequential context in British English, although the same token produced with a falling tone in T4 is familiar to British speakers in its function as an acknowledgement:

(16) Student: Did you lose a lot in the crash?
Aphasic: I would have done if I've had had . . . / but what I did do was hung on/ . . . so I just got my money back and perhaps peanuts/ but today today they're thirty-two/ if I'd have hung on another six months . . ./ when you talk about thirty-two of course you gotta multiply it by four if you're talking about figures/ y'know the pound   T1
Student: ˇright   T2

> Aphasic: say you've got to think about like say if
> you're moving twenty-five pence to twenty-
> six pence you've lost one if you like but
> you're actually four per cent   T3
> Student: 'right   T4

The student's T2 reveals that she has no difficulty here in identifying the final part of T1 as a presequence, as her minimal utterance orients to the aphasic speaker's T3. However, as we saw from Schegloff's analysis of (14) in Chapter 8, participants sometimes find recognition of pre-sequences problematic where there is no phonological reduction of the kind used by the aphasic speaker, and in our experience misidentification of utterance types which can function ambiguously as pre-sequences or requests for information is quite common. A routine trawl of two three-party conversations over a family lunch yielded two such misidentifications on one occasion and three on the other.

We should note finally that a further type of presequence is a *prerequest*. In (17) B has apparently recognized A's utterance as such, and simultaneously responds to the prerequest and the anticipated main request:

(17) A: Do you have any fresh yeast?
     B: Yes pet how much would you like?

This kind of conflation of presequence and target sequence is the basis of Levinson's reanalysis of indirect speech acts in conversation analytic terms (1983: 356).

An important interactional function of presequences appears to be to clear the ground so as to establish the relevance of a later sequence like a story, joke, or explanation (as in (16)) or to forestall unwanted responses like refusals of invitations or rebuffals of attempts to tell jokes. For that reason presequences are another aspect of conversational structure which may be associated with politeness phenomena and considered along with preference organization as a strategy for forestalling potential threats to face. Pre-sequences seem to be particularly prevalent in children's speech (*Mummy, guess what*, etc.), probably because of their preemptive function in claiming the right to speak.

OPENINGS AND CLOSINGS

Our account of turn-taking, adjacency pairs and embedded sequences has dealt with salient overall aspects of conversational organization, and now we turn to more localized structures. Extreme predictability of form is a very obvious property of conversational openings and closings; they are highly ritualized 'routines'. According to Laver's (1981) analysis, they exemplify the link between conversational organization and politeness phenomena particularly clearly, in that the beginning and end points of conversation constitute particular threats to face (Brown and Levinson, 1987). This is because in conversational openings social roles and interpersonal orientations are negotiated, while closings challenge participants' abilities to ease out of the interaction without appearing to snub the other or prevent him from having his say. Openings take a familiar enough form, typically an exchange of greetings followed by one or two *how are yous* and other highly conventionalized tokens of 'phatic communion' before any recognizable topic is introduced. Telephone call openings, which have been studied extensively (the classic examples being Schegloff, 1968, 1979), are even more complex in that the telephone bell may be seen as a summons, immediately responded to as in Sandy's first turn in (18). But overlaid on the greetings sequence here is the need for the caller to identify herself explicitly and the respondent (who in this case does not immediately identify her by her voice) to indicate recognition. All the familiar elements of the opening sequence are present in (18), the greetings sequence being followed by conventionalized exchanges and the entire opening sequence bounded by a brief pause before Laura tentatively indicates the purpose of her call with an utterance which Sandy evidently interprets as a prerequest:

(18)   1. Telephone rings
      2. Sandy: Douglas 12345 (.) hello
      3. Laura: hello Sandy(1.00) it's Laura
      4. Sandy: oh:: hi Laura(.) how are you?
      5. Laura: busy with the lambing but otherwise fine (.) and you?
      6. Sandy: very well thanks
      7. Laura: what time did you get back?
      8. Sandy: oh:: 'bout eightish

9. Laura: that's not too bad (0.5) erm is your mother busy?
10. Sandy: no (.) she's watching TV (.) do you want her?
11. Laura: yes please.

Closings too are worked on carefully and can be very extended, like the 'modest' example of a closing cited by Schegloff and Sacks (1973) which stretches to 12 turns. Typically, we find an identifiable *pre-closing* sequence which minimally and frequently takes the form of an exchange of conventional tokens such as *okay*, or *right*; phatic communion tokens regularly crop up in the form of expressions of solicitude or good wishes for the other such as *look after yourself; take care*; accountings such as *I'd better get ready to go out*, or platitudes like *I'm sure things'll turn out for the best*. The function of such pre-closing sequences seems to be to clear the ground for and give participants an opportunity to delay the imminent closing, the final exchange of *goodbye* tokens. The co-ordination of a pre-closing and closing sequence to a doorstep conversation is shown here:

(19) 1. B: but hh (.) still (.) I've got a bad tooth (.) right *see you love* I'd better get me ready
2. A: *see you*(.) see you again
3. B: have a nice holiday if I don't see you
4. A: okay (.) bye
5. B: tara

That participants recognize and orient to such pre-closing sequences is evidenced by their marking as 'misplaced' any introduction of a new topic after the launch of the pre-closing sequence. In (20) we find *oh gosh* apparently functioning as a *misplacement marker* to indicate that 'the talk that is going to occupy the turn . . . is something which has a proper place in conversation, but is about to be done outside its proper place' (Schegloff, 1987: 72; see also Levinson, 1983: 322; Schegloff and Sacks, 1973). The misplacement is further marked by upgrading:

(20) 1. C: fine
2. A: right then (.) see you on Friday
3. C: okay=
4. A: =okay then (.) okay then OH GOSH (.) COULD YOU BRING THAT BOOK TOO?

5. C: yes sure
6. A: okay then see you later *bye*
7. C: *right* bye
8. A: bye

We have spent some time elaborating the complexity of these opening and closing routines, since aphasic speakers are often assumed to be relatively skilled in routine and stereotyped aspects of linguistic behaviour. However, the undifferentiated notion of a stereotype covers a very wide range of phenomena, and the question of whether the ability to handle such elaborate conversational routines as these is impaired seems to be empirically verifiable, but as yet unresolved.

THE NOTION OF 'TOPIC' IN CONVERSATION

In the years since Schegloff's remark that 'nothing has yet appeared in print to describe "topic" as a sequential unit of analysis' (1979a: 270) relatively little progress has been made in showing how people move in and out of topics in a conversation. Like Schegloff we do not use the term here in any precise way, but rather loosely to refer to "what is talked about' through some series of turns at talk'. With a view to plugging this rather surprising gap in knowledge, some investigators have approached the issue of topic tangentially. The main problem seems to be that topical coherence and relevance, like other aspects of conversation, are better seen as created by participants than as previously given. Anything referred to can potentially be related to anything else.

In an unpublished lecture (discussed by Levinson, 1983: 313; Atkinson and Heritage, 1984: 165) Sacks insists that conversationalists work hard to achieve a *stepwise* topic relatedness, which is apparently preferred to *boundaried* topic movement where one topic is closed down and another initiated. Sharp topic jumps are avoided where possible and signalled where they do occur by various misplacement and discontinuity markers such as *by the way*, *hey* (Schegloff 1979a). Button (1987) has identified pre-closings of the type shown in (19) as a point where topic bounding takes place and new topics may be initiated in response to invitations such as *How are things?* or *What's new today?*. Several different topic initiation sequences and initiation procedures are discussed by Button and Casey (1984) and Jefferson (1984a) has examined stepwise transitions out of an emotionally charged topic in 'trouble-telling' sessions. Her data suggest that this is frequently achieved by addressing the concerns of the other in a way which is related to the topic of the trouble. What we do know is that explicit initiations such as *Let's talk about x now* do not appear as topic initiators in conversation, however characteristic they might be of classrooms and therapy sessions (Wilson, 1989).

A number of non-lexical particles and idiomatic expressions can be identified as marking topic boundaries in various ways. We have already mentioned the misplacement markers *by the way, oh gosh*, which signal a sharp topic shift, and pre-announcements such as *guess what/ you know what* seem in some sequential positions to function similarly; *anyway* often signals a return to a previous topic. Particles such as these (we shall return shortly to examine the function of some others) are difficult to describe in terms of sentence grammars, but are readily comprehensible in terms of their interactional function. Following up a footnote by Sacks, et al. (1974: 714), Fasold (1990: 71) has suggested that the sequential organization of topic is in effect a by-product of the turn-taking system which favours the production of utterances with minimum gap and overlap. If a gap does occur which is not attributable to any participant, speakers are free to assume that no-one has anything more to say about what is currently being talked about and introduce a new topic. The use of a gap as a topic boundary is illustrated by C. in (1) and by Laura in (18).

We have included a brief review of approaches to topic (see also Brown and Yule, 1983: 68ff. for an extensive general discussion), because topical coherence is a notion which often appears in studies of aphasic discourse ability or in assessment instruments (Penn, 1985; Terrell and Ripich, 1989). We need to bear in mind in interpreting such work the rather obscure nature of topic and the difficulty of handling it in normal conversation. Sometimes, indeed, topic is assumed to be a central concept in determining coherence – a doubly misleading assumption, in view of the difficulties in characterizing coherence also. Much of the material covered in these chapters has shown that co-herence is a problematic and abstract property of discourse which scholars have approached from a number of different perspectives. However, no-one has succeeded in analysing it in terms of topic.

REPAIR

There is a massive literature on repair in conversation to which we can refer only selectively, picking out issues of particular relevance to aphasic discourse. This literature also suggests a number of questions which might usefully be asked about the communicative abilities and strategies of aphasic conversationalists. Perkins (in progress) is currently investigating them in greater detail than is possible here (see also Milroy and Perkins, 1992). The term *repair* as used by conversation analysts covers many different ways of managing various sources of trouble in conversation, ranging from partial repetitions in the same turn to the third or fourth turn repair which is achieved over a larger sequence and is a response to a misunderstanding displayed in an interlocutor's turn. The repair process accounts for many backtrackings, false starts, repetitions and disfluency phenomena (see particularly (7) and (8) in Chapter 8). An excellent general discussion is supplied by Levinson (1983: 339–42).

'Repair' rather than 'correction' is the favoured descriptive term for a number of reasons, chiefly because the normative overtones of the latter are misleading. Problems in speaking, hearing and understanding are dealt with in an organized way in conversation, 'not limited or occasioned by independently establishable "error"' (Schegloff, 1979a: 261). Indeed speakers may revise their utterances where there is no noticeable error, and conversely ignore a clear error or ambiguity on the assumption that matters will become sufficiently clear as the discourse proceeds. Thus, the issue is not whether a speaker makes an 'error' or contributes 'inappropriately', but how the mechanism for sorting out a perceived trouble spot works. In the case of aphasic speakers the main question is whether the mechanism works in such a way as to avoid frequent prolonged or irretrievable communicative breakdown. If the communicative outcome *is* generally successful, we can ask whether the repair mechanism is the same as or different from the one used in non-aphasic conversation. The focus in a conversation analytic approach to aphasic and non-aphasic conversation alike is thus on *how participants together manage repair*, rather than on the independent 'correctness' or 'appropriateness' of a given speaker's contribution. We shall have more to say shortly about repair mechanisms in aphasic conversation, this being a particularly important topic often dealt with in the aphasic literature under the rubric of 'self-correction' (Busch and Brookshire, 1985; Davis, 1983; Marshall and Tompkins, 1982). However, we shall begin by looking at normal conversation, illustrating first with a brief example (taken from Schegloff, 1987) the reasons for rejecting the notion of an independently existing 'error' in any discussion of repair:

(21) (B. has just telephoned a report into a fire department, and the trouble spot in the conversation is the referent of the expression *that house number* in A's first turn).
A: now what was that house number you said *you were*
B: *no phone* (.) *no*
A: sir?
B: no phone at all
A: no I mean the uh house number *y-*
B: *thirty eight oh one?*
A: thirty eight oh one

We have here an evident mishearing and misunderstanding problem. Although the attention of both participants is focused on the house number mentioned by A, and indeed B reveals at the end of the sequence that he possesses the required information, his initial mishearing of *house number* as *phone number* is followed by a repair sequence. Thus, the original cause of the trouble is not an error in any commonly understood sense of the term, but rather a mishearing. What we want to focus on is the manner in which B's mishearing is sorted out rather than on the relatively uninteresting fact of the mishearing. Such mishearings and misunderstandings take place regularly, although problems arising from them are generally sorted out extremely rapidly. However, examples like (6) above suggest that they are likely to be more problematic in aphasic discourse.

The physical manifestations of repair, particularly evident at turn beginnings, reflect the cognitive processing and self-monitoring activities of speakers as they engage in planning their utterances under the constant threat of intervention by others. In their seminal exposition of repair, Schegloff, et al. (1977) make two important distinctions; first *self-initiated* versus *other-initiated* repair which refers to repair by a speaker respectively with or without prompting; second *self-repair*, carried out by the speaker is contrasted with *other-repair* carried out by another participant. Schegloff, et al. argue that repair is always carried out within a very limited domain – specifically within three turns of the *repairable* or item which caused the original problem (but see (14) in Chapter 8 for an example of the so-called fourth-turn repair more recently identified). We have already seen an example of an aphasic-with-normal conversation where a repair spanned a very much longer sequence, and this difference in repair sequence duration in aphasic verus non-aphasic discourse seems to be rather general. Schegloff, et al. emphasized an overwhelming preference for self-repair, particularly self-initiated self-repair, which generally takes place within the same turn as the repairable (or original trouble spot).

In a pilot study of the repair strategies adopted by two aphasic speakers and their families, Conway (1990) confirms this overwhelming preference for self-initiated self-repair by both aphasic and non-aphasic speakers. However, as Table 9.1 shows, the difference lies in the ranking of speaker preference for other types of repair. The non-aphasic speakers (family R and family

Table 9.1: Percentages of different types of repairables in conversations of two aphasic women (Mrs R and Mrs S) with their families

Type of repair	Mrs R	Mrs S	Family R	Family S
SISR	46.9	59.1	77.8	79.0
OISR	0.0	1.1	16.7	16.6
SIOR	20.7	11.8	0.0	4.2
OIOR	1.4	5.4	5.6	0.0
Failure to attempt	9.0	2.2	0.0	4.2
Failure of attempt	0.7	5.4	0.0	0.0
Specific aphasic repair	21.4	15.1		

Key
SISR = self-initiated self-repair
OISR = other-initated self-repair
SIOR = self-initiated other-repair
OIOR = other-initiated other-repair

S) follow the now extensively-confirmed pattern predicted by Schegloff, et al. in ranking *other-initiated self-repair* as the next preferred mechanism. Both aphasic speakers however (Mrs R and Mrs S) differed in following their first preference with a preference for *self-initiated other-repair* while other-initiated other-repairs were rare for both groups.

What this seems to amount to is that aphasic speakers like their partners to help them out of a conversational difficulty which they themselves have first identified (as exemplified in (29) below) while normal speakers expect their partners rapidly to draw their attention to a difficulty which they have overlooked, in order that they themselves might carry out the repair (see (22)). Barnsley (1987) points out that the detailed model of repair proposed by Schegloff, et al. is not particularly easily applicable to aphasic conversation, and offers a more suitable account of the characteristic structure of aphasic repairs. The difficulty arises largely because aphasic repairs span very much longer sequences than are accommodated by the standard model, but also because they are often accomplished strenuously and with great determination with recourse to a mixture of strategies. In Chapter 12 we shall suggest some ways in which this analysis might help in planning therapy for aphasic speakers and their relatives.

The well-documented preference for self-repair (extending also to aphasic speakers, as we have seen) partially reflects the way in which conversationalists habitually design utterances for particular recipients. They quickly change track if they seem not to be understood or if they spot a potential trouble source. It also means that the conversational repair mechanism can be encompassed within the *preference organization* system (cf. p. 194f. above). What this amounts to is that even though recipients spot errors, they prefer where possible to let speakers carry out their own repair in a manner which can be attributed to a desire to avoid threats to face. In non-aphasic conversation, dispreferred repair strategies resemble dispreferred second parts in that other-initiations and other-repairs are overtly *marked*; in (22) for example (cited by Schegloff, et al., 1977: 370) the other-initiated self-repair is preceded by a pause:

(22) A: Hey the first time they stopped me from selling
cigarettes was this morning
(1.0)

B: From *selling* cigarettes?
A: From buying cigarettes

Two further points, which are less prominent in the repair literature, are of particular relevance to aphasic communication. First, although repair is generally considered to be *retrospective* in that it takes place after the repairable, Schegloff reports that careful examination of his transcripts reveals that trouble is sometimes indicated in advance; for example what he describes as a 'sound-stretch' – effectively a lengthened syllable – often crops up as a harbinger of trouble ahead (Schegloff, 1984a: 268). Schlenk, et al. (1987) have coined the term *prepair*, to emphasize that aphasic repairs are usually *prospective*. Often the problem is lexical as the aphasic hunts for a word rather than backtracking to correct a preceding piece of talk, but Schegloff's comments suggest that the aphasic and non-aphasic repairs are structurally more similar than Schlenk, et al. imply.

Secondly, since repair may be carried out to the syntax, lexis or phonology of an utterance, a corresponding capacity is required to access particular items and structures. We have already seen some examples of phonological and lexical repairs in (7) in Chapter 8 (see particularly turns 6 and 11). The following examples, adapted and simplified from those quoted by Schegloff (1979a: 264) give some indication of the way in which speakers utilize a great deal of syntactic ability in accomplishing repairs, as they rapidly change the syntactic shape of utterances. The repair in (23) changes a main clause to a subordinate clause; in (24) a *yes/no* interrogative to a declarative; in (25) a *wh*-interrogative to a *yes/no* interrogative (relevant sequences are italicized):

(23) yeah *he – as* he was handing me the book and he told me 20 dollars I almost dropped it.
(24) A: We saw *Midnight Cowboy* yesterday.
     B: did you *s – you saw that?* it's really good.
(25) A: tell me uh *what – do you need a hot sauce.*
     B: hhh a Taco sauce.

These examples show that routine self-repair in conversation requires not only constant self-monitoring but frequently changes the lexical content and syntactic and phonological shape of utterances. We can confidently predict that this will cause difficulties for aphasic speakers with syntactic or lexical retrieval problems – see for example (12) above, and recall the communicative consequences described in Chapter 6 of lexical retrieval problems or impairment at the level of grammatical structure. Thus, since one important communicative consequence of these lexical or syntactic problems is difficulty in handling routine conversational repair, the question arises of how aphasic conversationalists actually achieve repair.

REPAIR IN APHASIC CONVERSATIONS

We shall concentrate in this section on some conversations involving aphasic speakers, in both clinical and non-clinical contexts. Both Lubinski, et al. (1980) and Barnsley (1987) point out the powerful effect of the clinical situation on successful repair. The reason for this seems fundamentally to be that in the domestic setting family members collaborate in accomplishing the repair as efficiently as possible, while in the clinical situation the therapist is often more concerned to encourage patients to carry out their own repairs. Extract (26), an excerpt from a single much longer sequence, is taken from a clinical session and exemplifies what Lubinski, et al. have called the 'hunt and guess' strategy with the patient hunting for a word and the therapist making a guess as to what he might intend, offering her own suggestions to cue him in. Sequences of this type seem to be common in clinical contexts and can be extremely lengthy. Here the (dialect-speaking) Tyneside patient J is trying to access a place name, while the therapist T is offering information to help him make a better guess:

(26) 1. J: it's er (3 sylls) gannin to (3 sylls)
      2. T: where
      3. J: (4 sylls)
      4. T: where are you?
      5. J: (4 sylls)
      6. T: are you in Newcastle?
      7. J: no not that way
      8. T: that way?
      9. J: yes
     10. T: which is that way?

11. J: it's (2 sylls) (.) (3 sylls)
12. T: no (.) are you in the North East?
13. J: aye
14. T: yeah (.) not in Newcastle?
15. J: no
16. T: Ashington?
17. J: (2 sylls
18. T: Bedlington?
19. J: oh aye
20. T: that's where we are now. Where are you talking about?
21. J: this is (2 sylls) oooh (.) how can I (3 sylls)? you know the M1?
22. T: yes
23. J: er you (3 sylls) right up
    (J draws on a piece of paper)
24. T: what's that you're talking about on the M1?
25. J: aye. massive. biggest town biggest
26. T: big town?
27. J: biggest
28. T: big roundabout?
29. J: oh yes
30. T: spaghetti junction?
31. J: yes (.) right up
32. T: are you talking about roadworks?
33. J: yes
34. T: or a place?
35. J: what an idiot!
36. T: is it a building?
37. J: aye up here same (3 sylls) 'ere ther's a (2 sylls)
38. T: what are all these? are these trees or something?
39. J: aye you got the (3 sylls)
40. T: archery?
41. J: yes
42. T: Sherwood Forest?
43. J: yes
44. T: Nottingham?
    J: (3 sylls)
                                        (2.0)
45. J: bloody hell!

Non-aphasic conversationalists do not seem to tolerate repair sequences as long as this, and unsuccessful word-finding attempts are quickly abandoned (as indeed they sometimes are in the clinic). Not all clinical repair sequences are like (26) however, and trouble spots are sometimes successfully sorted out relatively quickly. Typically, the therapist makes a series of guesses as the patient offers more information or sometimes merely confirms or disconfirms the guesses. The following piece of clinical discourse illustrates a successful and clearly co-operatively accomplished repair, concluding with a confirmation that it has been success-fully accomplished:

(27) 1. T: and what does your husband do? what work?
     2. H: in er
(3.0)
     3. H: what else can I say to you? Stowing it on the er (.) he was always fine
     4. T: uh huh. was it a factory?
     5. H: no (.) the next (.) what's next? (2 sylls) you know like
(1.0)
     6. H: what are they doing in the er (2 sylls)? the people who like in South Bank was years and years down there
     7. T: you mean steel works?
     8. H: that's it! that's where he worked
(Barnsley, 1987; 48)

Some sequences are shorter even than (27). Barnsley cites (28) to show that a self-repair may be accepted even when it gives obviously erroneous information (see p. 206f. above on the distinction between 'repair' and 'correction'):

(28) 1. P: She's the oldest one (.) no he's the first one (.) she's (.) no he's
(1.0)
     the oldest one is the youngest one/ right?
     2. T: Uhuh

This is not much different from normal conversation, where all kinds of ambiguities and contradictions are regularly allowed to pass, unless they have the effect of disrupting the conversation (Milroy, 1984).

Let us see now how aphasic conversationalists and their partners accomplish repair in everyday domestic settings. The following sequence illustrates both the eagerness of the non-aphasic partner to assist in achieving a successful outcome, and the aphasic speaker's resort to modality shift, using gesture and writing in the air in her strenuous attempts to overcome her communicative difficulties. P is the patient, H her husband, D her daughter, S her son and T the student therapist:

(29) 1. T: and write it down
   2. P: yes yes and er er er er er about half past (.) twelve (.) you get er your (demonstrates exercises) er er er oh dear

(1.0)

   3. H: exercises
   4. D: dad
   5. P: exe (waves hand) (ALL LAUGH) ex (ALL LAUGH)
   6. H: I know what she's trying to say you see (LAUGHTER)
   7. P: exercises (demonstrates exercises) that's like this (.) you know (waves hand) and er about five (.) after that it be dinner time (2.0) then we get our dinner (1.0) and then come back) and then (3 syll) they that they play um er (7.0; writes 'S' in the air; continues to make a waving gesture; 8.0) er (4.0) er er to do with er ah er scribble ah scrabble scrabble
   8. S: *scrabble*
   9. T: *uhuh*
   10. P: yes

(Conway, 1990: Appendix)

This resourcefulness and determination to communicate, using all means available and relying on the support of interlocutors is very characteristic of aphasic speakers. A notable feature of (29) is the frequency and length of within-turn pauses while P carries out the repair, the utimate success of which is collaboratively confirmed in turns 8–10.

The following extract is interesting in revealing the evident frustration of one speaker L whose husband H attempts to cue her in to a place name in a manner more characteristic of clinical discourse. This contrasts with the co-operation provided by the family in the previous extract:

(30) 1. T: so where do the other two live then?
    2. L: one lives up at (.) at er
                               (2.0)
    3. H: Ed- Ed- Ed-
    4. L: come on tell us pet! TELL US?
    5. H: Ed- Ed-
    6. L: NO PET TELL HER
    7. H: Edward Street
    8. T: oh (.) yes

(Barnsley, 1987: 60)

So far we have confined our attention to conversations between aphasic and non-aphasic speakers, emphasizing the role of the non-aphasic partner. However, conversations between pairs of aphasic conversationalists are particularly interesting for their capacity to reveal the extent to which speakers with limited communicative resources succeed in repairing the many trouble spots which result from their impairment. Extracts (31) and (32), taken from Fleming (1989) are transcribed from two ten-minute conversations, videotaped at a Speech after Stroke Club, between two pairs of seriously impaired conversationalists. The first pair are women, the second pair are men:

(31) 1. B: er er
    2. M: [krou] cherries
    3. B: [kou] yes uh (.) no
    4. M: [kou]
    5. B: no
    6. M: crocheries?
    7. B: (.) er(3.0) er oh dear [kos] er (2.0) oh dear
    8. M: I ca:nt
    9. B: [les] (.) [boi boidi]
    10. M: er broi:dery
    11. B: broidery (.) yes (.) oh dear

(32) 1. G: and the the one the bat in the er [pand] pant er
         pant
    2. R: pant?
    3. G: the er erm

   4. R: (.) ball is eh (2.0) oh the tennis ball
   5. G: yeh (3.0) the er (picks up paper and draws
        diagram of table tennis table, bats and balls)
   6. R: (.) yeh (6.0) yeh (.) cash with order (2.0)
   7. G: what's the er?
                            (3.0)
   8. R: oh
                            (2.0)
   9. G: the small (cups two hands together)
  10. R: (.) yes (BOTH LAUGH)
                            (4.0)
  11. G: the small [ba? bak]
  12. R: bat (1.0) bat
  13. G: uh bat
  14. R: bat
  15. G: yeah er small and uns
  16. R: small ball (G points to drawing)
  17. G: er the inch ball (.) yeah yeah
  18. R: yes yes
                            (3.0)
  19. G: yes
                            (5.0)
  20. R: yes
        (G puts pen and paper down and laughs)

Data such as these are very suggestive. Conversation analysis
offers a useful way of describing in detail how speakers achieve a
surprising degree of communicative efficiency, given the severity
of their impairment and the consequent limitations on their
ability to offer mutual support of the kind provided in (27). We
shall comment here on a few points of particular interest,
concentrating chiefly on (32). Both pairs of speakers run into
rather severe word-finding difficulties; in (31) B is searching for
the word 'embroidery', and after rejecting M's approximation to a
semantically related lexical item (crochet), she finally accomplishes
the repair with M's help. The obligation M seems to feel to offer
this support is particularly clear; she makes several attempts to
supply a candidate repair, before declaring her inability to help
(T8). However, her next contribution succeeds in helping B. to
locate the target item, to B's evident satisfaction.

In (32) G is apparently trying first to find the word 'bat' in which he is ultimately successful (and which he had in fact already uttered without accepting), and then the word 'ball'. R helps him first by initiating a repair and then by offering a candidate lexical item. G appears to accept 'ball' as relevant, but persists in his hunt for 'bat'. The collaborative nature of the repair activity is again particularly evident throughout the sequence. Interestingly, although R effectively communicates by means of a rather elaborate diagram early in the sequence, he continues to hunt for the target lexical items until he achieves a successful outcome. This bears on the question posed by Green (1984) of whether clinicians should aim to help patients achieve *normal* or simply *effective* communication. G shows clearly that he is not satisfied with effective communication, persisting in his search until he successfully retrieves each of the target items in turn.

One notable pattern emerges in (32) at the points where successful repair is ultimately (collaboratively) achieved. In T12–T15 and T17–T20, both speakers appear to confirm that this has been done to their mutual satisfaction (cf. also (27)). Exchanges of this type are reminiscent of pre-closing sequences with their characteristic exchange of 'okays' (cf. (20) above), but do not seem to be characteristic of normal repair. However, in one of a series of papers which attempt to develop a formal collaborative model of discourse, Clark and Schaefer (1989) argue that the establishment of mutual agreement and understanding is an important general organizing principle in conversation, a *contribution* consisting not merely of an utterance but of the joint expression of mutual understanding that the utterance has been understood 'well enough for current purposes'. This understanding is frequently expressed by means of repetition, paraphrase or minimal tokens of agreement as in the two examples from (32), and the occurrence of such a pattern at the conclusion of a repair seems to reflect the intersubjectively perceived need of impaired conversationalists to indicate explicitly the successful outcome of the repair activity. It seems reasonable to assume that speakers' notion of what constitutes an understanding 'good enough for current purposes' is likely to vary with a number of factors, including the difficulty which participants experience in communicating. Certainly (32) displays a repair strategy very different from the rapid and inconspicuous activity characteristic of normal repair.

The conversational extracts cited in this section illustrate various repair mechanisms utilized by aphasics both inside and outside of clinical contexts. Sometimes these are similar to non-aphasic repair strategies, sometimes they are clearly different. Collaborative activity is extremely important in achieving repair, even when both of the partners experience severe communicative difficulties. Aphasic speakers show remarkable tenacity in achieving successful repair, even where effective communication has already been achieved. Something approximating to normal communication appears to be the goal.

DISCOURSE MARKERS

Many of the conversational sequences considered in this chapter have contained minimal speech items whose chief function is to organize and structure interaction. Some such items like *hey*, *right*, *by the way*, *anyway* have been mentioned with reference to their topic bounding function, and Heritage (1989: 29) has used the label 'non-lexical speech objects' for an unspecified subset of tokens (*mm hm*, *yes*, *oh*, *really*) whose function seems to be describable only in interactional terms. Schiffrin (1987), from whose work the term 'discourse markers' is taken, has analysed the distribution and function of eleven items, *oh*, *well*, *and*, *but*, *or*, *so*, *because*, *now*, *then*, *y'know*, *I mean*. Her analysis reveals some interesting and not entirely obvious restrictions on their use; for example *now* is associated with disputes and contentious topics, *oh* with repairs and explanations. One of the strengths of her multi-level analysis is that it incorporates, but proceeds beyond, the strictly bottom-up methods of conversation analysis. Schiffrin argues that markers organize discourse at several levels. Some like *oh* and *well* are semantically empty and have a purely interactional function, while at the other extreme *y'know* and *I mean* have a semantic specification which influences their interactional function.

As we can see from the sequences transcribed in this chapter, discourse markers are quite extraordinarily prevalent in conversation (particularly, we might add, in aphasic conversation) but they crop up much less frequently in institutional talk where a premium is placed on 'fluency' and 'smoothness'. For example, during a radio chat show in which one of the authors participated, panel members were explicitly requested to suppress tokens such as *mm hm* with which they automatically marked continuing recipiency of the current speaker's contribution. One specific reason for the general dislike of telephone answering machines is probably the absence of such recipiency tokens which mark orientation to another speaker's extended unit of talk (cf. (11) Chapter 8).

Items such as *mm hm, yeah, oh, uhuh*, which in Schiffrin's terms are at the semantically 'empty' end of the scale, have often been labelled in an undifferentiated way as *response tokens*, and along with such phenomena as laughter and applause tend to be popularly regarded 'as responses indicative of some emotion, or of amusement or approval', with the implication that their production is in some way spontaneous or instinctive. However Atkinson and Heritage point out that their role is much more complex and differentiated than this assumption suggests (1984: 297). In the first place there is nothing unconstrained or disorganized about their production; they cannot be inserted just anywhere in the interaction and have different sequential implications depending on their placement. Moreover, objects such as *yeah, oh, mm hm* are not freely interchangeable. Clark and Schaefer's (1989) emphasis on the requirement that a recipient expresses understanding of an utterance before a conversation can proceed assigns to them a central role in discourse, since they are most commonly tokens of recipiency. Such an analysis also suggests one good reason for their pervasiveness in aphasic discourse, where constant confirmation of understanding would seem to be a highly efficient way of nipping in the bud incipient misunderstandings. We shall bear in mind these comments scholars have made in considering the use and distribution of discourse markers in aphasic conversation.

In extracts (10) and (18) above (see also (32)) we find examples of a distribution of *oh* noted by Schiffrin (1987), who associated it with repairs and explanations. Heritage (Atkinson and Heritage, 1984) similarly associates *oh* with successful receipt of a repair, but suggests a more general function as a *change of state token*, whereby the speaker marks acceptance of prior talk as informative and indicative of a change of state in knowledge, orientation or awareness. It can, however, occur in initiating as well as responding utterances, where it may indicate some disruption of the talk (see (20)). Its function is different from, for example, that of the so called continuers *mm hm, yeah* and *uhuh* in that it does not invite or request further information, but in Heritage's terms marks a 'strong' recipiency; compare *mm hm* in extract (11) in Chapter 8 and *oh* in (10) and (17) above.

Since the significance of these items varies according to placement in interaction, we cannot assume that they mean the same because they look and sound the same. Jefferson's (1984) analysis of *yeah* and *mm hm* as acknowledgement tokens reveals their distinctively different functions, dependent on sequential placement. These differences in function may also be marked prosodically (see Johns-Lewis, 1986). *Yeah* can function both as a topic shift marker and as a preparation to shift into 'speakership' from 'recipiency'. Jefferson comments that speakers sometimes exploit the functions of *mm hm* as a way of eliciting further talk and avoiding speakership – a function which she calls *passive recipiency*. Schegloff (1982) has similarly shown that the precise placement of items such as *uhuh, yes, mm hm* allows them to be heard variously as for example *acknowledgements*, which claim understanding of the talk, so passing an opportunity to initiate a repair, or *continuers*, which display an awareness that the unit of talk is incomplete. All this suggests that a description of these items simply as 'back channels' or 'signals of continued attention' substantially underestimates their interactional function. They are an excellent illustration of the role of sequential placement in determining meaning, and of the interactional significance of minimal, apparently meaningless, items. As Jefferson (1984: 197) points out, they also demonstrate that no conversational phenomenon, however apparently trivial, should be discarded in advance as 'garbage'. Certainly it does not seem reasonable to adopt an approach to aphasic conversation which idealizes away from such discourse markers and rejects them as 'performance' phenomena.

Similar comments apply to the role of *laughter* in interaction, which at first sight may seem an unpromising candidate for analysis. But its general role seems to be to display affiliation or alignment between participants (see excerpt (2) in Chapter 8 and also (33) below for an example from an aphasic conversation), or by its absence to indicate lack of such alignment (Jefferson, 1984a; 1987).

In view of their diversity of interactional function, limited linguistic substance and lack of semantic content it is not surprising if aphasic speakers make extensive use of these discourse markers. Fleming (1989) has analysed their distribution in a ten-minute conversation between a third aphasic pair, Jane and Avril, whom she also recorded on videotape at a Speech after Stroke club. Both women were judged by their clinician to be equally fluent and were less impaired than the other dyads studied (see (31) and (32)).

Fleming coded 45 per cent of all the turns in the Jane and Avril conversation as minimal responses; many of these were items such as *yeah/yes*, *mmhm*, *oh*, while others were *no*, or items generally classified as fillers such as *er* or *um*. However, in aphasic conversations such items themselves regularly constitute turns (cf. (32) above). Anyone who has worked with conversational materials is likely to be aware of the difficulties in making analytic decisions on such issues as what does or does not constitute a turn, a response, a back-channel or a filler (see Tottie, 1990).

Setting these analytic problems aside, Fleming's limited quantitative analysis of minimal responses turns out to be instructive, since the conversational partners do not use them to the same extent. Of all Avril's turns, 63 per cent were minimal responses, while the corresponding figure for Jane was 23 per cent. This suggests that Jane is taking a more pragmatically and linguistically active role in supporting the conversation. Furthermore, the figure of 63 per cent represents 79 utterances, and of these 51 are realized by the item *yes*. The following extract gives an idea of the interactional behaviour which lies behind these figures, suggesting that Avril, as well as Jane, can participate in a coherent conversation despite extremely limited linguistic substance:

(33) 1. Avril: what was your school days like? (quick point to Jane)
2. Jane: (.) not very good because the war is on
3. Avril: ah yes
4. Jane: we had er two (.) er (1.0) years where no school *at all*
5. Avril: *yeah yeah*
6. Jane: (1.0) an our an one school er er waz er year with no (1.0) erm (.) nother (1.0) I had to (.) er go up (lifts left hand briefly)
7. Avril: (.) yes yes
8. Jane: but no er schoo- er cooking or *anything*

    9. Avril: *mmhm*
    10. Avril: oh
    11. Jane: (.) I was er (.) fourteen
    12. Avril: mmhm yes
    13. Jane: but I had to I had to a a job then
    14. Avril: yes yes

After setting the ball rolling by initiating a new topic (line 1), Avril makes extensive use of minimal conversational tokens, one recognizable function of both *mmhm* and *yeah* being the so-called 'perverse passive'. This effectively places the onus of the conversation on her partner, enabling Avril to participate fully with only minimal recourse to lexical and syntactic resources.

Fleming reports that *oh* turns up particularly frequently in her data, sometimes recognizably in the functions outlined by Heritage such as acknowledging receipt of information (as apparently in T10 above; see also (32)). However, Schiffrin's association of *oh* particularly with repair sequences is reflected by a similar pattern in aphasic conversations where *oh* (or *oh dear*) seem commonly to function in identifying difficulties and initiating repair. Here is an example:

(34) 1. Avril: um (.) ah but um started to cry um oh=
     2. Jane: =with the mother?
     3. Avril: yes yes (BOTH LAUGH) yes
     4. Jane: and she wasn't (.) oh dear
              (AVRIL LAUGHS)

It is not surprising that quantitative differences in overall distribution of minimal turns in the Avril–Jane conversation should reflect relative levels of impairment, with the less able speaker using them strategically to achieve conversational participation and coherence. However, this is only part of the story. Perkins (in progress) has examined the distribution of such minimal turns relative to full turns in two conversations between a single aphasic speaker, E, and different partners. The first is a relative of E, and the second Perkins herself. The conversations are of rather different kinds. The relative is engaging in an exchange of chat, without any overt transactional goal. Perkins, on the other hand, while conversing informally in E's own home, is actively attempting to elicit both speech and information. In this conversation the proportion of *full* and *minor* turns (a category corresponding to Fleming's minimal responses) is roughly equal for both participants. However, in the conversation with the relative the distribution is quite uneven, with the aphasic using 22 minor turns and the relative only one. We find the converse pattern with regard to full turns, where the relative contributes 27 turns and the aphasic 10.

Again, some sequences drawn from these conversations give some idea of the interactional behaviour underlying the quantitative differences, which seem to reflect the different amount of help being given to the aphasic speaker by her two partners. In (35) the researcher, LP, seems to be attempting to elicit as much speech as possible, while making only a minimal contribution herself. In (36) the relative, R, carries the main conversational burden, as in (29) above:

(35) 1. LP: you went from *physio*
2. E: *yes* er no no er went through there
3. LP: mhm
4. E: into the toilet
5. LP: right
6. E: and er I [tə] took (2.0) [məmə] er put four letters through the letter box
7. LP: mhm

(36) 1. E: oh I thought she was living round here
2. R: she [w] she's living out she was living in Valley View=
3. E: =aye
4. R: er Letts Way but I don't know what er (.) three weeks since I was talking to her and she said well [wə] I'll be away shortly
5. E: aha=
6. R: = but I don't know whether she was with her

These examples suggest that discourse markers are likely to prove a fruitful area of investigation in aphasia. While semantically empty items are apparently used in a wide range of functions by aphasic speakers to achieve maximum conversational participation, their frequency of use varies in different conversations and reflects the amount of help provided by a given conversational partner. Analysis of their function in non-aphasic conversation has revealed that these apparently trivial items have a differentiated and sequentially constrained interactional meaning, suggesting that the interactional abilities of aphasic conversationalists might realistically be assessed by looking in detail at how these tokens are used and interpreted. A quantitative analysis of the kind used by both Fleming and Perkins cannot reveal these differences in function, but potentially could provide a sound basis for measuring and assessing interactional participation. We shall look further at this possibility in Chapter 12.

NON-VERBAL BEHAVIOUR

This topic has been much discussed in the clinical aphasiological literature (see, for example, Feyereisen and Seron, 1982, for a review) and the salience of various non-verbal behaviours in aphasic conversations is evident in several of our cited extracts. We conclude this chapter with a brief comment on a very large field of enquiry into an issue of great interactional importance.

Many conversation analysts are doubtful of the validity of the verbal/non-verbal distinction, since non-verbal and verbal moves can function in a similar way in conversation. For example headnods seem to mark recipiency in much the same way as the various non-lexical particles discussed in the previous section, and Heath's (1984) analysis of a doctor–patient dialogue shows that gaze and body orientation fulfil the same role. In (10) above the barman finally grants the customer's request non-verbally, but the granting could easily have been marked verbally, as in (8). This suggests that any assessment of aphasic conversationalists' non-verbal behaviour should examine it in its sequential context. However, both Penn (1985) and Prutting and Kirchner (1987) examine it globally, as one of several pragmatic parameters. Feyereisen and Seron (1982) report that both fluent and non-fluent aphasic patients produce more gesture than controls in a free conversational setting, but confirm that the way in which such patients regulate social interactions by use of non-verbal signals has not yet been studied. They comment that 'The present knowledge of gesture production in aphasics suggests, however, that social competence could be intact in aphasia' (p. 226).

Social psychologists have worked a great deal on non-verbal

behaviour in interaction, but their methods tend to differ from those of conversation analysts in that they concentrate on quantitative analyses and coding of phenomena such as gesture and gaze (see Roger and Bull, 1989, for a recent discussion of their approach). Conversation analytic research such as that carried out by Schegloff (1984), Heath (1984) and Goodwin (1981, 1984) gives greater emphasis to sequential positioning of phenomena in relation to ongoing talk. Schegloff has analysed gesture as a *speaker* phenomenon, with an organizational role in relation to the on-going talk. Hand-movements by *hearers* on the other hand tend (with some exceptions which he specifies) to be perceived as non-functional 'fidgeting'. Goodwin has shown in great detail the role of *gaze* in maintaining recipiency and the tendency of conversation to run into trouble if difficulties with gaze arise. Heath has examined the role of a number of non-verbal signals such as gaze and body orientation. Generally speaking, conversation analysts are sceptical of quantitative approaches, because they seem to posit a one-to-one relationship between any given nonverbal activity and its assumed meaning.

SUMMARY

This chapter started with an outline of overall conversational organization, emphasizing the highly skilled co-operative work and split-second timing involved in turn-taking and resolving overlap. We tried to indicate the kind of difficulties which aphasic conversationalists with syntactic or lexical retrieval problems were likely to encounter in managing the turn-taking system and the strategies which they are observed to employ in making contributions and forestalling interruption.

The systematic marking by conversationalists of dispreferred second parts of *adjacency pairs* invests apparently trivial pauses and vocalizations with profound communicative significance. Hearers can be shown to infer from pauses or vocalizations the imminence of a dispreferred second part, and we illustrated the interactional consequences in an aphasic conversation of an erroneous inference arising from this preference marking system. Partners of aphasic conversationalists need to be aware that the communicative significance of pauses varies greatly according to their sequential placement, and to be alert to the inferences which they are likely to trigger in specific sequential contexts. In general, the various communicative problems which spring from difficulties in aligning the timing of conversational contributions with normal timing patterns need much more careful analysis than they have received. This dimension of communicative behaviour in aphasia has hardly been studied at all, and a simple quantitative analysis of contextually undifferentiated pause patterns can grant only limited insight into the problems which might predictably emerge.

Speakers seem to be able to suspend their expectation of the second part of a pair, such as a response to a question. Simultaneously they cope with the complex layers of embedding regularly displayed in insertion sequences, while still orientating themselves to the conditionally relevant second part. Although there is little clear evidence of how aphasic conversationalists fare with such embedded structures, their complexity and conspicuous absence in our data has led us to suggest that they may present particular difficulties.

Turning next to more local aspects of conversational organization, we discussed opening and closing sequences, and the difficulty of handling the popular notions of topic or topic boundary, since sharp topic jumps are typically avoided in normal conversation. Where they occur they are usually marked – for example by a pre-sequence or gap, or by a preface such as *hey* or *anyway*. Repairs in normal and aphasic conversations were compared, with examples showing how extensive repair sequences can be in aphasic speakers as they seek to communicate effectively despite their linguistic impairments. We then described the varied interactional functions of so-called 'discourse markers' such as *mm*, *oh* and *yeah* which are very salient in normal conversation. Their minimal linguistic form means that they can be used by aphasic speakers so as to allow interlocutors to carry the main interactional burden as they strive to maintain a conversation. We concluded with a brief outline of the way in which conversation analysts (as opposed to psychologists) characteristically handle non-verbal behaviour in conversation.

PART III:
IMPLICATIONS AND APPLICATIONS

In Part II we attempted to identify the somewhat different contributions of psycholinguistic and pragmatic models to aphasia studies. The first chapters in Part II indicated the fairly narrow, but detailed, focus of psycholinguistic studies of acquired language disorder. Later chapters surveyed more discursively some general principles which might be applied in studying the pragmatics of aphasia, before focusing on conversation analysis as a framework which seemed particularly suitable for the description and analysis of aphasic conversation. The sharp differences in theory, method and approach between psycholinguistic and pragmatic orientations will have been obvious from the differences in style between the first and later chapters, as will the extent to which they have each been translated into applications to aphasia.

In Part III we wish to emphasize not these sharp differences, but the extent to which these two approaches can beneficially be viewed as complementary rather than conflicting. Aphasiologists have always borrowed from a range of disciplines, and are generally comfortable with the idea of approaching their patients' language problems from a number of different angles. This is surely sensible, since no single model or approach can offer exclusive insight into the nature or management of aphasia. What seems to be required is a combination of approaches where strengths and weaknesses are in complementary distribution, much as with the two approaches presented here.

Psycholinguistic procedures are hypothesis-based, set out to solve precisely specified problems, and tend to centre on identification of deficits and assets. Pragmatic approaches on the other hand are not generally hypothesis-based, take a global rather than a molecular view of language, and orientate to

communicative strengths rather than to specific mental operations. Psycholinguistics attempts to answer questions about the
mental processing of language by the individual, as far as
possible abstracting from the complexities of situational context.
Pragmatics offers a set of detailed and theoretically principled
procedures for describing and analysing contextually situated
conversational behaviour. A clear point of contact with psycholinguistic modes of investigation arises from the need to consider
communicative consequences in everyday conversation of the
deficits which psycholinguistics can locate and specify.

Our goal in this final part is to examine in turn the
complementary applications of psycholinguistics (Chapters 10
and 11) and pragmatics (Chapter 12). Reflecting the different
stages of application which psycholinguistics and pragmatics
have so far achieved, there is a greater emphasis in Chapter 11 on
studies in which a cognitive neuropsychological assessment has
been applied to the analysis of an individual's disorder as a basis
for therapy; several such studies have now been published and
are described here. In Chapter 12, in contrast, the application of
pragmatics is still primarily directed at analysis and assessment,
with very few studies which have translated this into actual
intervention. The contrast between the two approaches is also in
part, but not entirely, a contrast between direct therapy for the
individual (predominantly in a clinical setting) and indirect
forms of management which include communication partners in
non-clinical settings as well as the aphasic person. We therefore
discuss these two facets of intervention, both of them being
generally recognized by speech-language therapists as central to
their roles, and complementary rather than conflicting.

In our concluding chapter, Chapter 13, we attempt to pull
together the two themes which have been developed in parallel
throughout the book, and to indicate how we think both may
develop in the future to the advantage of the patients with whom
we are concerned.

TEN

Applying psycholinguistics to intervention: some preliminary considerations

In the chapter which follows this one we shall be reviewing some of the studies which have attempted to apply psycholinguistic modelling as a basis for devising programmes of direct intervention for aphasic patients. There are, however, some theoretical and methodological issues which arise in the practice of applying psycholinguistics in this field. The present chapter therefore considers these as a preliminary to our review of therapy studies.

We begin by acknowledging, and attempting to answer, some of the fundamental objections which have been raised against directly applying the types of model described in Chapters 4 and 5. We then discuss the methodological issues which arise in applying psycholinguistic theory to intervention and evaluating its efficacy.

THEORETICAL ISSUES: RESERVATIONS FROM COGNITIVE NEUROPSYCHOLOGY

Cognitive neuropsychologists have been diffident about extrapolating from their analyses to implications for language remediation. Wilson and Patterson (1990) argue that, although studies of brain-damaged patients have contributed substantially to the development of theories of normal cognition, these theories have done little in turn to inform therapy. Caramazza (1989) discusses the gap between *clinical* neuropsychology (as a study which necessarily has remediation amongst its concerns) and *cognitive* neuropsychology. Although he proposes that the difference is one of degree rather than category, he sees clinical neuropsychology (and, in association, language remediation) as still dominated by interest in anatomical localization and classification into syndromes. Consequently, he suggests, the methodology used by the two disciplines is inherently different: the clinical seeks patterns from group studies, while for the cognitive 'only single-patient research allows valid inferences about cognitive mechanisms from the analysis of cognitively impaired performance' (pp. 385–6). This position is not supported by all cognitive neuropsychologists, and the appropriateness of including group studies in neuropsychological methodology has been debated in a special issue of the journal *Cognitive Neuropsychology*, edited by Caramazza himself. In this issue, for example, Newcombe and Marshall (1988) propose that choice of a group as opposed to an individual as the basis of the study depends on the theoretical claim being investigated, rather than on any difference of philosophy; cognitive neuropsychologists, for example, might well use group studies rather than single case studies if they are seeking evidence of *associations* in cognitive functions. Continuing his emphasis on the different methods of clinical and cognitive neuropsychology, however, Caramazza chastizes rehabilitation studies which apply cognitive neuropsychological models but still employ a syndrome-oriented approach, referring to patients as suffering from the syndromes of deep dyslexia, agrammatism, and so on.

More fundamentally he suggests that the models so far developed by cognitive neuropsychologists still present major problems of specification of detail. Giving the postulated graphemic output buffer as an example (see Chapter 4, p. 59), he points out that 'Unless we articulate in greater detail our claims about the graphemic buffer we will not be able to provide motivated accounts for important aspects of dysgraphic patients' performance' (p. 389). Other components of the proposed mental architecture of language such as the phonological lexicon are even more complex, and, he claims, will require even more specification before their relevance to therapy becomes clear.

Caramazza suggests that, in the present state of knowledge, strategic choices in therapy could be based as much on mere observation of the patient as on a psycholinguistic explanation. For example observation that a dysgraphic patient spells very short words almost flawlessly could be sufficient to prompt the therapeutic strategy of teaching him to spell words syllable by syllable. Caramazza takes another example of the application of a psycholinguistic theory in analysing a patient's disorder, that is attributing a deficit to mapping meaning onto syntactic structure (Byng, 1988), and asks how the therapeutic strategy inferred from such an analysis would differ from one deriving from an analysis of the deficit as in processing the referential dependencies of traces (Grodzinsky, 1986; Caplan and Hildebrandt, 1988). (See Chapter 5 for a discussion of these different proposals.) Caramazza concludes that the main contribution of cognitive neuropsychology to language remediation is in its diagnostic *methodology* applied to individual cases, but that the *content* of cognitive theories 'does not constrain in any obvious way the nature of possible therapy-determined modifications of a system' (p. 393).

We may, therefore, sum up Caramazza's reservations about applying psycholinguistic models to intervention as essentially fourfold:

1. these models are underspecified;
2. clinical neuropsychologists (and, by implication in association, aphasia therapists) have a different orientation from cognitive neuropsychologists, in that they are necessarily concerned with the neurological basis of disorders, and hence with syndromes;
3. no theory of cognitive rehabilitation has yet been developed;
4. the content of cognitive neuropsychological theories has not been linked with rehabilitation in any non-trivial way, that is beyond what could have been inferred from routine clinical observation.

We shall attempt now to respond to some of these reservations.

A REPLY TO COGNITIVE NEUROPSYCHOLOGY

Caramazza's first point, that psycholinguistic models are under-specified, is not controversial. It is, however, no counter-indication to applying models in therapy which can feed back into development of the models. The response of patients to model-motivated therapy is a potentially fruitful and as yet underused means of further specifying the nature of the components in these models and the interactivation between them. For example unexpected generalization from a targeted behaviour in therapy to an untargeted one would seem to be potentially illuminating concerning interactions in the model. Coltheart and Byng (1989) found that visual mnemonic strategies used by a patient with a form of surface dyslexia generalized to untreated words, and suggest that this supports a model of distributed lexical representations rather than item-specific ones. In contrast Scott and Byng (1989) report no generalization in another patient from recognition of the reading comprehension of homophones to the ability to spell them. Generalization therefore seems to have relatively untapped potential as a test of the validity of present models. The reason why the potential of response to therapy has been underused is not because of any inherent difficulties, but because of the hitherto professional separation of cognitive neuropsychologists (who have seen themselves predominantly as scientist-researchers) and aphasia therapists (who have seen themselves predominantly as practitioners); we shall come back to this theme later. Using response to therapy as a means of refining psycholinguistic models would go some way also to meeting criticisms of the models as focusing on operations at one point in time rather than being dynamically and evolutionarily motivated.

There is, moreover, an empirical justification for aphasia therapists in applying psycholinguistic modelling. The specification of the model of cross-modal word processing in Fig. 4.1 is already considerably more detailed than any neurologically based model in its relevance to therapy. Moreover, aphasia therapists are necessarily obliged to work eclectically, pending the nirvana of *the* definitive model of language processing and its relationship to brain damage.

Caramazza's second point is that clinical neuropsychology has a different orientation from cognitive neuropsychology. We take it from the context in which this point was made that Caramazza sees clinical psychology as including the rehabilitation of the language disordered, and as therefore subsuming aphasia therapy. Clinical neuropsychology (with aphasia therapy) and cognitive neuropsychology are indeed distinctive, in that practitioners of the first discipline are generally based in a medical setting and those of the second in an academic setting. This becomes increasingly uninfluential, however, as clinical neuropsychologists incorporate cognitive neuropsychology into their thinking and practice. The suggested dissociations between the two are of a very different kind from the dissociation between theoretical linguistics and aphasiology which we discussed in Chapter 3. The two do not operate at different levels of abstraction. Cognitive neuropsychological models claim a psychological validity, and therefore should be relevant to the study of the mental functioning of brain-damaged patients, whether they be located in a hospital or in a university laboratory. The main difference is that clinical neuropsychologists have to translate their observations into a form which makes sense to medical practitioners who are also interested in the anatomy and physiology of the brain damage. In reply to Caramazza's objection to the use of syndrome labels, we might therefore note the pragmatic utility of these labels in communication with neurologically orientated investigators. Caramazza is unrealistic in objecting to a juxtaposition of terminology in an essentially interdisciplinary study. The pressures of clinical practice dictate the use of the shorthand of syndrome labels, and a terminology which is comprehensible to colleagues in the medical disciplines, provided that it is recognized that a syndrome label is 'a code-word for a lengthy message whose detailed content is changing continuously' (Holladay and Poole, cited by Newcombe and Marshall, 1988: 552). Indeed we must note that the description of a patient as suffering from aphasia is itself a classification into a (gross) syndrome, which may itself be questioned as having fuzzy edges (e.g. in the conventional exclusion of some but not all people with right brain damage or the bilateral damage which underlies most forms of dementia). Caramazza himself has frequently used syndrome labels to characterize patients, not only when writing for a medically oriented readership (e.g. Hillis and Caramazza in *Brain and Language*, 1989, refer to two patients 'with acquired dysgraphia'), but also when writing for the cognitive psychological literature (e.g. Caramazza, et al., 1987). The question is to what extent these shorthand compromises reflect constraints on our understanding of an individual's disorder, and the answer is, in respect of language rehabilitation, very little. In fact the majority of the psycholinguistic studies of intervention we report in the next chapter have attempted to make their findings comprehensible to medical clinicians by showing how their cases can be related to conventional syndromes.

Still concerning Caramazza's second point we might also note that the use of 'single-case studies' is in fact germane to the practice of aphasia therapy. The majority of speech-language therapists (we make this claim securely of Britain, and believe it to be so in most countries) apply an individualized approach to therapy, with intervention aimed at each patient's own needs. This is very much in tune with the single-case hypothesis-testing method of investigation advocated in cognitive neuropsychology. This individualized approach in aphasia therapy of course includes many other dimensions besides the patient's putative psycholinguistic deficits (witness the preceding and following chapters of this book on the minutiae of conversational analysis); it adopts cognitive neuropsychological theory as only one addition to its repertoire.

Caramazza's second point also reflects another assumption, that is that aphasia therapists are necessarily concerned with neuroanatomical localization. We would argue that this reflects a cultural bias. In Britain, where much of the development of cognitive neuropsychology occurred, aphasia therapy is largely conducted without any hard information as to neuroanatomical site of lesion. Expensive (and sometimes invasive) brain-imaging technology is generally only used where it assists in a neuro-logical diagnosis, and insurance considerations have less influence on the unneccessary performance of such tests. This means that the majority of the aphasia therapist's clients in Britain are referred not only without a CT or MRI scan, but often without even a clinical neurological screening, if the referral has come direct from a physician or a general medical practitioner. Given the limitations of present-day brain-imaging in providing accurate information as to functional sites of lesion, and the limited knowledge which the infant science of neurolinguistics has yet been able to provide about the link between the mental processes of language and the brain, the lack of neurological data about an individual patient for aphasia *therapy* is at present not a major disadvantage, except in so far as *reliable* neuroimaging data have the potential for influencing therapeutic decisions by assisting in forming a prognosis. Brain-imaging has an enormous and exciting potential in the development of aphasiology and neurolinguistics, and eventually perhaps on aphasia therapy too, but its present direct relevance to decisions about intervention is overstated by Caramazza. Most aphasia therapy in the UK has developed independently from a neuroanatomical focus.

With Caramazza's third point, that no theory of cognitive

rehabilitation has yet been developed, we cannot but agree. However, it is more realistic to expect a theory of cognitive rehabilitation to develop from the evidence of response to model-based cognitive rehabilitation, rather than to be a precondition of it. As we noted in Chapter 2, already some preliminary proposals have been made, distinguishing the effects of cognitive rehabilitation as being due to reactivation, reorganization or deliberately adopted relays circumventing dysfunctions (to this we may also add a fourth 'r' – revelation – when affective barriers to the use of what language abilities remain are removed). We should like to emphasize the value of rehabilitation studies which apply psycholinguistic theories in preparing the groundwork for such a theory, and also for feeding back necessary modifications to the models.

Caramazza's fourth point begs the question as to what routine clinical observation consists of, given that the observer perceives only what his/her preconceptions enable to be perceived. The 'mere' clinical observation that Caramazza suggests is adequate to inform therapy is only as good as the perceptions of the observer. It may seem obvious to the well-read clinician that the patient has less difficulty with short words than long, or with content words than grammatical words, or with syntactically complex sentences than non-reversible Subject-Verb-Object (SVO) structures. But these perceptions themselves are based on psycholinguistic theory, and reflect not only the observer's training in psycholinguistics but the limitations of that training. For example, it is clear from the discussion of pronouns in Chapter 6 that linguists generally make much finer discriminations amongst what psycholinguistic theory currently categorizes as 'grammatical words', relating them also to their contextual functions. The relationship of the observer's perceptions to the observer's theoretical bias is therefore far from trivial. The kinds of observations that we have illustrated are (often) not ones that the layman would make, most particularly the patient and spouse themselves. Moreover, one important aspect of therapy based on psycholinguistic models and pragmatic theory is to sharpen, not only the therapist's observation and understanding of the case, but also the patients' and families' own understanding of the nature of the disorder which has been inflicted on them.

Aphasia therapists who are familiar with models such as the one illustrated in Fig. 4.1 perceive more than those whose familiarity with naming disorders is restricted to scores on a standard clinical test of naming. Furthermore, they use these differential perceptions to guide their choice of what appropriate therapy might be. Therapy applying these models does not use any radically new methods (other than incidentally applying advances in technology, such as computers). The techniques used are part of classical lore; the difference is in selecting a particular technique for a particular aspect of a patient's disorder at a particular time in recovery, based on a theoretical analysis of what the key malfunction is. Caramazza proposes that simple clinical observation is sufficient to dictate the selection of the appropriate technique. To take the specific example he gives, Caramazza claims an irrelevance to therapy for sentence production of a distinction between a mapping disorder and a difficulty in handling traces. According to the model discussed in Chapter 5, however, the therapeutic implications of such a differential diagnosis are distinct; one disorder affects the transition from meaning to syntax, the other is contained within the syntactic planning of sentences. Remediation for the first could be targeted at the understanding of thematic roles (as reported in Jones, 1986; Byng, 1988). Remediation for the second could be targeted specifically at gap location and identifying referential dependencies, distinguishing between those which GB theory proposes occur in S-structure rather than in D-structure. Response to such different therapies could inform the model. If the model seemed to be supported in this respect, it could lead to therapists being more exact in selecting economical remediation for an individual patient. Such is already the case with disorders of naming, in which subtypes of naming difficulties are more efficiently targeted by different techniques (Lesser, 1989; Nettleton and Lesser, 1991).

THEORETICAL ISSUES: SOME RESERVATIONS FROM APHASIA THERAPY

Reservations about the relevance of cognitive neuropsychological modelling to aphasia therapy have come not only from practitioners in cognitive neuropsychology but from aphasia therapists as well, and we shall state these also, as well as attempting to reply to them in the next section. One of the aphasia therapists who has expressed reservations about the value of applying psycholinguistic models to practice in aphasia therapy is Basso (1989). She also worries about the application on four grounds, although these are rather different from Caramazza's:

1. psycholinguistically based (cognitive neuropsychological) rehabilitation is well grounded only if the underlying model is correct;
2. her own data on recovery do not provide any support for the claim of modular organization of language;
3. the rehabilitation strategies associated with these models are appropriate only for patients who have selective impairments and these are rare;
4. in adopting psycholinguistic modelling aphasia therapists are taking a step backwards, ignoring the pragmatic level of language.

She also makes a fifth point, which reflects a strong medical influence on her conceptualization of the role of the aphasia therapist, and is in contrast to the view of the aphasia therapist as scientist-practitioner which we promulgate in this book. Basso's viewpoint is best illustrated in the following extract:

> As in all disciplines, in speech language therapy there is a time for research and a time for application . . . The clinical speech pathologist['s] . . . task is to apply what he has learnt, to learn from his clinical experience and provide treatment for all patients who request it. It is not his task to demonstrate that what he does is effective. It would be the same as asking the general practitioner to demonstrate each time he prescribes a drug that the drug is effective.
>
> (Basso, 1989a: 79)

In the next section we attempt a reply to the first four points, and comment on the limitations which Basso's separation of research and its application imposes.

A REPLY TO RESERVATIONS FROM APHASIA THERAPY

Basso's first point, that model-based rehabilitation is well-grounded only if the model is correct, is not dissimilar to

Caramazza's that the models are underspecified. It should be noted that the psycholinguistic models which have been applied (both in respect of single lexical items and sentences) were based on experimental results obtained from normal subjects, and that they therefore have an *a priori* claim to validity independent of clinical data. The models, however, are still developing, and 'correctness' is perhaps too much to hope for at the present state of development of any theories of mental processing. This does not make psycholinguistically based intervention any different from any other form of intervention in aphasia. Therapy has traditionally been based on only the sketchiest of theoretical foundations, and psycholinguistically based intervention has in fact gone further along these lines than any other so far. Rehabilitationists cannot afford to wait for the nirvana of the exactly specified 'correct' model. Patients exist in the here and now, and any theory which offers promise of a rationale for selecting therapeutic techniques economically for individual patients' problems cannot be ignored. It would be neglectful of rehabilitators not to evaluate such a promise by well-designed studies of its application. However much the reification of a psycholinguistic model may be necessary before it can be mapped onto brain physiology, it is not necessary before it can be used as a rationale for therapy, given the potential of therapy, as we have already stated, for refining such models.

Basso's second point is also easily answered. The Italian studies of recovery she refers to have all been large-scale, and individual patients have not been described in the detail associated with a psycholinguistic model. The absence of support in the data collected in these studies for claims that language is organized in a modular way is therefore not surprising: the investigators were not seeking this evidence, the standard assessments used in these studies were not such as to lend themselves to extraction of this detail, and the data must therefore remain neutral on this claim. This is in itself an interesting illustration of the limitations of 'mere' clinical observation, as we have already pointed out in commenting on Caramazza's proposal that such observation is sufficient to inform therapy.

Basso's third point, that rehabilitation strategies associated with the models are appropriate only for the rare patients with selective disorders, can be refuted. The models were originally based on studies of patients with *relatively* selective disorders (particularly of reading), since these were the ones who were most likely to show dissociations of function (and were the ones most likely to stand up to extended investigation, and for whom access for investigation by cognitive psychologists was therefore the more readily agreed). The detail of the model has been developed through study of patients who are not at all atypical of a speech therapy clinic's case load in aphasia. Published papers may give the impression of selectivity by focusing on one aspect of a patient's disorder. Patient EST, for example, appears in one paper (Kay and Patterson, 1986) as an example of surface dyslexia, in another (Kay and Ellis, 1987) as an example of anomia, both analyses giving illuminating insights into the nature of language processing. (We referred in Chapter 4, p. 75, to the way a psycholinguistic model can account for the relationship between one form of anomia and one form of surface dyslexia.) Many aspects of the models have been elaborated through patients described as being globally aphasic. One example is Warrington and McCarthy's (1987) study of the semantic disorder in globally impaired patient VER; another is Blanken, et al.'s (1988) interpretation of the nature of recurrent stereotypic utterances in a severe form of aphasia. Both these studies deal with patients whose disorders affect many aspects of language and who can hardly be described as being selectively impaired. The remediation studies based on psycholinguistic models which we shall describe later in this chapter have been on cases with multifaceted disorders, similar to those which form the bulk of the aphasia therapist's referral load. The fact that direct language therapy focused on one aspect of a disorder at a time does not mean that other elements in the patient's language pathology and needs were ignored.

Basso's fourth reservation presumes that psycholinguistically based therapy displaces functionally based therapy. This seems to be a misconception of the situation. It is more common for model-based therapy and pragmatically based therapy to be used in complement to each other. Direct work on a hypothesized dysfunction (if the analysis indicates that this is appropriate) uses functionally relevant materials and is linked with work aimed at using the acquired technique or restored function in everyday life. As we describe in Chapter 12, much of pragmatic therapy is indirect, and is mediated through the patient's communicative partners. Psycholinguistic analyses of patients' disorders, when shared with partners, can contribute to their understanding of the nature of trouble spots which occur in everyday conversations, making it easier to develop strategies to accommodate these. There is no justification for the belief that psycholinguistically based therapy needs to displace pragmatically based therapy.

We comment finally on the orientation to the role of aphasia therapists which the quotation we cited from Basso reflects. Again we suggest that Basso's orientation shows a cultural bias, in this case due to the separation of research training from the training of speech therapists in her country (as in some others). In other countries the education of speech therapists has fostered a research orientated approach, premised on the belief that each patient provides a detective challenge to the therapist. The development of single-case methodology has allowed the direct translation of this research-orientated approach into clinical practice. In contrast to the approach advocated by Basso, the hypothesis-testing method which permeates most UK clinics sees the work to be carried out with each patient as a mini-research exercise; a necessary part of this is evaluation of whether the intervention achieved its stated objects, essential as a means not only of justifying clinical practice but also of acquiring insights into the nature of aphasia. The only gap between the 'researcher' and the 'applier' (to take Basso's distinction) is in the time each can devote to this study. The practising clinician contributes to the development of the field, and brings to it the benefit of an extending and intimate knowledge of the continuing nature of the disorder, rather than receiving and applying prescriptions formulated elsewhere. Demonstration of effectiveness or otherwise with patients who share a common feature amongst their individualisms, and refinement of our understanding of the nature of aphasia, can be achieved through compilation of these clinical studies. Hence arises the need for practising clinicians to be allowed time and space for publishing their observations, without which the wealth of experience and insight gained through continuing interaction with evolving patterns of aphasia is lost to a wider circle. Particularly if response to therapy is to feed back into the development both of models and of further refinement of therapy, as we have advocated, a separation of scientist-researcher and applier-therapist is not tenable.

METHODOLOGICAL ISSUES: EXPERIMENTAL DESIGN

It is germane to the approach that we have advocated that therapy needs a means of ascertaining whether it is effective. The effects of social and personal support must be distinguished from the effects of the direct intervention with language itself. Large-scale group studies have not been able to make a contribution at this level, despite the use of randomized controlled trials (Lincoln, et al., 1984). The methodological problems which afflict such randomized controlled trials have been fully discussed (Pring, 1986; Howard, 1986), and need not be rehearsed here (but see Fitz-Gibbon, 1986; Siegel and Young, 1987; and Allen, 1990 for a defence of group designs in intervention research).

The alternative methodology which has been developed to evaluate the cognitive neuropsychological approach to therapy is that of single case studies, an approach which is essentially in tune with current clinical practice of planning individualized therapy, albeit requiring a more rigorously quantifiable approach. Since evaluative designs with $n = 1$ form the basis of the therapy studies reported in the next chapter, we shall briefly summarize the principal options available. Accessible reviews of these are available in McReynolds and Thompson (1986), Kearns (1986), Connell and Thompson (1986) and Howard and Hatfield (1987).

The simplest design which has been applied in single-case evaluative research in aphasia is to compare a period without active intervention (an 'A' phase) with a period with intervention (a 'B' phase). If the patient has reached a stable point in recovery (though as we noted in Chapter 2 there is some dispute as to when this may have been reached), and if the B phase shows an improvement over the A phase, it may be attributable to the intervention. It may, of course, also just be attributable to someone taking an interest in the patient, and coming along with a programme which both patient and therapist expect to be effective. It may also be due to some unanticipated general improvement in the patient's health or other circumstances. The effects of these can be partly disentangled through various means.

First an unrelated 'non-linguistic' task (such as copying stick designs), or an unrelated 'linguistic' task (such as repeating non-words), which is not to be the subject of therapy, can be used as a comparator for assessment at the beginning and end of the intervention phases. If scores on this do not change, the sheer effect of interaction with an interested therapist, or of a general improvement in circumstances, can be largely discounted. Another method is to divide the therapy materials into two equivalent lists B_u and B_t, one of which (B_u) will remain untreated, while the other (B_t) is used in therapy. Unless there is generalization from one to the other, B_t will be expected to improve more than B_u. This method has often been used in naming therapy. If set B_u does show improvement, however, the results can be difficult to interpret: is this a non-specific effect of any treatment, or a specific generalization between the two sets due to their similar nature? To control for this, multiple baseline designs may in addition compare different kinds of treatment for set B_t (treatments B_{t1} and B_{t2}). If, in such a design, the results of treatment B_{t1} differ significantly from those of treatment B_{t2}, this eliminates the possibility of a non-specific effect of treatment as such in itself; any improvement in the untreated B_u items is more reliably attributable to generalization between items. Since generalization is the hoped-for aim of much therapy, the analysis may consist of a comparison of a mild trend for improvement in B_u items over the therapy period, with the trends for improvement (or otherwise) which have occurred in B_t items during treatments B_{t1} and B_{t2}.

A further method is to repeat the A phase (ABA), to test if a reduction of ability occurred during the second A phase. Since an aim of therapy is lasting improvement, the second A phase would be hoped to maintain the level achieved during the B phase, though not expected to exceed it. These A periods may coincide with intervals when the patient has been put on review from the clinic, or after holiday breaks (a coincidence which usefully lends itself to student projects in evaluation of therapy). A further refinement is to add another B phase, to test whether performance improves again (ABAB). These designs, however, imply that therapy gains are likely to switch on and off; most aspects of remediation in aphasia are not designed to achieve such effects, so the ABAB design has been less popular in aphasia research than in other branches of remediation.

A cross-over design is advocated by Coltheart (1983), using two tasks, X and Y. Both are assessed at the beginning of the study, then treatment is undertaken for X only, with reassessment of both at the end, followed by treatment for Y only, concluding with a reassessment of both. This differs from the B_t and B_u design, in that tasks X and Y can be unrelated. Again, however, results from this will only emerge clearly if the language components targeted for therapy are indeed independent of each other; and, as we have discussed above this is one of the critical questions in cognitive neuropsychological theory.

Other designs have been suggested by Kearns (1986), for example investigation of components in the treatment package by comparing periods in which one method of treatment is used in isolation in the B phase and then in combination with another (C) in a BC phase. Kearns cites as an example a study by Simmons of a blind patient who acquired aphasia with apraxia of speech after a stroke; the patient was treated both through auditory stimulation and through Braille, through an A-B-BC-B-BC design (the conclusion was that the combined condition was more effective than auditory stimulation on its own).

Whatever the design used in the evaluation of aphasia therapy, Willmes (1990) notes that three types of effects have to be evaluated statistically. These are:

1. increase of competence (improvement) for a treated linguistic function;
2. differential improvement for treated and non-treated sets of items assessing the same or a related linguistic function;
3. improvement for a treated function and no improvement for an unrelated non-treated function.

(Willmes, 1990: 427)

Reviews of single-case experimental designs used in the evaluation of aphasia therapy, and of some statistical factors which have to be born in mind, can be found in Howard (1986), Pring (1986), Howard and Hatfield (1987) and Willmes (1990).

METHODOLOGICAL ISSUES: ASSESSMENT MATERIALS

Evaluation of the effectiveness of therapy requires reliable assessment measures for test-retest purposes. We shall discuss this in Chapter 12 in respect of the most important criterion for the success of therapy in aphasia, the use of language (and/or other means of communication) in everyday life. Where the aim of a particular therapy programme has been circumscribed (e.g. to improve naming), measurement is simplified: the evidence of success (if any) will be the change in the number of items named before and after the period of therapy (provided that the method has kept constant such niceties as the amount of time to be given, whether first or final attempts are to be used, and how intelligible the response is required to be).

For improvement targeted at specific modules in a psycholinguistic model, a more comprehensive resource of materials is required. This also needs to be one which directly addresses the distinctions proposed in the models. Therapists could design specific tasks for each patient, and compare before-and-after performances, or search the now extensive cognitive neuropsychological literature for precedents in which the important variables have been controlled. Either of these would be too time-consuming for a practising clinician. Material which is standardized rather than one-off also has the advantage of improving meaningful interpretation of results across therapists and clinics. One such collection of tests, Psycholinguistic Assessments of Language Processing in Aphasia (PALPA) has been developed by Kay, et al. (1992). It is intended to be used as a resource by speech-language therapists as well as cognitive neuropsychologists. It consists of tasks which assess components involved in the phonological, orthographic, lexical-semantic, morphological and syntactic-semantic processing of language. Variables which experiments suggest are relevant to distinguishing processing disorders in aphasia have been controlled, e.g. word frequency, length, morphological complexity, imageability, semantic distance. The resource, for example, includes materials which can be used in the diagnosis of types of auditory comprehension or reading disorders described in Chapter 4. From results on a combination of tests, selected as appropriate to develop initial hypotheses about a patient's disorder, it is possible to profile the patient's psycholinguistic processing as a basis for planning therapy (Lesser and Perkins, in preparation). Many of the studies described in the next chapter have used either tests from PALPA or similar assessments for their before/after therapy comparisons.

It is also important that the quantity, nature and type of

intervention should be specified, in order to facilitate replication of the study with other patients who share similar features. This is one of the criticisms which can be made of most group studies of the effectiveness of aphasia therapy. Details of the intervention used with the patients are not given. Sometimes it is referred to as 'standard', or as 'tailor-made for each subject so they embodied what was felt to be personally meaningful and immediately utilitarian to that individual' (Hagen, 1973: 456). Such reports make interpretation of the results difficult, and replication impossible.

An example of a group study in which treatment principles and materials are specified in great detail is Shewan and Bandur's (1986) report on their Language Oriented Therapy (LOT) approach. This selected patients according to syndrome, however, rather than according to their psycholinguistic profile, and hence describes the intervention patterns used in the study only in terms of mean number and duration of sessions on five modalities (auditory, visual, gestural, oral and graphic) in five groups of patients (Global, Broca's, Wernicke's, Anomic and Conduction). Given the polythetic nature of these syndromes, replication of this study could only be approximate. Although Shewan (1979) referred to LOT as 'a psycholinguistic approach to aphasia therapy' (in the sense that it is based on information about language and its processing rather than on general claims about the need for language stimulation), we are using *psycholinguistic* in a more restricted sense as related to specific models of language processing.

SUMMARY

In this chapter we have reviewed some preliminary considerations concerning the application of psycholinguistics to aphasia therapy. We itemized the reservations expressed both by some cognitive neuropyschologists and by some aphasia therapists about the relevance of psycholinguistic models to aphasia therapy. We attempted to show that these were in part based on misapprehensions, on unrealistic expectations and on cultural biases. In particular we advocated a research-orientated perspective on aphasia therapy, in which hypotheses are derived about the nature of each patient's disorder, therapy is designed on the basis of these hypotheses, clinically and experimentally acceptable designs are used to evaluate the effectiveness of the therapy, and the results of the intervention are used not only to inform decisions about whether to continue or change the therapy but to feed back into refinement of the models used as a basis for planning therapy. Some designs were outlined, together with an account of assessment materials for use in pre- and post-therapy testing.

ELEVEN

Applying psycholinguistics to intervention: some clinical studies

For the reasons we gave in the last chapter, our review of psycholinguistic interventions in aphasia is largely restricted to single case studies in which the following conditions are met: the nature of an individual's disorder in terms of a psycholinguistic model is specified, the nature of the intervention used is itemized in detail, and a single-case experimental design has been used which allows some inferences to be made about the effects of the intervention. This is not to deny that therapy can achieve *clinically* significant results which are not necessarily reflected by *statistically* significant results, as Pring (1986) has pointed out (see also our comments in Chapter 8 on the preference in conversational analysis for qualitative rather than quantitative descriptions). If the cognitive neuropsychological approach to aphasia therapy is to achieve certain other aims, however, it is statistically valid results which are at present of most interest. Without statistical probability measured, the aims cannot be met of, first, convincing a healthily sceptical scientific community that aphasia therapy is effective, and, secondly, feeding back into psycholinguistic models information which is useful in their development.

This is a growing field, particularly as an increasing number of speech-language therapists employ this approach as part of their clinical practice (see the five case studies reported in the proceedings of a conference of the British Aphasiology Society, Jones, 1989). Our review is not intended to be exhaustive, but to illustrate the approach which can be used, drawing on this theoretical base. (For other reviews of direct language intervention in aphasia, including group studies which have applied some elements from psycholinguistic models, see Chapey, 1986; Howard and Hatfield, 1987; and Lesser, in press.) We have grouped the studies which meet the requirements we have stated (some better than others) under five main headings. These address, respectively, *disorders of naming, auditory comprehension, sentence production, reading* and *spelling*. To facilitate an overall view of current practice at the time of writing, we provide here summary tables of the various studies under these five main headings (see Tables 11.1–11.5).

NAMING THERAPY

We begin our review of studies of therapy with examples of applications of psycholinguistic models to therapy for difficulties in confrontation (picture) naming, a common deficit in aphasia. For ease of reference, Table 11.1 provides a survey of all the individual cases used in these examples. The table also summarizes the methods used, the time taken and the statistical probability of the outcome being achieved by chance, where this is reported. We have restricted the survey to studies where a psycholinguistic model has been specifically applied. Naming difficulties are targeted in therapy not because of their direct utility but because of their expected generalization to word finding difficulties in conversations and the frustrations these can cause in everyday speech. As we discussed in Chapter 5 there is reason to believe that difficulties in lexical retrieval (particularly of verbs) may not only be germane to problems in constructing sentences but may also compound syntactic difficulties through the need to trade-off computational space between lexical-semantic and syntactic processing.

As a preliminary, we first outline one of the first examples of this approach, albeit using the then preferred paradigm of a group study rather than detailed single case studies. Seron, et al. (1979) undertook their study of four patients not so much as a test of the effectiveness of therapy as an investigation of whether their naming difficulties were due to problems of access to the phonological lexicon rather than to a loss of the semantics of the words. The argument was that, if the difficulty was in access, then strategies aimed at improving access would result in generalization from drilled words to words which had not been used in therapy. The patients were classed as anomic (two), Wernicke's or Broca's aphasics (one of each). They were given two months of intensive therapy on the naming of 40 words, ten in each category of clothes, houses, tools and action verbs. In each category five words were of high frequency and five of low. The words were selected from those in a list of 240 which the patients had been unable to name. A control set of words in each category was also selected to form an untreated set. In addition a further set of words was used in pre- and post-testing, comprising 40 high and low frequency words in two different categories, food and animals, which were not included in therapy. It was thus possible to see whether any effects of treatment on the drilled words had generalized either to untreated words in the same categories or to untreated words in different categories. The type of therapy is not described in detail in Seron, et al.'s paper, but was drawn from a resource of methods, adapted for each subject, all of which aimed at improving access to the lexicon, for example using gestures, lead-in phrases, word associations. Another group of four patients acted as controls in that they were given 'traditional language therapy' (again not described) without any restriction on words used.

The results of Seron, et al.'s study were suggestive, but not conclusive. First, they indicate that the intensive therapy on the restricted set of words may have been more effective than the diffuse therapy: three of the four 'experimental' patients produced highly significantly ($p < 0.001$) fewer errors on the naming test after two months of treatment, while only one of the control group did. Secondly, two of the experimental patients showed significant improvement on the undrilled words which had been taken from the same categories as the drilled words. Thus it seemed that there had been within-category generalization in these two patients (though not in the other two). In all the three experimental patients who improved significantly, there was also generalization of naming ability to categories which had not been included in the therapy. Furthermore, in the two more successful patients this significant improvement showed in a semantic classification test as well as in naming.

These results indicate that the putative distinction in the psycholinguistic model between a semantic disorder and a disorder of access to the phonological output lexicon has potential value for its implications in therapy. The variable success of Seron, et al.'s patients also shows that detailed specifications of a patient's naming difficulties need to be made as a preliminary to targeting therapy accurately. As a confirmation of the effectiveness of therapy the study is a little more questionable, however. The patients were stated as being at least one month after the onset of aphasia, but the design did not account for the possible effects of continuing spontaneous recovery. Although the control group's less successful results seem to show that the improvement in the three patients given experimental therapy was not due to the placebo effect of a therapist's interaction, the principles on which the patients were allocated to either treatment are not stated, and we cannot be sure that the groups were matched on important variables. A further restriction on the usefulness of this early study is the lack of specification of just what the therapy comprised. Consequently the study also does not allow for interpretation of the results as endorsing *reactivation* of semantic-phonological links or the acquisition of cognitive *relay strategies* for retrieval (as described in Chapter 2). Two of the remaining four studies to be outlined here fall more clearly within the intervention paradigm of adoption of a relay strategy, while the other two fall within that of reactivation.

RELAY STRATEGIES IN NAMING THERAPY

In the first case the relay strategy is externalized through a computer as an aid. Bruce and Howard's (1987) study was of five cases, three women and two men, in all of whom the naming difficulty was diagnosed as due to need for extra activation of the phonological output lexicon. Their problems were therefore similar to those of patient S in extract (1) in Chapter 4. Further details of these five aphasic patients are given in Table 11.1. All the patients had failed to name more than 50 pictures out of a set of 100, but could indicate the initial letters of between 43 per cent and 79 per cent of the words they did not name. It could be deduced therefore that they were able to retrieve the semantic representation of most of the words (in that they had access to at least part of its orthographic representation), but they were unable to achieve the full phonological representation needed for pronunciation of the word. Three of the subjects also benefited if a therapist supplied them with the initial sound of the picture name they were seeking; they were, however, unable to utilize their own retrieval of initial letters by converting them into phonemic cues themselves.

Bruce and Howard used a computer to provide the missing link (for words beginning with one of nine consonants). They trained the patients in five sessions to press the right key for the picture's initial letter, listen to the corresponding sound produced by the computer and then name the word. A therapist stood by to provide the sound cue, or if necessary the whole picture name, if the patient failed to respond satisfactorily. The list of words used was divided into two sets, one for use in therapy, and the other as a control set. The experimental design compared the patients' abilities to produce the names without and then with the aid of the computer.

At the end of the study four of the patients were naming significantly better through use of the computer than they had been at the beginning, and in two of these there was generalization of the skill to the untreated control words. In the fifth patient, PAB, naming without use of the computer had improved so dramatically that the aid was not necessary; he appeared to have internalized the strategy of generating his own 'phonemic cues' from initial letters. As Robertson (1990) has pointed out, this study shows the effectiveness of the prosthetic use of the computer in assisting recall of words in general, after a relatively brief training. Moreover, it provides evidence that some patients can learn cognitive relay strategies which produce functional improvements giving independence from the computer.

Bruce and Howard's study is open to the criticism made by Caramazza of the weak link between psycholinguistic modelling and aphasia therapy in that the therapy could be derived from common clinical observation, that is that these patients could spontaneously say the initial letters of words they could not name, and could benefit from phonemic cues. A similar procedure was recommended and applied by Berman and Peelle (1967) in the era before psycholinguistic modelling and computers entered aphasia therapy. The psycholinguistic model in fact only provides a better account of how this condition occurs, rather than itself providing original prescriptions for intervention. The explanation it provides is that insufficient activation was reaching the phonological output lexicon from the semantic

Table 11.1: Case studies of naming therapy

Authors	Subject	Age	Sex	Months post-onset	Type	Main psycho-linguistic target	Intervention type
Bruce & Howard (1987)	OLI	53	F	50	Broca	activation of phono-logical output lexicon	relay via computer
	LIN	42	F	41			
	MAA	39	F	19			
	DAV	57	M	9			
	PAB	47	M	17			
Bachy-Langedock & de Partz (1989)	SP	31	M	c7	deep dyslexic & oral anomia	phonological output lexicon or phonemic assembly	relay via written form
Marshall, et al. (1990)	RS	45	M	c10	anomia (verbs)	semantics to phonological output lexicon link	reactivation
	IS	76	F	c3	non-fluent anomia + apraxia	semantic?	
	FW	76	F	c5	anomia + apraxia	semantic	
Nettleton & Lesser (1991)	PD	55	M	6	fluent anomia	semantic	reactivation
	FF	68	M	36	Wer-nicke	semantic	
	DF	63	F	12	anomia	phonological output lexicon	
	MC	57	F	96	agram-matism	phonological output lexicon	
	MH	72	F	8	fluent	phonological assembly buffer	
	NC	74	F	36	fluent	phonological assembly buffer	

Intervention method	Experimental design	Total therapy time	Effectiveness	Generalization
naming pictures with computer generated phonological cues	B_u/B_T	5 sessions	$p < .05$	no
			$p < .05$	yes, on use of computer
			$p < .01$	yes
			$p < .01$	no
			'dramatic'	yes
construct mental image of written word	ABA	36 sessions	reduction from 48 to 16% errors	yes
match pictures to 1 of 5 written words	B_u/B_T	3 hours	$p < .01$	no
match written words to drawing or definition	cross-over	10 hours	$p < .02$	no
match picture to 1 of 4 written words	B_u/B_T	7 hours	$p < .02$	yes, non-specific
semantic therapy	ABA	16 sessions	$p < .05$	?
semantic therapy	ABA	16 sessions	not significant	
phonological therapy	ABA	16 sessions	$p < .03$	no
phonological therapy	ABA	16 sessions	$p < .01$	yes
semantic therapy	ABA	16 sessions	not significant	
semantic therapy	ABA	16 sessions	not significant	

system, although the latter was presumably intact and was able to generate an at least partial orthographic lexical output. Readers may wish at this point to refer back to the model in Chapter 4, see page 57. Provision of the initial sound, either by the computer, or, in the case of PAB, by the patient himself, was sufficient to provide the additional activation needed of the item in the phonological lexicon. Improvement was achieved over the short span of five sessions.

In the second study of application of a relay type of therapy for anomia, the therapy was again based on a common clinical observation, but again one which a psycholinguistic model helps to explain and justify as part of a coherent model of single-word processing. This is Bachy-Langedock and de Partz's (1989) study of SP, a 31 year old man who had recovered from a Wernicke's aphasia to a type more corresponding to conduction aphasia. His condition included deep dyslexia, and naming difficulties which were greater in the spoken medium than the written. We shall describe the therapists' treatment of his reading disorder later; here we discuss the improvement in oral naming which they effected.

This study took place over a much longer period than Bruce and Howard's (see Table 11.1), and, in respect of naming, was concerned entirely with the internalising of a cognitive relay strategy. SP had only 52 per cent success on naming 108 line-drawings, the majority of errors being 'no responses'. Assessment indicated no difficulty in the semantic system, at least in respect of the pictured and concrete stimuli used in the programme. Errors were most common on low frequency and multi-syllabic words. SP could occasionally write a word he could not orally name. For pictures SP failed to name, providing him with the first written syllable of the word achieved success in 83 per cent of cases. He was also shown to have good phonological lexical representations of mono-syllabic words. This was tested in several ways through the use of homophones and rhyming words. For example he was shown four pictures of objects and asked which two had names pronounced the same. In terms of the psycholinguistic model, SP's naming difficulty appeared to be in accessing the full phonological representations of multi-syllabic words, and/or accomplishing the phonemic assembly stage. He could achieve the first syllable correctly (in 63 per cent of bi-syllabic words and in 55 per cent of three- and four-syllabic words) but not the entire pattern, with his typical error being not to respond when asked to name a long word. When he made errors they were clearly phonemic rather than phonetic in nature; the 'phonemes were separately well realized with regard to their articulatory features, but their seriation was inadequate' (Bachy-Langedock and de Partz, 1989: 230). These errors did not occur in reading aloud. Reference to the model in Fig. 4.1 will show that this is consistent with the additional use of orthographic input into the phonological output lexicon and phonological output buffer in order to achieve phonological output. It should be possible to distinguish whether the additional orthographic influence was on the phonological output lexicon or on the buffer, by examining the effect of regularity of spelling. An influence of reading restricted to regular words would suggest it occurred directly on the buffer. The researchers, however, did not provide data to clarify this point.

The implication to be drawn from the observation that reading of multi-syllabic picture names was superior to their oral naming is that a therapeutic 'relay' strategy would be appropriate. The relay therapy the therapists employed for SP was to get the patient to construct a mental image of the word in its written form (using the orthographic lexicon), decode the word as if reading it, rehearse the word sub-vocally and then pronounce it aloud. This capitalized on the assistance that the additional orthographic information gives to phonemic assembly, and allowed for rehearsal before the sequence was committed to an utterance.

A simple experimental design was used to evaluate effectiveness of therapy in the case of SP. It consisted only of test-retest changes on a control set of words (which included no words used in the treatment programme). The measure was therefore of generalization of the relay strategy in naming (assuming that this was indeed what the patient was applying) rather than of drill on the targeted words. The changes were a reduction in naming errors from 48 to 16 per cent after 36 sessions, with a further reduction to 11 per cent after another 36 sessions. Gains continued until a year after the initial assessment, by which time naming was almost normal (6 per cent errors), as was word-finding in spontaneous speech. Although the naming programme was not initiated until about seven months after SP's cerebral haemorrhage, and therefore after the maximum period of spontaneous recovery, the design of this intervention does not exclude the possibility that the improvement was achieved by supportive contact with concerned therapists rather than the therapy programme itself. However, the fact that improvement was measured on non-drilled words suggests that the patient was indeed applying the cognitive relay strategy he had been taught in therapy.

REACTIVATION NAMING THERAPIES

Marshall, et al.'s (1990) study is an example of what can be classed as reactivation rather than relay therapy, and has a more elaborate experimental design. Since two of the three patients whom they studied may still have been at a stage where some spontaneous recovery might have accounted for improvement, control measures of other language tasks were used. The study is remarkable for the short duration of the therapy needed before gains in naming were achieved (from 3 to 10 hours) (see Table 11.1).

Marshall, et al.'s three cases were diagnosed in terms of the psycholinguistic model as having either semantic difficulties or impairment in the link from the semantic system to the phonological output lexicon. RS and IS could read words aloud which they could not produce as names for pictures, and which they had difficulty comprehending. This suggested that they could make use of the direct route from orthographic input lexicon to phonological output lexicon which by-passes the semantic system. In the case of IS this was confirmed by her difficulties in reading non-words, indicating that she could not read by orthographic-to-phonological conversion. For both patients it was concluded that their impairment was not in the phonological lexical representation itself, but was related to the semantic system. RS's semantic difficulty was limited to low-imagery words, and it was thought that his essential problem might lie in the link between the semantic system and the phonological output lexicon. Like IS the third case, FW, showed a more general semantic difficulty on comprehension tests.

Therapy was therefore aimed at enhancing semantic abilities, and consisted of matching pictures to written words amongst sets which were semantically related. For all these three cases success on naming of a list of treated words before and after therapy was compared with that on untreated words. RS was significantly better on treated than untreated words after about three hours of therapy over two weeks, and this effect lasted when he was retested a month after the conclusion of the therapy programme. This does indicate a specific effect of the therapy on the drilled words, as distinct from a general placebo effect or spontaneous recovery, which would have affected the untreated words as well. Lack of generalization, however, restricts the usefulness of such a programme, although Marshall and her colleagues note that there was some evidence of generalization to words which had been used as semantic foils. In the case of IS a cross-over design was used, with a group of words treated for two weeks and then a previously untreated group treated in turn. After treatment there were significant improvements on the treated lists but not on untreated items. There was also improvement on control tests of semantic comprehension which had been used (attributed by the researchers to spontaneous improvement of semantics), but not on control tasks of sentence comprehension and reading aloud. With FW (who also had a semantic disorder) the picture-word matching semantic therapy showed only a slight improvement on treated words at the end of three weeks (equivalent to about three and a half hours of therapy), but when this was continued for a further three weeks improvement on the treated and untreated lists was similar and the pooled results were significantly better than before therapy began.

Marshall, et al. also report the group results of a further study in which similar therapy was used with seven patients, who all had superior oral reading of names to picture naming. The therapy was given as a home package to supplement the group therapy they were also receiving. This study again showed a significant improvement in treated items, with maintenance of the improvement at reassessment about a month later. A follow-up study over a year later showed that treated pictures were still named better than their untreated controls (Pring, et al., 1990).

As with Bachy-Langedock and de Partz's study (1989), the interventions in Marshall et al.'s (1990) study were undertaken on patients admitted to clinics for 'routine' speech therapy for complex aphasias, and the interventions summarized above were only part of the therapists' involvement with the cases. Patients were also receiving therapy for other aspects of their disorder, together with supportive counselling both of themselves and their families. These studies therefore have a direct applicability to clinical practice, although, as Marshall, et al. note, theirs was designed in order to evaluate a method which might be used in therapy, rather than as an evaluation study of the therapy itself. The method they illustrate is, of course, the application of psycholinguistic modelling.

In the second study to be described in this section, the motivation was also to evaluate a method which is being used in therapy – in fact the adoption of 'semantic therapy' similar in principle to that described by Marshall and her colleagues, and to question how important it is to select patients identified as having semantic disorders. Howard, et al.'s (1985) group study of a comparison of semantic and phonological therapy for anomia has lead some therapists to an inference that semantic therapy may be the method of choice in *any* anomic aphasia. This in fact seems to have been the basis of Marshall, et al.'s choice of therapy, as they comment that Howard et al.'s 'results suggest that tasks which require access to the semantic system may benefit subsequent naming. By comparison phonological cues that may be assumed to operate by activating entries in the phonological output lexicon appear to have immediate but little lasting benefit' (1990: 173). Nettleton and Lesser (1991) questioned whether 'semantic therapy' is appropriate for all patients with anomia, and proposed that patients with naming difficulties should be selected on the basis of their more exactly specified psycholinguistic naming dysfunctions.

Six cases were studied (see Table 11.1) whose naming abilities on the Boston Naming Test ranged from 10 to 42 per cent. Like the patients already discussed in this and the last section, they all made more than 50 per cent errors of a naming task, and would be characterized as having severe naming difficulties as a predominant feature of their aphasia. In PD and FF this naming disorder was accompanied by comprehension errors on a semantic test of word-picture matching from PALPA, by greater facilitation of naming by semantic than phonemic cuing, by a predominance of semantic paraphasias in naming errors, and by acceptance of cued semantic associates of a target word as the target word itself. The naming disorder of these two patients was therefore diagnosed as having a significant semantic component, and as appropriate for a programme of semantic therapy. DF and

MC in contrast had good comprehension on the PALPA semantic test, produced predominantly anomic circumlocutions when failing to name, were not assisted by semantic cuing on the Boston Naming Test, rejected cued semantic associates and repeated heard words relatively well. They were diagnosed as having a disorder related to the phonological output lexicon, rather than to the semantic system, and considered appropriate for a programme of lexical-phonological therapy. MH and NC also had good scores on the PALPA semantic test, were not helped by semantic cues and rejected cued semantic associates. In these cases, however, the errors were predominantly phonemic paraphasias, and the patients' repetition percentiles on the BDAE were below their auditory comprehension percentiles. On the psycholinguistic model, therefore, they appeared to have a deficit concerning the phonological assembly buffer. To test the claim that semantic therapy might be of general benefit for anomic patients, they were given semantic therapy, like PD and FF, although this was inappropriate to the psycholinguistic diagnosis.

Semantic therapy consisted of word-picture matching amongst semantic associates, semantic judgements and category sorting. It did not include any actual practice in naming by the patient, since the psycholinguistic model would predict that this should not be necessary in order to effect improved naming. Phonological therapy consisted of name repetition, rhyme judgements using pictures and naming with phonemic cuing. The experimental design involved both an extended baseline of eight measures of naming ability before treatment compared with eight measures of untreated words during the therapy phase (as a measure of generalization) and a direct comparison of naming of treated words at two points before therapy, after therapy and after a maintenance period without therapy. The amount of time spent on therapy for each patient was 16 hour-long sessions, although some of this was used on supportive counselling.

In the outcome, after a stable baseline before treatment, phonological therapy for the two patients for whom the model had predicted it would be appropriate resulted in significantly better naming of the treated words. One of them, MC, also showed some evidence of generalization to untreated words. Of the two cases where semantic therapy had been considered appropriate it resulted in statistically significantly improved naming only in one, PD. There were signs, however, of qualitative changes in the other patient, FF, in that he produced fewer semantic paraphasias and these were rated by independent judges as closer to the target. The significant improvement in PD, it should be noted, was achieved through a programme of therapy which did not itself involve the patient in the production of names – a result consistent with the supramodal nature of the semantic system attributed by the psycholinguistic model. For the two patients for whom semantic therapy had not been considered appropriate, MH and NC, the predicted lack of a significant improvement was found. As the authors note, stronger evidence of this being due to the inappropriacy of the therapy itself would have been obtained had these patients then been demonstrated to improve following appropriate therapy.

The results of Nettleton and Lesser's study broadly support the utility of applying a psycholinguistic model in the diagnosis of a patient's disorder, although firm conclusions cannot be drawn from such a limited study with some equivocal findings. In as much as its tentative findings are sound, it does question Caramazza's statement that 'Perhaps, though not auspiciously, *any* detailed analysis would do as well' as an analysis guided by cognitive (psycholinguistic) theory (1989: 395). If a detailed analysis such as that provided by a standard clinical test (e.g. the Boston Diagnostic Aphasia Examination) is what Caramazza considers to be the alternative, all the studies in our last two sections indicate that the information obtained from such a test (e.g. 'below the 50th percentile for naming') would not be sufficient to guide therapy.

THERAPY FOR AUDITORY COMPREHENSION

We now move to a consideration of the application of psycholin-guistic theory to therapy for another modality of impairment, auditory comprehension. Despite the precision with which disorders of auditory lexical comprehension have been identified in a psycholinguistic model (Franklin, 1989), there are few studies which have specifically examined the effectiveness of applying such a model to therapy for these disorders. Indeed it is notable that no implications for therapy were drawn from a meticulous mapping by two therapists of the dysfunctions of a patient with significant auditory comprehension impairment onto a single-word processing model (Howard and Franklin, 1989). Moreover, the unspecified therapy given to their patient is reported by these two authors as not having been effective. Some of the studies in our previous section have, of course, concerned people with semantic disorders which necessarily affect auditory comprehension as well as other linguistic modalities, but the focus of therapy in these studies has been on improving naming rather than comprehension.

One reason for the present dearth of psycholinguistic case studies of amelioration of auditory comprehension disorders is that such patients tend to divide themselves into two categories. Auditory comprehension disorders are more prominent immediately after the onset of aphasia, and in many patients appear to resolve spontaneously. Direct intervention in respect of comprehension may therefore not be considered appropriate, or, if it is, presents particular problems of evaluation during spontaneous recovery. In the other group of patients with lasting comprehension impairment, the condition is one which is classically thought to be intransigent, as in global aphasia, word-deafness or persistent jargonaphasia. Word-deaf patients may be best helped through lip-reading (a prosthetic strategy), rather than direct therapy on their dysfunction. For jargonaphasic patients also in whom the disorder persists, Martin (1981) suggests that the appropriate intervention may be more through improving the family's understanding, than through direct therapy with the patient. For patients with auditory comprehension difficulties such as these, therefore, the applications made of the analysis of the disorder fall under our heading of pragmatics rather than psycholinguistics (see Chapter 12).

Nevertheless there is a body of lore, first formalized by Luria (1963), as to how acoustic-agnostic or 'sensory' aphasia might be treated at a phonemic and lexical level, the presumption here being (in terms of the psycholinguistic model that we have used) that the patient's deficit lies in auditory phonological analysis. This principle has been applied in a clinically (rather than psycholinguistically) based programme aimed at ameliorating comprehension disorders secondary to impaired phonemic discrimination (the Sentence Level Auditory Comprehension programme of Naeser, et al., 1986). Gielewski (1989) also describes such a programme of work on phonemic discrimination using sets of minimal pairs and rhyming words. The 45 year old woman who was treated in this way improved over a period of three and a half months, but the programme had been initiated within six weeks of her stroke, and attribution of the improvement only to the therapy is therefore questionable. Mitchum and Berndt (1991) describe a programme of training in word segmentation into phonemes undertaken by an aphasic college professor with impaired comprehension. As the prime aim of this programme, however, was to improve reading, it will be described in a later section.

An early application of a psycholinguistic model to therapy for a patient with a severe disorder of auditory comprehension is that of Clark (1979) (see Table 11.2). In this case the model was Marslen-Wilson and Welsh's (1978) model of lexical access in comprehension, in which contextual constraints from the sentence interact with the auditory analysis to effect word recogni-

Table 11.2: Case studies of therapy for auditory comprehension

Authors	Subject	Age	Sex	Months post-onset	Type	Main psycho-linguistic target	Intervention type
Clark (1979)	un-named	67	M	35	trans-cortical sensory	'lexical activation'	reactivation
Byng & Coltheart (1986) – see also Byng (1988)	BRB	46	M	60	Broca	mapping of syntax on to semantics	relay
	BRB	46	M	65	Broca	semantics of abstract words	reactivation
Behrmann & Lieberthal (1989)	CH	57	M	3+	global	semantic represent-ations (categorical)	reactivation

tion. This intervention study of a 67 year old man, with severe comprehension problems nearly three years after a stroke, was conducted as a test of this model through the changes that occurred with therapy. Seventy-two hours of therapy were devoted to practice in selecting appropriate words to fill sentence gaps, with the gap varying in location and in the lexical category of the appropriate filler. Distractor choices were given of semantically congruent or anomalous words, or of phonemically similar or dissimilar non-words.

In this study the patient's auditory discrimination of words was not facilitated by semantically anomalous contexts (as in 'I pay the —— soap'), but it was by semantically related words in an appropriate sentential context (as in 'The —— melted the snow' facilitating the selection of 'sun' from a choice of non-words or semantically related words). Moreover, although non-words which were grossly dissimilar phonemically to the target

Intervention method	Experimental design	Total therapy time	Effectiveness	Generalization
choosing words for gaps	ABA	72 hours	60 to 85% improvement on words in sentences	52.5% improvement on single words. 36.7% on commands
colour coded cues to re-learning reversible locative sentences	cross-over	2 weeks	Increase from 60 to 100%	yes, from comprehension of active to passive sentences
synonym generation	cross-over	4 weeks	Increase from 16 to 94%	
learning super-ordinates & category subordinates	B_u/B_T	15 hours	Increase from 10 or 40% to 95 or 100% depending on category	yes, within categories no, to untreated categories

words interfered with lexical access, the sentence context overrode this effect when the non-words were phonemically close. Clark concludes that this provides support for the Marslen-Wilson and Welsh model. The patient's performance improved over four months of this reactivation therapy; comprehension of sentence-final nouns improved by up to 85 per cent, of sentence-initial nouns by 60 per cent and of sentence-medial prepositions by 80 per cent. Tests of generalization to recognition of single words and commands also showed improvement (52.5 and 36.7 per cent respectively).

We include in this section a study of therapy aimed at restoration of semantic representations, although this necessarily does not only implicate auditory comprehension. Behrmann and Lieberthal's (1989) patient, CH, was an engineering graduate whose stroke left him with global aphasia and unintelligible speech described as 'babbling'. A psycholinguistic examination indicated a supra-modal disorder of semantic representations. There was some evidence that gross distinctions of meaning could still be made. CH's comprehension of six categories was assessed (animals, colours, transport, food, body parts and furniture). Animals were sorted into their appropriate category more accurately than any other group (79 per cent compared to from 30 to 9 per cent for the others). Therapy was directed at improving comprehension of three categories (transport, body parts and furniture), with words in each category divided into treated and non-treated sets. Over a period of six weeks, 15 hours of therapy were directed at teaching first the general features of the categories and then the specific identification of its members. The programme was backed up by home assignments. There was a significant improvement on all treated sets, with within-category generalization to untreated words for two of them (transport and body parts) but not from treated to untreated words within the furniture category. There was no generaliza-tion, however, to two of the categories which had not been treated (animals, colours) although food words were classified significantly better. A test of sentence comprehension which had been used as a control measure showed, as predicted, no change. This supported the claim that the improvements noted could be attributed to the reactivation (the researchers call it 'reinstate-ment') therapy targeted at improving semantic representations. This study, like that of Seron, et al. (1979) described at the beginning of our account of naming therapies, provides further psycholinguistic support for the categorical organization of semantics.

The final study we shall describe in this section shows considerable progress in achieving a synthesis between theory and therapy, and in evaluating intervention through a more robust design. It is a well-controlled study applying both an aspect of the lexical psycholinguistic model we described in Chapter 4 and the model of sentence processing we described in Chapter 5. Byng and Coltheart's (1986) patient, BRB, was diagnosed as having both a limited lexical disorder which affected his comprehension of abstract words and a deficit in mapping syntactic constituents onto thematic roles in sentence comprehension, which affected his understanding of plausibly reversible sentences. The latter was deduced from a comparison of his intact ability to judge syntactic illegalities in sentences (confirming adequate parsing ability) but difficulty comprehending single verbs, as tested through matching them to videotaped scenes in which words such as *buy* and *sell* or *come* and *go* were contrasted. Lexical retrieval for the type of words used in the sentences was intact.

This study used a cross-over design in which the mapping deficit was treated first, followed by the deficit in comprehension of abstract words. Therapy for the first focused on reversible locative sentences, such as 'The pan is in the jug' and used colour-coded clues which were faded out, in order to develop a cognitive relay strategy. Therapy for the second comprised picture-word matching and assignments to look up words and their definitions in a dictionary. This kind of re-learning is presumably aimed at reactivation of old knowledge. Both procedures were designed so that BRB could undertake the work at home, with only weekly contact with the therapist. Two weeks of therapy on locative sentences were sufficient to effect a significant improvement on sentence comprehension which generalized to comprehension of passive sentences (improvement from 60 per cent on the sentence test to 100 per cent). This was followed by the second period of therapy, aimed this time at improving comprehension of abstract words. Four weeks on this was sufficient to effect an improvement from 16 to 94 per cent on the abstract words, even though these had shown no benefit from the first period of mapping therapy in which they had not been targeted. There was, therefore, justification in the claim that it was the intervention programme which had achieved the changes in this patient who was five years post-onset of aphasia. The results were also consistent with the proposed distinctions made in the models between relative independence of abstract and concrete semantics, and lexical, parsing and mapping procedures in sentence comprehension.

THERAPY FOR SENTENCE PRODUCTION

Byng and Coltheart's programme, being addressed to central syntactic-semantic aspects of comprehension, would be expected to effect improvement in sentence production as well as comprehension, in a similar way to the effect of semantic therapy (conducted without speech from the patient) on spoken naming that we described earlier in this chapter. Hatfield and Elvin (1978) used this approach explicitly in treating the sentence production difficulties of two agrammatic aphasics by means of comprehension exercises. Hatfield was a research speech therapist who pioneered the application of psycholinguistic modelling to aphasia therapy in Britain. We shall refer to her work again in the section on psycholinguistically based therapy for spelling disorders. The model of sentence production which she applied in the 1970s distinguished four stages:

A the idea
B the prelinguistic proposition, in which lexical content elements and accessory factors such as concepts of location in time and plurality were separable
C phonemic (or graphemic) realization
D production of the final sentence.

In Hatfield and Elvin's study the two agrammatic patients were diagnosed as having difficulty with word order in speech. One, for example, described how a dog had chased his grandson as 'Andrew . . . dog . . . chasing'. The other, wishing to convey that his football team (Chelsea) had lost, said 'Chelsea beaten Manchester'. This latter example could be deletion of passive *be* and agentive *by* rather than a word order problem. However, testing showed that the patients also had difficulty in understanding reversible sentences and sentences with locative prepositions, although they understood the meaning of locatives in isolation. Hatfield and Elvin had observed that one patient often substituted a noun for a preposition, for example *top* for *on*, thus demonstrating understanding of the preposition's meaning. Hatfield and Elvin interpreted these findings as indicating that the patients' difficulties did not lie in stages A or B. The intervention used was explicitly of a relay type in intent, that is making use of cognitive strategies as a substitute for automatic processing. The strategy both were employing spontaneously in comprehending reversible sentences was to take the first noun as agent. (This also supports the interpretation of 'Chelsea beaten Manchester' as a word order problem rather than deletion of the passive.) Their strategy succeeded with active sentences, when the subject was animate and had the thematic role of *agent*, but not with sentences in which the subject was inanimate and had the role of *instrument*. The difference between the thematic roles was taught in therapy, through comparison of such sentences as 'The man scratched the rock with a glass', 'The glass scratched the rock' and 'The rock was scratched by the glass'. The comprehension of sentences which included locatives was also enhanced by an emphasis on the semantic aspects of locative prepositions, drawing on the patients' retained understanding of locative relationships when these were presented in isolation.

Although this early study is not reported as using a formal experimental design, Hatfield and Elvin would appear to have used a cross-over design. Comprehension of sentences which did not include locatives was worked on first, with improvement in both patients, followed by work on locative sentences, in which further improvement was only shown in the younger (22 year old) man (see Table 11.3).

Diagnosis of the sentence production disorder at a different level was made in another pioneering report in 1982. Beauvois and Derouesné's patient AD, classed as having dynamic (transcortical motor) aphasia, was thought to have a difficulty at the most central level of speech production, the co-ordination of verbal thought, or the transformation of ideas to language (stage A in Hatfield and Elvin's model). His naming, comprehension and processing of function words and inflections were shown to be unimpaired, and he could arrange long sentences from single

Table 11.3: Case studies of therapy for sentence production

Authors	Subject	Age	Sex	Months post-onset	Type	Main psycho-linguistic target	Intervention type
Hatfield & Elvin (1978)	un-named	67	M	'a few years'	Broca	comprehension of reversible sentences and	relay
	un-named	22	M	'a few years'	Broca	comprehension of locative relations	reactivation
Beauvois & Derouesné (1982)	AD	62	M	18	trans-cortical motor	transformation of thought to language	relay
Jones (1986)	BB	47	M	72	Broca	access to mapping information needed for assignment of verb arguments	relay
Byng (1988)	JG (see also BRB in Table 11.2)	59	M	54	Broca	mapping, parsing and verb comprehension. Also short-term memory	relay

Intervention method	Experimental design	Total therapy time	Effectiveness	Generalization
understanding of thematic roles as Experiencer or Instrument; enhancement of semantics of locatives	cross-over	3 months (10 sessions)	20% sentence comprehension; n.s. on locatives	sentence comprehension generalized to speech
		3 months (5 sessions)	62%	comprehension of sentences & locatives generalized to speech
structuring ideas through answering questions on relationships between concepts; then self-generation of the questions	AB	2 months (30 sessions)	$p < .001$	yes, to speech
understanding of thematic roles	AB	6 months	sentence comprehension errors reduced from 48 to 23%	yes, to speech
(a) colour cues to comprehension of locative relations.	cross-over	(a) 6 weeks	n.s.	
(b) understanding of thematic roles		(b) 3 months (= 24 hours)	auditory sentence comprehension errors reduced from 28 to 13%. Verb errors reduced from 22 to 9%	yes, to speech (use of 2-argument structures, $p < .001$)

Table 11.3 continued

Authors	Subject	Age	Sex	Months post-onset	Type	Main psycho-linguistic target	Intervention type
Kohn, et al. (1990)	CM	74	M	9	con-duction	phono-logical assembly buffer	relay
Nickels, et al. (1991)	AR	68	M	36	Broca	as JG above, but better verb com-prehension	relay

words, and repeat long sentences. Yet his spontaneous speech was very limited. The intervention devised for him was aimed at getting him to structure his ideas before speech; he was given two words, and made to answer questions about the relation-ships between the concepts expressed by these words. This was a strategy which he eventually learned to use on his own without help from the therapist – a cognitive relay strategy. After two months of the programme, he improved significantly on the ability to put his thoughts into long and correctly structured sentences.

The kind of disorders in comprehending reversible sentences shown by Hatfield and Elvin's patients have been reinterpreted by later investigators as 'mapping' deficits, in terms of Schwartz's (1987) model described in Chapter 5. In other words these patients may be unable to co-ordinate descriptions of sentence form (achieved through syntactic parsing) and sentence meaning through relating verb arguments to their thematic roles. As we saw in the previous section this would be expected to affect both

Intervention method	Experimental design	Total therapy time	Effectiveness	Generalization
sentence repetition directed at fluency not accuracy	AB	2 months (= 10 hours)	n.s. on sentences, p < .01 on content words, p < .03 on multi-syllabic words	
(a) colour cued comprehension of agent/theme roles	cross-over	(a) 6 weeks (= 18 hours)	p = .06	no generalization to other thematic roles
(b) sentence construction in speech, using personal names		(b) 8 weeks (= 24 hours)	p < .001 on 2-argument structures	

sentence comprehension and sentence production. Jones (1986) therefore employed therapy aimed at improving comprehension of thematic roles with the specific intent of improving an agrammatic patient's speech, which had failed to respond to therapy during the six years following a stroke. BB was able to parse sentences into phrases, but conversely had difficulty in re-assembling sentences which he had previously divided at phrase boundaries, for example *John/ paid/ £2/ for a new spanner*. In a therapy programme which lasted about six months, BB was taught to identify which was the verb in a sentence, and then gradually to recognize thematic roles identified as answering *who, what, where, when, why* and *how* questions about relationships in the sentence. Eventually he was asked to identify these roles in sentences with embedding or subordination. A substantial improvement in both elicited speech and spontaneous use of spoken language followed, although at this stage no formal work on encouraging speech production had been undertaken.

Le Dorze, et al. (1991) have partially replicated Jones'

programme with a more severely impaired aphasic man. In addition to limited speech, severe word-finding difficulties and some articulatory impairment, MG had poor reading, both for comprehension and reading aloud. His naming of verbs was also worse than Jones' patient BB. The therapy was therefore modified from Jones' programme, although maintaining the same principle of working on comprehension to improve production. Since written materials could not be used, pictorial sentences (sequences of pictures) were employed to accompany drawings of scenes. Given an auditory sentence, MG had to identify the verb in the first part of the therapy programme, then the actor in phase two, then the patient/theme, and then the prepositional phase. In the final fifth phase he was asked to identify and correct pictorial sentences with a missing element. After a month his spoken descriptions of the pictures showed significant improvement in the number of verbs and noun-verb combinations produced. There was also generalization to ten sentences which had not been treated. Reading comprehension, the control measure which had not been treated, did not improve. This replication endorses the effectiveness of this type of therapy, in a patient 14 months post-onset and therefore beyond the period of 'spontaneous recovery'. It shows that the improvement was not simply due to the placebo effect of supportive interest, as it was specific to the treated task. That it was not specific to the drilled items themselves, but generalized across the task, also shows that a general reorganization took place or that a relay strategy was learned, making the therapy functionally useful.

Like Jones' patient and Le Dorze, et al.'s patient, Byng and Coltheart's case (BRB) improved significantly in speech after a programme of mapping comprehension therapy, as described in the last section. In order to test the reliability of such a diagnosis with associated therapy, Byng (1988) reports a study of another patient, JG, for comparison with BRB. Use of similar diagnostic measures suggested that JG not only had a similar mapping deficit, but also additional difficulties with parsing, verb production and with short-term memory. JG also appeared to have non-linguistic conceptual difficulties, too, shown in inability to sort pictures into those which showed actions and those which did not. JG proved unable to cope with the therapy programme using colour coding for locative relations, which had been effective with BRB, and instead a programme targeted at improving perception of agent and theme roles in sentences was devised for him. Testing after three months showed significant improvement on verb comprehension, and non-locative sentence comprehension. There was, however, no significant improvement on reversible locative sentences. Although these had not been the subject of therapy, the mapping hypothesis would have predicted generalization of improvement to all types of reversible sentences. As Byng points out this is a difficult result for the mapping theory to account for, and she stresses the need for further studies of this kind. There was, however, an improvement in JG's speech, as the hypothesis that his difficulties lay in mapping would claim. A higher proportion of words were produced in sentences (although still classed as ill-formed due to omission of function words), with an increase in number of words per sentence and in the number of constructions in which a verb plus two arguments were realized. There was generalization of the therapy also to improved single-word comprehension of both concrete and abstract words.

A replication of the approach used with JG has been undertaken by Nickels, et al. (1991) on a patient with a similar psycholinguistic diagnosis. AR had better comprehension of single verbs than JG, and colour cued sentence comprehension tasks were used with him first. This study addressed both the comprehension and production of sentences. Using a cross-over design, it began with six weeks of a programme aimed at comprehension of reversible sentences, followed by two months of a production programme, with testing before and after each type of therapy. Again a limited set of thematic roles was used, that is agent and theme. The therapy proved successful in that at the end of the three and a half months AR was producing significantly more verb-plus-2-argument structures, and was bordering on significance (p = 0.06) on improvement of comprehension of agent-theme reversible sentences. There was no generalization to other types of thematic roles in comprehension, however, nor did comprehension improve significantly by the end of the first six-week therapy programme. Since baseline measures (of lexical decision, non-word repetition, etc.) did not change over the period, the improvement found in sentence production can safely be attributed to the specific effects of the therapy. Like JG. AR was well past what is considered to be the significant period for spontaneous recovery. Nickels and her colleagues point out that the specificity of AR's improvement to the thematic roles used in the programme has implications for psycholinguistic theory; mapping procedures may be differentiated in terms of the thematic roles that are to be mapped onto other representations:

> the assignment of thematic roles to phrases proceeds partly by reference to lexical information and partly by means of general procedures. For pairs of thematic roles such as Agent/Theme, the mapping can be done by a general procedure which maps Agent onto the Subject, and the Theme onto the Object.

> (Nickels, et al., 1991)

The final paper we shall discuss in this section addresses a different kind of problem in sentence production. Kohn, et al.'s (1990) case, CM, had dysfluent speech which comprised a large number of *conduite d'approche* phonemic paraphasias. His frequent attempts to correct his paraphasias resulted in the production of numerous word fragments and extraneous syllables, giving his speech a stuttering-like quality. His comprehension, reading and writing were relatively preserved and Kohn (1989) diagnosed his difficulty in terms of a psycholinguistic model of single word processes as at the 'phonemic string' stage (phonemic assembly buffer) of word production. Kohn suggests that his 'phonemic perseverations (both anticipatory and perseveratory copies) could be conceived of as a deficit in clearing information from a buffer that is used for constructing phonemic strings (a planning phrase at a time)' (1989: 235). In this case the therapy devised rested not only on the analysis of the psycholinguistic deficit, but on the clinical observation that phonemic paraphasias were fewer when CM was asked to repeat sentences than in spontaneous speech. (This finding is difficult to accommodate in a psycholinguistic model which is restricted to single word processing, like the one illustrated in Fig. 4.1.) For this patient, a two-month programme was instigated which consisted of sentence repetition, using increasingly longer and more demanding sentences (more words, more syllables, greater semantic content), with an emphasis on fluency rather than phonemic accuracy. A baseline of picture description repeated before therapy indicated that his performance was stable; after therapy his picture description had improved in that fewer syllables were produced per concept conveyed. Although the overall change in number of sentences repeated correctly after the therapy period was not significant, there was significant improvement on the number of content words produced and on the number of multi-syllabic words uttered fluently. There was also a reported, but not quantified, improvement on spontaneous speech at home. This therapy again seems to have used a cognitive relay process in that a malfunctioning automatic process was brought under cognitive control. The fact that this generalized from the repetition procedure, where he had the external help of the therapist, to picture description, where he lacked this, indicates some internalization of the strategy. An alternative behaviourist interpretation of the change would be that an acquired stuttering-like habit of speech was masking the recovery which had taken place, and that the therapy rewarded him for fluency. With such an interpretation this would be a 'revelatory' therapy (see Chapter 2, p. 17) rather than a cognitive relay therapy. This patient's disorder has some resemblances to the condition described clinically as 'acquired stuttering' (reviewed by Helm, et al. 1978). Future psycholinguistic analyses and evaluations of intervention may help to clarify the nature of this disorder.

READING THERAPY FOR PHONOLOGICAL AND DEEP DYSLEXIA

The pioneering report of Beauvois and Derouesné (1982) on the application of cognitive neuropsychological modelling to aphasia, which we have already referred to in the context of sentence production disorders, includes two case studies of therapy for different types of acquired reading disorders. One concerns a case of pure alexia, and interprets the disorder as due to visuo-verbal interference. Although it provides an excellent illustration of the relay method of therapy, we will not discuss it here, since it goes beyond the psycholinguistic models we have outlined. The other is a case of phonological dyslexia, the symptom-complex in which sublexical orthographic to phonological conversion is impaired, making it difficult to read novel words or non-words. It is distinguished from deep dyslexia by the absence of semantic paralexias, although in both types reading of free grammatical morphemes with low semantic content is impaired. This was the case with RG, making the reading of sentences particularly difficult. Moreover, he made more errors in sentence contexts on grammatical words with a high semantic content (such as prepositions) than he did in reading them in isolation.

This may therefore have been due to a trade-off between lexical-semantic and syntactic processing such as we described in Chapter 5.

The rehabilitation strategy devised for RG was to inhibit his tendency to read texts rapidly for meaning without retaining lexical and syntactic information for attention (as normal readers do). Instead he was instructed to read texts word by word. Again this was a cognitive strategy, although in this case the process to be controlled was a normal one, with the substitution of an abnormal behaviour better adapted to drawing his attention to single words with which he could cope. At the end of one month of practice in this word-by-word technique RG's reading of all words, including grammatical words and inflected verbs, in texts had improved significantly, although remaining unchanged when words were read in isolation (see Table 11.4). The improvement could therefore have been due to allowing more computational time for sentence processing. As Beauvois and Derouesné note, this result indicates that the change could be attributed specifically to the strategy induced by the programme rather than to an improvement in the capacity to read these categories of words as such.

There are reports of intervention also in two cases of the more severe symptom-complex of deep dyslexia, patients SP (de Partz,1986; Bachy-Langedock and de Partz, 1989) and LP (Mitchum and Berndt, 1991). Deep dyslexia compounds the features of phonological dyslexia with semantic difficulties. In SP, for example, 42 per cent of his errors in reading aloud were nil responses, and 12 per cent semantic paralexias. His reading difficulty was severe, with an error rate of 72 per cent on the total reading battery used. He made errors in matching letters cross-case and in reading them aloud, and appeared unable to perform any sub-lexical or grapheme-phoneme conversion, such as contributes to the ability to read non-words. The therapy strategy was aimed at using the patient's better preserved lexical knowledge to relearn grapheme-phoneme links – a cognitive relay strategy again. It started with simple associations of letters with family names and common words (as in a child's first alphabet book, although the words were chosen by the patient as of personal relevance to him). The next stages were to identify the letters with the first phonemes of these words, and then to blend singly pronounced letters into the pronunciation of monosyllabic non-words. Complex graphemes were then associated with words as mnemonic relays to their pronunciation, for example AU with 'eau' (water). At this stage the percentage of errors made by the patient had been reduced from 72 to 14 per cent, with the predominant error type now being in misapplication of grapheme-phoneme conversion, showing that the patient was indeed using the taught strategy. The consequent teaching of context-sensitive grapheme-phoneme conversion rules (e.g. that S is pronounced as /z/ when between two vowels) reduced his reading errors to 2 per cent. This was a long rehabilitation programme, spread over 18 months. Although it was initiated at three months past the patient's cerebral haemorrhage, within the possible period of some spontaneous recovery, the later improvements were so substantial as probably to be due to the intervention programme, despite the fact that control measures were not incorporated. The dovetailing of this reading therapy with naming therapy (as described in our earlier section) is reported in Bachy-Langedock and de Partz (1989).

Mitchum and Berndt's (1991) deep dyslexic patient was more handicapped than de Partz's, although her premorbid occupation as a university professor and writer suggested a former high level of literacy. Thirteen years after a stroke she remained agrammatic and anomic with impaired comprehension. Unlike SP her auditory analysis and segmentation abilities appeared to be impaired, and Mitchum and Berndt examined the effect that this had on her ability to read aloud. Their first therapy programme, which consisted of training in segmentation, showed that LR could segment phonemes from whole words, but had a reduced ability to retain a series of segmented phonemes in order to reproduce them as a phonological pattern. The assessment of segmentation abilities prior to therapy had the unanticipated effect of improving letter-sounding from 75 to 100 per cent, suggesting a rapid learning of the distinction once it was demonstrated through the assessment. However, a cognitive relay programme of re-teaching grapheme-phoneme correspondences (letter sounds) in words, based on that used with SP and lasting 22 sessions, resulted in no improvement on non-word reading. This was attributed to LR's difficulties in short-term storage of the phonological patterns. There was some benefit, nevertheless, from the improved knowledge of letter sounds; this reduced the number of semantic paralexias, as the patient could

Table 11.4: Case studies of reading therapy

Authors	Subject	Age	Sex	Months post-onset	Type	Main psycho-linguistic target	Intervention type
Beauvois and Derouesné (1982)	RG	not stated	M	not stated	phono-logical dyslexia	grapheme-phoneme conversion; grammatical morphemes	relay (cognitive control)
Byng & Coltheart (1988) – see also Coltheart & Byng (1989)	EE	40	M	9	surface dyslexia + anomia	orthographic input lexicon	relay
de Partz (1986) – see also Bachy-Langedock & de Partz (1989)	SP	31	M	3–18	deep dyslexia	grapheme-phoneme conversion; grammatical morphemes	relay
Scott & Byng (1989)	JB	24	F	8	surface dyslexia anomia & surface dys-graphia; fluent	link from orthographic input lexicon to semantics & from semantics to orthographic output lexicon	reactivation
Mitchum and Berndt (1991)	LR	63	F	156	deep dyslexia & anomia; non-fluent	grapheme-phoneme conversion. letter sounding; access to abstract & low frequency words	relay

Intervention method	Experimental design	Total therapy time	Effectiveness	Generalization
reading word by word	AB	one month	$p < .05$ on grammatical morphemes in sentence reading	not generalized to grammatical morphemes presented in isolation
mnemonics (pictures)	cross-over B_u/B_T	6 weeks (plus)	$p < .001$	yes
(a) mnemonics (place names)	AB	(a) 9 months	reduction in errors from 72 to 14%	
(b) learning rules of grapheme pronunciation		(b) 65 sessions	reduction in errors from 14 to 2%	
computer-aided practice on homophones, using multiple choice	B_u/B_T	10 weeks	$p < .05$	yes, to untreated homophones; no, to irregular words; no, to spelling
(a) auditory analysis of spoken words	AB	(a) 8 sessions	$p < .001$ on letter sounding *prior* to therapy	reduction in semantic paralexias
(b) learning rules of grapheme pronunciation		(b) 22 sessions	n.s. on non-word reading	

check that their initial letters did not correspond to those of the target pronunciation. As the authors note, the negative findings of therapy studies can be informative; in this case they suggest that the psycholinguistic model needs to be revised so as to reflect the importance of short-term storage of the phonological output during grapheme-phoneme conversion.

READING THERAPY FOR SURFACE DYSLEXIA

The remaining two cases we describe had a different kind of reading disorder, characterized as surface dyslexia. In EE (Byng and Coltheart, 1986; Coltheart and Byng, 1989) the surface dyslexia was of the type where heterographic homophones are misread as having the wrong meaning. It was therefore concluded that his impairment could be attributed to damage affecting visual word recognition (the orthographic input lexicon or its link with the semantic system). From this, therapy aimed at reinforcing visual word recognition would seem to be indicated. This was implemented through use of mnemonic aids for words, that is cards associating the printed word with a picture showing the meaning of the word – again a cognitive strategy, using the picture as a relay to word recognition. This was done in a sequence of three programmes for different types of words: the phonographemically anomalous -OUGH words such as *through, cough, enough*, high frequency and low frequency words. With all of these, relatively short periods of therapy effected significant improvements on treated words. There was significant improvement also on untreated words, although a stable baseline for these had previously been demonstrated. As we noted in Chapter 10, Coltheart and Byng comment that such unexpected results of generalization from a therapy designed to provide relay mnemonics for specific words gives support to a model of distributed representation of processing rather than item specific models. This provides another example of feedback to psycholinguistic theory from the results of controlled studies of intervention. It also suggests that a therapy intended to develop a cognitive relay proved in fact to be a reactivation one.

The young head-injured nurse, JB, studied by Scott and Byng (1989) also had a surface dyslexia of a similar type, together with anomia and a surface dysgraphia. She too misdefined homophones, and the psycholinguistic examination suggested that the links between both the orthographic input lexicon and the semantic system on the one hand and between the semantic system and the orthographic output lexicon on the other were impaired. Therapy was directed at re-establishing (re-activating) the input-semantic link for a set of 135 homophone pairs. Half of these pairs were treated through a computer program, Homotrain. In this case the computer was used not as a prosthesis but as a teaching device. The program displayed a written sentence with a gap, together with a choice of six numbered words. These comprised the two homophones with visual and pseudo-homophone distractors. The computer gave immediate feedback to JB on her success, and cued the correct word for any errors. JB also had to type in the correct word before the program proceeded. Post-therapy testing on a number of measures showed that there was significant improvement, in respect of the treated homophones, on measures which required judgement of the correct homophone for a sentence, and production and recognition of definitions of homophones. There was also significant improvement on the untreated lists for all except recognition of definitions. The generalization, however, did not extend to writing homophones to dictation or to the spelling of irregular words. The improvement was therefore specific to tasks which involved the orthographic input – semantic link, as predicted. Again, as in Coltheart and Byng's study, this was shown to be not item-specific but distributed (as evidenced by the generalization to untreated homophones). The minimum amount of spelling practice in Homotrain did not have a significant influence on JB's surface dysgraphia, though, as we see in the next section, programmes specifically aimed at this have proved effective. The lack of generalization from reading to spelling is also consistent with the psycholinguistic model on which the remediation for JB was based.

THERAPY FOR SPELLING DISORDERS

Hatfield's 1982 paper describes therapy for four aphasic patients' writing disorders, three of them characterized as deep dysgraphic, one as surface dysgraphic. In Table 11.5 we have summarized the

Table 11.5: Case studies of writing (spelling) therapy

Authors	Subject	Age	Sex	Months post-onset	Type	Main psycho-linguistic target	Intervention type
Hatfield (1982) – see also Hatfield & Patterson (1984)	BB	43	M	24	deep dys-graphia, deep dyslexia, Broca's	grammatical morphemes	relay
	TP	51	F	18	surface dys-graphia, anomia, fluent	semantic to orthographic output link & depen-dency on impaired phoneme-grapheme conversion	relay
Behrmann (1987)	CCM	54	F	10	surface dys-graphia, conduc-tion aphasia	semantic to orthographic output lexicon link	relay
Carlomagno & Parlato (1989)	Un-named	60	M	12	severe dys-graphia, surface dyslexia, fluent	lexical and sublexical routes	relay

findings on one of the deep dysgraphic patients, BB, who was also the subject of Jones's study of sentence production reported above. Hatfield's interpretation of BB's writing disorder at this stage (two years post stroke) was that the impaired phonological-grapheme routine leads to a dependence on semantic information and on visuo-spatial patterns of word forms in writing (Hatfield, 1985). The therapy she devised was directed at BB's particular difficulties with free grammatical morphemes. The emphasis was on creating cognitive relay links between the grammatical words and homophones with more semantic and imageable content, as

Intervention method	Experimental design	Total therapy time	Effectiveness	Generalization
mnemonics for grammatical morphemes (content words)	AB	Not stated	improved from 34 to 63.5%	
learning phoneme-grapheme rules; mnemonics for homophones	AB	5 sessions	improved from 60 to 80% 55 to 85% on words applying spelling rules	
mnemonics (pictures)	multi-baseline B_u/B_T	6 sessions	$p < .01$	no, to untreated homophones; yes, to untreated irregular words
(a) auditory analysis into syllables (b) syllable linked with proper name	AB	40 sessions	$p < .001$	yes, to non-word reading

in linking *in* with *inn*. After an unstated period of therapy, conducted twice a week, BB's ability to write to dictation a set of 18 prepositions, auxiliaries and pronouns improved from 34 per cent to 63.5 per cent. No therapeutic implications were drawn from BB's use of visuo-spatial patterns in reproducing words.

For the surface dysgraphic patient in Hatfield's study, TP, the analysis indicated not only an impaired semantic-to-orthographic-output routine but also some impairment of the phoneme-grapheme conversion rules on which surface dysgraphic patients typically depend. Therapy therefore incorporated reteaching of some of these rules – rules such as consonant doubling (*rub /rubbing*) and the dropping of final E before an affix (*love /lovable*) – in order to strengthen the routine on which the patient principally relied. Other therapy was aimed at strengthening the deficient semantic-to-orthographic link, by using cognitive relay mnemonics. TP was shown how alternative spellings for vowel phonemes can be recalled through association with meaning, for example the AI spelling for /ei/ in the words in 'The rain in Spain falls mainly on the plain'. After five sessions of therapy a change had been effected in both these areas (see Table 11.5).

In Behrmann's (1987) case of surface dysgraphia, CCM, a similar cognitive relay strategy of linking the separate meanings of homophones to pictures was employed. A six-session course of treatment after a stable baseline was confirmed as sufficient to effect a significant improvement in the homophones treated, but without generalization to a set of 20 untreated homophones. A control measure of sentence comprehension showed no change. This had been predicted, since sentence comprehension involves a set of processes which the model does not link to the processes involved in writing words to dictation. Although there was no generalization to untreated homophones, a different list of untreated (non-homophonic) irregular words was significantly better spelled. Behrmann suggests this may have been due to a combination of improvement of CCM's lexical route in writing and practice in visual checking through the therapy procedure. It appeared, however, from this study that the spelling of homophones requires word-specific attention, and does not improve simply because of improved lexical processing.

In our final account the dysgraphic patient was Italian (Carlomagno and Parlato, 1989). Since Italian is an orthographically regular language with few irregular spellings (for example when /k/ is realized as Q instead of C as in 'quota') surface dysgraphia cannot be easily detected. Stress assignment errors, however, can indicate use of a non-lexical routine, consistent with a diagnosis of surface dyslexia. This (unnamed) patient was given a diagnosis of surface dyslexia with a severe dysgraphia, the latter described in terms of the psycholinguistic model as compromising both the lexical and phoneme-grapheme conversion routines. However he was able to write the initial syllables of dictated words correctly, and therapy capitalized on this. He was asked to fragment the words he heard for dictation into syllables, and then to use the cognitive relay of associating each syllable with a proper name with which he was familiar. As he had been a railway clerk this was generally the name of an Italian town. The programme began with real words and then continued with non-words so as to include all possible Italian syllables.

After five months of therapy the number of errors in a 36-word list was reduced from 31 to 5. That the improvement was linked to his use of the taught strategy was evidenced by two features. First he used the strategy in reading non-words, which also improved significantly, showing transfer of learning. Secondly, his errors showed misapplication of the strategy, for example in using an incorrect phonemically similar town name. The errors he made in indicating stress placement or apostrophe position in writing were those consistent with a surface dysgraphia, indicating that his writing was accomplished by the syllable-graphic routine which had been taught. There was also an improvement of spontaneous writing by the patient, supported by a self-dictation strategy. Interestingly, there is support for the application of a psycholinguistic analysis as a prologue to therapy in this study, in that this patient had previously been unsuccessfully treated by a general visuo-kinetic method of therapy for writing (copying words, copying from memory and then writing without a model). This programme was not predicated upon any psycholinguistic analysis of his disorder. It could be considered as appropriate for patients with an afferent dysgraphia, a peripheral disorder which we briefly described in Chapter 4. It does not appear that this patient's disorder was of that kind. Here then we have some further tentative corroboration of the claim made in our section on naming that model-inappropriate therapy does not work. It is, however, too soon to make any real judgements of this. –

CONCLUSION

Preliminary though they are, the few single case studies reviewed in the above sections all point to the conclusion that therapy motivated by the detailed psycholinguistic investigation of individuals can be measurably effective. In some cases this can be achieved over a short span of contact with the patient, although these studies say nothing about the amount of time the therapist has to spend at present in testing the patient's disorder, devising an appropriate intervention strategy, preparing therapy materials and so on. While the results in most cases are consistent with predictions from the models, they may also be consistent with other models as yet to be applied. In some cases the results indicate the need for revision of the present models – for example to include a dynamic processing element of storage capacity or computational space. In whatever way the models may change, however, as Byng (1988) comments, they will need to incorporate the findings of the changes which occur in language as a result of therapy – an additional contribution of aphasiology to the study of the mental processes in language.

All these studies have been of direct therapy. They have used a direct confrontational approach to the patients' deficits, even when the therapy has consisted of adoption of a relay strategy, with a focus in most cases on ameliorating the deficit rather than avoiding it and using compensatory indirect methods of intervention. It is these we turn to in the next chapter.

SUMMARY

In this chapter we reviewed over 30 case studies in which psycholinguistic models have been applied to the interpretation of the patient's disorder as a basis for planning therapy. Most of these studies have also attempted to use experimental designs from which the effectiveness of the intervention could be evaluated. Therapies for naming disorders were distinguished according to whether they used relay strategies or reactivation. The patients reported include ones diagnosed as having different types of naming disorders: in semantic representations, in the link from the semantic system to the phonological output lexicon, or in the phonological output lexicon itself. Some of these patients were able to access parts of names for writing when they could not do so for speech. Our review of therapy for auditory comprehension disorders was briefer. We suggested that one reason for the relative dearth of psycholinguistic studies in this area was that a pragmatic approach may be more appropriate in many cases. Our next section on psycholinguistically based therapies for sentence production showed how they have worked on the patient's understanding of thematic roles and on clarification of the ideas the patient wished to express. We also summarized one study in which the repetition of sentences was used with the aim of ameliorating a disorder affecting the phonological output buffer. Therapies for patients with reading disorders were contrasted according to whether the patients had phonological, deep or surface dyslexic symptoms. Finally, we described four studies evaluating therapies for spelling disorders related to different types of central dysgraphias. The majority of these studies bear testimony to the effectiveness of therapy based on psycholinguistic models.

TWELVE

Applying pragmatics in intervention

In our last chapter we were able to review the substantial progress which has been made in applying psycholinguistics to intervention in aphasia, illustrating our review with over 30 published cases where progress had been evaluated. The situation is very different for pragmatics. Although 'functional communication' has long been the acknowledged target of much aphasia therapy, we can cite very few evaluative studies. Even the informed assessment of patients' pragmatic abilities lags far behind psycholinguistic assessment, and some of the procedures in current clinical use are based on questionable postulates. We therefore cannot present the same kind of review as we did in Chapters 10 and 11. Instead we begin this chapter with an account of the present clinical perspective on applying pragmatics in intervention in aphasia, and end it with ideas on how the review of pragmatics we have given in Chapters 6 to 9 suggests that this clinical pragmatic approach might be adjusted and extended.

In the clinical survey with which we start, we have divided our discussion into three main sections. The first of these deals with approaches which have been used in developing strategies of functional communication in the patient – whether these are concerned with helping the patient to convey messages in speech (writing, drawing, etc.) or through an external prosthesis such as a computer. Like the psycholinguistic approach, this involves *direct* intervention. In the second section we discuss an alternative approach which has been used in *indirect* intervention, that is the development of functional strategies in the patient's conversational partners – generally, of course, members of the caring family. This strategy has sometimes been described as changing the patient's 'communicative environment'. The third section deals with the important question of how the success of such pragmatic interventions can be evaluated, a question which hinges on the suitability of present methods of assessing functional communication. We shall discuss this in relation to the range of approaches to pragmatics outlined in Chapters 6 to 9. Evaluation is, however, quite problematic, since some perspectives which figure prominently in the applied literature (speech act theory is a good example) are highly controversial within pragmatics. One recent paper which deals with the psycholinguistics of discourse comprehension in relation to aphasia devotes a very large amount of space to speech-act approaches, reflecting their continuing popularity despite the conceptual problems associated with them as outlined in Chapter 7 (Murphy, 1990).

This focus on evaluation leads naturally to a discussion in the final part of the chapter on the role which the linguistically informed pragmatic studies we have described can contribute to *interactive* assessments specifically by means of a conversational analysis approach. This approach, discussed in Chapters 8 and 9, focuses on everyday situated speech not as an independently existing text produced and comprehended by the patient, but as a collaborative achievement by at least two conversationalists. We shall be arguing that this orientation makes it a particularly useful and hitherto underexplored tool for the aphasia therapist. We shall conclude by trying to show how assessments which take into account the insights of conversation analysis can lead to more exactly targeted strategies for achieving communicative success in everyday life. However, we need to offer the caveat that these ideas have not yet been subject to controlled testing like the more formalized psycholinguistically oriented interventions discussed in Chapter 11. Difficulties in designing adequate testing procedures arise chiefly because it is much easier to find ways of testing relatively decontexualized psycholinguistic abilities than conversational abilities which are sensitive to myriad contextual constraints and incentives which are difficult to reproduce either over time in everyday contexts or in laboratory or clinical conditions. This seems to be an inevitable consequence of any approach to conversation which has, in Holland's expressive phrase, 'high ecological validity' (Holland, 1991: 199), and reflects the conversation analysts' insistence that each conversation is a uniquely contextualized event.

DEVELOPING FUNCTIONAL STRATEGIES IN THE PATIENT

In our last chapter we described some applications of strategies using cognitive relays to substitute for impaired processes. Here we look at a different kind of strategy, an overt adaptation of speech behaviour aimed at enhancing communicative efficiency and/or social acceptability.

The basis for aphasia therapists to encourage development of these strategies is observation of those used by patients who are good communicators despite their aphasia. It has often been observed that global communicative ability is remarkably well preserved even where linguistic deficits are quite severe (Holland, 1991; Gardner, 1990). It is a general tenet of aphasia therapy that the therapist should identify and foster those aspects of the patient's speech which facilitate communication. However, we should emphasize at this point that not all compensatory strategies adopted by patients are facilitatory; recall the example of Edwards and Garman's Mr V. whose tendency to talk excessively until interrupted seemed to constitute a strategy for dealing with lexical retrieval problems (see p. 46 above). We review here, in contrasting types of patients, two further examples of strategies which simply do not seem to work; it is probable that linguistic impairments at grammatical, lexical or semantic levels are in general likely to inhibit the effectiveness of compensatory strategies, as seems to be the case with Mr V.

Hand, et al.'s (1979) study (already referred to in Chapter 3) reported on the adoption, observed four years after her stroke, of abnormal syntactic compensations by a 42 year old teacher. She had agrammatic speech, with particular difficulties in verb retrieval. One of her strategies was to substitute an introductory filler ('this is') when she was unable to retrieve a following verb (as in 'This is Eddie the telephone' for 'Eddie worked for the telephone company'). She also used 'it was' or 'this is' as a substitute for prepositions (as in 'Mother was alright it was Christmas' for 'Mother was alright at Christmas'; 'I was born this is Charlton Avenue' for 'I was born on Charlton Avenue'). As Hand, et al. note, these compensatory devices, although maintaining fluency and partially disguising the patient's telegrammatic problems, may result in incomprehensible utterances, and in fact be counter-productive to communication. The researchers suggest that they may be an unfortunate by-product of therapy in which naming practice has been stressed ('This is . . . (picture name)'). On the other hand, it should be noted that the strategies described in this paper did on some occasions at least assist communication, and that, if listeners were aware of what strategies were being used, they might have the key to better understanding. It is this latter notion which underlies the indirect functional approach to be discussed shortly.

Fluent patients also develop their own compensatory strategies, as has been described by Panzeri, et al. (1987) in an Italian case of jargon aphasia. Observed over a period of three years, this patient's speech showed a significant reduction of neologisms which could not be related to target words (Butterworth's Type B neologisms) and an increase in phonemic paraphasias (Type A neologisms in Butterworth's terminology). Since phonemic paraphasias imply partial retrieval of an intended word, while Type B neologisms are considered to be non-lexical gap fillers, this might suggest that the patient had achieved some recovery of language. The authors point out, however, that the apparent change was due to an increase in the use of stereotypic phrases and that the variety of vocabulary items used had decreased rather than increased. The patient had not improved as a functional communicator, despite appearing to be a more 'competent social agent', and able to 'participate better in the ordinary processes of turn-taking' (Panzeri, et al., 1987: 931–2).

A comprehensive taxonomy of compensatory strategies used by aphasic adults has been proposed by Penn (1984). She studied 20-minute videotaped patient–therapist conversations. The 18 patients, aged 24 to 72, were of varying degrees of severity of aphasia; 11 were fluent and 7 non-fluent and all had been aphasic for at least six months. In addition to the strategies used by their interlocutors and to the patients' non-verbal behaviour strategies, she found five categories of compensatory behaviour employed by the aphasic adults. The first was described as simplifying or condensing the message. Patients shortened their conversational turns in order to promote communication, changing the order of words so that salient aspects of the message were placed near the beginning of the utterance. Sentences did not begin with an unstressed syllable, and direct speech was preferred to indirect speech (cf. p. 114 above). One simplification strategy – of using proforms without clear reference – was counter-productive. This type of reference problem in aphasia is discussed in Chapter 6.

The second strategy described by Penn was the use of various kinds of elaboration, stemming apparently from word-finding difficulties. Falling into this category are circumlocution, elimination strategies ('It's not Monday but Tuesday'), post-modification and co-ordination or embedding of clauses, apparently to maintain a conversational turn. This seems to be the general type of strategy adopted by Mr V.

Various kinds of repetition constituted a third strategy – repetition of the patient's own productions, repetition of adverbs or adjectives as an alternative to phrasal constructions with intensifiers such as *very, extremely*, paraphrases of the proposition which the patient is attempting to express, and repetition by the patient of all or part of the interlocutor's preceding utterance. This last type of repetition might in some sequential contexts be viewed as a time-gaining device to facilitate comprehension. Where the patient is responding to a first part of a pair produced by the partner rather than initiating a novel utterance, such a strategy can be remarkably successful in disguising the level of impairment. This is because in normal everyday conversation repetition of a first part of a pair by the next speaker routinely accomplishes a range of pragmatic functions, such as confirmation, acceptance and agreement (see Chapter 9 above). Consider the following extract from the closing stages of a therapy session with Mr E., whose comprehension is intact but whose lexical retrieval and syntactic abilities are severely impaired. These impairments are, however, not at all evident here:

(1) T: So Helen and I will see you on Tuesday
     Mr E: on Tuesday (.) mm [nods]
     T: and I'll come myself on Wednesday morning
     Mr E: Wednesday morning (.) good
     T: so we'll see you twice next week
     Mr E: yes (.) twice

A fourth strategy described by Penn (also noted by Hand, et al., 1979, and Panzieri, et al., 1987) was apparently adopted to maintain fluency during lexical search. This involves the use of stereotypical 'learnt' chunks of language such as 'you know what I mean', of filled pauses and so-called placeholders like 'well' and 'let me see'. On the whole, aphasic speakers seem to be sensitive to the function and distribution of these discourse markers, as described in Chapter 9. Some use these particularly effectively on the telephone, where the communication channel is restricted to speech. Non-fluent speakers in particular may develop their own fluent stereotyped utterances such as 'Oh my dear'.

Penn's fifth category comprised strategies particularly related to what she describes as 'sensitivity to the sociolinguistic demands of the situation'. Examples of these are self-corrections, requests for clarification, pausing and topic shift at a point of breakdown. Again, aphasic speakers who employ this type of strategy are demonstrating their general sociolinguistic sensitivity; they seem to be employing normal procedures for maintaining a coherent conversation generally to the extent required for current purposes. Holland (1991) cites some recent research which suggests that this kind of sociolinguistic sensitivity is relatively intact in aphasia, although difficulties in talking and understanding may mean that the conversation is frequently disrupted by the use of such strategies.

Penn comments that identical compensatory strategies could be used with entirely different communicative consequences in different patients, depending on the frequency and (as we might expect from our account of conversational structure in Chapters 8 and 9) on the sequential placement of the items used. This sequential placement seems to be what Penn means by 'timing'. She cites the example of dysfluencies which might be felt by observers to be facilitatory, in that they reflect normal searching and conversational management procedures, provided they do not occur too frequently. Self-corrections and comment clauses are similarly interpreted sometimes as supportive and sometimes as counter-productive, depending on frequency and sequential context. The implication Penn draws for the therapist is that, while communicative strategies may need to be taught to some patients, spontaneously acquired but maladaptive strategies may need to be unlearned by others.

'TOTAL COMMUNICATION'

Teaching of productive strategies has become the basis of a functional approach in aphasia therapy, now known as 'total communication'. It has a long history in traditional practice in British clinics, with their emphasis on use of materials which are of relevance to the patient's everyday life and interests, and on linking speech therapy work with activities in occupational therapy. It received a boost in American clinics from Wepman's (1976) paper, which suggested that indirect *thought-provoking* therapy was more beneficial than direct work on language. By 'thought-provoking', Wepman meant therapy which concentrated on increasing the patients' thinking about other things than how to express themselves in speech. He gave as an example procedures for helping an aphasic lawyer to understand a current case of litigation. This patient had not responded to a programme of direct work on speech, but this focus on meaning rather than medium produced more effective results. Howard and Hatfield (1987) comment that focus on meaning, and in particular on the mapping of meaning on to syntax, can be justified for some patients by a psycholinguistic model, as we discussed in Chapters 5 and 11.

Chapey (1981,1986) developed this emphasis on thought-therapy into a programme of cognitive intervention in aphasia, concerned with stimulation of cognition and memory, and of divergent and evaluative thinking as a complement to the convergent thinking (e.g. description of common activities and objects) which forms the basis of much clinical work in aphasia therapy clinics.

One of the recent formulators of the total-communication approach in Australia is Green (1982). She has analysed the type of productive strategies which can most profitably be taught, emphasizing that while therapists should try to develop those which are as socially acceptable as possible, 'to communicate with any strategy is better than no communication at all' (1982: 21). She suggests seven expressive and four comprehension strategies. For expressive strategies, the patients can attempt to learn to:

1. use an alternative communication system, for example drawing, pointing;
2. give the listener cues about words they are searching for, for example by using circumlocutions or writing an initial letter;
3. give the listener an associated word;
4. avoid silences by producing a word even if it is known to be wrong, and then self-correcting;
5. use approximate pronunciations of words if the full representation is not available;

6. use fillers to maintain attention;
7. request help.

For comprehension strategies Green suggests:

1. requesting repetitions;
2. telling the speaker that you do not understand;
3. clarifying what was said by repeating it;
4. asking questions.

The way to tackle the teaching of strategies, Green proposes, is first to determine whether there are any naturally occurring strategies and, if there are, assess how much they help communication. One might then test the usefulness of other strategies by trying them out in various situations, and then practising the strategies which have been shown to be useful. This can be done by instruction, demonstration and rehearsal in a variety of situations.

One such situation is the clinical application of a procedure known as Promoting Aphasics' Communicatory Efficiency (PACE), developed by Davis and Wilcox (1985; Davis, 1986). This sets up some of the parameters of natural conversation in a structured way in the clinic, so that the aphasic person can 'practise hint-and-guess sequences and resultant natural communicative behaviors such as resolution, revision and repair' (Davis, 1986: 261). The patient has information (on concealed cards) to communicate to the therapist and vice versa. Thus both participate equally as receivers and senders of messages, and there is an exchange of new information between them. The patients can use any means whatsoever of getting the message across, and receive immediate feedback as to whether the message has indeed been understood. The therapists model what are expected to be productive strategies in the course of their own participation. PACE has become a popular procedure in many clinics, with the publication of a ready-made kit (Edelman, 1987) and lends itself to quantifiable measures to test the effectiveness of this approach to teaching communicatory strategies. Despite its development from the knowledge base provided by pragmatics, however, the use of PACE as a treatment has been criticized as being 'as far from true communication as one can imagine' (Howard and Hatfield, 1987: 85).

Nevertheless the PACE type of procedure is attractive to clinicians as a manageable method of rehearsing word-finding strategies. Its links with speech-act theory have also been developed. Pulvermuller and Roth (1991) have introduced a development of the PACE procedure, making explicit not only its links with Searle's speech-act theory but also with Wittgenstein's similar analysis of types of communicative interaction as *language games*. Pulvermuller and Roth describe the application to aphasia therapy of a method aimed at encouraging two of these speech acts or language games, requesting and bargaining. The stimulation of requests is achieved through a procedure similar to that used by Perkins (see p. 125) in that the participants are divided by a screen and one has to seek information from the other. In this case, however, both have identical sets of picture cards, and the 'game' is for each participant in turn to request from description a matching card from the other. The difficulty can be varied by changing the complexity of the cards and the degree of similarity amongst them. The clinicians can also elicit rejections by asking for a card which is not present in the patient's set. For the bargaining 'game', five cards are placed on the table in full view of both the patient and the therapist, each card representing an activity (e.g. swimming). The participants bargain as to who should be assigned each activity. This is aimed at eliciting speech acts such as proposing, rejecting and arguing. To increase the difficulty and the resemblance to natural exchanges, the cards can be removed after the initial presentation. These kinds of 'language game' procedures have advantages over the PACE system in that they emphasize the collaborative nature of conversational negotiations, rather than the transfer of information.

Pulvermuller and Roth report results of this 'communicative aphasia treatment' with three women (two anomic and one with Broca's aphasia) and five men with global or Broca's aphasia. All of them were at least six months post-onset. As instruments for measuring functional communication were not available for this German study, change in verbal comprehension on the Token Test was used as the measure of improvement. Both the anomic women and three of the men improved significantly on this measure after up to 18 sessions (over three or four weeks) of this type of therapy. The performance of two of the men was also compared with that after three weeks of 'conventional' therapy;

the latter effected no significant change on the Token Test scores. With these same two patients, however, communicative therapy was shown to effect improvements of from 50–60 per cent to 80–90 per cent on a measure of spoken communication, that is the ability to give adequate answers to questions with alternative choices, such as 'Do you want tea or juice?'. This type of communicative therapy therefore seems to be worth further development and evaluation as part of the aphasia clinician's resources.

Aten (1986) has also described some more global procedures which contribute to what he labels as Functional Communication Therapy (FCT). Here the emphasis is on the patient's development of general communicative strategies, rather than on training in specific speech acts. These strategies are seen as usefully practised in one-to-one therapy as a preliminary to group therapy, where they can be consolidated in a more natural communicative setting. FCT begins by attempting to eliminate non-productive strategies, such as hurrying to produce responses or 'press of speech'; this is done by encouraging the patient to 'wait a second'. Patients who feign understanding can be similarly encouraged to stop the interlocutor and ask for clarification. Training is socially orientated, with an initial emphasis on greetings, and use of personal names. Since it is often assumed that most aphasic patients' comprehension benefits from the redundancy which is a regular characteristic of conversation, Aten advocates therapeutic procedures based on therapist–patient interactions, rather than concentrating on decontextualized words or sentences. An example Aten gives of a topic which can be introduced by the therapist as a basis for interaction is the following:

> Here's a short article from today's newspaper. It mentions three places to go to for inexpensive dinners. I'll read the story, then we'll talk about it.

After one-to-one interactive therapy, group therapy can provide a half-way stage before the patient attempts to generalize to an unsheltered real-life situation the strategies which have been learned.

Another pioneer in the development of the application of pragmatics in the assessment and treatment of aphasia, Holland (1991) has developed a method of helping the patient to practise learned communicative strategies which she calls Conversational Coaching. This involves the preparation of a short 'script', designed to be just too difficult for the patient to produce spontaneously. This obliges the patient to draw on communicative strategies, and is intended to provide a bridge to the spontaneous use of strategies in patient-initiated conversations. The script is rehearsed with guidance from the therapist on what strategies to use in order to communicate the desired message; the patient then, with prompting from the therapist, communicates the message to a family member to whom it is unfamiliar. The family member's comprehension of the script is then checked, the interaction being videotaped so that it can be discussed by the participants. The procedure is subsequently repeated with a less familiar listener. Scripts can be made to vary in their difficulty by (for example) including gossip or unlikely events. Holland comments that one patient even used the scripts prepared in the clinic as conversational devices at home with his family and friends. This, however, is not the goal of Conversational Coaching, which is intended as a procedure for generalizing the strategies to be used in communication, rather than supplying the content of a conversation.

NON-LINGUISTIC MEDIA OF COMMUNICATION

Before passing on to the important question of facilitating communication through the aphasic person's partners, we conclude this section on strategies which a patient may learn to use with a brief account of the use of non-linguistic media of communication. These also draw on communicative strategies, but these are ones which it is unlikely that the patient will achieve spontaneously. We describe briefly the teaching of drawing skills (recall the example of the patient who used these in conversation in Chapter 9) and the use of symbols. We also describe the use of computers as a dictionary and as a means of communication (in contrast to their use as a vehicle for therapy exercises as decribed in Chapter 11).

Drawing has been relatively neglected as a means of enhancing communication in aphasia, despite the evidence that this ability can be remarkably unaffected by left brain damage (see the review by Van Dongen, 1974). Hatfield and Zangwill (1974) successfully encouraged a patient with 'expressive aphasia' to draw narrative sequences as a means of communicating ideas. Pillon, et al. (1980) extended the application of this strategy to global aphasia and to the use of drawing as a facilitator of language as well as a substitute for it. They monitored the recovery of drawing over two years in a 36 year old cartoonist. At a time when he was producing no spontaneous speech, he was able to draw objects by name and verbal description and then to write and read their names. This later stimulated the production of spontaneous, though agrammatic, speech. The clinicians then used his drawing to encourage the production of verbs and sentences. By a year post-onset, this patient was able to draw a sequence of cartoons to illustrate a story. His written expression as captions to such a story was superior to both his spontaneous speech and writing, in which he showed confusions of word order ('la rivière pêche un poisson' – the river fishes a fish). Pillon and colleagues suggest that the effect on language of using drawings was achieved by the stimulation of the right cerebral hemisphere activating the residual language of the left hemisphere. A somewhat different explanation would be that externalization of ideas through picture sequences in this patient overcame the initiation problems he experienced in language (like those in transcortical motor aphasia), by clarifying concepts as a preliminary to mapping them onto language structures.

Other therapists have continued to explore the use of drawing as an element in functional communication. Nicholas and Helm-Estabrooks (1990) describe a treatment programme devised by Morgan and Helm-Estabrooks which they called *Back to the Drawing Board* (BDB). Its use is reported with a globally aphasic 57 year old engineer, who made significant improvements several months after his stroke on drawing cartoons to express actions in scenes. With some prompting he also used drawing in functional communication. Trupe (1986) has reported use of a similar technique with 15 aphasic patients, in which the training in drawing began with tracing and matching, and proceeded to drawing unseen objects.

The therapeutic approach to the use of drawing by Trupe and by Morgan and Helm-Estabrooks can be contrasted with that of Lyon and others in which the emphasis in training is on communicative function right from the start, rather than on copying. Lyon and Sims (1989) and Lyon and Helm-Estabrooks

(1987) have used a *response-elaboration* technique similar to that advocated by Yedor and Kearns (1987). The patient's own initial attempts at communicating by drawing are developed by the use of strategies by the communicative partner. For example, for unclear drawings the partner asks the patient to indicate the most important part of the picture, to show which orientation was used or to draw an important section larger. Instructions such as these can be used not only by the patient's family for enhancing functional communication, but can also be transferred to written guidelines which the patient can show to less familiar communicators. As in the study by Pillon and colleagues, Lyon and Helm-Estabrooks report that improved communication by drawing can lead in turn to improved language skills, perhaps through clarification of the ideas involved. In terms of a psycholinguistic model, then, it seems that trained drawing may become a facilitator for patients who have a central semantic disorder, whereas it is likely to be best used as a complement to verbal communication (rather than a facilitator) by patients whose restricted speech follows impairment at a more peripheral level. A psycholinguistic analysis may therefore help in the assessment of a patient's suitability for training in drawing, and for anticipating whether it will facilitate language or substitute for it in functional communication.

The same applies to the second kind of communication strategy we discuss here, the use of symbols. There have been reports of the successful use of a visual logographic system, Blissymbols, as an alternative system of communication. Bailey (1989) for example gives an account of how a 30-month programme of therapy using Blissymbols improved communication for a 55 year old scientist when it was initiated nine months after he acquired a severe aphasia with articulatory apraxia. Such reports might suggest a potential for these systems in supplementing restricted functional communication. This implies, however, that patients may be able to use such pictographic symbols more successfully than written language symbols. Bailey's study does not in fact support this interpretation, since her patient rejected use of Blissymbols for writing at the end of his programme.

The possibility that the use of pictographic symbols is limited by the patients' linguistic capabilities was investigated in two severely aphasic patients by Funnell and Allport (1989) with less promising results. The patients' language processes were investigated, applying a psycholinguistic model, to ascertain their linguistic characteristics, and the patients were then given 18 months of weekly training on the use of a vocabulary of 140 Blissymbols in meaningful, friendly, conversational situations. Both patients learned content words, but had difficulty in learning the symbols for 'I' and 'you' and in learning words with non-specific reference. Neither could the patients recall the order of symbols necessary to express questions versus statements. Funnell and Allport conclude that the patients' difficulty in the use of Blissymbols reflected the limits of their processing capacities for natural language, and did not therefore offer the possibility of extending their functional communication by this alternative means; 'whenever a symbol could be learned and used, so too could an equivalent written word sharing the same conceptual base' (p. 299). As the authors point out, the familiar form of written language is a more acceptable base for functional communication than a system of pictographic symbols.

More realistic visual logographic representations than Blissymbols may however provide a more adequate functional means of communication, particularly if they are accompanied by the written forms of the words. Such a set of representations has been used by Weinrich (1991) and his colleagues in developing a computerized system of visual communication. This spares the aphasic patient any phonetic and morphosyntactic processing, and may be of particular relevance to those agrammatic patients who have a specific difficulty in producing verbs. The computer supplies the patient with the equivalent of stacks of cards organized in piles as proper nouns (using digitized pictures of family members, etc.), common nouns, verbs, modifiers and punctuation marks. Weinrich describes how two patients whose spontaneous speech consisted only of recurring verbal stereotypes learned to send messages in the telegraphic style of the system (e.g. 'Maureen buy hot sandwich'). The communicatory potential of this system, C-VIC, is therefore promising for severely impaired patients, but depends on the development of a portable computer which can use this software. There is also a possibility, which still remains to be tested, that training on the computer might facilitate the return of some natural language functions.

The use of a portable computer for people with anomia, in

supplying the users with words they are unable to retrieve on their own in conversation has already been described (Colby, et al., 1981). This replicates the word-finding strategies which such patients might use, that is in seeking to identify the topic area, the first or last or middle letters in the word and any associated words (these can be personalized to the user). If this procedure is too laborious, such aids may lend themselves better to therapy exercises for word-retrieval rather than functional communication, since the conversational partner's collaborative help may be excluded from solving the word-finding problem when it is transferred to a computer.

There has been even more controversy about the potential of gesture as a substitutory means of communication in aphasia than there has about the use of pictorial symbols. There is less of a prima facie case for expecting gestural communication to be preserved than communication through visual symbols, given the frequent co-occurrence of aphasia and limb apraxia (McCarthy and Warrington, 1990: 114–5). However, we should note that the selection of visual symbols involves gesture, and the interpretation of gesture involves vision. Consequently it may seem unlikely, given Funnell and Allport's finding that the restrictions on the use of a visual symbol system were the same as restrictions as natural language, that gesture should fare any better. There does indeed seem to be a close relationship between severity of aphasia and difficulty in learning AmerInd signs for high frequency words, with a threshold of severity below which successful acquisition of signs is negligible (Coelho and Duffy, 1987). In individual cases, however, success has been reported (see Di Simoni, 1986, for a review); one example is with a case of fluent aphasia without hemiplegia reported by Simmons and Zorthian (1979). Eleven months after a stroke, a programme of training in AmerInd-based signs was initiated with this 51 year old woman, and seven months later her family reported spontaneous use of the taught gestures in communicating at home. Two months later she was generating new signs herself. Since there was no change on a standard test of verbal expression and comprehension it seemed that in this case, the teaching of gesture as a communicatory strategy had extended her ability in functional communication.

This use of AmerInd, an explicit system of signs, is of course different from the use of gesture as a normal component of conversation, in which we are all 'naturally multi-modal com-municators' (Green, 1982: 19). Herrmann, et al., (1988) analysed videotaped conversations between severely nonfluent aphasic adults, their partners and a third individual (described as a 'talk master' whose function was to maintain the dyadic communica-tion). They found that the patients employed non-verbal behaviour significantly more often as speech substitutes than their partners. Much of this was codified gesture (nodding, shrugging, etc.), and it was noted that their partners themselves used more of such codified or descriptive gesture than would be expected in normal conversation. This would appear to be a spontaneous modelling by the partners of a strategy which it was advantageous for the patients to use. Aphasia therapists may need to be aware of the utility of encouraging such behaviour in relatives who do not use it spontaneously.

INDIRECT THERAPY

There are different interpretations of this term. For some it includes the supportive counselling given to patients, the recruiting of other help for the patients' social and financial needs and the use of psychosocial techniques to help the patients to come to terms with their emotions (as reviewed by Brumfitt and Clarke, 1989). Important though these facets of intervention are, we shall not deal with them here in the context of pragmatic approaches to therapy, but will restrict ourselves to a definition of indirect therapy as therapy which, although focused directly on spoken communication, is mediated through other people. Within this definition, moreover, we shall concentrate on methods by which conversational partners can improve interac-tions, excluding the extensive range of studies where spouses or other helpers are used as substitutes for therapists in carrying out direct intervention programmes. It is worth noting at this point the relevance of conversation analysis to such indirect therapy methods, given its focus on the collaborative nature of conversa-tional management.

Martin (1981) echoes this orientation by drawing attention to the fact that a disruption of communicative interaction, in which one of the participants is aphasic, may be due to 'the failure of either or both participants as a receiver-sender in the exchange'

(p. 313). In indirect therapy, as we have defined it, the focus is on the non-aphasic partners in respect of their communications with their aphasic partner in the conversation. This is particularly relevant in respect of communicating with aphasic patients who have persistent comprehension disorders, as in chronic jargonaphasia. Martin notes the importance of considering comprehension as holistic, including visual input as well as speech, and stresses the need for the conversational partner or therapist to support comprehension with gesture. This again is quite in keeping with the orientation of conversation analysis, which analyses gestures as equivalent or parallel to verbal conversational contributions with respect to their function and sequential placement in the conversation (see p. 224f. above). Martin also points out that context can sometimes disambiguate what at first seems to be unintelligible speech e.g. 'I bike Perro' can be interpreted if the patient is holding an album of Perry Como records. An awareness of any patterns of distortion produced by the patient can facilitate the listener's comprehension. This can be checked by seeking clarification, thus obliging the jargon speaker to move from the role of sender to receiver, a move which may need to be reinforced by some gesture such as touching. If the patient's family is to be involved in the therapy, they need to be as well informed as possible about the nature of the patient's disorder and the limitations which it imposes, and to be trained by the therapist in the techniques of using gesture, interpretation and seeking clarification. Again, the detailed descriptions provided by conversation analysis offer a principled basis for such training. The family's superior knowledge of the patient's circumstances will generally give them an advantage over the therapist, once training has been accepted.

Green (1982) recommends use of this kind of indirect intervention not only with jargonaphasic speakers but with aphasic patients in general. She suggests that the therapist needs to inform the families of four areas in particular, which are relevant to the development of more successful communication. These are as follows:

1. which strategies might best help the patient to communicate;
2. which contextual factors might affect the level of communication (e.g. number of people in the conversation, or surrounding stimuli);
3. what to do if the message from the patient is not understood;

4. how to structure their own conversational contributions to foster the patient's understanding.

Green suggests that the last is best done, not by formal instruction, but by encouraging members of the family to try out these techniques under the therapist's supervision. In this way the therapist is primarily developing conversations between the aphasic person and the family rather than conversations with the therapist. It is likely that conversational analysis as described in Chapters 8 and 9 will be relevant in applying these principles. In so far as it provides detailed descriptions of the structure of everyday conversation and offers insights into the reasons for communicative successes and failures, it offers a principled basis for building and testing strategies.

Some examples of how comprehension can be facilitated by adjusting the linguistic structure and content of utterances have been given by Pierce (1981, 1982). He demonstrated that aphasic patients generally find sentences of a subject-verb-object type the easiest to understand, and are helped to understand sentences with past time reference if the *have +en* verb form is used. Future time reference is also more easily understood by patients if it is expressed by the form *be going to* + V rather than *will* + V. On the basis of experimental results Pierce (1982) recommends encouraging relatives to use adverbial expressions of time like 'tomorrow', 'yesterday', 'already' in conjunction with verb forms in order to facilitate comprehension of time reference (described rather misleadingly by Pierce as 'tense'). He also recommends expanding other sentence types with redundant expressions (e.g. 'The man takes the boy *over to* the girl', in preference to '*to* the girl'.

EVALUATING PRAGMATIC THERAPY: DESIGNING THE ASSESSMENTS

We might ask now whether there is any evidence of the effectiveness of either of these approaches in pragmatic therapy, direct or indirect, parallel to the evidence which is being collected of the efficacy of psycholinguistically based therapy. The answer is not much, at least so far. We have already commented that one reason for this lack of evaluative evidence is the 'ecological validity' of pragmatic approaches to therapy which base themselves on situated speech in naturalistic contexts, and this makes them difficult to control. A further reason, however, has been alluded to throughout this book – the lack of adequate and sufficiently principled instruments of assessment geared to examining the pragmatic aspects of communication. The difficulty in designing such instruments is largely a consequence of the diversified and contentious nature of the knowledge base in pragmatics upon which they draw. Nevertheless reliable assessments before and after intervention are essential if the efficacy of the intervention is to be judged.

There are in fact several assessment procedures which have attempted to profile pragmatic aspects of language, but all have limitations. They fall roughly into two types, elicitation and observation schedules. In the first the therapist conducts a structured interview in the clinic, using a test-like format, and analyses the elicited samples of the patient's behaviour against predetermined categories. These are often rather loosely based on some of the pragmatic approaches discussed in this book. In the second, carers' or therapists' ratings are used for several parameters of communication to summarize interactive behaviour. All of these assessments employ what we have described as a top-down type of analysis, in that they approach the data with a predetermined set of categories. This contrasts with a possible approach, not yet developed in language pathology as far as we are aware, which tries to profile recurrent patterns in interactive discourse with as few prior assumptions as possible of how these patterns will turn out.

The best known of the elicitation schedules is Holland's (1980) well-standardized instrument for examining communicative activities in daily living (CADL). Making use of the general insights underlying speech-act theory, it asks the patient to perform a range of such acts, many of them through the medium of role playing. It makes use of props such as a doctor's jacket, and draws on various contextual situations like shopping and telephoning. Other items in CADL are presented as more formal tasks, such as choosing an appropriate picture for a metaphor.

Role play in everyday life situations is also the basis of the Everyday Language Test devised by Blomert, et al. (1987; see also Blomert, et al., 1990). The tester describes a situation such as the following: 'You must arrange a dinner for a wedding. You are now in the restaurant. I am the owner. What do you say to me?'.

The patient's responses are scored according to whether they contain the necessary basic information ('I'd like to arrange a dinner for a wedding') and appropriate amplifying information ('It's for October 20, and for 50 people').

The pilot study of elicited conversation described by Copeland (1989) applies speech act theory. Twenty 'communicative acts' were elicited informally in a conversation in the patient's own home, with stimuli and cards to act as prompts if needed. These acts were rated on a five-point scale by a judge listening to the audiotape . The following acts were elicited: greetings, personal introduction, informing, reporting, explaining, arguing, estimation of time and numbers, correction of misunderstanding and misinformation, agreement, negotiation, assertion, questioning, ordering, requesting, advising, warning, imagining and problem-solving. Copeland notes that this proved to be an incomplete list of the communicative acts which occurred spontaneously, a comment reflecting one of the chief conceptual difficulties besetting speech-act theory, namely the provision of a finite and principled set of acts (see p. 149 above). Copeland also remarks that message (topic) extension was an important dimension which this conversation assessment did not include, a point which we shall return to later.

Turning now to the observation schedules, we find that they differ in their complexity. Some require considerable expertise on the part of the therapist for analysis and ratings, while others can be filled in by the patients' family or other carers. Observation schedules have the general advantage of avoiding the artificiality of role-play, something which some aphasic people find hard to use as it involves metacommunicative rather than communicative ability. Therapist-conducted analyses include Prutting and Kirchner's (1983) Pragmatic Protocol (with its later modifications by Goldblum (1985) and by Prutting and Kirchner themselves (1987)); Penn's (1985) Profile of Communicative Appropriateness (PCA); and the Edinburgh Functional Communication Profile (EFCP) (Skinner, et al., 1984; Revised EFCP, Wirz, et al., 1990). Another protocol has been developed by Gerber and Gurland (1989), the Assessment Protocol of Pragmatic Linguistic Skills (APPLS). As this is exceptional in analysing conversation as collaborative in nature, we shall discuss it in more detail later in this section, after summarizing the currently more commonly used functional assessments. Like CADL, all these draw in part on the notion of speech acts as current in the 1980s. Both the Pragmatic Protocol and PCA rate samples of the patients' speech as appropriate or inappropriate on various dimensions. We have already commented on the intrinsic problems besetting the notion of appropriacy (see p. 152 above), which derive chiefly from two related sources: the considerable amount of inferential activity normal in any kind of discourse interpretation and the wide range of contextual information routinely used in situated speech.

The Pragmatic Protocol includes ratings of varied aspects of discourse, grouped broadly as verbal, paralinguistic and non-verbal. The verbal group of parameters includes turn-taking and topic control; the paralinguistic includes voice quality and intelligibility, while the non-verbal includes posture, gesture and facial expression. It is, as the authors acknowledge, a global appraisal of the patient's system on the principle that 'if we operate on the premise that assessment is conducted for the purpose of designing intervention programs, then the level of assessment for the client should be no finer than would be functional in a therapeutic sense' (Prutting and Kirchner, 1983: 44).

The PCA recognizes the need for a finer scrutiny than the Pragmatic Protocol. Penn uses a five-point rating scale of appropriacy and, while keeping items on non-verbal and paralinguistic aspects, includes more detail on topic use, response to the interlocutor, cohesion, fluency and 'sociolinguistic sensitivity'. This last category includes such diverse items as placeholders and fillers (surface features of talk of the kind handled by conversation analysis), sarcasm and humour, and indirect speech acts. All Penn's categories are derived from a socially orientated view of pragmatics and are represented as products of the communicative setting and the operation of Grice's maxims combined with 'rules for communicating' (Penn, 1985: 19).

The Edinburgh Functional Communication Profile (Skinner, et al., 1984) also provides an observation schedule for rating the patient's responses in conversation. Although more limited in scope than the PCA, it covers greeting, acknowledging, respond-ing, requesting, propositional communication and verbal problem-solving. The revised version (Wirz, et al., 1990) is also based on speech-act theory. As well as providing a communication performance analysis framed by the speech acts of greeting, acknowledging, responding, requesting and initiating, it offers an interaction analysis. The latter accommodates 'severely disordered communicators whose ability to convey speech acts is severely restricted' (p. 2) through a global rating of effectiveness of communication and the modalities used. This revised version also incorporates a Supplementary Interview through which speech acts can be elicited and topics initiated.

All the observational schedules reviewed above require the therapist's skills and time in rating and analysis, but there are other assessments which can be undertaken by relatives or other carers. These have the attraction of providing a quicker, although necessarily very limited, summary of patients' communicative success, at least as interpreted by those most involved in their care. They therefore have a particular attractiveness as pre- and post-measures of intervention. These are the Functional Communication Profile (FCP) (Taylor, 1965) and the Communicative Effectiveness Index (CETI) (Lomas, et al., 1989). The FCP was the first schedule to become popular for assessing functional communication. Although it was originally designed for use 'by experienced clinicians, having access to hundreds of aphasic patients in any given year', it has been widely used by speech therapists with a less extensive case load of aphasic patients, by other therapists and carers and by relatives of patients. It has also been used frequently, as a complement to formal language testing, in evaluation studies of the effectiveness of intervention. It adopts a 9-point rating scale for five modalities of communication: (non-verbal) movement, speaking, understanding, reading and 'other', the last including writing and calculating. Each category is divided into a number of activities; for example the 'understanding' category includes recognition of family names and comprehension of complicated verbal directions. Since the ratings are intended to reflect the patient's voluntary control over the activities in the course of daily life, the ratings when given by a therapist should be based on informal interaction with the patient. A conversion chart allows for the deriving of an overall percentage score of functional communication, for test-retest purposes.

The designers of CETI (Lomas, et al., 1989) have pointed out the incomplete psychometric documentation on measures such as the much earlier FCP. They have also drawn attention to its poor correlation with a scale of non-verbal communication during conversational exchanges (Behrmann and Penn, 1984). CETI is intended to be a reliable and valid measure of functional communication, for use specifically by patients' 'significant others' after a brief explanation and training period. It uses a visual analogue scale for ratings on a 16-item questionnaire concerned with everyday communication. Item Four, for example, deals with communicating emotions, and the explanation given to the rater is 'Does he/she intentionally let you know how he/she is feeling rather than you "reading" his/her emotions?'. The analogue scale is converted into numbers from 1 to 100 by a template. Preliminary results indicate that CETI reliably measures change in functional communicative ability. However, the fact that this change does not correlate significantly with change on a standard test of aphasia (the Western Aphasia Battery of Kertesz, 1982) gives support to Lomas, et al.'s claim that in recovery there is a separate dimension of functional communication which is not measured by standard clinical tests. Penn (1988) and Green (1984) similarly stress the mismatch between measures of syntactic ability and measures of pragmatic ability.

We have so far reviewed a variety of measures of pragmatic aspects of communication in current use, all primarily based on some kind of top-down analysis of communication, and many of them fairly heavily dependent on an underlying model of speech act theory. They differ in their potential for reliably measuring change in functional communication, and in the demands they make on the therapist's time. Like formal clinical batteries of language tests, the direct implications for intervention which can be drawn from them are somewhat tenuous. Despite their limitations, their main clinical utility at present is as test-retest measures of an elusive dimension of communication which standard batteries do not capture.

One protocol, however, represents a considerable advance on these methods: this is Gerber and Gurland's APPLS, which we referred to earlier. It is exceptional in four ways. It employs a bottom-up analysis of natural conversation; it views conversation as collaborative rather than concentrating only on the patient's performance; it acknowledges the interdependence of linguistic and pragmatic abilities; and it provides specific guidance on intervention. We shall discuss these four advances in turn.

First, APPLS is based on analyses of two samples of

conversation, one between the patient and a familiar partner (the spouse), the other between the patient and a newcomer (the clinician). It therefore enables some inferences to be made about the influence on conversation of the degree of shared knowledge between the participants, and the extent to which the patient's behaviour reflects this. It also permits a comparison of how the patient functions with two conversational styles. Secondly, APPLS' focus on the collaborative nature of conversation allows the assessment of aphasic breakdowns to be objective. Judgement of whether such a breakdown has actually occurred, and whether a repair is successful, is made on the basis of the partner's reactions. In contrast to all the functional assessments we have just reviewed, this judgement is not made from the subjective perspective of an external rater. The analysis made centres on repairs, which are identified through one of the partners signalling that the message has not been understood, and not through any externally applied criterion of 'inadequacy'. The detailed evolution of each breakdown-repair sequence, through however many conversational turns are required, can then be examined, with particular note taken of the strategies used by both partners to effect resolution of the breakdown. Gerber and Gurland propose that, as well as a qualitative examination of these sequences, the outcome of the analysis can be quantified. Specifically, two calculations can be undertaken, that is the percentage of conversational turns in which breakdowns occurred, and the average number of consecutive unsuccessful turns that breakdown-repair sequences take. The third advance made by APPLS is the scope it provides for relating linguistic and pragmatic abilities. The consequences of linguistic disabilities (phonological, syntactic-semantic and in lexical access) are examined within a context in which their interaction with pragmatic abilities can be studied. The particular pragmatic problems which can occur are identified as problems with contextual relevance, presuppositional referencing, topic maintenance and shift and turn-taking. As an example of the interaction between linguistic and pragmatic abilities, the authors show how use of pronominal forms for previously unidentified referents indicates an area where a word-finding problem and a presuppositional referencing problem enmesh. Of particular value is the examination of the linguistic-pragmatic strategies both participants use during these breakdown-repair sequences, and this brings us to the fourth way in which this protocol is at present unique in its field; this is in drawing specific inferences for therapy from its functional analysis.

This is best illustrated from an extract which Gerber and Gurland give from a conversation between a 79 year old patient and his wife, recorded eight months after his stroke. In this extract the wife has just mentioned a friend's daughter:

> (2) Wife: You know, she's coming in. Isn't she coming in this week?
>
> Patient: She's coming in. Yeah. And tell her when you get here. When do you get to visit them? When do you? What day? What time do you visit them?
>
> Wife: Visit who, visit who?
>
> Patient: If they want to.
>
> Wife: What do you mean?
>
> Patient: They gonna call a girl up. They gonna call name up to see if you want to talk to your patient too. When I'm not here with them. You understand or not?
>
> Wife: No, say it again, I'll understand.
>
> Patient: You'll have to talk to me for a while. And then the girl, whosoever there will want to talk to you. Start asking you a few questions. See?
>
> Wife: Yeah. You'll be able to answer.
>
> (Gerber and Gurland, 1989: 275)

This is an example of a breakdown which is (apparently) resolved after five unsuccessful turns. The wife uses explicit requests for more information ('visit who?') and directives ('say it again'). The patient is responsive to these bids, but his linguistic impairment impedes his ability to provide the required information; his attempted revisions show continued pragmatic difficulties of pronominal referencing and what may be an unmarked topic shift. The therapeutic implications which Gerber and Gurland draw from this extract, and a comparison of it with the other conversation with the unfamiliar partner, are summarized under the headings of four goals. First, the patient's presuppositional referencing problems should be addressed. This could be undertaken through, for example, self-monitoring and practice in establishing referents in discourse through a combination of the patient's linguistic strengths and non-linguistic contexts (gestures, pictures). Secondly, when breakdowns occurred, the wife could be encouraged to make her bids for specific information through supplying alternatives rather than giving conversational directives. For example, in seeking clarification of her husband's 'What time do you visit them', she could ask 'Visit the family or the speech therapists?'. The third therapeutic goal that Gerber and Gurland set from the analysis is that the clinician should develop a core of shared information with the patient, in order to negotiate the conversational flow while training the targeted skills. They suggest that this might include routine events such as going to the office for coffee, so as to develop functionally useful dialogue scripts. The fourth implication for therapy was drawn from the observation that the patient himself did not make any requests for clarification, and the authors suggest that he may need to be trained in this through modelling or prompts. We have seen that requests for clarification (other-initiated repairs) are relatively uncommon in normal conversation, as participants generally allow minor problems and ambiguities to pass with the expectation that meanings will progressively emerge through its continuation. However, aphasic people who have comprehension difficulties may need specifically to learn to give clear signals that they have not understood.

In summary, APPLS is a clinical procedure orientated to the bottom-up approach of conversational analysis, which we have suggested is one of its strengths. Although the protocol restricts its detailed analysis to breakdown-repair sequences, it makes considerable advances over other current procedures for assessing functional communication, not the least of which is its capacity for deriving specific recommendations for therapeutic procedures. However, at the time of writing, it has not yet to our knowledge been reported as having been used in evaluations of such therapeutic procedures. It is to such evaluations that we turn next, before we come back to the important question of what might be included in a detailed conversational-analysis approach to intervention.

EVALUATING PRAGMATIC THERAPY: EXPERIMENTAL STUDIES

Although the FCP has been used frequently as one of the assessment measures to evaluate the success of conventional therapy, there seem at present to be relatively few well-controlled studies which have aimed at quantifying changes following pragmatic therapy of the kind we described in the first two sections of this chapter. One such study, by Aten, et al. (1982) used CADL in order to test the effectiveness of a programme of functional therapy, using group role play. This was a study of seven men, all of whom had a chronic aphasia with agrammatism, of between nine months and nearly 22 years duration. They had all received extensive conventional therapy, lasting for at least seven months. The assumption was therefore that they had all reached a relatively stable level, and that an evaluation study of intervention would not be invalidated by continuing spontaneous recovery. The 12-week programme of functional therapy consisted of role playing focused on six situational contexts requiring communicative abilities: shopping, giving and following directions, social greetings, supplying personal information, reading signs and directories and using gesture to express ideas. These situations were derived from those listed in CADL, but CADL test items were not used as such, and the materials were selected to be personally relevant to the men concerned. In the first of the twice-weekly sessions, the therapist provided cues and modelled appropriate responses, but in the second session the patients were encouraged to respond without this help. CADL was used as the instrument to assess communication at the beginning, middle and end of the programme, and six weeks after treatment was completed. A standardized formal clinical test, the Porch Index of Communicative Effectiveness (PICA), was also the comparator measure of language behaviour. In the outcome there was significant improvement on the CADL scores but not on the PICA scores. Although this was a well controlled study, using different assessors and therapists, the conclusions would have been more convincing had the items used in the therapy programme not been so similar to the items measured by CADL, and had a measure of generalization of the therapy to non-clinical situations been incorporated.

Our second example of a study measuring change in communicative behaviour also illustrates the use of direct intervention in a clinical setting to improve functional communication. Kearns (1985) incorporated what he called 'loose training' in assisting a patient with a three-year history of Broca's aphasia to elaborate his responses and produce creative language in a conversational setting. Picture stimuli were used for this, with the therapist giving in his own speech models for expansion of the patient's minimal utterances, and prompting further elaboration by cueing with questions such as 'Why is he . . .?'. Although this procedure may at first sight seem to resemble normal collaborative strategies for achieving successful reference (see Chapter 8), in fact it more closely resembles the test questions characteristic of the classroom discourse analysed by Sinclair and Coulthard (see p. 162 above). This is because the information to be communicated was already known to the therapist, since the pictures were placed in full view of both interlocutors. Furthermore, the intervention was metalinguistic in a manner quite uncharacteristic of naturally occurring conversations, in that the therapist suggested repetitions of successful utterances and praised them. Although generalization to spontaneous conversations was not examined in this study, the experimental design allowed the effectiveness of the intervention to be examined by testing whether the patient generalized his responses to pictures which had not been used in the programme. A multiple baseline design was also used, with half of the pictures forming a second set which was not used in therapy until 17 sessions had been spent on the first set.

A well-controlled study by Doyle, et al. (1989) was designed to facilitate the production of requests by patients with Broca's aphasia. It follows the behaviourist tradition in intervention by assuming that subjects can indeed perform the targeted activity in a rudimentary fashion, but that it needs to be shaped and encouraged through modelling and rewards. Requests were defined as any utterance which 'solicited the hearer to affirm, negate, or confirm the proposition of the speaker's utterance or solicited information about the identity, location, or property of any object, event or situation' (p. 159). The patients were expected to mark questions by means of an interrogative structure or by rising intonation. For each of their four patients Doyle, et al. used three therapists and a number of volunteers. To establish a baseline for the amount of requesting used by the patients before therapy, a series of sessions was conducted three times weekly until a stable level was recognized. Each session consisted of six separate five-minute conversations with one of the three therapists and three volunteers in turn. A topic was suggested for each session, and the patient was told to ask as many questions about it as possible. The therapy which followed consisted of 36 to 40 sessions; in each session the therapist set a topic, and looked expectantly at the patient for up to 20 seconds until the patient responded with a request for information on the topic. The reward for successful requesting was praise and being given the requested information. After 20 seconds without an adequate response, the therapist provided prompts and, if necessary, models. In the case of one patient cue cards were also provided dealing with topics on which questions could be asked, for example focusing on 'personal information' in relation to home, family, career, neighbourhood and so on. Each week a conversation with a volunteer took place, acting as a probe measure, until four probes had been conducted for each of the three topics which were targeted (personal information, leisure activities, health). The multiple baseline design allowed for detection of whether requesting abilities had generalized to untrained topics, and whether the use of requests on trained topics was maintained when these were no longer the subject of therapy. Also included in this study was a control group of 72 volunteers, who met separately in unfamiliar pairs. These volunteers were given similar instructions to those given to the patients, with a view to testing how much requesting behaviour might be expected to occur under these circumstances. The results showed that, for all four experimental subjects, requesting behaviour generalized, particularly in the conversations held with the therapists, who had become familiar partners. One of the patients, who had a co-occurring apraxia of speech, showed less generalization to conversations with the volunteers, who were strangers to him (in these naturalistic conversations responses were frequently expected following a delay of less than 20 seconds). Treatment did not, however, result in generalization of requesting behaviour across topics, which the authors consider may have been a consequence of the training method discouraging off-topic requests. These four patients used intonational questions much more frequently than syntacticized interrogatives. From a baseline which was below that of the controls (for all except the topic of health with one subject), subjects reached a normal level after treatment. The only exception was the verbally apraxic patient's conversations on 'leisure'. Subjects were also rated as significantly more talkative than before the therapy programme began.

All these studies have used direct therapy to improve conversational abilities in aphasia. However, although they deal with impairment at a pragmatic level, they focus on the impairment as a disability of the individual rather than on the handicap which results from the impairment. Use of indirect therapy which would emphasize the communicative consequences of the impairment through intervention with the family has long been advocated (see Wahrborg, 1989, for a brief survey). However, so far this type of intervention has been primarily psychotherapeutic in its formulation, and instruments for measuring family interactions (e.g. Mulhall's 1978 Personal Relations Index) have analysed emotional reactions to communication failures and successes rather than the conversational mechanisms which give rise to these different conversational outcomes. Supportive counselling for spouses has also been evaluated (Hartman and Landau, 1987; Rice, et al., 1987). There has been a number of reports describing the training of aphasic people's spouses to employ strategies to improve functional communication, but none, as far as we know, has yet been evaluated for effectiveness through the detailed 'bottom-up' analysis of natural conversation. The advice which has been given to relatives has been based on behaviourist techniques or on general expectancies of strategies which might be used for types of aphasia. Unlike the psycholinguistic interventions it has not been based on a detailed individual assessment – which would, in the case of the pragmatic approach, need to be of the conversational interactions between individual patient and partner rather than of the patient alone. One way of approaching this task is by means of a detailed specification of particular conversation management procedures as identified by conversation analysis, and we consider in the final section of this chapter the details of how this might be done.

A CONVERSATION ANALYTIC APPROACH TO INTERVENTION

One of the goals of conversation analysis, as described in Chapters 8 and 9, is the provision of a precise description of how interlocutors collaborate in achieving a successful conversation with relatively little gap or overlap, sharing conversational time and overcoming difficulties and misunderstandings to their mutual satisfaction. Some of more intensively studied conversational management procedures such as turn-taking and repair have, as we have seen, found their way into the aphasic literature and seem to be particularly prominent in the observation schedules reviewed in this chapter. Both appear in some form, along with other conversation analytic categories, in Prutting and Kirchner's (1983) Pragmatic Protocol, while Penn's (1985) Profile of Communicative Appropriateness (PCA) includes phenomena such as self-correction, revision, pauses and fillers which relate to repair and turn-taking. However, as so often happens in applied pragmatics, the interpretation and application of these notions are very different from those current in the original field of study, and in this case may be only indirectly related to the conversation analytic principles outlined in Chapter 8. We shall argue in this section that it is important to attend to these principles, while preserving the eclecticism characteristic of current applications of pragmatics to intervention in aphasia. Aphasiologists have always borrowed from other disciplines, and in the case of pragmatics we are suggesting no more than that the borrowing needs to be a little more principled and judicious than it usually is. Chapters 6 and 7 introduced a range of topics which, while figuring informally in conversation analysis, do not form the basis of its approach to situated speech; examples are *reference* and *indirectness*. However, such topics find a prominent place in the aphasiological literature, and we shall continue to make informal reference to them here while developing a generally conversation analytic perspective on aphasic conversation. Of all the clinical procedures which we have reviewed, Gerber and Gurland's APPLS (1989) approximates most closely to the approach which we develop in the remainder of this chapter.

Conversation analytic techniques are, for a number of reasons, a promising basis for accountable and testable intervention procedures for enhancing functional communication ability. Because conversation analytic descriptions of normal conversation are so detailed and precise, it is in general likely that they can give clinicians a clearer idea of what they are investigating and what they are teaching to both patients and carers. Many clinicians have, like Copeland (1989: 305) found that 'assessing communicative acts and conversational sequence is . . . very complex'. We shall begin by summarizing more specifically the advantages of a conversation analysis approach to aphasic communication, in the context of its underlying philosophy, orientation and method as outlined in Chapters 8 and 9. Readers are referred at various points in the following discussion to the samples of both aphasic and non-aphasic conversation which are discussed in those chapters. We pay particular attention to differences of orientation between this approach and those of the schedules and profiles discussed in the previous sections of this chapter. This is because, given a more principled orientation, it is likely that these instruments could profile communicative ability more effectively and validly than they do at present. To a more limited extent we shall comment on similarities and affinities, especially with Gerber and Gurland's APPLS. As we have already remarked, this protocol embodies many of the advantages of a conversation analysis approach, the chief of which are as follows.

First, since conversation analysis is a bottom-up procedure, aphasic (like non-aphasic) conversations are approached with minimum prior imposition of analytic categories. Nor is a set of interactional behaviours initially defined, with respect to which individual conversationalists are rated as appropriate or inappropriate. Conversation analysis starts with the working assumption that all recorded data are potentially relevant, until the analyst has reason to conclude otherwise. As Levinson (1983) points out, this data-driven approach has illuminated the apparently irregular, unstructured casual conversations of everyday life. It compares favourably in this respect with top-down approaches such as speech act theory and the exchange analysis developed initially by Sinclair and Coulthard for the analysis of classroom interaction. Since it is a set of procedures for analysing *unidealized* contextually situated data, there is no reason to suppose that it cannot be applied equally successfully to other kinds of irregular, non-standard data like aphasic discourse, whose relationship to 'normal' discourse is simply not known. Conversation analysis is the only approach to pragmatics which explicitly takes account of the minutiae of conversation such as filled and unfilled pauses, overlaps, repetitions and repairs. This is particularly relevant to aphasic discourse, which is generally replete with these phenomena.

Secondly, pragmatic competence is frequently said to be well preserved in aphasia, and we noted earlier that measurable changes in linguistic ability may not necessarily correspond to changes in functional communication ability (Green, 1984; Copeland, 1989). However, as far as we can judge from a reading of the relevant research (see for example Joanette and Brownell, 1990) this assumed preservation of pragmatic ability is chiefly at the level of propositional and logical structure of discourse, and at the level of larger scale 'textual' organization. Inferencing ability of the kind illuminated by Gricean theory (along with its later developments) and speech act theory also seems to be relatively intact.

Even if pragmatic competence at this level is typically intact, the conversational ability of aphasic speakers cannot be said also to be unimpaired, since certain interactional consequences spring from limitations of working verbal memory and difficulty in accessing lexical items and processing utterances at the level of syntactic and semantic structure. For example, many of the samples of aphasic conversation cited in Chapter 9 reveal difficulties not generally encountered by normal speakers in rapidly repairing trouble spots in the conversation. It is often relatively difficult for aphasic speakers either to revise current utterances ('self-repair') or to respond to requests for clarification ('other-repair'); recall that this is the important area tackled by Gerber and Gurland's APPLS procedure. Aphasic speakers also find it hard to control placement and length of pause both within and between turns, a difficulty which has potentially far-reaching pragmatic consequences, since in certain sequential contexts pauses themselves have the capacity to trigger predictable inferences (see (11) and (12) in Chapter 9). Conversation analysis is therefore the approach which addresses itself most directly to the level of pragmatic difficulty typically experienced by aphasic patients. It enables the therapist to seek explanations for communicative success or failure with reference to the structural characteristics of patients' language and limitations imposed by their impairment (as exemplified by Gerber and Gurland's example (1) above) rather than stressing the separateness of linguistic and pragmatic problems. Conversation analysis provides tools for describing with some precision the likely communicative consequences of a particular patient's impairment.

Thirdly, conversation analysis explicitly treats a successful conversation as a *collaborative* process, and the onus of achieving a satisfactory outcome is placed jointly upon the patient and communicative partner. Conversational management procedures such as repair, turn-taking, opening and closing are thus seen as jointly negotiated rather than (as in most schedules with the exception of APPLS) a potential area of pragmatic impairment in the patient. This collaborative orientation clearly aligns well with the current interest in indirect therapy described on p. 303 above, which seeks to involve the patient's relatives and carers in intervention. Conversation analysis offers a means of deriving from observation of everyday interaction a set of precise instructions to patients and relatives which make explicit their respective roles in the interaction. As we shall see later, this emphasis on collaboration does not, however, preclude a further analysis of the patient's own contribution which may illuminate both strengths and weaknesses and the nature of his or her overall contribution to the conversation.

Fourthly, conversational behaviours are analysed and interpreted in their sequential context. This is the general point made by Penn (1984) in her discussion of strategies adopted by aphasic patients, but conversation analysis allows us to follow through the implications of her point that similar behaviours are interpreted differently on different occasions (see p. 293 above). Thus, for example, although we might use a measure of mean length of pause between turns as part of a very general account of the characteristics of the patient's conversational ability, we need to recognize that a pause following the first part of an adjacency pair is likely to receive a different interpretation from a pause in other between turn positions. The utterance following the pause would also be important in the analysis. Equally, the 'meaning' of discourse markers such as *oh* or *mm* varies with sequential context, as Schegloff (1987) has shown. Nor would indirect speech acts be considered independently of their context, and the relevant issue would not be the patient's control of or response to an independently defined series of acts, but whether an act such as requesting, offering, or disagreeing (in conversation analytic terms different types of 'first pair parts' – see Chapter 9, p. 193 above) was successfully accomplished. Evidence for success or failure would be sought in the interlocutor's response and the subsequent interactional outcome. Analysis of non-verbal behaviours such as gesture is also informed by this principle, in that behaviours are not simply described and measured, but their place in structure and their function are examined, as evidenced by the response of the interlocutor(s). Examples of functions of gestures in aphasic conversation already discussed in Chapter 9 are in referring, repairing, and as turn-holding devices.

This focus on sequential context has a number of further implications for the way conversational data are approached, which contrast sharply with current approaches to intervention described earlier in this chapter. The most important perhaps is that quantitative analysis is seen as being of only limited value, at best being supplementary to qualitative analysis of the kind illustrated in Chapter 9. We alluded above to the difficulties inherent in quantifying particular behaviours such as between-turn pauses as a means of characterizing the patient's conversational strengths and weaknesses when different pauses have different communicative functions. A finer-grained quantification of sub-types would however require an unrealistically large corpus of data. A qualitative analysis, on the other hand, requires larger single sequences of conversation than are generally used to illustrate or analyse behaviour; consider for example the length of the repair sequence in (32) in Chapter 9 which ends with expressions of mutual satisfaction that understanding has been achieved. It is on the basis of the final turns in this sequence that an analysis of the repair as successful is validated, the unit of analysis thus being the sequence, rather than the turn or the pair of turns.

This leads to the fifth and final point which we need to make about the applicability of conversation analysis to aphasic data. The concept of appropriacy, so commonly used in rating the behaviour of aphasic speakers but so problematic in practice (see further Chapter 7), is replaced with a concept of success or failure of the interaction. Rather than using criteria such as measures of inter-judge reliability to validate judgements of appropriacy on a two- or five-point scale, behaviours like self-correction or indirect speech acts (to cite but two items profiled in Penn's PCA) can be judged as effective or otherwise with reference to the subsequent interactional outcome. Evidence for the analyst's judgement is therefore sought not in measures of probability but in the observable behaviour of participants. For instance, if an act of anaphoric reference was unsuccessful, the central issue would not be the appropriacy or otherwise of that act of reference as judged by a non-participating third party, but whether any difficulty experienced by the interlocutor in identifying the antecedent of the anaphor gave rise to a successful repair (see (2) above for an example). A further clinically relevant question might be how the repair was achieved – by the speaker spontaneously (self-repair), after some comment by the partner (other-initiated self-repair) or by some kind of collaborative act (see (26)–(32) in Chapter 9 for a variety of relevant examples).

In the following section we shall suggest more concretely how this approach might be implemented by the clinician to assess the strengths and weaknesses of a patient's functional communicative ability, and to derive guidelines for both direct clinical work and indirect therapy involving relatives and other carers. The procedure is presented in the form of a 'checklist' to be used for identifying conversational strengths and weaknesses. Specific inferences for therapy can also be drawn in a manner similar to the APPLS procedure, which is restricted to repair and clarification sequences (see p. 310f. above).

A BOTTOM-UP PROCEDURE FOR ANALYSING APHASIC CONVERSATION

The basic data required are audio-tape recordings in a familiar setting of relatively small samples of conversation between the aphasic patient and a familiar partner. Patient–therapist interaction can also be analysed (cf. the APPLS procedure) always allowing for the special characteristics of 'institutional' discourse (see p. 162 above). Ten-minute samples seem to be sufficient for most purposes and may indeed sometimes be too much to cope with, since conversation analysis typically focuses intensively upon very small fragments of data. Samples are most useful when information is included on length of pause, filled pauses, overlap, repetition, searching behaviour and unintelligible sequences. The simple transcription system recommended by Crystal, et al. (1981) is generally quite adequate, although we have used an expanded set of conversation analytic transcription conventions based on those of Levinson (1983), which are listed at the beginning of this book.

The general procedure is to scan the conversational sample using as an analytic framework a checklist which is organized round the five major conversational management procedures discussed in Chapter 9:

1. turn-taking and the structure of conversational pairs
2. repair
3. embedding of sequences
4. routines
5. discourse markers.

This list is not intended to be prescriptive. Some items might be omitted if they seem irrelevant and others might be included if the list proves inadequate for a particular conversation. McTear (1985), whose eclectic approach to situated speech is less oriented to conversation analysis (focusing on the patient rather than on both participants) offers some useful suggestions. For example, he proposes a detailed examination of the patient's initiation and response patterns, with attention to the realization of responses as minimal or with additional content. He also considers various forms which initiations might take – such as interrogatives, statements, vocatives, or gestures (McTear, 1985: 55f.).

The purpose of the checklist is to identify the patient's strengths and weaknesses in so far as they are evident in the conversation. The major questions are whether and how particular conversational mechanisms are handled by the participants, and whether specific communicative problems as evidenced by the behaviour of participants can plausibly be attributed to an independently established impairment, such as a lexical retrieval difficulty.

In the following checklist the patient is referred to as P, and assumed to be male, the interlocutor as I and assumed to be female. Clinicians may find it useful to score some behaviours as occurring 'frequently' or 'occasionally', rather than as being categorically present or absent. Further relevant observations may be included in a 'Comment' box at the end of each section of the checklist.

CHECKLIST OF CONVERSATIONAL ABILITIES

A. *Turn-taking:*

1. Does P hand over turns to I (as opposed to running on until interrupted)?
2. Conversely, does P take his turn when explicitly selected as next speaker?

3. If he does is this after an excessive pause?
4. Does P signal intent to take the floor?
5. Is there evidence of intolerance by either party of 'processing' pauses as a result of the pressures of the turntaking system (for example P might rush to take a turn before processing the utterance or I might start to speak before P can do so)?
6. Conversely, is there evidence that pauses between turns are triggering incorrect inferences?
7. Does P initiate talk - that is speak even when he is not under an obligation to do so as opposed to responding to an explicit handover of the turn by I?
8. Does P limit himself to minimal responses when selected as next speaker?
9. Does P use turn-holding strategies interpreted by I to indicate that his turn is in progress?

COMMENTS ON SECTION A:

B. *Repair:*

10. Is P able to locate and spontaneously repair trouble spots in the conversation?
11. Is there evidence that any particular behaviour of either participant gives rise to conversational difficulty?
12. Can P carry out a repair in response to a request for clarification or a difficulty otherwise indicated by I?
13. Is there evidence of a particular difficulty with lexical, phonological or syntactic repair?
14. Do P and I achieve repair collaboratively?
15. Is repair achieved extralinguistically, by for example modality-shift or gesture?
16. Do participants indicate the successful outcome of a repair sequence?

COMMENTS ON SECTION B:

C. *Embedding of sequences:*

17. Is there evidence that P uses and responds to summonses and other presequences which orient participants to a later target sequence?

18. Is there evidence that P can introduce topics by presequences (as opposed to non verbally or by means of vocatives?

19. If insertion sequences appear in the data, are they particularly troublesome to P?

COMMENTS ON SECTION C:

D. *Routines:*

20. Do P and I work together to accomplish mutually acceptable opening and closing routines?

COMMENTS ON SECTION D:

E. *Discourse markers:*

21. Is P able to make use of discourse markers in such a way as to signal to I:
    topic change
    response
    distress
    surprise
    acknowledgment or agreement
    other (specify in comments box)

22. Does P make disproportionate use of discourse markers as minimal responses?

COMMENTS ON SECTION E:

This checklist allows the specific *functions* of P's contributions to be examined in their sequential context, offering a procedure for seeking answers to questions such as the following: 'How is he using gesture, pause, fillers, discourse markers?' 'Are they being employed as strategies to help the interaction?' 'Does the subsequent interaction suggest that they facilitate effective communication?' 'If communication seems to be unsatisfactory for the participants, can the source of the breakdown be located and a collaborative strategy devised for avoiding it?' and so on.

We have already seen how quite detailed implications for

therapy can be drawn from Gerber and Gurland's protocol. For example it is clear from (2), quoted on p. 312 above, that P's use of personal pronouns without clear referents gives rise to a long repair sequence. This suggests not only therapeutic work with P's interlocutor on how such repair sequences might best be handled, but may alert the therapist to the need to consider whether direct work with P on strategies for adequately identifying referents should be attempted at this time. While the checklist is similar to APPLS in its general orientation, it attempts to move beyond repair and breakdown sequences in offering a more comprehensive framework for examining aphasic conversations. It can also offer guidelines for both direct and indirect therapy. For example, interlocutors may be alerted to problems associated with pauses in certain contexts (but not necessarily pauses in general); or both parties may need to be taught to be tolerant of gaps between turns; or to be alert to problems posed by embedded sequences.

In view of the particular complexities associated with aphasic repair sequences (see Chapter 9, extracts (26)–(32)) it may be worth looking closely at these, as Gerber and Gurland have done. For example, it may be useful to help the non-aphasic partner to understand the circumstances in which it is preferable to avoid an overt other-repair and to assist the aphasic speaker in giving clear signals that s/he is engaged in a lengthy repair sequence. The failure of the therapist in (12) in Chapter 9 to understand this and the absence of any clear signal by the aphasic speaker appears to have contributed to a prolonged conversational breakdown.

We have alluded several times to the particularly close affinity between the APPLS protocol and the approach developed here, but it is clear that the analysis embodied in the checklist also reflects the major preoccupations of much other current work on intervention, Penn's work on strategies (see p. 291f. above) being a clear example. She suggests that while communicative strategies may need to be taught to some patients, spontaneously acquired but maladaptive strategies may need to be unlearned by others; many of the strategies identified partly correspond to the behaviours set out in the checklist. We would suggest that the checklist can supplement work such as Penn's in enabling the therapist to identify quite precisely both facilitative strategies (which need to be taught) and maladaptive strategies (which need to be unlearned). At present it is not clear how these strategies might reliably be identified from current assessments.

QUANTITATIVE ANALYSIS

In this section we shall look at the advantages (and some of the difficulties) of attempting a supplementary quantitative analysis of the behaviours examined in the checklist. We noted earlier the conversation analytic orientation of Gerber and Gurland's protocol, which proposes a framework for primarily *qualitative* analysis. However, the authors also quantified the outcome of that analysis; they undertook calculations both of the percentage of conversational turns in which breakdowns occurred and the average duration (measured in consecutive turns) of breakdown-repair sequences.

While a sound qualitative analysis offers a basis for intervention in enabling the therapist to identify accurately areas of strength and weakness, the chief advantage of a quantitative analysis is in facilitating *comparison* of various kinds – for example between speakers or between the same speaker in different situational contexts or at different times. This allows evaluation of whether intervention has effected any change in communicative behaviour. Here are some examples of measures which are likely to be relevant to comparison and assessment:

1. average length of turn;
2. length of pause between or within turns;
3. frequency of discourse markers and minimal responses relative to those of the conversational partner;
4. relative frequency of non-verbal contributions.

An example of such simple quantitative analysis may be found in Chapter 9, p. 223 above, where the frequency of an aphasic and a non-aphasic partner's minimal response tokens are compared. Conversations with two different partners (student interviewer and relative) were examined, and the analysis revealed a reliance by the aphasic partner on mimimal response tokens with the relative but not with the interviewer. While this information is potentially useful as a basis for deciding to encourage the aphasic speaker to take a more active part and the relative a less active part in the conversation, quantitative analysis supplements rather than replaces qualitative analysis. The example of non-verbal behaviour makes this clear; for some partners it may be useful to examine quantitatively the proportion of verbal and non-verbal contributions by each participant. But the sequentially constrained functions of, for example, gesture would also need to be recognized, since gesture can accomplish a number of different tasks such as turnholding and repair (see Chapter 9, (5) and (29)). It is quite likely that qualitative analysis would suggest that the non-verbal behaviour was more successful in one sequential context than another, while a purely quantitative analysis would tend to submerge important distinctions.

Distortions arising from the lumping together of physically similar but functionally different behaviours are not the only hazard of quantitative analysis. In a recent pilot study which monitored the evolution of communication abilities over a six-week span in acute and chronic aphasic speakers, Crockford (1991) used a measure of the number of consecutive turns necessary to complete repairs, similar to that of Gerber and Gurland (see p. 311 above). While other measures suggested that one patient's functional communication had improved, Crockford found that the average duration of repair sequences had actually increased. Closer qualitative analysis revealed the explanation for this apparent paradox, namely that the patient's conversational partner (his wife) had responded to his improved conversational ability by collaborating less on repair sequences, forcing the patient to carry out his own repair work. Some kind of quantitative analysis is clearly needed for evaluation of therapy or to provide evidence on which to base decisions about continuing, changing, or concluding intervention. However, Crockford's work offers a clear illustration not only of its advantages, but also of its hazards.

In conclusion, the checklist which we have informally presented here is intended to supplement and refine rather than replace existing assessment schedules. It should help clinicians identify rather precisely communicative strengths and weaknesses, and provide a principled basis for both direct and indirect therapy. Because it is an open-ended bottom-up procedure rather than a defined protocol, it should be capable of offering more than we have been able to specify here. It is intended at present as a framework for approaching varied and intransigent data rather than a formal assessment procedure.

SUMMARY

In this chapter we focused on direct applications of pragmatic principles to aphasia. We began with examples of both maladaptive and functionally useful pragmatic strategies reported in studies of aphasia, with particular reference to Penn's classification. The kind of strategies which could be taught in a direct intervention which had the aim of 'total communication' were described, both in naturalistic and clinical settings. Amongst these we discussed the use of drawing, symbols (including computerized ones) and gesture. For indirect therapy, for example intervention mediated through changing the patient's 'communicatory environment', the procedures used in conversation analysis are particularly relevant. They facilitate a detailed understanding of the extent to which the aphasic impairment results in a communicative handicap. We reviewed some of the current assessment procedures which attempt to address this issue, examining both elicitation and observation schedules. Within the latter category we distinguished schedules which require expert analysis from those which can be used by relatives.

None of these assessment procedures is entirely satisfactory in offering a principled and reasonably comprehensive framework for examining functional communication. A few experimental studies were described which have applied pragmatic principles to therapy and attempted a global evaluation of its success. Finally, we pointed out some of the advantages of therapists incorporating conversation analytic methods into their assessments of aphasic patients. A procedure incorporating a (conversation analytic) collaborative model of conversation was presented in the form of a checklist. This is intended to offer as a further resource to clinicians a framework for the analysis of functional communication. The use of the checklist to provide a basis for supplementary quantitative analysis was also discussed.

THIRTEEN

Contrast and complement: some concluding remarks

Many times throughout this book we have drawn attention to sharp contrasts between those aspects of psycholinguistics and pragmatics which we have selectively described; we have particularly attempted to highlight the contrast between their approaches and manner of application to assessment and intervention in aphasia. The goal of this final chapter is to draw together these rather scattered observations which have arisen in the course of a number of different arguments, so that we might formulate some more general conclusions. We shall not only focus on the differences between psycholinguistic and pragmatic orientations, but will also point to the affinities and similarities between them from the broader perspective of aphasia studies. Finally, we shall suggest how both might complement each other in refining clinical practice in aphasia therapy.

DIFFERENCES

We can begin with a brief restatement of the essential difference between the two approaches, a topic dealt with in some detail in Chapter 1: psycholinguistics is concerned with the individual language user's mental processes, while pragmatics deals with the relationship between the individual's language use and the context in which his or her utterances are situated. Two further differences have emerged clearly in the course of the last dozen chapters. First, psycholinguistics is multimodal, dealing with the processing of linguistic information in all four modalities of listening, speaking, reading and writing. In contrast, the approach to pragmatics which we have chosen to develop focuses chiefly on spoken language (including non-verbal communication). Its emphasis on the collaborative nature of conversation entails that comprehension and production of spoken language are of equal interest. Secondly, the domains of enquiry of each field are somewhat different. Psycholinguistics concerns itself with phonological, orthographic, lexical, syntactic, and semantic processing up to the level of the sentence (at least in the well-developed applications to aphasia we have described, although potential applications go beyond sentence level). Pragmatics on the other hand is concerned with discourse, a level of analysis which goes beyond the isolated sentence or utterance.

The radical differences in orientation and methodology between the two approaches are more profound than these relatively simple dichotomies suggest. Psycholinguistics employs a theory-driven top-down procedure, in that it starts from an experimentally derived model, which is then applied to analyse the patient's language processing. Although some applications of pragmatics to aphasia also employ types of top-down procedure, we have argued that the most productive way to examine the aphasic speaker's pragmatic abilities is from the opposite direction, bottom-up, through a data-driven conversation analytic approach. The reason for this contrast in orientation springs partly from differences in the maturity of each applied field. Benefiting particularly from a cognitive neuropsychological input and from the substantial amount of empirical data which has already accrued, psycholinguistics has had time to collect sufficient evidence for provisionally coherent models to be proposed. These models currently show the influence of an allied field, artificial intelligence, in their application of modular theory. With the development of neural network theory using parallel processors we may expect to see corresponding changes in the psycholinguistic models which are applied to aphasia. In contrast, the wider field of pragmatics is characterized by many partly developed theories of which the application is unclear, and those researchers who have adopted a conversation analytic framework have not yet developed *data-driven* models of how normal conversation works which can serve as comparators for any examination of aphasic conversations (but see Clark and Schaefer, 1987, 1989 for a move in this direction). We can draw a parallel between the present stage of development of conversation analytic approaches to aphasia and the anti-theoretical behaviourist views on aphasia of the 1970s, as exemplified by Sidman (1971). In contrast we can predict from a psycholinguistic model that, for example, particular types of naming disorder will have different consequences on conversation – uncorrected semantic confusions in the case of a disorder of the semantic system, circumlocutory strategies involving collaborative work in the case of disorders related to the phonological output lexicon, phonemic paraphasias open to other-repair in the case of disorders of phonemic assembly.

The two approaches also differ in the extent to which they lend themselves to qualitative or quantitative analysis. Quantitative measurement is the norm in psycholinguistic analyses of aphasia, and the relative ease with which test-retest scores can be compared is one of the benefits of applying this approach to intervention. But in conversational analysis quantification is fraught with hazards. With so many variables uncontrolled and uncontrollable in naturally occurring data, the identification for quantification purposes of recurrent instances of the 'same' phenomenon is problematic. One of the most influential variables may be who the conversational partner is (Green, 1984). However, de Bleser and Weisman's (1986) study of the way non-aphasic partners communicate with aphasic patients in both simulated and spontaneous dialogues shows quite clearly that partners do modify their style of interaction to accommodate the patient's needs. This brings in another variable if conversational analysis is used for test-retest comparisons; even if the partner is the same person, there may have been changes in him or her as well as in the patient (for an example see p. 329 above). Nevertheless some quantification is desirable if the success of pragmatically oriented intervention is to be evaluated, and we showed in Chapter 12 how a judicious use of measurement of duration and types of repairs may provide a foundation for such a comparison. We shall return to this point shortly, with a further example.

These very different levels of development achieved by applied psycholinguistics and applied pragmatics have been reflected at many points in this book. The psycholinguistic assessment of aphasic patients is becoming a standard procedure in case studies reported in the aphasiological literature, and even to some extent in the neurological journals; it has also made considerable inroads into clinical practice in speech-language therapy clinics. The socially oriented style of pragmatics we have emphasized in this book as potentially the most useful has yet to have much influence either in published research or in clinical practice, although it does offer a systematic framework within which everyday clinical practice can be developed. It is for this reason that we have devoted a considerable amount of space in this book to expounding conversation analytic procedures, clarifying basic principles and locating them within the broader field of pragmatics.

SIMILARITIES

It would be wrong to conclude, however, that the two approaches we have selected as particularly promising are worlds apart in the way they tackle the phenomena of aphasia, and in their potential utility to aphasia therapists. Here we briefly comment on some of their similarities. We can note first that while both are broadly linguistic approaches, they are rather distant from the abstract theoretical linguistic orientations which once dominated the aphasiological literature. Both seek to use empirically accountable evidence, collected in the one case using controlled experimental techniques and in the other as far as possible in naturally occurring settings. Both attempt to avoid the intuitive and subjective, in the case of psycholinguistics through seeking explicit responses to explicit input, in the case of conversational analysis through using partners' reactions to validate a judgement that understanding has or has not been achieved rather than the investigator's assumption of intended meaning or of pragmatic appropriacy.

This avoidance of the impressionistic and the subjective leads in both approaches to an emphasis on the mechanics of linguistic structure, focusing in one case on word or sentence level and in the other on the level of the conversational sequence. Although operating at these different levels of language structure, both use an essentially reductionist method, in their concentration on fine analysis of detail. This is in contrast, for example, to the holistic interpretations of aphasia employed by some aphasiologists and psychiatrists (Darley, 1982; Sarno, 1981). Furthermore, both take as the starting point for their analysis the behaviour of non-aphasic people, making the assumption that aphasic language is not a novel kind of behaviour, but is produced by normal speakers' adaptations to abnormal constraints. Despite this reductionist orientation, both approaches nevertheless emphasize the holistic inferences which can be made from their analysis of detail – see, for example, Howard and Franklin's (1987) claim that their psycholinguistic analysis of patient MK provided an integrated interpretation of disparate data which had resulted in his being classified as suffering from several clinical aphasia syndromes. Consider also the inferences about the nature of the patient's functional communication problem which could be drawn from the detailed analysis of turn-taking difficulties in sequences (6) and (12) in Chapter 9.

Although our perspective on psycholinguistics has been restricted in the interests of emphasizing its applications to aphasia, it is important here to acknowledge the increasing concentration in cognitive psychology on the relevance of psycholinguistic and other aspects of the study of cognition to the world outside the laboratory. This focus offers a point of intersection with the central concerns of a socially orientated applied pragmatics. Reed (1982: vii) for example describes the increasing interest in studying complex, real-world tasks as the 'most exciting development in the field of cognitive psychology'. An illustration of this increasing interest may be found in Smyth, et al.'s (1987) book, which expounds the relevance to everyday life of various cognitive capacities such as those involved in reading words, categorizing objects, planning and understanding speech and reading a book. It has been proposed that pragmatic competence should be viewed as a branch of cognition, and the need articulated for a psychologically valid model of conversational inference which takes account of the manner in which inferenced meanings are collaboratively negotiated, rather than uniquely deducible from a previously worked out set of principles (Gibbs, 1987). It has also been recognized that the pragmatic dimension is an important extension to psycholinguistic modelling in aphasia (see for example Townsend and Bever's (1991) and Tyler's (1987) use of pragmatic probability).

It is probably at present in the search for a synergy of discourse and sentence-level linguistic abilities that the most likely progress is to be made in marrying the two approaches we have discussed in this book, as Patry and Nespoulous (1990) recommend. We suggest here some particular candidates for this. One is the analysis of pauses in conversational speech from both a psycholinguistic and a conversation analytic perspective, based on the principles discussed in Chapters 8 and 9. Another is an examination of the effects which word-finding difficulties, differentiated on psycholinguistic principles, might have on conversation and communication. We need to tease out the extent to which these difficulties can be interpreted as phonological, syntactic or semantic in nature, so that specifically targeted advice can be given to the partner. One area in which a conversation analysis of aphasic interaction may illuminate psycholinguistic analysis more effectively than experimental laboratory studies is in specifying the effects of limited computational space and/or attention, in that competition for resources will be involved. It is under naturalistic conditions that real-life pressures, springing from the need to communicate, expose restrictions on the communicator's capacity to do so. Laboratory conditions can change this into a metalinguistic exercise, which may impose different parameters and give rise to different behaviours from those which emerge when language is used spontaneously. Consider Caplan and Waters' (1990) comprehensive review of neuropsychological studies of the role of short-term memory in sentence comprehension. The inferences made are based on formal tasks such as sentence repetition and sentence comprehension through picture selection and judgement tasks. Such inferences do not necessarily hold true for the constraints imposed on short-term memory when artefacts of response are omitted and the pressure of a pragmatic need to understand a fellow speaker or speakers is imposed, as in everyday conversation.

CLINICAL APPLICATIONS

We would suggest that the essential link between psycholinguistic and pragmatic approaches to aphasic intervention springs from the complementary nature of their respective contributions (a point stressed by Holland, 1991). At present they are represented in the literature as forming parallel streams, each of which needs to be followed separately by the aphasia therapist in the search for a clinically relevant analysis of the patient's current language abilities. There are, however, already some respects in which the streams converge in their clinical applications, since therapies based on a psycholinguistic analysis are often pragmatic in nature. This is most obviously the case when substitutory strategies or devices are employed. For example lip-reading may be the appropriate technique to recommend as a therapy for word-sound deafness. Shindo, et al. (1991) studied four patients 'with word deafness or auditory agnosia without aphasia', whose disorder, according to the psycholinguistic analysis presented in Chapter 4, would appear to have been word-*sound* deafness as they had poor discrimination of non-words. All four patients in this study however showed improved auditory comprehension when lip-reading support was provided, although one of them had not previously used this technique in everyday life. Again demonstrating the over-simplification of our psycholinguistic model, it seemed that lip-read information on its own was not adequate for comprehension, but needed to be supported by the sounds of the words or short sentences. Lip-reading was therefore functioning not simply as a substitutory relay, but as a means of enhancing the impaired system of auditory phonemic analysis. Perhaps we should not be too surprised by this in view of the lip-reading experiments with normal subjects which have demonstrated that 'both auditory and visual sources of information are utilized in speech perception' (Massaro, 1987: 56).

In the example of lip-reading above, it could be argued that psycholinguistic modelling appears to have added little more to our understanding of these patients' disorders, other than to show how they relate to other possible patterns of function and dysfunction. Psycholinguistic modelling can however make a greater contribution than this. A case in point is where it offers an explanation for a counter-intuitive phenomemon. Pierce and DeStefano (1987) observed that a group of 11 aphasic subjects whom they tested were impeded rather than facilitated by the supportive context in which words were heard. The patients heard short narratives such as:

(1) Mother and I went shopping today
    We forgot to buy [word]
    We'll have to go again tomorrow

The key words varied in their predictability from the context. Having heard the narrative, patients were asked a question such as 'What did we forget to buy?', and were invited to select the target word from a choice of four. Contrary to prediction they made more errors when the words were highly predictable from the context than when they were not. In the highly predictable condition (where the number of acceptable words was by definition restricted, and semantic links amongst the possible set of words were close) they tended to choose appropriate alternative words. Under these conditions the patients found it harder to distinguish amongst the alternatives, due to their semantic closeness. This study presents individual results for all eleven patients; apart from one person who scored almost at ceiling, all made more errors on the 'high context' condition than on the low. This counter-intuitive result is however consistent with the psycholinguistic proposal that semantic representations become degraded through brain damage. It also reminds us that it may not be advisable to try to help some aphasic patients' word-finding difficulties by supplying semantically related words. For patients who have been assessed as having some semantic difficulties, this may be a pragmatic strategy which is best avoided.

We have indicated in this book various principled methods and specific techniques which aphasia therapists can apply in examining two complementary aspects of their patients' behaviour, the psycholinguistic and the pragmatic. To improve its clinical relevance, model-based psycholinguistic analysis needs to move towards something which can cope better with the realities of everyday life, while the analysis of natural conversation needs to develop quantifiable measures which can be used for test-retest purposes to assist in the evaluation of direct or indirect pragmatic intervention. Crockford's (1991) pilot study of the utility to speech-language therapists of conversation analytic procedures compared to two other current methods of examining functional communication provides an example of an attempt to work out quantifiable measures, such as we described in Chapter 12. Crockford also includes measurement of the increasingly important factor of how much of the therapist's time this takes. Although the conversation analytic procedure emerged as more time-consuming than the comparative methods (spouse's questionnaire and a role-playing exercise), it was the only instrument to detect finer aspects of change in the patients, and to provide information which therapists could use for specific guidance to the patients' communicative partners.

Intervention in aphasia is multi-faceted. Psycholinguistic

analysis is becoming part of routine clinical practice in many speech-language clinics, not as a detached intellectual or research exercise but as a necessary prerequisite to therapy. Cook for example, writing as a practising aphasia therapist, has described how the analysis of a patient's naming disorder led her to devise an appropriate and successful programme for him (Cook, 1991). The patient, MD, was similar to the patient described in Chapter 4 who was able sometimes to retrieve partial spelling information about a word he could not retrieve for speech. Cook diagnosed his deficits as consisting of partially impaired phonological and orthographic output lexicons without a functional phoneme-grapheme conversion link. Her therapy was aimed at establishing this link, and consisted of two phases. MD first worked on producing 'phonemes' for letters in isolation and in words, using simple drawings ('pictograms') as mnemonics. In phase two the tasks were directed at enabling him to identify the first sounds of words, so that he could then apply his newly learned ability to match them to letters. The aim was to give him a strategy whereby he could combine the partial information he had in each output lexicon. Each phase was accompanied by improvement in the targeted activity, producing at the end of the therapy programme a significantly better score on a naming test. Control tests of written lexical decision and synonym judgement did not show any changes, supporting the interpretation that it was the targeted therapy which had effected the change. The patient's spontaneous speech became fluent. Both he and his wife attributed this to the greater confidence he now had in speaking, through applying the strategy he had learned. Interestingly, this functional improvement was maintained when he was re-tested some time after conclusion of the programme, even though his score on the naming test had then reverted to the pre-therapy level. The dramatic improvement in sentence production and conversational ability had not been predicted from a programme teaching him strategies to apply in picture naming; moreover the effect on spontaneous speech lasted even though he did not maintain the conscious strategy in the later naming test. Results such as this remind us how far we have to go in developing a knowledge of the interactions amongst various dimensions of language processing, and between that and other factors influencing cognition, such as confidence and motivation. The application of psycholinguistic methods as part of clinical routine, as in Cook's example, has the potential to produce a vast amount of data to use in amplifying this knowledge, as well as to structure therapy efficiently for individual patients.

Psycholinguistic analysis, which at first sight appears to be the scientific face of aphasia therapy, needs to be tempered by acknowledgement of its limitations and of the sketchiness of its foundations. Pragmatic intervention, which originated quite differently in a more intuitive global recognition of the importance of 'functional communication', is beginning in its turn to provide a structured and objective means of analysis. We have suggested that, for aphasia, this can be best achieved through the application of the detailed procedures of conversation analysis. Notwithstanding their very different frames of reference, both psycholinguistic and conversation analyses need to combine the detailed with the global. The relevance of both to therapy is evident although their applications contrast; for the psycholinguistic approach it will be predominantly direct and one-to-one, while for the pragmatic it will be predominantly through a three-way partnership of patient, carer and therapist.

Our recognition of how very skilled aphasia therapists need to become has been evident throughout this book. The education of such therapists has traditionally laid much emphasis on their training in neurology, and we do not minimize the contribution of this training. Although we recognize the potential of aphasia for enlarging our knowledge of the relationship between brain and behaviour (Lesser, 1990a), we have in this book dissociated our approach from the neurological base of aphasia. We have concentrated instead on two other fields in which the aphasia therapist needs to become a skilled practitioner: psycholinguistics and pragmatics, with a special focus on conversational analysis. Although we have given several examples in Chapters 11 and 12 of the applications of such psycholinguistic and conversational analyses to the remediation of aphasic disorders, we must emphasize again that there is no one-to-one prescription of therapy arising from these analyses (such as medical science might claim from many of its diagnoses). The selection of appropriate interventions depends on the therapist's judgement of a number of factors, of which the patient's cognitive state and functional communication are but two. Nonetheless, we believe that the ability to make use of the two approaches we have described in this book forms an important contribution to the aphasia therapist's rational planning of both direct and indirect intervention.

References

Abbeduto, L., Furman, L. and Davis, B. (1989) Identifying speech acts from contextual and linguistic information. *Language and Speech* 32, 189–203.

Abercrombie, D. (1965) Conversation and spoken prose. In D. Abercrombie (ed.) *Studies in Phonetics and Linguistics*. Oxford: Oxford University Press.

Ahlsen, A. (1985) Discourse patterns in aphasia. *Gothenburg Monographs in Linguistics*, 5. Department of Linguistics, University of Gothenburg.

Aitchison, J. (1989) *The Articulate Mammal* (3rd edn). London: Hutchinson.

Albert, M. L. (1988) Aphasia is now treatable, *Hospital Practice*, 23, 31–38.

Albert, M. L., Bachman, D. L., Morgan, A. and Helm-Estabrooks, N. (1988) Pharmacotherapy for aphasia, *Neurology*, 38, 877–79.

Albert, M. L., Sparks, R. W. and Helm, N. A. (1973) Melodic intonation therapy for aphasia, *Archives of Neurology*, 29, 130–31.

Allen, C. M. C. (1990) Trials and tribulations in speech therapy, *British Medical Journal*, 301, 302–3.

Allport, D. A. (1984) Speech production and comprehension: one lexicon or two? In W. Prinz and A. F.Sanders (eds) *Cognition and Motor Processes*. Berlin: Springer.

Allport, D. A. and Funnell, E. (1981) Components of the mental lexicon. *Philosophical Transactions of the Royal Society of London*, B295. London, Royal Society, pp. 397–410.

Ansell, B. J. and Flowers, C. R. (1982) Aphasic adults' understanding of complex adverbial sentences, *Brain and Language*, 15, 82–91.

Arbib, M. A., Caplan, D. and Marshall, J. C. (1982) *Neural Models of Language Processes*. New York: Academic Press.

Armstrong, E. M. (1991) The potential of cohesion analysis in the analysis and treatment of aphasic discourse, *Clinical Linguistics and Phonetics*, 5, 39–52.

Armus, S. R., Brookshire, R. H. and Nicholas L. E. (1989) Aphasic and non-brain-damaged adults' knowledge of scripts for common situations, *Brain and Language*, 36, 518–28.

Aten, J. L. (1986) Functional communication treatment. In R. Chapey (ed.) *Language intervention strategies in adult aphasia*. Baltimore: Williams and Wilkins.

Aten, J. L., Caligiuri, M. P. and Holland, A. (1982) The efficacy of functional communication therapy for chronic aphasic patients. *Journal of Speech and Hearing Disorders*, 47, 93–6.

Atkinson, J. M. and Drew, P. (1979) *Order in Court: the Organisation of Verbal Interaction in Judicial Settings*. London: Macmillan.

Atkinson J. M. and Heritage J. (1984) *Structures of Social Action: Studies in Conversation Analysis*. London: Cambridge University Press.

Austin, J. L. (1962) *How to do Things with Words*. Oxford: Clarendon Press.

Bach, K. and Harnish, R. M. (1979) *Linguistic Communication and Speech Acts*. Cambridge, Mass.: MIT Press.

Bachman, D. L. and Albert, M. L. (1990) The pharmacotherapy of aphasia: historical perspective and directions for future research, *Aphasiology*, 4, 407–13.

Bachman, D. L. and Morgan, A. (1988) The role of pharmacotherapy in the treatment of aphasia: preliminary results. *Aphasiology*, 2, 225–8.

Bachy-Langedock, N. and de Partz, M-P. (1989) Coordination of two reorganization therapies in a deep dyslexic patient with oral naming disorders. In X. Seron and G. Deloche (eds) *Cognitive Approaches in Neuropsychological Rehabilitation*. Hillsdale, New Jersey: Lawrence Erlbaum.

Bailey, S. (1989) Blissymbolics and aphasia therapy: a case study. In C. Code and D. Muller (eds). *Aphasia Therapy*, 2nd edn. London: Cole and Whurr.

Barnsley, G. (1987) Repair strategies used by aphasics and their conversational partners. Unpublished BSc dissertation, University of Newcastle upon Tyne.

Basso, A. (1989) Spontaneous recovery and language rehabilitation. In X. Seron and G. Deloche (eds) *Cognitive Approaches in Neuropsychological Rehabilitation*. Hillsdale, New Jersey: Lawrence Erlbaum.

Basso, A. (1989a) Therapy of aphasia. In F. Boller and J. Grafman (eds) *Handbook of Neuropsychology, Vol. 2*. Amsterdam: Elsevier.

Bates, E., Hamby, S. and Zurif, E. (1983) The effects of focal brain damage on pragmatic expression, *Canadian Journal of Psychology*, 37, 59–84.

Bates, E. S., McNew, B., MacWhinney, A., Devescovi, A. and Smith, S. (1982) Functional constraints on sentence processing. *Cognition*, 11, 245–99.

Beattie, G. (1989) Review of T. van Dijk (ed.) (1985) Handbook of discourse analysis, *Journal of Language and Social Psychology*, 8, 69–75.

Beauvois, M-F. and Derouesné, J. (1981) Lexical or orthographic agraphia, *Brain*, 104, 21–49.

Beauvois, M-F. and Derouesné, J. (1982) Recherche en neuropsychologie et rééducation: quels rapports? In X. Seron and C. Laterre (eds) *Rééduquer le Cerveau*. Brussels: Mardaga.

Behrmann, M. (1987) The rites of righting writing: homophone remediation in acquired dysgraphia. *Cognitive Neuropsychology*, 4, 365–84.

Behrmann, M., Black, S. E. and Bub, D. (1990) The evolution of pure alexia: a longitudinal study, *Brain and Language*, 39, 405–27.

Behrmann, M. and Lieberthal, T. (1989) Category-specific treatment of a lexical-semantic deficit: a single-case study of global aphasia, *British Journal of Disorders of Communication*, 24, 281–99.

Behrmann, M. and Penn, C. (1984) Nonverbal communication of aphasic patients, *British Journal of Disorders of Communication*, 19, 155–68.

Berman, M. and Peelle, L. M. (1967) Self-generated cues: a method for aiding aphasic and apractic patients, *Journal of Speech and Hearing Disorders*, 32, 372–6.

Berndt, R. S. (1987) Symptom co-occurrence and dissociation in the interpretation of agrammatism. In M. Coltheart, G. Sartori and R. Job (eds) *The Cognitive Neuropsychology of Language*. Hillsdale, New Jersey: Lawrence Erlbaum.

Berndt, R. S. (1988) Category-specific deficits in aphasia, *Aphasiology*, 2, 237–40.

Berwick, R. C. and Weinberg, A. (1985) Deterministic parsing and linguistic explanation, *Language and Cognitive Processes*, 1, 109–34.

Bilmes, J. (1988) The concept of preference in conversation analysis, *Language in Society*, 17, 161–82.

Black, M. and Chiat, S. (1981) Psycholinguistics without 'psychological reality', *Linguistics*, 19, 37–61.

Black, M., Nickels, L. and Byng, S. (1991) Patterns of sentence processing deficit: processing simple sentences can be a complex matter. *Journal of Neurolinguistics*, 6, 79–101.

Black, S. E., Behrmann, M., Bass, K. and Hacker, P. (1989) Selective writing impairment: beyond the allographic code, *Aphasiology*, 3, 265–77.

Blakemore, C. and Greenfield, S. (eds) (1987) *Mindwaves: Thoughts on Intelligence, Identity and Consciousness*. Oxford: Blackwell.

Blakemore, D. (1988) The organisation of discourse. In F. Newmeyer (ed.) *Language: the Sociocultural Context*. Volume 4, *Linguistics: The Cambridge Survey*. Cambridge: Cambridge University Press.

Blanken, G., Dittmann, J., Haas, J-C. and Wallesch, C-W. (1988) Producing speech automatisms (recurring utterances): looking for what is left, *Aphasiology*, 2, 545–56.

Blomert L., Koster, C., Kean, M-L., Schaap, T., Von Stockert, T., Buslach, D. and Junker, D. (1990) The Amsterdam-Nijmegen everyday language test: standardised Dutch version and a preliminary study of a German adaptation. Paper presented at the Eighth European Workshop on Cognitive Neuropsychology, Bressanone.

Blomert, L., Koster, C., van Mier, H. and Kean, M-L. (1987) Verbal communication abilities of aphasic patients: the everyday language test, *Aphasiology*, 1, 463–74.

Blumstein, S. E., Milberg, W. and Shrier, R. (1982) Semantic processing in aphasia: evidence from an auditory lexical decision task, *Brain and Language*, 17, 301–15.

Brinton, B., Fujiki, M., Loeb D. F. and Winkler E. (1986) Development of conversational repair strategies in response to requests for clarification, *Journal of Speech and Hearing Research*, 29, 75–81.

Brown, G. (n.d.) Definite and indefinite reference in conversational discourse. Mimeo. Department of Language and Linguistics, University of Essex.

Brown, G. (1989) Making sense: the interaction of linguistic expression and contextual information, *Applied Linguistics*, 10, 98–108.

Brown, G. and Yule, G. (1983) *Discourse Analysis*. Cambridge: Cambridge University Press.

Brown, G. D., Sharkey, A. and Brown, G. (1987) Factors affecting the success of referential communication, *Journal of Psycholinguistic Research*, 16, 535–49.

Brown, P. and Levinson, S. (1987) *Politeness*. London: Cambridge University Press.

Bruce, C. and Howard, D. (1987) Computer-generated phonemic cues: an effective aid for naming in aphasia, *British Journal of Disorders of Communication*, 22, 191–201.

Bruce, C. and Howard, D. (1988) Why don't Broca's aphasics cue themselves? An investigation of phonemic cuing and tip of the tongue information, *Neuropsychologia*, 26, 253–64.

Brumfitt, S. and Clarke, P. (1989) An application of psychotherapeutic techniques to the management of aphasia. In C. Code and D. Muller (eds) *Aphasia Therapy*, 2nd edn. London: Cole and Whurr.

Bryan, K. (1989) Language prosody and the right hemisphere, *Aphasiology*, 3, 285–99.

Bub, D. and Kertesz, A. (1982) Deep agraphia, *Brain and Language*, 17, 146–65.

Buffery, A. W. H. and Burton, A. (1982) Information processing and redevelopment: towards a science of neuropsychological rehabilitation. In A. Burton (ed.) *The Pathology and Psychology of Cognition*. London: Methuen.

Busch, C. R. and Brookshire, R. H. (1985) Referential communication abilities of aphasic speakers. In R. H. Brookshire (ed.) *Clinical Aphasiology*. Minneapolis: BRK.

Butterworth, B. (1979) Hesitation and the production of verbal paraphasias and neologisms in jargonaphasia, *Brain and Language*, 8, 133–61.

Butterworth, B. and Howard, D. (1987) Paragrammatisms, *Cognition*, 26, 1–37.

Buttet, J. and Aubert, C. (1980) La therapie par l'intonation melodique. *Revue Médicale de la Suisse Romande*, 100, 195–9.

Button, G. (1987) Moving out of closings. In G. Button and J. R. Lee (eds) *Talk and Social Organisation*. Clevedon: Multilingual Matters.

Button, G. and Casey, N. (1984) Generating topic: the use of topic initial initiators. In J. M. Atkinson and J. Heritage (eds) *Structures of Social Action: Studies in Conversation Analysis*. London: Cambridge University Press.

Byng, S. (1988) Sentence processing deficits: theory and therapy, *Cognitive Neuropsychology*, 5, 629–76.

Byng, S. and Black, M. (1989) Some aspects of sentence production in aphasia, *Aphasiology*, 3.3, 241–63.

Byng, S. and Coltheart, M. (1986) Aphasia therapy research: methodological requirements and illustrative results. In E. Helmquist and L. G. Nilsson (eds) *Communication and Handicap: Aspects of Psychological Compensation and Technical Aids*. North Holland: Elsevier.

Caplan, D. (1987) Contrasting patterns of sentence comprehension deficits in aphasia. In M. Coltheart, G. Sartori and R. Job (eds) *The Cognitive Neuropsychology of Language*. Hillsdale, New Jersey: Lawrence Erlbaum.

Caplan, D. (1991) Agrammatism is a theoretically coherent aphasic category. *Brain and Language*, 40, 274–81.

Caplan, D. and Hildebrandt, N. (1988) *Disorders of Syntactic Comprehension*. Cambridge, Mass: MIT Press.

Caplan, D. and Waters, G. S. (1990) Short-term memory and language comprehension: a critical review of the neuropsychological literature. In G. Vallar and T. Shallice (eds) *Neuropsychological Impairment of Short Term Memory*. London: Cambridge University Press.

Caramazza, A. (1984) The logic of neuropsychological research and the problem of patient classification in aphasia, *Brain and Language*, 21, 9–20.

Caramazza, A. (1989) Cognitive neuropsychology and rehabilitation: an unfulfilled promise? In X. Seron and G. Deloche (eds) *Cognitive Approaches in Neuropsychological Rehabilitation*. Hillsdale, New Jersey: Lawrence Erlbaum.

Caramazza, A. and Berndt, R. S. (1985) A multicomponent deficit view of agrammatic Broca's aphasia. In M. L. Kean (ed.) *Agrammatism*. New York: Academic Press.

Caramazza, A. and Hillis, A. E. (1989) The disruption of sentence production: some dissociations, *Brain and Language*, 36, 625–50.

Caramazza, A., Miceli, G., Villa, G. and Romani, C. (1987) The role of the Graphemic Buffer in spelling, *Cognition*, 26, 59–83.

Carlomagno, S. and Parlato, V. (1989) Writing rehabilitation in brain-damaged adult patients: a cognitive approach. In X. Seron and G. Deloche (eds) *Cognitive Approaches in Neuropsychological Rehabilitation*. Hillsdale, New Jersey: Lawrence Erlbaum.

Chapey, R. (1981) *Language Intervention Strategies in Adult Aphasia*, Baltimore: Williams and Wilkins.

Chapey, R. (1983) Language-based cognitive abilities in adult aphasia: rationale for intervention, *Journal of Communication Disorders*, 16, 405–24.

Chapey, R. (1986) *Language Intervention Strategies in Adult Aphasia*, 2nd edition, Baltimore: Williams and Wilkins.

Chapman, S. B. and Ulatowska, H. K. (1989) Discourse in aphasia: integration deficits in processing reference, *Brain and Language*, 36, 4, 651–69.

Chiat, S. (1982) If I were you and you were me: the analysis of pronouns in a pronoun-reversing child, *Journal of Child Language*, 9, 359–79.

Chiat, S. and Jones, E. V. (1988) Processing language breakdown. In M. J. Ball (ed.). *Theoretical Linguistics and Disordered Language*. Beckenham: Croom Helm.

Chomsky, N. (1965) *Aspects of the Theory of Syntax*. Cambridge, Mass.: MIT Press.

Chomsky, N. (1981) *Lectures on Government and Binding*. Dordrecht: Foris.

Cicourel, A. V. (1987) Review article: on John A. Searle's *Intentionality*, *Journal of Pragmatics* 11, 641–60.

Clark, H. (1979) Responding to indirect speech acts, *Cognitive Psychology*, 11, 430-77.

Clark, H. and Marshall, C. (1981) Definite reference and mutual knowledge. In A. Joshi, B. Webber and I. Sag (eds) *Elements of Discourse Understanding*. London: Cambridge University Press.

Clark, H. H. and Schaefer, E. F. (1987) Collaborating on contributions to conversations, *Language and Cognitive Processes*, 2, 19–41.

Clark, H. H. and Schaefer, E. F. (1989) Contributing to discourse, *Cognitive Science*, 13, 259–94.

Clark, H. H., and Wilkes-Gibbs, D. (1986) Referring as a collaborative process. *Cognition*, 22, 1–39.

Clark, L. W. (1979) Processing interactions and lexical access during word recognition in continuous speech for a severe fluent aphasic. Paper presented at ASHA conference, Atlanta.

Code, C. (1987) *Language, Aphasia and the Right Hemisphere*. Chichester: Wiley.

Coelho, C. A. and Duffy, R. J. (1987) The relationship of the acquisition of manual signs to severity of aphasia: a training study, *Brain and Language*, 31, 328–45.

Colby, K. M., Christinaz, D., Parkison, R. C., Graham, S., and Karpf, C. (1981) A word-finding computer program with a dynamic lexical-semantic memory for patients with anomia using an intelligent speech prosthesis, *Brain and Language*, 14, 272–81.

Coltheart, M. (1983) Aphasia therapy research: a single case study approach. In C. Code and D. Muller (eds) *Aphasia Therapy*. London: Edward Arnold.

Coltheart, M. and Byng, S. (1989) A treatment for surface dyslexia. In X. Seron and G. Deloche (eds.) *Cognitive Approaches in Neuropsychological Rehabilitation*. Hillsdale, New Jersey: Lawrence Erlbaum.

Coltheart, M. and Funnell, E. (1987) Reading and writing: one lexicon or two? In D. A. Allport, D. G. Mackay, W. Prinz and E. Scheerer (eds) *Language Perception and Production: Shared Mechanisms in Listening, Reading and Writing*. London: Academic Press.

Connell, P. J. and Thompson, C. K. (1986) Flexibility of single-subject experimental designs. Part 3: using flexibility to design or modify experiments, *Journal of Speech and Hearing Disorders*, 51, 214–25.

Conway, N. (1990) Repair in the Conversation of Two Dysphasics with Members of their Families Unpublished undergraduate dissertation; Department of Speech, University of Newcastle upon Tyne.

Cook, V. J. (1988) *Chomsky's Universal Grammar*. Oxford: Blackwell.

Cook, K. (1991) An investigation into self-cuing techniques used by a high-level Broca's dysphasic client. Paper presented at British Aphasiology Society symposium on Therapeutic Approaches in Aphasia. Newcastle upon Tyne.

Cooper, J. A. and Flowers, C. R. (1987) Children with a history of acquired aphasia: residual language and academic impairments, *Journal of Speech and Hearing Disorders*, 52, 251–62.

Copeland, M. (1989) Assessment of natural conversation with Broca's aphasics, *Aphasiology*, 3, 391–6.

Coulmas, F. (ed.) (1986) *Direct and Indirect Speech*. Berlin: Mouton de Gruyter.

Coulthard, M. (1985) *An Introduction to Discourse Analysis*, 2nd edn. London: Longman.

Coulthard, M. and Montgomery, M. (eds) (1981) *Studies in Discourse Analysis*. London: Routledge and Kegan Paul.

Crockford, C. (1991) Assessing functional communication in aphasic adults: a comparison of three methods. Unpublished undergraduate dissertation; Department of Speech, University of Newcastle upon Tyne.

Crystal, D. (1982) *Profiling Linguistic Disability*. London: Edward Arnold.

Crystal, D. (1987) *Clinical Linguistics* (paperback edn). London: Edward Arnold.

Crystal, D. (1991) *A Dictionary of Linguistics and Phonetics*, 3rd edn. Oxford: Blackwell.

Crystal, D., Fletcher, P. and Garman, M. (1976, 1981) *The Grammatical Analysis of Language Disability*. London: Arnold.

Damon, S. G., Lesser, R. and Woods , R. T. (1979) Behavioural treatment of social difficulties in an aphasic woman and a dysarthric man, *British Journal of Disorders of Communication*, 14, 31–8.

Darley, F. L. (1982) *Aphasia*. Philadelphia: W. B. Saunders.

Davidson, J. (1984) Subsequent versions of invitations, offers, requests and proposals dealing with potential or actual rejection. In J. M. Atkinson and J. Heritage (eds) *Structures of Social Action: Studies in Conversation Analysis*. London: Cambridge University Press.

Davis, G. A. (1983) *A Survey of Adult Aphasia*. Englewood Cliffs: Prentice-Hall.

Davis, G. A. (1986) Pragmatics and treatment. In R. Chapey (ed.) *Language Intervention Strategies in Adult Aphasia*, 2nd edn. Baltimore: Williams and Wilkins.

Davis, G. A. and Ball, H. E. (1989) Effects of age on comprehension of complex sentences in adulthood, *Journal of Speech and Hearing Research*, 32, 143–50.

Davis, G. A. and Wilcox, M. J. (1985) *Adult Aphasia Rehabilitation: Applied Pragmatics*. Windsor: NFER-Nelson.

Davis, G. A., Wilcox, M. J. and Leonard, L. (1978) Aphasics' comprehension of contextually conveyed meaning, *Brain and Language*, 6, 362–77.

de Bleser, R., Dronsek, C. and Bayer, J. (1988) Morphosyntactic processing in German agrammatism: a replication and revision of von Stockert and Bader (1976). *Cortex*, 24, 53–76.

de Bleser, R. and Weisman, H. (1986) The communicative impact of non-fluent aphasia on the dialog behaviour of linguistically unimpaired partners. In F. Lowental and F. Vandamme (eds) *Pragmatics and Education*. New York: Plenum Press.

Delis, D., Wapner, W., Gardner, H. and Moses, J. A. (1983) The contribution of the right hemisphere to the organisation of paragraphs, *Cortex*, 19, 43–50.

Dell, G. S. (1986) A spreading-activation theory of retrieval in sentence production, *Psychology Review*, 93, 283–321.

Demeurisse, G. and Capon, A. (1989) Language recovery in aphasic stroke patients: clinical, CT and CBF studies, *Aphasiology*, 1, 301–15.

de Partz, M-P. (1986) Reeducation of a deep dyslexic patient: rationale of the method and results, *Cognitive Neuropsychology*, 3, 149–77.

Di Simoni, F. (1986) Alternative communication systems for the aphasic patient. In R. Chapey (ed.) *Language Intervention Strategies in Adult Aphasia*, 2nd edn. Baltimore: Williams and Wilkins. 345–58.

Doyle, P. J., Goldstein, H. and Bourgeois, M. S. (1987) Experimental analysis of syntax training in Broca's aphasia: a generalization and social validation study, *Journal of Speech and Hearing Disorders*, 52, 143–55.

Doyle, P. J., Goldstein, H., Bourgeois, M. S. and Nakles, K. O. (1989) Facilitating generalized requesting behavior in Broca's aphasia: an experimental analysis of a generalization training procedure, *Journal of Applied Behavior Analysis*, 22, 157–70.

Drew, P. and Wootton, A. J. (1988) *Exploring the Interactional Order*. London: Polity.

Duncan, S. (1972) Some signals and rules for taking speaking turns in conversation, *Journal of Personality and Social Psychology*, 23, 283–92.

Dunham, M. and Newhoff, M. (1979) Melodic intonation therapy: rewriting the song. In R. H. Brookshire (ed.) *Clinical Aphasiology* Minneapolis: BRK.

Early, E. A. and VanDemark, A. A. (1985) Aphasic speakers' use of definite and indefinite articles to mark given and new information in discourse. In R. H. Brookshire (ed.), *Clinical Aphasiology*. Minneapolis: BRK.

Edelman, G. (1987) *Promoting Aphasics' Communicative Effectiveness*. Bicester, Bucks: Winslow.

Edwards, S. and Garman, M. (1989) Case study of a fluent aphasic: the relation between linguistic assessment and therapeutic intervention. In P. Grunwell and A. James (eds) *The Functional Evaluation of Language Disorders*. London: Croom Helm.

Ellis, A. W. (1987) Intimations of modularity, or, the modelarity of mind: doing cognitive neuropsychology without syndromes. In M. Coltheart, G. Sartori and R. Job (eds) *The Cognitive Neuropsychology of Language*. Hillsdale, New Jersey: Lawrence Erlbaum.

Ellis, A. W. and Beattie, G. (1986) *The Psychology of Language and Communication*. London: Lawrence Erlbaum.

Ellis, A. W., Flude, B. M. and Young, A. W. (1987) 'Neglect dyslexia' and the early visual processing of letters in words, *Cognitive Neuropsychology*, 4, 439–64.

Ellis, A. W. and Young, A. W. (1988) *Human Cognitive Neuropsychology*. Hove: Lawrence Erlbaum.

Fairclough, N. (1989) *Language and Power*, London: Longman.

Fasold, R. (1990) *The Sociolinguistics of Language*. Oxford: Blackwell.

Fazzini, E., Bachman, D. and Albert, M. L. (1986) Recovery of function in aphasia, *Journal of Neurolinguistics*, 2, 15–46.

Fenwick, P. (1989) A Family Mealtime: Conversation Analysis of Turntaking Patterns. Unpublished paper, Department of Speech, University of Newcastle upon Tyne.

Ferry, G. (1989) The nervous system: repairs to the network, *New Scientist*, 1668, Inside Science, 23, 1–4.

Feyereisen, P. and Seron, X. (1982) Nonverbal communication and aphasia: a review, *Brain and Language*, 16, 191–212, 213–36.

Fillmore, C. J. (1982) Towards a descriptive framework for spatial deixis. In R. J. Jarvella and W. Klein, (eds) *Speech, Place and Action: Studies of Deixis and Related Topics*. Chichester: Wiley.

Fitz-Gibbon, C. (1986) In defence of randomised controlled trials, with suggestions about the possible use of meta-analysis. *British Journal of Disorders of Communication*, 21, 117–24.

Fleming, C. (1989) An analysis of the communication strategies employed by aphasics when conversing with other aphasics. Unpublished undergraduate dissertation; Department of Speech, University of Newcastle upon Tyne.

Fletcher, P. and Garman, M. (eds) (1986) *Language Acquisition*. Cambridge: Cambridge University Press.

Fletcher, P. and Garman, M. (1988) Normal language development and language impairment: syntax and beyond, *Clinical Linguistics and Phonetics*, 2, 97–11.

Fodor, J. A. (1983) *The Modularity of Mind*, Cambridge, MA: MIT Press.

Fodor, J. A. and Garrett, M. F. (1966) Some reflections on competence and performance. In J. Lyons and R. Wales (eds) *Psycholinguistics Papers*. Edinburgh: Edinburgh University Press.

Foldi, N. S. (1987) Appreciation of pragmatic interpretations of indirect commands: comparison of right and left hemisphere brain-damaged patients, *Brain and Language*, 31, 88–108.

Franklin, S. (1989) Dissociations in auditory word comprehension: evidence from nine fluent aphasic patients. *Aphasiology*, 3, 189–207.

Frazier, L. and Friederici, A. (1991) On deriving the properties of agrammatic comprehension, *Brain and Language*, 40, 51–66.

Frederiksen, C. H., Bracewell. R. J., Breuleux, A. and Renard, A. (1990) The cognitive representation and processing of discourse: function and dysfunction. In Y. Joanette and H. H. Brownell (eds) *Discourse Ability and Brain Damage*. New York: Springer.

French, P. and Local, J. (1983) Turn-competitive incomings. *Journal of Pragmatics*, 7, 17–38.

Funnell, E. (1983) Phonological processes in reading: new evidence from acquired dyslexia, *British Journal of Psychology*, 74, 159–80.

Funnell, E. and Allport, A. (1989) Symbolically speaking: communicating with Blissymbols in aphasia, *Aphasiology*, 3, 279–300.

Gainotti, G., Caltagirone, C. and Miceli, G. (1983) Selective impairment of semantic-lexical discrimination in right brain damaged patients. In E. Perecman (ed.) *Cognitive Processing in the Right Hemisphere*. New York: Academic Press.

Gallagher, T. M. and Craig, H. (1982) An investigation of overlap in children's speech, *Journal of Psycholinguistic Research*, 11, 63–75.

Gardner, H. (1982) *The Shattered Mind: the Person after Brain Damage*. New York: Alfred A. Knopf.

Gardner, H. (1990) Foreword to Y. Joanette and H. Brownell (eds) *Discourse Ability and Brain Damage*. New York: Springer.

Gardner, H., Zurif, E.B., Berry, T. and Baker, E. (1976) Visual communication in aphasia, *Neuropsychologia*, 11, 95–103.

Garman, M. (1989) The role of linguistics in speech therapy: assessment and interpretation. In P. Grunwell and A. James (eds) *The Functional Evaluation of Language Disorders*. London: Croom Helm.

Garrett, M. (1980) Levels of processing in sentence production. In B. Butterworth (ed.) *Language Production, 1: Speech and Talk*. London: Academic Press.

Garrett, M. (1982) Production of speech: observations from normal and pathological use. In A. W. Ellis (ed.) *Normality and Pathology in Cognitive Functions*. New York: Academic Press.

Garrett, M., Bever, T. G. and Fodor, J. A. (1966) The active use of grammar in speech perception, *Perception and Psychophysics*, 1, 30–2.

Gasparrini, B. and Satz, P. (1979) A treatment for memory problems in left hemisphere c.v.a. patients, *Journal of Clinical Neuropsychology*, 1, 137–50.

Gerber, S. and Gurland, G. B. (1989) Applied pragmatics in the assessment of aphasia. *Seminars in Speech and Language*, 10, 263–81.

Geschwind, N. (1965) Disconnexion syndromes in animals and man, *Brain*, 88, 237–94.

Gibbs, R. (1983) Do people always process the literal meanings of indirect requests? *Journal of Experimental Psychology: Learning, Memory and Cognition*, 9, 524–33.

Gibbs, R. W. (1987) Mutual knowledge and the psychology of conversational inference, *Journal of Pragmatics*, 11, 561–88.

Gibbs, R. W., Mueller, R., and Cox, R. (1988) Common ground in asking and understanding questions, *Language and Speech*, 31, 321–35.

Gielewski, E. J. (1989) Acoustic analysis and auditory retraining in the remediation of sensory aphasia. In C. Code and D. Muller (eds) *Aphasia Therapy*, 2nd edn. London: Cole and Whurr.

Givon, T. (ed.) (1979) *Syntax and Semantics*, Vol. 12. New York: Academic Press.

Gleason, J. B., Goodglass, H., Green, E., Ackerman, N. and Hyde, M. R. (1975) The retrieval of syntax in Broca's aphasia, *Brain and Language*, 2, 241–71.

Glosser, G. and Deser, T. (1990) Patterns of discourse production among neurological patients with fluent language disorders, *Brain and Language*, 40, 67–88.

Glosser, G., Wiener, M., and Kaplan E. (1986) Communicative gestures in aphasia. *Brain and Language*, 27, 345–59.

Goffman, E. (1981) *Forms of Talk*. Oxford: Blackwell.

Goldblum, G. M. (1985) Aphasia: a societal and clinical appraisal of pragmatic and linguistic behaviors, *South African Journal of Communication Disorders*, 32, 12–18.

Goldfarb, R. (1981) Operant conditioning and programmed instruction in aphasia rehabiliation. In R. Chapey (ed.) *Language Intervention Strategies in Adult Aphasia*, Baltimore: Williams and Wilkins.

Goodglass, H. (1976) Agrammatism. In H. Whitaker and H. A. Whitaker (eds) *Studies in Neurolinguistics*, Vol. 1. New York: Academic Press.

Goodglass, H., Blumstein, S. E., Gleason, J. B., Hyde, M. R., Green, E. and Statlender, S. (1979) The effect of syntacic encoding on sentence comprehension in aphasia, *Brain and Language*, 7, 201–9.

Goodglass, H. and Kaplan, E. (1983) *The Assessment of Aphasia and Related Disorders*. Philadelphia: Lee and Febiger.

Goodkin, R. (1969) Changes in word production, sentence production and relevance in an aphasic through verbal conditioning. *Behavior Research and Therapy*, 7, 93–9.

Goodwin, C. (1981) *Conversational Organisation*. New York: Academic Press.

Goodwin, C. (1984) Notes on story structure and the organisation of participation. In J.M. Atkinson and J. Heritage (eds) *Structure of Social Action: Studies in Conversation Analysis*, Cambridge: Cambridge University Press.

Green, D. W. (1986) Control, activation and resource: a framework and a model for the control of speech in bilinguals, *Brain and Language*, 27, 210–23.

Green, G. (1982) Assessment and treatment of the adult with severe aphasia: aiming for functional generalisation. *Australian Journal of Human Communication Disorders*, 10, 11–23.

Green, G. (1984) Communication in aphasia therapy: some of the procedures and issues involved, *British Journal of Disorders of Communication*, 19, 35–46.

Grice, P. (1975) Logic and conversation. In P. Cole and J. Morgan (eds), *Syntax and Semantics 3: Speech Acts*, London: Academic Press.

Grodzinsky, Y. (1986) Language deficits and the theory of syntax, *Brain and Language*, 27, 135–59.

Grodzinsky, Y. (1988) Unifying the various language-related sciences: aphasic syndromes and grammatical theory. In M. Ball (ed.) *Theoretical Linguistics and Disordered Language*. Beckenham: Croom Helm.

Grunwell, P. and James, A. (1989) *The Functional Evaluation of Language Disorders*. London: Croom Helm.

Gumperz, J. J. (1982) *Discourse Strategies*. Cambridge: Cambridge University Press.

Hagen, C. (1973) Communicative abilities in hemiplegia: effect of speech therapy, *Archives of Physical Medicine and Rehabilitation*, 54, 454–65.

Halliday, M. A. K. (1985) *An Introduction to Functional Grammar*. London: Edward Arnold.

Halliday, M. A.K. and Hasan, R. (1976) *Cohesion in English*. London: Longman.

Hand, C. R., Tonkovich, J. D. and Aitchison, J. (1979) Some idiosyncratic strategies utilized by a chronic Broca's aphasic, *Linguistics* 17, 729–59.

Hartman, J. and Landau, W. M. (1987) Comparison of formal language therapy with supportive counselling for aphasia due to acute vascular stroke, *Archives of Neurology*, 44, 646–9.

Hatfield, F. M. (1972) Looking for help from linguistics, *British Journal of Disorders of Communication*, 7, 64–81.

Hatfield, F. M. (1982) Diverses formes de désintégration du langage écrit et implications pour la rééducation. In X. Seron and C. Laterre (eds) *Rééduquer le Cerveau*, Brussels: Mardaga.

Hatfield, F. M. (1983) Aspects of acquired dysgraphia and implications for re-education. In C. Code and D. Muller (eds) *Aphasia Therapy*. London: Edward Arnold.

Hatfield, F. M. (1985) Visual and phonological factors in acquired dysgraphia, *Neuropsychologia*, 23, 13–29.

Hatfield, F. M. and Elvin, M. D. (1978) Die Behandlung des Agrammatismus bei Aphasikern, *Stimme – Sprache – Gehör*, 4, 145–51.

Hatfield, F. M. and Patterson, K. (1983) Phonological spelling, *Quarterly Journal of Experimental Psychology*, 35A, 451–68.

Hatfield, F. M. and Patterson, K. (1984) Interpretation of spelling in aphasia: the impact of recent developments in cognitive neuropsychology. In F. C. Rose (ed.) *Recent Advances in Neurology, 42: Progress in Aphasiology*. New York: Raven.

Hatfield, F. M. and Zangwill, O. (1974) Note: ideation in aphasia: the picture-story method, *Neuropsychologia*, 12, 389–93.

Hatfield, G. (1988) Neuro-philosophy meets psychology: reduction, autonomy and physiological constraints, *Cognitive Neuropsychology*, 5, 723–46.

Hawkins, P. (1989) Discourse aphasia. In P. Grunwell and A. James (eds) *The Functional Evaluation of Language Disorders*. London: Croom Helm.

Heath, C. (1984) Talk and recipiency: sequential organisation in speech and body movement. In J. M.Atkinson and J. Heritage (eds) *Structures in Social Action: Studies in Conversation Analysis*. Cambridge: Cambridge University Press.

Helm, N., Butler, R. B. and Benson D. F. (1978) Acquired stuttering, *Neurology*, 28, 1159–65.

Helm-Estabrooks, N. (1983) Exploiting the right hemisphere for language rehabilitation: Melodic Intonation Therapy. In E. Perecman (ed.) *Cognitive Processing in the Right Hemisphere*. New York: Academic Press.

Helm-Estabrooks, N., Fitzpatrick, P. M. and Barresi, B. (1981) Response of an agrammatic patient to a syntax stimulation program for aphasia, *Journal of Speech and Hearing Disorders*, 46, 422–7.

Helm-Estabrooks, N., Fitzpatrick, P. M. and Barresi, B. (1982) Visual action therapy for global aphasia, *Journal of Speech and Hearing Disorders*, 47, 385–9.

Heritage, J. (1989) Current developments in conversation analysis. In D. Roger and P. Bull (eds) *Conversation: an Interdisciplinary Perspective.* Clevedon: Multilingual Matters.

Herrmann, M., Reichle, T., Lucius-Hoene, G., Wallesch, C-W. and Johannsen-Horbach, H. (1988) Nonverbal communication as a compensatory strategy for severely nonfluent aphasics? A quantitative approach, *Brain and Language*, 33, 41–54.

Herzog, J., Hutchinson, J., Richardson, A. and Marquardt, T. (1982) Agrammatism in Broca's aphasia: a test of verb tense manipulation. Paper presented to the American Speech-Language-Hearing Association Convention: Toronto.

Hildebrandt, N., Caplan, D. and Evans, K., (1987) The man$_i$ left$_i$ without a trace: a case study of aphasic processing of empty categories, *Cognitive Neuropsychology*, 4, 257–302.

Hillis, A. E. and Caramazza, A. (1989) The graphemic buffer and attentional mechanisms, *Brain and Language*, 36, 208–35.

Holdcroft, D. (1979) Speech acts and conversation – 1, *Philosophical Quarterly*, 29, 125–41.

Holland, A. (1980) *Communicative Abilities in Daily Living.* Baltimore: University Park Press.

Holland, A. (1991) Pragmatic aspects of intervention in aphasia, *Journal of Neurolinguistics*, 6, 197–211.

Holland, A., Greenhouse, J. B., Fromm, D. and Swindell, C. S. (1989) Predictors of language restitution following stroke: a multivariate analysis, *Journal of Speech and Hearing Research*, 32, 232–8.

Howard, D. (1986) Beyond randomised controlled trials: the case for effective case studies of the effects of treatment in aphasia, *British Journal of Disorders of Communication*, 21, 89–102.

Howard, D. and Franklin, S. (1989) *Missing the Meaning? A Cognitive Neuropsychological Study of Processing of Words by an Aphasic Patient.* Cambridge, Mass.: MIT Press.

Howard, D. and Hatfield, F. M. (1987) *Aphasia Therapy: Historical and Contemporary Issues.* Hove: Lawrence Erlbaum.

Howard, D., Patterson, K., Franklin, S., Orchard-Lisle, V. and Morton, J. (1985) The treatment of word retrieval deficits in aphasia: a comparison of two therapy methods, *Brain*, 108, 817–29.

Huddleston, R. (1984) *Introduction to the Grammar of English.* Cambridge: Cambridge University Press.

Hurford, J. and Heasley, B. (1983) *Semantics: a Course Book.* Cambridge: Cambridge University Press.

Ince, L. P. (1968) Desensitization with an aphasic patient, *Behavior Research and Therapy*, 6, 235–7.

Ince, L. P. (1973) Behavior modification with an aphasic man, *Rehabilitation Research and Practice Review*, 4, 37–42.

354   REFERENCES

Isaacs, E. A. and Clark, H. H. (1987) References in conversation between experts and novices. *Journal of Experimental Psychology: General* 116, 26–37.

Jefferson, G. (1972) Side sequences. In D. Sudnow (ed.) *Studies in Social Interaction*. New York: Free Press.

Jefferson, G. (1984) Notes on a systematic deployment of the acknowledgment tokens yeah and mm hm, *Papers in Linguistics*, 17, 197–216.

Jefferson, G. (1984a) On stepwise transition from talk about a trouble to inappropriately next-positioned matters. In J. M. Atkinson and J. Heritage (eds) *Structures of Social Action: Studies in Conversation Analysis*. Cambridge: Cambridge University Press.

Jefferson, G. (1984b) On the organisation of laughter in talk about troubles. In J. M. Atkinson and J. Heritage (eds) *Structures of Social Action: Studies in Conversation Analysis*. Cambridge: Cambridge University Press.

Jefferson, G. (1987) On exposed and embedded correction in conversation. In G. Button and J. R. E. Lee (eds) *Talk and Social Organisation*. Clevedon: Multilingual Matters.

Joanette, Y. and Brownell, H. H. (1990) *Discourse Ability and Brain Damage*. New York: Springer.

Johns-Lewis, C. (ed.) (1986) *Intonation in Discourse*. London: Croom Helm.

Johnson-Laird, P. N. (1988) *The Computer and the Mind*. London: Fontana.

Jones, E. V. (1984) Word order processing in aphasia: effect of verb semantics. In F. C. Rose (ed.) *Advances in Neurology, 42: Progress in Aphasiology*. New York: Raven.

Jones, E. V. (1986) Building the foundations for sentence production in a non-fluent aphasic, *British Journal of Disorders of Communication*, 21, 63–82.

Jones, E. V. (1989) A year in the life of EVJ and PC. In E. V. Jones (ed.) *Advances in Aphasia Therapy in the Clinical Setting*. Proceedings of Cambridge symposium on aphasia therapy. London: British Aphasiological Society.

Joshi, A. K., Webber, B. and Sag, I. A. (1981) *Elements of Discourse Understanding*. Cambridge: Cambridge University Press.

Katz, J. (1981) *Language and Other Abstract Objects*. Oxford: Blackwell.

Kay, J. and Ellis, A. E. (1987) A cognitive neuropsychological case study of anomia: implications for psychological models of word retrieval, *Brain*, 110, 613–29.

Kay, J., Lesser, R. and Coltheart, M. (1992) *Psycholinguistic Assessments of Language Processing in Aphasia*. Hove: Lawrence Erlbaum.

Kay, J. and Patterson, K. (1986) Routes to meaning in surface dyslexia. In K. E. Patterson, J. C. Marshall and M. Coltheart (eds) *Surface Dyslexia: Neuropsychological and Cognitive Studies of Phonological Reading*. London: Lawrence Erlbaum.

Kean, M-L. (1977) The linguistic interpretation of aphasic syndromes: agrammatism in Broca's aphasia, an example, *Cognition*, 5, 9–46.

Kearns, K. P.(1985) Response elaboration training for patient initiated utterances. In R. H. Brookshire (ed.) *Clinical Aphasiology*. Minneapolis: BRK.

Kearns, K. P. (1986) Flexibility of single-subject experimental designs. Part 2: design selection and arrangement of experimental phases, *Journal of Speech and Hearing Disorders*, 51, 204–14.

Keenan, E. O. (1976) The universality of conversational implicature. *Language in Society*, 5, 67–80.

Kelly, J. and Local, J. (1989) On the use of general phonetic techniques in handling conversational material. In D. Roger and P. Bull (eds) *Conversation: an Interdisciplinary Perspective*. Clevedon: Multidisciplinary Matters.

Kertesz, A. (1982) *Western Aphasia Battery*. New York: Grune and Stratton.

Kinsbourne, M. (1971) The minor cerebral hemisphere as a source of aphasic speech, *Archives of Neurology*, 25, 302–6.

Knopman, D. S., Rubens, A. B., Selnes, O. A., Klassen, A. C. and Meyer, M. W. (1984) Mechanisms of recovery from aphasia: evidence from serial xenon 133 cerebral blood flow studies, *Annals of Neurology*, 15, 530–5.

Kohn, S. E. (1989) The nature of the phonemic string deficit in conduction aphasia, *Aphasiology*, 3, 209–39.

Kohn, S. E., Lorch, M. P. and Person, D. M. (1989) Verb finding in aphasia, *Cortex*, 25, 57–69.

Kohn, S. E., Smith, K. L. and Arsenault, J. K. (1990) The remediation of conduction aphasia via sentence repetition: a case study, *British Journal of Disorders of Communication*, 25, 45–60.

Kolk, H. (1987) A theory of grammatical impairment in aphasia. In G. Kempen (ed.) *Natural Language Generation*. Dordrect: Martinus Nijhoff.

Kolk, H. H. J. and Van Grunsven, M. F. (1985) Agrammatism as a variable phenomenon, *Cognitive Neuropsychology*, 2, 347–84.

Labov, W. (1966) *The Social Stratification of English in New York City*. Washington, DC: Center for Applied Linguistics.

Labov, W. and D. Fanshel (1977) *Therapeutic Discourse*. New York: Academic Press.

Laver, J. (1981) Linguistic routines and politeness in greeting and parting. In F. Coulmas (ed.) *Conversational Routines*. The Hague: Mouton.

Lecours, A. R., Osborn, E., Travis, L., Rousillon, F. and Lavallee-Huynh, G. (1981) Jargons. In J. W. Brown (ed.) *Jargonaphasia*. New York: Academic Press.

Le Dorze, G., Jacob, A. and Coderre, L. (1991) Aphasia rehabilitation with a case of agrammatism: a partial replication, *Aphasiology*, 5, 63–85.

Leech, G. N. (1980) *Language and Tact*. Amsterdam: Benjamins.

Leech, G. N. (1983) *Principles of Pragmatics*. London: Longman.

Leech, G. and Thomas, J. (1990) Language, meaning and context: pragmatics. In N. E. Collinge (ed.) *An Encyclopedia of Language*. London: Routledge.

Lesser, R. (1974) Verbal comprehension in aphasia: an English version of three Italian tests, *Cortex*, 10, 247–63.

Lesser, R. (1976) Verbal and non-verbal memory components in the Token Test, *Neuropsychologia*, 14, 79–86.

Lesser, R. (1976a) Verbal comprehension after brain damage. PhD thesis. University of Newcastle upon Tyne.

Lesser, R. (1984) Sentence comprehension and production in aphasia: an application of lexical grammar. In F. C. Rose (ed.) *Advances in Neurology, 452: Progress in Aphasiology*. New York: Raven.

Lesser, R. (1985) Aphasia therapy in the early 1980s. In S. Newman and R. Epstein (eds) *Current Perspectives in Dysphasia*, Edinburgh: Churchill Livingstone.

Lesser, R. (1989) *Linguistic Investigations of Aphasia*, 2nd edn. London: Cole and Whurr.

Lesser, R. (1989a) Some issues in the neuropsychological rehabilitation of anomia. In X. Seron and G. Deloche (eds) *Cognitive Approaches in Neuropsychological Rehabilitation*. Hillsdale, New Jersey: Lawrence Erlbaum.

Lesser, R. (1989b) Selective preservation of oral spelling without semantics in a case of multi-infarct dementia, *Cortex*, 25, 239–50.

Lesser, R. (1990) Superior oral to written spelling: evidence for separate buffers, *Cognitive Neuropsychology*, 7, 347–66.

Lesser, R. (1990a) Language in the brain: neurolinguistics. In N. E. Collinge (ed.) *Encyclopaedia of Language*. London: Routledge.

Lesser, R. (in press) Aphasia therapy. In J. Dittman and C. Wallesch (eds) *Handbook of Linguistic Disorders and Pathologies*. Berlin: Walter de Gruyter.

Lesser, R. and Perkins, L. (in preparation) *Applications of Psycholinguistic Assessments in Aphasia Therapy*.

Levinson, S. C. (1979) Activity types and language, *Linguistics*, 17, 356–99.

Levinson, S.C. (1981) The essential inadequacies of speech act models of dialogue. In H. Parret, M. Sbisa and J. Verschueren (eds), *Possibilities and limitations of pragmatics*: Proceedings of the conference on pragmatics at Urbino. Amsterdam: John Benjamins.

Levinson, S. C. (1983) *Pragmatics*. Cambridge: Cambridge University Press.

Levinson, S. C. (1988) Putting linguistics on a proper footing: explorations in Goffman's concepts of participation. In P. Drew and A. J. Wootton (eds) *Exploring the Interactional Order*. London: Polity.

Lincoln, N. B., McGuirk, E., Mulley, G. P., Lendrem, W., Jones, A. C. and Mitchell, J. R. A. (1984) Effectiveness of speech therapy for aphasic stroke patients: a randomised controlled trial, *Lancet* 1, 1197–200.

Linebarger, M., Schwartz, M. F. and Saffran, E. M. (1983) Sensitivity to grammatical structure in so-called agrammatic aphasics, *Cognition*, 13, 361–92.

Local, J. (1986) Patterns and problems in a study of Tyneside intonation. In C. Johns-Lewis (ed.) *Intonation in Discourse*. London: Croom Helm.

Local, J., Kelly, J. and Wells, W. H. G. (1986) Towards a phonology of conversation: turn-taking in Tyneside English, *Journal of Linguistics*, 22, 411–38.

Lomas, J., Pickard, L., Bester, S., Elbard, H., Finlayson, A. and Zoghaib, C. (1989) The communicative effectiveness index: development and psychometric evaluation of a functional communication measure for adult aphasia, *Journal of Speech and Hearing Disorders*, 54, 113–24.

Lowental, F., and Vandamme, F. (1986) *Pragmatics and Education*. New York: Plenum.

Lubinski, R., Duchan, D. and Weitzner-Lin, B. (1980) Analysis of breakdowns and repairs in aphasic adult conversation. In R. Brookshire (ed.) *Clinical Aphasiology Conference Proceedings* Minneapolis: BRK Publishers.

Luria, A. R. (1963) *Restoration of Function after Brain Injury*. Oxford: Pergamon.

Lyon, J. and Sims, E. (1989) Drawing: its use as a communicative aid with aphasic and normal adults. In T. Prescott (ed.) *Clinical Aphasiology*, Vol. 18. Boston: College Hill Press.

Lyon, J. and Helm-Estabrooks, N. (1987) Drawing: its communicative significance for expressively restricted aphasic adults, *Topics in Language Disorders*, 8, 61–71.

Lyons, J. (1977) *Semantics* (2 vols). Cambridge: Cambridge University Press.

Lytton, W. W. and Brust, J. C. M. (1989) Direct dyslexia: preserved oral reading of real words in Wernicke's aphasia, *Brain*, 112, 583–94.

Marr, D. (1982) *Vision*. San Francisco: Freeman.

Marshall, J., Pound, C., White-Thomson, M. and Pring, T. (1990) The use of picture/word matching tasks to assist word retrieval in aphasic patients, *Aphasiology*, 4, 167–84.

Marshall, R. C. and Phillips, D. S. (1983) Prognosis for improved verbal communication in aphasic stroke patients, *Archives of Physical Medicine and Rehabilitation*, 64, 597–601.

Marshall, R. C. and Tompkins, C. A. (1982) Verbal self-correction behaviours of fluent and non-fluent aphasic subjects, *Brain and Language* 15, 292–306.

Marslen-Wilson, W. D. and Welsh, A. (1978) Processing interactions and lexical access during word recognition in continuous speech, *Cognitive Psychology*, 10, 29–63.

Martin, A. D. (1981) Therapy with the jargonaphasic. In J. W. Brown (ed.) *Jargonaphasia*. New York: Academic Press.

Massaro, D. W. (1987) Speech perception by ear and eye In B. Dodd and R. Campbell (eds) *Hearing by Eye: the Psychology of Lip-reading*. London: Lawrence Erlbaum.

Matthews, P. H. (1979) *Generative Grammar and Linguistic Competence*. London: Allen and Unwin.

McCarthy, R. and Warrington, E. K. (1985) Category specificity in an agrammatic patient: the relative impairment of verb retrieval and comprehension, *Neuropsychologia*, 23, 709–27.

McCarthy, R. and Warrington, E. K. (1986) Phonological reading: phenomena and paradoxes, *Cortex*, 22, 359–80.

McCarthy, R. and Warrington, E. K. (1990) *Cognitive Neuropsychology: a Clinical Introduction*. London: Academic Press.

McMahon, M. K. E. (1972) Modern linguistics and aphasia, *British Journal of Disorders of Communication*, 7, 54–63.

McNeil, M. and Prescott, T. (1978) *The Revised Token Test*. Springfield, Illinois: Charles C. Thomas.

McReynolds, L. V. and Thompson, C. K. (1986) Flexibility of single-subject experimental designs. Part 1: review of the basics of single-subject designs, *Journal of Speech and Hearing Disorders*, 51, 194–203.

McTear, M. (1985) Pragmatic disorders: a question of direction, *British Journal of Disorders of Communication*, 20, 119–27.

McTear, M. (1985a) *Children's Conversation*. Oxford: Blackwell.

Mesulam, M-M. (1990) Large-scale neurocognitive networks and distributed processing for attention, language and memory, *Annals of Neurology*, 28, 597–613.

Metter, E. J. (1987) Neuroanatomy and physiology of aphasia: evidence from positron emission tomography, *Aphasiology*, 1, 3–33.

Mey, J. L. and Talbot, M. (1988) Review article: Computation and the soul, *Journal of Pragmatics*, 12, 743–89.

Meyerson, R. and Goodglass, H. (1972) Transformational grammars of three agrammatic patients, *Language and Speech*, 15, 40–50.

Miceli, G., Silveri, M. C. Villa, G. and Caramazza, A. (1984) On the basis of the agrammatic's difficulty in producing main verbs, *Cortex*, 20, 207–20.

Miller, J. (1990) Speaking, writing and language acquisition. Mimeo, Department of Linguistics, University of Edinburgh.

Milroy, L. (1984) Communication in context: successful communication and communicative breakdown. In Trudgill, P. (ed.) *Applied Sociolinguistics*. London: Academic Press.

Milroy, L. (1987) *Observing and Analysing Natural Language*. Oxford: Blackwell.

Milroy, L. and McTear, M. (1983) Linguistics for social skill training. In R. Ellis and D. Whittington (eds) *New Directions in Social Skill Training*. London: Croom Helm.

Milroy, J. and Milroy, L. (1991) *Authority in Language*, 2nd edn. London: Routledge and Kegan Paul.

Milroy, L. and Perkins, L. (1992) Repair strategies in aphasic discourse: towards a collaborative model, *Clinical Linguistics and Phonetics*, 6, 27–40.

Mitchum, C. C. and Berndt, R. S. (1991) Diagnosis and treatment of the non-lexical route in acquired dyslexia: an illustration of the cognitive neuropsychological approach, *Journal of Neurolinguistics*, 6, 103–37.

Molloy, R., Brownell, H. H. and Gardner, H. (1990) Discourse comprehension by right hemisphere stroke patients: deficits of prediction and revision. In Y. Joanette and H. H. Brownell (eds) *Discourse Ability and Brain Damage*. New York: Springer.

Mulhall, D. (1978) Dysphasic stroke patients and the influence of their relatives, *British Journal of Disorders of Communication*, 13, 127–34.

Muller, J. (1989) 'Out of their minds': an analysis of discourse in two South African science classrooms. In D. Roger and P. Bull (eds) *Conversation: an Interdisciplinary Perspective*. Clevedon: Multilingual Matters.

Murphy, G. L. (1990) The psycholinguistics of discourse comprehension. In Y.Joanette and H. H.Brownell (eds) *Discourse Ability and Brain Damage*. New York: Springer.

Naeser, M. A., Haas, G., Mazurski, P. and Laughlin, S. (1986) Sentence level auditory comprehension treatment program for aphasic adults, *Archives of Physical Medicine and Rehabilitation*, 67, 393–9.

Nespoulous, J-L. and Dordain, M. (1990) Agrammatism: a disruption of the phonological processing of grammatical morphemes? In J-L Nespoulous and P. Villiard (eds) *Morphology, Phonology and Aphasia*. New York: Springer.

Nespoulous, J-L., Dordain, M., Perron, C., Ska, B., Bub, D., Caplan, D., Mehler, J. and Lecours, A. R. (1988) Agrammatism in sentence production without comprehension deficits: reduced availability of syntactic structures and/or grammatical morphemes? A case study, *Brain and Language*, 33, 273–95.

Nettleton, J. and Lesser, R. (1991) Application of a cognitive neuro-psychological model to therapy for naming difficulties, *Journal of Neurolinguistics*, 6, 139–57.

Newcombe, F. and Marshall, J. C. (1988) Idealisation meets psycho-metrics: the case for the right groups and the right individuals, *Cognitive Neuropsychology*, 5, 549–64.

Nickels, L. Byng, S. and Black, M. (1991) Sentence processing deficits: a replication of therapy, *British Journal of Disorders of Communication*, 26, 175–99.

Nicholas, M. and Helm-Estabrooks, N. (1990) Aphasia, *Seminars in Speech and Language*, 11, 135–44.

Ochs, E. (1979) Transcription as theory. In E. Ochs and B. B.Schiefflin (eds) *Developmental Pragmatics*. New York: Academic Press.

Owen, M. (1989) Review of Schiffrin, D. (1987) Discourse markers, *Journal of Linguistics*, 25, 255–7.

Panzeri, M., Semenza, C. and Butterworth, B. (1987) Compensatory processes in the evolution of severe jargon aphasia, *Neuropsychologia*, 25, 919–33.

Parisi, D. (1983) A procedural approach to the study of aphasia, *Brain and Language*, 26, 1–15.

Pashek, G. V. and Holland, A. L.(1988) Evolution of aphasia in the first year post onset, *Cortex*, 24, 411–23.

Patry, R. and Nespoulous, J-L. (1990) Discourse analysis in linguistics: historical and theoretical background. Inn Y. Joanette and H. H.Brownell (eds) *Discourse Ability and Brain Damage*. New York: Springer.

Patterson, K. (1986) Lexical but nonsemantic spelling? *Cognitive Neuropsychology*, 3, 341–67.

Patterson, K. and Shewell, C. (1987) Speak and spell: dissociations and word-class effects. In M. Coltheart, G. Sartori and R. Job (eds) *The Cognitive Neuropsychology of Language*. Hillsdale, New Jersey: Lawrence Erlbaum.

Penn, C. (1984) Compensatory strategies in aphasia: behavioural and neurological correlates. In K. W. Grieve and R. D. Griesel (eds) *Neuropsychology II*. Pretoria: Monicol.

Penn, C. (1985) A profile of communicative appropriateness: a clinical tool for the assessment of pragmatics, *The South African Journal of Communication Disorders*, 32, 18–23.

Penn, C. (1988) The profiling of syntax and pragmatics in aphasia, *Clinical Linguistics and Phonetics*, 2, 179–208.

Penn, C. and Behrmann, M. (1986) Towards a classification scheme for aphasic syntax, *British Journal of Disorders of Communication*, 21, 21–38.

Perkins, L. (1989) Reference in aphasia: an investigation. Unpublished undergraduate dissertation, Department of Speech, University of Newcastle upon Tyne.

Perkins, L. (in progress) The impact of cognitive neuropsychological impairments on conversational ability in aphasia: an investigation. PhD thesis, University of Newcastle upon Tyne.

Petersen, S. E., Fox, P. T., Posner, M. I., Mintun, M. and Raichle, M. E. (1988) Positron emission tomographic studies of the cortical anatomy of single-word processing, *Nature*, 331, 585–9.

Peterson, L. N. and Kirshner, H. S. (1981) Gestural impairment and gestural ability in aphasia: a review, *Brain and Language*, 14, 333–48.

Pierce, R. S. (1981) Facilitating the comprehension of tense related sentences in aphasia, *Journal of Speech and Hearing Disorders*, 46, 364–8.

Pierce, R. S. (1982) Facilitating the comprehension of syntax in aphasia. *Journal of Speech and Hearing Research*, 25, 408–13.

Pierce, R. S. and DeStefano, C. C. (1987) The interactive nature of auditory comprehension in aphasia, *Journal of Communication Disorders*, 20, 15–24.

Pillon, B., Signoret, J. L., Van Eeckhout, P. and Lhermitte, F. (1980) Le dessin chez un aphasique: incidence possible sur le langage et sa rééducation. *Revue Neurologique (Paris)*, 136, 699–710.

Pinker, S. (1990) *Learnability and Cognition: the Acquisition of Argument Structure*. Cambridge, Mass.: MIT Press.

Pomeranz, A. (1984) Agreeing and disagreeing with assessments: some features of preferred/dispreferred turn shapes. In J. M. Atkinson and J. Heritage (eds) *Structures of Social Action: Studies in Conversation Analysis*. Cambridge: Cambridge University Press.

Power, R. J. D. and Dal Martello, M. F. (1985) Methods of investigating conversation, *Semiotica*, 53, 237–57.

Pring, T. (1986) Evaluating the effects of speech therapy for aphasics: developing the single case methodology, *British Journal of Disorders of Communication*, 21, 103–15.

Pring, T., White-Thomson, M., Pound, C., Marshall, J. and Davis, A. (1990) Picture/word matching tasks and word retrieval: some follow-up data and second thoughts, *Aphasiology*, 4, 479–83.

Prutting, C. and Kirchner, D. (1983) Applied pragmatics. In T. Gallagher and C. Prutting (eds) *Pragmatic Assessment and Intervention Issues in Language*. San-Diego: College Hill Press.

Prutting, C. A. and Kirchner, D. M. (1987) A clinical appraisal of pragmatic aspects of language, *Journal of Speech and Hearing Disorders*, 52, 105–19.

Pulvermuller, F. and Roth, V. M. (1991) Communicative aphasia treatment as a further development of PACE therapy, *Aphasiology*, 5, 39–50.

Quirk, R., Greenbaum, S., Leech, G. and Svartvik, J. (1972) *A Grammar of Contemporary English*. London: Longman.

Rapp, B. C. and Caramazza, A. (1989) Letter processing in reading and spelling: some dissociations, *Reading and Writing*, 1, 3–23.

Reed, S. K. (1982) *Cognition: Theory and Applications*. Monterey, Calif.: Brooks/Cole.

Resnick, L. B., Levine, J. and Teasley, S. D. (eds) (1991) *Socially Shared Cognition*. Washington, DC: American Psychological Association.

Rice, B., Paull, A. and Muller D. (1987) An evaluation of a social support group for spouses of aphasic partners, *Aphasiology*, 1, 247–56.

Robertson, I. (1990) Does computerized cognitive rehabilitation work? A review, *Aphasiology*, 4, 381–405.

Roger, D. and Bull, P. (1989) *Conversation: an Interdisciplinary Perspective*. Clevedon: Multilingual Matters.

Sacks, H., Schegloff, E. and Jefferson, G. (1974) A simplest systematics for the organisation of turntaking in conversation, *Language* 50, 696–735.

Saffran, E., Berndt, R. S. and Schwartz, M. (1989) The quantitative analysis of agrammatic production: procedure and data, *Brain and Language*, 37, 440–79.

Saffran, E. and Martin, N. (1990) Neuropsychological evidence for lexical involvement in short-term memory. In G. Vallar and T. Shallice (eds) *Neuropsychological Impairments of Short-term Memory*. London: Cambridge University Press.

Sarno, J. (1981) Emotional aspects of aphasia. In M. T. Sarno (ed.) *Acquired Aphasia*. New York: Academic Press.

Sarno, M. T. and Levita, E. (1971) Natural course of recovery in severe aphasia. *Archives of Physical Medicine and Rehabilitation*, 52, 175–9.

Schacter, D. L., McAndrews, M. P. and Moscovitch, M. (1988) Access to consciousness: dissociations between implicit and explicit knowledge in neuropsychological syndromes. In L. Weiskrantz (ed.) *Thought Without Language*. Oxford: Oxford University Press.

Schegloff, E. (1968) Sequencing in conversation openings, *American Anthropologist*, 70, 1075–95.

Schegloff, E. (1972) Notes on a conversational practice: formulating place. In D. N. Sudnow (ed.) *Studies in Social Interaction*, New York: Free Press.

Schegloff, E. (1979) The relevance of repair to syntax for conversation. In T. Givon (ed.) *Syntax and Semantics*. Vol. 12. New York: Academic Press.

Schegloff, E. (1979a) Identification and recognition in telephone conversation openings. In G. Psathas (ed.) *Everyday Language: Studies in Ethnomethodology*. New York: Irvington.

Schegloff, E. (1982) Discourse as an interactional achievement; some uses of 'uh huh' and other things that come between sentences. In D. Tannen (ed.) *Analysing Discourse: Talk and Text*. Georgetown University Round Table on Language and Linguistics. Georgetown : Georgetown University Press.

Schegloff, E. (1984) On some gestures' relation to talk. In J. M. Atkinson and J. Heritage (eds) *Structures of Social Action: Studies in Conversation Analysis*. Cambridge: Cambridge University Press.

Schegloff, E. (1984a) On some questions and ambiguities in conversation. In J. M. Atkinson and J. Heritage (eds) *Structures of Social Action: Studies in Conversation Analysis*. Cambridge: Cambridge University Press.

Schegloff, E. (1987) Some sources of misunderstanding in talk-in-interaction, *Linguistics*, 25, 201–18.

Schegloff, E. (1988) Discourse as an interactional achievement II; an exercise in conversation analysis. In D. Tannen (ed.) *Linguistics in Context: Connecting Observation and Understanding*. New Jersey: Ablex.

Schegloff, E. (1988a) Presequences and indirection: applying speech act theory to ordinary conversation, *Journal of Pragmatics*, 12, 55–62.

Schegloff, E., Jefferson, G. and Sacks, H. (1977) The preference for self-correction in the organisation of repair in conversation, *Language*, 53, 361–82.

Schegloff, E. and Sacks, H. (1973) Opening up closings, *Semiotica*, 7, 289–327. Reprinted in R. Turner (ed.) (1974) *Ethnomethodology*. Harmondsworth: Penguin.

Schienberg, S. and Holland, A. (1980) Conversational turn-taking in Wernicke aphasia. In R. Brookshire (ed.) *Clinical Aphasiology*. Minneapolis: BRK.

Schiffrin, D. (1987) *Discourse Markers*. Cambridge: Cambridge University Press.Schiffrin, D. (1988) Conversation analysis. In F. Newmeyer (ed.) *Language: the Social Context*. Vol. 4, *Linguistics. The Cambridge Survey*. Cambridge: Cambridge University Press.

Schlenk, K. J., Huber, W. and Willmes, K. (1987) 'Prepairs' and repairs: different monitoring functions in aphasic language production, *Brain and Language*, 30, 226–44.

Schneider, W. (1987) Connectionism: is it a paradigm shift for psychology? *Behavior Research Methods, Instruments and Computers*, 19, 73–83.

Schuell, H., Jenkins, J. and Jiménez-Pabón, E. (1964) *Aphasia in Adults*. New York: Harper.

Schwartz, M. (1987) Patterns of speech production deficit within and across aphasia syndromes: application of a psycholinguistic model. In M. Coltheart, G. Sartori and R. Job (eds) *The Cognitive Neuropsychology of Language*. Hillsdale, New Jersey: Lawrence Erlbaum.

Schwartz, M. Linebarger, M. and Saffran, E. (1985) The status of the syntactic theory of agrammatism. In M-L. Kean (ed.) *Agrammatism*. New York: Academic Press.

Schwartz, M., Saffran, E., and Marin, O. S. M. (1980) The word order problem in agrammatism: 1 Comprehension, *Brain and Language*, 10, 249–62.

Scott, C. and Byng, S. (1989) Computer assisted remediation of a homophone comprehension disorder in surface dyslexia. *Aphasiology*, 3, 301–20.

Searle, J. R. (1975) Indirect speech acts. In P. Cole and J. L. Morgan (eds) *Syntax and Semantics: 3: Speech Acts*, New York: Academic Press.

Searle, J. R. (1979) *Expression and Meaning*. Cambridge: Cambridge University Press.

Searle, J. R. (1983) *Intentionality, an Essay in the Philosophy of Mind*. Cambridge: Cambridge University Press.

Searle, J. R. (1986) Introductory essay: notes on conversation. In D. G. Ellis and W. A. Donahue (ed.) *Contemporary Issues in Language and Discourse Processes*. Hillsdale: Lawrence Erlbaum.

Seidenberg, M. (1988) Cognitive neuropsychology and language: the state of the art, *Cognitive Neuropsychology*, 5, 403–26.

Seron, X. and Deloche, G. (1989) Introduction. In X. Seron and G. Deloche (eds) *Cognitive Approaches in Neuropsychological Rehabilitation*. Hillsdale, New Jersey: Lawrence Erlbaum.

Seron, X., Deloche, G., Bastard, V., Chassin, G. and Hermand, N. (1979) Word-finding difficulties and learning transfer in aphasic patients, *Cortex*, 15, 149–55.

Shallice, T. (1988) *From Neuropsychology to Mental Structure*. London: Cambridge University Press.

Shallice, T. and Butterworth, B. (1977) Short term memory impairment and spontaneous speech, *Neuropsychologia*, 15, 729–35.

Shallice, T. and Warrington, E. K. (1977) The possible role of selective attention in acquired dyslexia, *Neuropsychologia*, 15, 31–41.

Shankweiler, D., Crain, S., Gorrell, P. and Tuller, B. (1989) Reception of language in Broca's aphasia, *Language and Cognitive Processes*, 4, 1–33.

Shapiro, L. P., Zurif, E. and Grimshaw, J. (1987) Sentence processing and the mental representation of verbs, *Cognition*, 27, 219–46.

Shattuck-Hufnagel, S. (1983) Sublexical units and suprasegmental structure in speech production planning. In P. F. MacNeilage (ed.) *The Production of Speech*. New York: Springer.

Shewan, C. M. (1979) A psycholinguistic approach to aphasia therapy. Paper presented at ASHA Convention, Atlanta.

Shewan, C. M. and Bandur, D. L. (1986) *Treatment of Aphasia: a Language-oriented Approach*. London: Taylor and Francis.

Shindo, M., Kaga, K. and Tanaka, Y. (1991) Speech discrimination and lip reading in patients with word deafness or auditory agnosia, *Brain and Language*, 40, 153–61.

Sidman, M. (1971) The behavioral analysis of aphasia. *Journal of Psychiatric Research*, 8, 413–22.

Siegel, G. M. and Young, M. A. (1987) Group designs in clinical research, *Journal of Speech and Hearing Disorders*, 52, 194–99.

Simmons, N. N. and Zorthian, A. (1979) Use of symbolic gestures in a case of fluent aphasia. In R. H. Brookshire (ed.) *Clinical Aphasiology*. Minneapolis: BRK.

Sinclair, J. M. and Coulthard, R. M. (1975) *Towards an Analysis of Discourse: the English used by Teachers and Pupils*. London: Oxford University Press.

Skinner, C., Wirz, S., Thompson, I. and Davidson, J. (1984) *Edinburgh Functional Communication Profile*. Buckinghamshire: Winslow Press.

Smith, S., Butters, N., White, R., Lyon, L. and Granholm, E. (1988) Priming semantic relations in patients with Huntington's disease, *Brain and Language*, 33, 27–40.

Smyth, M. M., Morris, P. E., Levy, P. and Ellis, A. W. (1987) *Cognition in Action*. London: Lawrence Erlbaum.

Sparks, R., Helm, N. and Albert, M. (1974) Aphasia rehabilitation resulting from Melodic Intonation Therapy, *Journal of Speech and Hearing Disorders*, 41, 287–97.

Spencer, A. (1988) The role of linguistics in psycholinguistic theory construction. In M. J. Ball (ed.) *Theoretical Linguistics and Disordered Language*. London: Croom Helm.

Sperber, D. and Wilson, D. (1986) *Relevance*. Oxford: Blackwell.

Sproat, R. (1986) Competence, performance and agrammatism: a reply to Grodzinsky, *Brain and Language*, 27, 160–67.

Stubbs, M. (1983) *Discourse Analysis*. Oxford: Blackwell.

Taylor, M. (1965) A measurement of functional communication in aphasia, *Archives of Physical Medicine and Rehabilitation*, 46, 101–7.

Terrell, B. Y. and Ripich, D. N. (1989) Discourse competence as a variable in intervention. *Seminars in Speech and Language*, 10, 282–973.

Tottie, G. (1990) Conversational style in British and American English: the case of backchannels. Mimeo, Department of English, University of Uppsala.

Townsend, D. J. and Bever, T. G. (1991) The use of higher-level constraints in monitoring for a change in speaker demonstrates functionally distinct levels of representation in discourse comprehension, *Language and Cognitive Processes*, 6, 49–77.

Trupe, E. H. (1986) Training severely aphasic patients to communicate by drawing. Paper presented at Convention of the American Speech-Language-Hearing Association: Detroit.

Tyler, L. K. (1985) Real-time comprehension processes in agrammatism: a case study, *Brain and Language*, 26, 259–75.

Tyler, L. K. (1987) Spoken language comprehension in aphasia: a real-time processing perspective. In M. Coltheart, G. Sartori and R. Job (eds) *The Cognitive Neuropsychology of Language*. Hillsdale, New Jersey: Lawrence Erlbaum.

Tyler, L. K. (1989) Syntactic deficits and the construction of local phrases in spoken language comprehension, *Cognitive Neuropsychology*, 333–55.

Ulatowska, H. K. (1979) Application of linguistics to treatment of aphasia. In R. H. Brookshire (ed.) *Clinical Aphasiology*. Minneapolis: BRK.

Ulatowska, H. K., Doyel, A. W., Stern, R. F. and Haynes S. M. (1983) Production of procedural discourse in aphasia, *Brain and Language*, 18, 315–41.

Ulatowska, H. K., Freedman-Stern, R. F., Doyel, A. W. and Macaluso-Haynes, S. (1983a) Production of narrative discourse in aphasia, *Brain and Language*, 19, 317–34.

van der Linden, M. and van der Kaa, M-A. (1989) Reorganization therapy for memory impairments. In X. Seron and G. Deloche (eds) *Cognitive Approaches in Neuropsychological Rehabilitation*, Hove: Lawrence Erlbaum.

van Dijk, T. A. (1977) *Text and Content: Explorations of the Semantics and Pragmatics of Discourse*. London: Longman.

van Dijk, T. A. and Kintsch, W. (1983) *Strategies of Discourse Comprehension*. New York: Academic Press.

van Dongen, H. R. (1974) Impairment of drawing and intelligence in aphasia. In Y. Lebrun and R. Hoops (eds) *Intelligence and Aphasia*. Amsterdam: Swets and Zeitlinger.

van Eeckhout, P., Meillet-Haberer, C. and Pillon, B. (1979) Apport de la mélodie et du rythme dans quelques cas de réductions sévères du langage, *Rééducation Orthophonique*, 17, 353–69.

van Lancker, D. R., Cummings, J. L., Kreiman, J. and Dobkin, B. H. (1988) Phonagnosia: a dissociation between familiar and unfamiliar voices. *Cortex*, 24, 195–209.

van Lancker, D. and Klein, K. (1990) Preserved recognition of familiar personal names in global aphasia, *Brain and Language*, 39, 511–29.

van Sommers, P. (1989) A system for drawing and drawing-related neuropsychology. *Cognitive Neuropsychology*, 6, 117–64.

Varney, N. R., Damasio, H. and Adler, S. (1989) The role of individual differences in determining the nature of comprehension deficits in aphasia, *Cortex*, 25, 47–55.

Vicher, A. and Sankoff, D. (1989) The emergent syntax of presentential turn-openings, *Journal of Pragmatics*, 13, 81–97.

Villiard, P. (1990) Agrammatism: evidence for a unified theory of word, phrase and sentence formation processes. In J-L. Nespoulous and P. Villiard (eds) *Morphology, Phonology and Aphasia*, New York: Springer.

von Stockert, T. and Bader, L. (1976) Some relations of grammar and lexicon in aphasia, *Cortex*, 12, 49–60.

Wahrborg, P. (1989) Aphasia and family therapy, *Aphasiology*, 3, 479–82.

Wales, R. (1986) Deixis. In P. Fletcher and M. Garman (eds) *Language Acquisition*. Cambridge: Cambridge University Press.

Warrington, E. K. and McCarthy R. (1984) Category specific language impairments, *Brain*, 107, 829–54.

Warrington, E. K. and McCarthy R. (1987) Categories of knowledge: further fractionations and an attempted integration, *Brain*, 110, 1273–96.

Watson, H. (1989) Discourse analysis: profiling the characteristics of normal and dysphasic conversation. Unpublished undergraduate dissertation, Department of Speech, University of Newcastle upon Tyne.

Weinrich, M. (1991) Computerized visual communication as an alternative communication system and therapeutic tool, *Journal of Neurolinguistics*, 6, 159–76.

Wells, G. (1985) *Language Development in the Preschool Years*. Cambridge: Cambridge University Press.

Wepman, J. M. (1976) Aphasia: language without thought or thought without language? *Asha*, 18, 131–6.

Wepman, J. M. and Jones, L. V. (1966) Studies in aphasia: classification of aphasic speech by the noun-pronoun ratio, *British Journal of Disorders of Communication*, 1, 46–54.

Weylman, S. T., Brownell, H. H., Roman, M. and Gardner, H. (1989) Appreciation of indirect requests by left- and right-brain-damaged patients: the effect of verbal context and conventionality of wording. *Brain and Language*, 36, 580–91.

Wilcox, M. J., Davis, G. A. and Leonard, L. (1978) Aphasics' comprehension of contextually conveyed meaning, *Brain and Language*, 6, 362–77.

Willmes, K.(1990) Statistical methods for a single-case study approach to aphasia therapy research, *Aphasiology*, 4, 415–36.

Wilson, J. (1989) *On the Boundaries of Conversation*. London: Pergamon.

Wilson, B. and Patterson, K. (1990) Rehabilitation for cognitive impairment. Does cognitive psychology apply? *Applied Cognitive Psychology*, 4, 247–60.

Winner, E. and Gardner, H. (1977) Comprehension of metaphor in brain damaged patients, *Brain*, 100, 717–29.

Wirz, S. L., Skinner, C. and Dean, E. (1990) *Revised Edinburgh Functional Communication Profile*. Tucson, Arizona: Communication Skill Builders.

Wolfson, N. (1982) *The Conversational Historic Present in American English Narrative*. Dordrecht: Foris.

Yamaguchi, F., Meyer, J. S., Sakai, F. and Yamamoto. M. (1980) Case reports of three dysphasic patients to illustrate rCBF responses during behavioral activation, *Brain and Language*, 9, 145–8.

Yedor, K. and Kearns, K. (1987) Establishing communicative drawing in severe aphasia through response elaboration training. Paper presented at American Speech-Language-Hearing Convention: New Orleans.

Zaidel, E. (1977) Unilateral auditory language comprehension on the Token Test following cerebral commissurotomy and hemispherectomy, *Neuropsychologia*, 15, 1–17.

Zingeser, L. B. and Berndt, R. S. (1988) Grammatical class and context effects in a case of pure anomia: implications for models of language production, *Cognitive Neuropsychology*, 4, 473–516.

Zurif, E. B. (1980) Language mechanisms: a neuropsychological perspective, *American Scientist*, 68, 305–11.

Author Index

Subject Index

(Page number references to tables are shown in italics)